AMERICAN PROTEUS

Narrative Self-Making in the Novels of

Charles Brockden Brown

JOHN WENKE

MERCER UNIVERSITY PRESS
Macon, Georgia

MUP/ P729

Published by Mercer University Press
1501 Mercer University Drive
Macon, Georgia 31207

29 28 27 26 25   5 4 3 2 1

Books published by Mercer University Press are printed on acid-free paper that meets the requirements of the American National Standard for Information Sciences—Permanence of Paper for Printed Library Materials.

Printed and bound in the United States.

This book is set in Adobe Garamond.

Cover/jacket design by Burt&Burt.

ISBN 978-0-88146-992-9 (Print)
978-0-88146-993-6 (eBook)

Cataloging-in-Publication Data is available from the Library of Congress

Contents

To Jacqueline, Joseph, Benjamin, and Gabriel

American Proteus

In his compelling and fun-to-read *American Proteus*, John Wenke offers new perspectives on authorial voice in Brockden Brown's major fiction of the 1797–1801 period. Wenke, a scholar and fiction writer himself, has an acute understanding of Brown's experiments in narrative storytelling, and he offers one of the best readings we have of Brown's relatively neglected *Memoirs of Carwin the Biloquist*. I learned much about Brown the writer from Wenke's exemplary study.

—Robert S. Levine, distinguished professor of English,
University of Maryland, College Park;
and general editor of *The Norton Anthology of American Literature*

John Wenke's *American Proteus* returns our attention to one of the most important figures in the development of the American novel. Wenke offers a rich analysis of Charles Brockden Brown's career and evolution as an artist, setting his novels against historical, cultural, literary, and biographical contexts. Of particular significance to scholars of early American literature is Wenke's deft and thorough exploration of Brown's experimentation with various narrative forms. Instructors and students will appreciate the book's treatment of salient questions regarding perception and truth (and the epistemological horrors these questions can uncover) and their relationship to the creation of individual and national identity.

—Dana Edwards Prodoehl, associate professor
of Literature, Writing, and Film,
University of Wisconsin-Whitewater

MERCER UNIVERSITY PRESS

Endowed by

TOM WATSON BROWN

and

THE WATSON-BROWN FOUNDATION, INC.

Abbreviations for Frequently Cited Sources by Charles Brocken Brown

A *Alcuin; A Dialogue* with *Stephen Calvert*, edited by Sydney J. Krause, S. W. Redi, and Robert D. Arner, Kent State University Press, 1987.

A M *Arthur Mervyn; or Memoirs of the Year 1793, First and Second Parts*, edited by Sydney J. Krause, S. W. Reid, Norman S. Grabo, and Marvin L. Williams, Jr., Kent State University Press, 1980.

EH *Edgar Huntly; or, Memoirs of a Sleep-Walker*, edited by Sydney J. Krause and S.W. Reid, Kent State University Press, 1984.

L *Letters and Early Epistolary Writings. The Collected Writings of Charles Brockden Brown*, vol. 1, edited by Philip Barnard, Elizabeth Hewitt, and Mark L. Kamrath. Bucknell University Press, 2013.

M *Memoirs of Carwin the Biloquist. Wieland; or, The Transformation. An American Tale, with Related Texts*, edited, with an Introduction and Notes by Philip Barnard and Stephen Shapiro, Hackett Publishing, 2009.

O *Ormond; or, The Secret Witness*, edited by Sydney J. Krause, S. W. Reid, and Russel B. Nye, Kent State University Press, 1982.

R *The Rhapsodist and Other Uncollected Writings*, edited by Harry R. Warfel. 1943, rpt. Scholars' Facsimiles & Reprints, 1977.

W *Wieland; or, The Transformation: An American Tale* with *Memoirs of Carwin the Biloquist*, edited by Sydney J. Krause, S. W. Reid, and Alexander Cowie, Kent State University Press, 1977.

Extracts

So I spoke, and she, shining among the goddesses, answered:
"See, I will accurately answer all that you ask me.
The ever-truthful Old Man of the Sea ranges in these parts.
This is the Egyptian, immortal Proteus, and he knows
all the depths of the sea."

(Homer, *Odyssey*, Book IV, lines 382–86)

"Now I will tell you all the devious ways of this old man.
First of all he will go among his seals and count them,
but after he has reviewed them all and noted their number,
he will lie down in their midst, like a herdsman among his sheep-
flocks.
Next, as soon as you see that he is asleep, that will be
the time for all of you to use your strength and your vigor,
and hold him there while he strives and struggles hard to escape you.
And he will try you by taking the form of all creatures that come
forth
and move on the earth, he will be water and magical fire."

(Homer, *Odyssey*, Book IV, lines 410–18)

For thou hast said in thine heart, I will ascend into heaven, I will exalt my throne above the stars of God: I will sit also upon the mount of the congregation, in the sides of the north: I will ascend above the heights of the clouds; I will be like the most High.

(Isaiah, 14:13–14)

"That since a large proportion of the most useful and distinguished men of every profession, and in every age, have sprung from humble life, the friends of the American Education Society have a peculiar reason to expect that in consequence of their efforts, a great addition will be made to the piety, talent, and effective influence of the Christian ministry"....Professor N[ewman] directs the attention first to that peculiar and important class of persons in our country whom he styles ["]self made men"....The following striking example is introduced...to fix the attention on an individual instance. I will mention Roger Sherman of Connecticut. He was the son of poor parents. The business marked out to him for life, was the sedentary and laborious employment of a shoemaker. But while his hands wrought in this humble, though useful occupation, a providential occurrence led him to aspire after a higher station in life.... Neither, at that time, were there kind liberal patrons, or generous associations, to which he might look with the hope of assistance. He saw, that all his resources were in himself.

([Professor Newman's Address] 7)

And out of what context did these transformations arise—out of what historical drama, acted unsuspectingly by its little protagonists, played out in classrooms and kitchens looking nothing at all like the great theater of life? Just what collided with what to produce the spark in us?

(Philip Roth, *American Pastoral* 44)

Preface

American Proteus seeks to explain what it means for Charles Brockden Brown to have created out of his life-experiences and encompassing cultural milieu a novel kind of fiction for a new kind of country. Drawing on archival evidence, biographical materials, and a rich tradition of scholarly and critical findings, this study charts the emergence of Brown's authorial voice as it developed throughout an amorphous, multifaceted, and conflicted apprenticeship. This period of literary experimentation established the foundations for his brief yet momentous career as a publishing novelist that lasted from 1798 through 1801.

Even as a teenager, Brown was a practiced multitasker. A precocious student, reader, thinker, and writer, Brown exercised mutually supporting talents in composing letters, journal entries, poems, inchoate novels, fictional fragments, and essays during more than a decade ranging from 1787 to 1798. Out of these originating ventures—which included his address to the Belles Lettres Club, his "Rhapsodist" essays, his epistolary interchanges with close friends, and his faux courtship "Henrietta Letters"—developed his insistent preoccupation with narrative self-making—an aesthetic vision of the authorial self as an emergent, performative voice and actor. In its most realized manifestations, this protean quality informs the creation of Brown's disruptive figures of power—like Carwin, Ormond, and Welbeck—who view other people and the social order as providing opportunities for manipulation and domination. For Brown, it was a liberating notion to imagine, and then dramatize, how voice, character, and behavior were not confined by religious strictures or social class, but that a self—a conspicuously *American* self—could be *authored* in ways that became both subversive and revolutionary.

In 1798, with the publication of *Alcuin; A Dialogue*, "The Man at Home," and *Wieland; or the Transformation: An American Tale*, Brown's literary apprenticeship gave way to his prolific, four-year career as a publishing novelist. *Wieland* in particular was a breakthrough work, especially as it reconfigured the dialectical intensities generated within *Alcuin* and the protean aesthetic depicted in "The Man at Home" into narrator Clara Wieland's Gothicized epistolary improvisations, on the one hand, and Francis Carwin's poetics and politics of imposture, on the other. *Wieland*'s most striking innovations relate to aesthetic and cultural implications that derive from Clara's precise assertion of a determinant, deific authorial power, the conviction that God Himself insistently impinged upon and *inscribed* her thoughts: "It was surely no vulgar agency that gave this form to my fears. He to whom all parts of time are equally present, whom no contingency approaches, was the author of that spell which now seized upon me" (*W* 87). Clara's belief in God as intrusive "author" stands in diametrical, perhaps inimical, opposition to human assertions of authorial agency, especially as manifest through self-making in word or deed. Under Brown's hand, and manifest most powerfully in *Wieland*, the determinate power of deific authorship appears not as an extrinsic fact but as a postulation that energizes the magnetizing force of its antithesis—the revolutionary premise that protean, self-making artificers can usurp the divine prerogative, internalize this ostensibly autonomous power, and then use "imposture" for purposes of manipulation and domination within the social sphere (*W* 201). Throughout Brown's apprenticeship pieces and his novels, authorship appears variously as a compositional act, a histrionic process, and a form of political provocation and domination.

From this perspective, self-making involves a consciously aesthetic activity that has distinct personal and political ramifications. In Brown's case, the poetics and politics of self-making led him to create synergistic versions of the "American Tale" out of the importation, and transfiguration, of a host of transatlantic literary and ideational materials. By drawing on, and reconfiguring Gothic and epistolary forms as well as Enlightenment ideologies, Brown reveals how his protean artist-figures reject ideological confinements of attending social forms, whether theological or political. In their attempts to control the social "stage" (*W* 50)—an informing trope throughout his novels—they seek to challenge, disrupt, or destroy those conventional modes that allow society to operate.

Within Brown's novels, a succession of problematic, self-reflexive first-person narrators portray dire situations afflicting characters turned loose in a frightening, destabilized world. In *Wieland*, Clara's father suffers a strange, incendiary death. Later, his two orphaned children experience a multitude of consequences that attend the irruption of (ostensibly) supernatural voices—voices that mysteriously appear to have something to do with the elder Wieland's passing. In two novels—*Ormond; or The Secret Witness* (1799) and *Arthur Mervyn; or Memoirs of the Year 1793, First and Second Parts* (1799–1800)— a plague ravages residents of Philadelphia and eviscerates the social order. In the unfinished *Memoirs of Carwin the Biloquist*, the social compact may lie under an insidious threat from a conspiratorial body of foreign, utopian atheists. In *Edgar Huntly; or, Memoirs of a Sleep-Walker* (1799), Brown's most radical and unsettling novel, avenging, marauding Indians commit random murders and terrorize the frontier in their bid to re-take stolen, ancestral lands. In this work, the narrator and his deranged counterpart discover that beneath the fragile, frayed textures of social identity and conscious intention resides the transformative domain of an autonomous unconscious. In this outré, pre-Poe underworld of the mind, madness, murder, and other inducements impel the peripatetic gyrations of Brown's haunted sleepwalkers.

The following study is divided into a prologue, six chapters, and a coda. Chapter One, "Rhapsodic and Epistolary Antecedents," examines selective literary materials that give shape and substance to Brown's creative foreground. These materials include his precocious address to the Belles Lettres Club; the first two "Rhapsodist" essays; Brown's explosive 1791–92 letters to Joseph Bringhurst, Jr. and William Wood Wilkins; and the remarkable "Henrietta Letters." His 1792 revision of the "Henrietta" materials constitutes a pivotal, transformative experience that consolidated the gains he had made in earlier compositional ventures. This embryonic process looked forward to, and made possible, the completion of his literary apprenticeship in late 1797 and early

1798 as Brown prepared to publish *Sky-Walk; or, The Man Unknown to Himself—An American Tale*, while also planning for the publication of *Alcuin* and "The Man at Home," thirteen serial fictional pieces published in the Philadelphia *Weekly Magazine* in the early months of 1798. Throughout his literary apprenticeship, Brown dramatized how the procreant mind revealed itself in the very activity of writing and provided the impetus for the development of his protean, authorial voice.

In the aftermath of these early experiments, Brown delineates a host of conflicting "double-tongued" imperatives in *Wieland* (*W* 1). Chapter Two, "Competing Voices: *Wieland* and the Limits of Disclosure," explores Brown's innovative reconfigurations of epistolary and Gothic forms. As a "double-tongued" narrator, Clara Wieland delivers a *sensation* narrative describing what she felt, thought, and believed *then* as well as a *critical* narrative detailing what she feels, thinks, and believes *now*. These oscillations in narrative perspective dramatize the following complexes: Clara's problematic attempt to find a stable point of narrative origination; her father's failure to realize newness in America—a venture culminating in his catastrophic death; the irruption of disembodied voices; the disruptive antics of Carwin as both covert and overt performer; Theodore Wieland's murderous rampage; and culminating complications associated with Clara's presentation of competing first-person, inset narratives.

In Chapter Three, "Imposture and Subversion: *Memoirs of Carwin the Biloquist*," Brown develops foundational, aesthetic complexes that inform his attempts to articulate the emergent contours of a new American poetics and politics of self-making. *Memoirs of Carwin* should not merely be seen as an abortive addendum to *Wieland* or as a promising beginning to a truncated prequel. Instead, through the youthful Carwin, Brown depicts how the nascent American artist-figure's suffocating and repressed relationship with his patrimonial, Calvinistic heritage provides the stimulus for discovering (and literally internalizing) revolutionary powers inherent in nature's hidden forms. Carwin's covert self-empowerment achieves self-reflective expression through a transatlantic, allusive matrix connecting John Milton's *A Mask* with William Shakespeare's *The Tempest.* The early pages of this unfinished prequel constitute an illuminating act of aesthetic self-definition composed as Brown was entering his greatest period of writerly achievement.

Chapter Four, "Toward a Supreme Fiction: *Ormond; or, The Secret Witness,*" presents insurgent tricksters operating in a social world riven by the yellow fever epidemic. As depicted by narrator Sophia Courtland, the conniving Thomas Craig and the self-deifying Ormond stand in opposition to Constantia Dudley and her ethos of proto-feminist self-empowerment. In this expansive narrative, the fragility of social constructs makes possible the predatory power of self-making. Sophia, the frequently intrusive narrator, uses her discursive meditations on Constantia's incorruptible virtue and Ormond's mendacious role-playing to launch intermittent, meta-critical forays that find issue in strategic assertions of expanded, hermeneutical access. What emerges is a dialectic among alternative possibilities that is directed and modified by the recurrent imposition of aesthetic and histrionic tropes.

Chapter Five, "Arthur and the Ambiguities: *Arthur Mervyn; or, Memoirs of the Year 1793. First and Second Parts,*" explores shifting, mock-oral delineations of Mervyn's protean identity. Once this second son leaves the home of his abusive father, he finds that he is no one—a man without a plot—until a series of serendipitous encounters impel his recurrent attempts at self-making. In appearing as both tyro and raconteur, Mervyn becomes the ambiguous sum of his performative avatars, assuming roles that oscillate between the extremes of altruistic beneficence and insidious manipulation.

Chapter Six, "American Novelty: *Edgar Huntly; or, Memoirs of a Sleep-Walker,*" explores Brown's adaptation of the epistolary form not as a record of conventional social manners celebrated, flaunted, or satirized, but as an investigative device designed to reflexively explore the cognitive limitations of Edgar Huntly's conscious mind, especially the vacillating track of his protean consciousness, as well as the inchoate revelations of a constructed authorial self that Huntly believes he knows and controls. This putatively stable self is repeatedly challenged, undermined, and re-invented by the uncontrolled activities of his autonomous (and irruptive) unconscious mind. This novel dramatizes the relationship between psychological disintegration and the encompassing colonial/ political matrix, especially insofar as protean energies characterizing the expanding nation suggest a moral and political critique of the Eurocentric, colonial enterprise.

Coda: 1801 offers a concluding, speculative essay on intersections between Brown's courtship letters to Elizabeth Linn, the future Mrs. Charles Brocken Brown, and his futile attempts to salvage his career. By the end of 1801, after publishing the conventional, epistolary *Clara Howard; in A Series of Letters* and *Jane Talbot, A Novel*, Brown ended his career as a publishing novelist.

To contemporary sensibilities, all too attuned to the province of irony and the sweep of deconstructive energies, intended or otherwise, Brown's professed desire to seek truth-in-fiction might seem like a quaint anachronism, a pious genuflection toward orthodoxy, or a sardonic joke that only the clever few might discern. Nevertheless, Brown—or at least a part of him—did seem to think that the narrators he created were exploring a multitude of moral issues and that some, if not all, were deeply concerned with providing useful instruction on matters of ethics and justice. Frequently, in his own authorial voice or through a narrator, Brown inscribes prefatory materials that direct readers toward considering "the moral constitution of man" (*W* 3). Some "moral painters" (*W* 3) like another "moral painter" (*EH* 3) present stories that allow "the moral observer" to find "new displays of the influence of human passions and motives" (*AM* 3). Significantly, however, Brown as "moral painter" uses his palette not to construct didactic lessons depicting categorical axioms or reductive bromides, but to incite mystery and dramatize interpretive possibilities dialectical in nature. One reason for this disposition is that Brown, like Carwin and Welbeck, was himself an American Proteus, a sly, provocative, literary shape-shifter— "[H]e will be water and magical fire" (Homer, line 418)—mercurial, slippery, difficult to pin down before sliding away to assume other figurations—a writer who uses stories about "new displays of the influence of human passions and motives" to excite provocative questions about scheming artificers that have no easy answers.

Acknowledgments

It is a little disturbing to my Franklinian sensibilities when I recall how long I've worked on this project, but along the winding way, with some years on and some years off, I have had the good fortune to incur a number of debts. I am grateful to the department chairs of Salisbury University's English department—Connie Richards, Elizabeth Curtin, Adam Wood, and David Johnson—who have supported my efforts in bountiful fashion. I am grateful to Maarten Pereboom, Dean of Salisbury University's Fulton School of Liberal Arts, for fostering an atmosphere wherein teaching and scholarship are recognized as reciprocal processes. The libraries of the University of Maryland system never failed to supply my requests for easy- and hard-to-find materials. A number of friends and colleagues have helped me in ways too numerous to specify. My heartfelt thanks go out to Hershel Parker, Milton R. Stern, Thomas Werge, Stuart Warner, John Bryant, Gary Harrington, Diane Lubkeman, Lisa Jones, John Nieves, Christine Spillson, Chris Vilmar, Ryan Habermeyer, Manav Ratti, and Joshua Downes. Jo Wenke and Jim Wenke encouraged me to find my way through various difficulties. I am grateful to Marion Rust and *Early American Literature* for publishing a standalone version of Chapter Three. I am especially grateful to Marc Jolley for the opportunity to publish this book through Mercer University Press. I tender special thanks and abiding love to my children, to whom this book is dedicated.

Carriages rumbled through the streets to pick up the dying and the dead during the 1793 yellow fever epidemic in Philadelphia. Woodcut shows Stephen Girard on an errand of mercy.

(Bettmann/Corbis)

Prologue

During the summer of 1798, New York City was a horrible place: yellow fever ravaged rich and poor, saints and reprobates. Mounting corpses and agitated invalids were neglected or attended. Distraught survivors watched the unfolding disaster and awaited the body-heat of first symptoms (Nye 304–05). While the epidemic claimed victims within and without his circumference of friends, Charles Brockden Brown inhabited a serene, creative space.[1]

Come death if it may, he was intent on advancing his fledgling literary career, even though proofs of his first completed novel, the ill-fated Sky-Walk, *were either misplaced, withheld, or lost following the yellow fever death of printer James Watters. On July 23, 1798, Brown delivered to printers Thomas and James Swords a large portion of his hastily composed novel, even as he attempted, in consultation with members of the New York Friendly Club, to stage its concluding catastrophe and tie up loose ends. As if this juggling were not enough, Brown was also producing chapters of*

[1] Clark summarizes conditions in the late eighteenth century that led to frequent outbreaks of yellow fever (160–61). See Brown's letters (*L* 412–42) during this period and editorial discussions that illuminate Brown's circumstances: "The 1798 New York epidemic was a particularly severe one....After heavy rains, the mortality rate began to climb dramatically between August 15 and 20....The mortality rate was highest during September (a daily average of 38), somewhat lower in October, and tapered off in November as cold weather began to kill the mosquitoes that spread the disease" (*L* 414, Note 2). In a July 26, 1799 letter to his brother James, Brown describes dreadful conditions from a year before when he pushed himself to complete his second novel amid the yellow fever devastation: "My sensations, in this state of things are so different from my sensations last summer, that I look back with astonishment. I do not wonder that I then remained in the city, but that my mind retained its tranquility in the midst of perils the most imminent; that I could muse and write cheerfully in spite of the groans of the dying and the rumbling of hearses, and in spite of a thousand tokens of indisposition in my own frame, is now almost incredible. I perceive that this tranquility and courage is utterly beyond my reach at present" (*L* 457–58).

Arthur Mervyn *for serial publication in the* Weekly Magazine *and working on a prequel to* Wieland, *what became the unfinished* Memoirs of Carwin the Biloquist. *By September 3, 1798, Brown had penned his prefatory "Advertisement" and on September 14, 1798* Wieland; or the Transformation: An American Tale *was published by Hocquet Caritat. Handsomely bound, it cost the considerable sum of one dollar (Cowie 321–22).*[2]

[2] Davidson notes, "A common day laborer in Massachusetts had to work two days to buy a copy of *Wieland* (1798). For the same amount, he could purchase a bushel of potatoes and a half bushel of corn" (*Revolution* 25).

1

Rhapsodic and Epistolary Antecedents

Foreground

Wieland owes its completion not only to Charles Brockden Brown's death-defying compositional energies, but to a long creative foreground that spanned at least eleven years. The springs feeding Brown's literary life flowed from a profusion of personal, educational, political, cultural, and aesthetic resources. His Quaker upbringing imbued him with an active, moralizing—and highly critical, even disputatious—conscience that found expression in the free exercise of thought. As Philip Barnard and Stephen Shapiro note, "Brown was shaped by that community's history of dissenting relations to mainstream Protestant and Anglo-American culture, and by Philadelphia's importance as both a political center and a major port connected with Atlantic and global mercantile networks" (xiii).[1] His closely-knit family valued a form of commercial success that aspired to become the public embodiment of ethical citizenship. In the Brown family, the sons were cast as the agents responsible for establishing the family fortunes and eradicating the unsettling, even humiliating, political and economic legacy that for many years afflicted their father, Elijah Brown.[2]

---

[1] For a detailed examination of Brown's Quaker heritage, especially the relationship between his ancestry and immediate family, see Kafer, 1–65. He explores the "historical horrors that had shadowed the Brown family ever since the 1650s and 1660s, when, in the Midlands of England, they first turned to the *light* that was Quakerism" (xxi, emphasis in original).

[2] Elijah Brown was imprisoned in September 1777, legally abducted as (ostensibly) a potentially seditious Quaker by a vigilance committee of the Philadelphia Revolutionary militia. Kafer unravels this complicated affair that found Elijah caught between agents of Revolution and factions within the Quaker community. The disappearance of Elijah Brown for seven months in 1777–78 was the first great trauma

In preparing for his future, Brown contended with a longstanding vocational dilemma that found issue in his pursuit of a dual apprenticeship. From the age of sixteen into his early twenties, he wavered between the respective demands of legal studies and literary ventures. He aspired to be the good son and brother and earn his family's approbation by preparing to establish a respectable legal practice, even as he most deeply desired to fulfill the decidedly unconventional dictates associated with becoming a professional man of letters. What informed his dual commitment, what kept him oscillating between two careers, was his faith that these paths did not have to diverge. Perhaps a career in law could provide a foundation for, as well as a complement to, his vocation as a writer. Brown's eventual rejection of the legal profession in 1793 in favor of a tenuous and wholly unpromising literary life was not conceived as a form of economic martyrdom. Rather, this devotion was fueled by the hope that he could make an acceptable living as a writer of poems, novels, histories, pamphlets, and essays. An inchoate world of literary opportunism lay before him. As William Dunlap argues in his 1815 biography, his late friend worked assiduously to achieve eminence in the fledgling literary marketplace that he helped to create:

> Charles Brockden Brown was among the earlier adventurers into the world of fiction and the painful path of public amusement or instruction, by the pen and the press, which the United States of America produced.... Those who first saw the propriety of men in a new and better political state,

---

in the life of six-year-old Charles. In 1784, Elijah was imprisoned for debt, when Charles was thirteen, a fact that informs the prominence of debtor's prison in Brown's fiction (Kafer 162–64). Christophersen notes, "[T]he tenets of Quakerism may at least have sensitized [Brown] at an early age to the dangers of violence, whether ordained, self-defensive, or politically justified—a theme that pervades his fiction and that haunted Federalist America" (6). For a biographical summary of Brown's early life and times and its relation to post-Colonial America, to revolutions abroad, and to an array of Enlightenment philosophers, see Barnard and Shapiro, xiii–xvii.

throwing off the shackles of an absurd prejudice in favour[3] of European opinion and writing, as they had thrown from them the proffered chains and rejected the pretensions of European tyranny...saw the necessity of establishing a literature for their own country...[and] saw the advantages of publications suited to a new state of manners and political economy, and which should not only produce original instruction, but point out and sever the good from the bad in the literature and institutions of Europe. (*The Life*, I, 9–10)[4] Brown's career in letters became part of the cauldron of cultural and

[3] In citing Brown's letters and other primary sources, I have maintained his original spelling, which sometimes seems to have errors.

[4] See Bennett, "Introduction," for an account of the relationship between Paul Allen's failure to fulfill the promises stipulated by his "Proposals for Publishing The Life of the Late Charles B. Brown" (VIII) and the difficult conditions under which William Dunlap in 1815 completed and published *The Life of Charles Brockden Brown*. Essentially, co-literary executors Elizabeth Linn Brown, Charles' widow, and Elijah Brown, Jr., Charles' brother, dismissed Allen from the project for cause. Allen was over-extended, had a reputation for laziness, and prioritized other professional commitments to the detriment of Brown's biography. As Bennett notes, "The Browns had every reason to feel betrayed" ("Introduction xxi). Mrs. Brown was not only upset that Allen padded the biographical narrative with hundreds of pages selected from Brown's letters and (mostly) unfinished manuscripts, but she did not appreciate the critical tenor of some of Allen's assessments. Whereas Allen's biography was never published as planned, it *was* printed in at least a single copy, which Dunlap used to perform his salvage operation. Bennett details how Dunlap was forced to delete and add materials in exact measure to retain as much of the (costly) original typesetting as possible. The entire work, when completed, was published under Dunlap's name, but many of the words that Allen wrote and the selections he made from Brown's manuscripts remain part of the two-volume biography. Allen ceded the entire project to the executers—a matter that obviates potential charges of plagiarism that may arise regarding Dunlap's editorial decision to retain, and adapt, Allen's writing (Bennett, "Introduction," XII). Also see Cody, "Allen offers a largely negative view of [Brown's] output" (523).

economic conditions roiling the nation in the early decades of its existence.[5]

The tensions associated with Brown's dual apprenticeship aligned him with very powerful forces shaping the cultural and political domain of the nascent republic. As Jay Fliegelman demonstrates, Brown's eventual (partial and conflicted) rejection of his family's conventional, bourgeois path reflects in personal terms an encompassing cultural phenomenon: the affective and aesthetic consequences of the age's revolution against patriarchal authority (5). As Steven Watts contends, the advent of Brown's literary career was buoyed and defined by the dominant economic forces that shaped the evolving republic.[6] Brown emerged not simply as the aspirant proto-Romantic seeking to express his soul; instead, he was intent on finding ways to synthesize his

---

[5] Davidson engages complex issues associated with competing claims to literary "firstness" (84), essentially with how to rank the cohort of novelists who were Brown's contemporaries. These writers include William Hill Brown, Susanna Rowson, Peter Markoe, and Aphra Behn, among others. See Davidson, *Revolution* 83–109. An important issue attending the creation of literary history is how, and why, Brown for a time assumed canonical status as the first "major" American novelist, with *Wieland* as a canonical work. Faherty argues, "The novel's importance for our collective understanding of the development of American literary history does not reside in its claims to firstness; rather, the critical history of the novel demonstrates how it has routinely served as a crucial compass for larger arguments about the development of cultural production in the early republic" (57). Silyn Roberts argues, "....Brown is viewed no longer as the paternal forefather of an 'American' novelistic tradition but as a prominent node on a dense, multidirectional Atlantic matrix of ideas contoured by shifting flows of material and cultural exchange" (440).

[6] Watts examines Brown's life and works within the context of his responses to various market forces, especially the young nation's encompassing transformation from a republican mode to a liberal economic mode (8). In situating Brown in relation to the de-centering of patriarchal power, Hinds explains how for Brown economic issues could not be dissociated from gender politics: "In his four major novels and *Alcuin*. . .Brown created economies as equivocal as his own slippery class position. Money or class is always at issue in these works.... Moreover, Brown created two distinct sets of virtues for his male and female characters. His characterization of gendered virtue rests in between the two poles of U. S. economic possibility during the 1790s" (11–12).

creative capital with the unstable energies animating his social and political sphere. Brown's mature work of the late eighteenth and early nineteenth centuries—especially his four major novels—gave expression to dialectical forces pitting a republican paternal tradition in opposition to individualizing energies that shaped a revolutionary culture of bourgeoisie capitalism. These dialectical forces animating Brown's work extended beyond issues related to patriarchal authority and liberal capitalism and informed the development of his complex, multifaceted range of thought and sensibility. In fact, it is the impress of these hybrid forces that allows Brown to be reasonably understood within the critical debate as revolutionary and/or orthodox, as liberal and/or conservative—an unsettled matrix that derives, at least partly, from his eclectic reading during his teenage and early adult years.

The fusion of social, political, and economic energies cannot be dissociated from Brown's assimilation of multiple aesthetic influences that informed and shaped his literary ambitions and achievements in overt and covert ways. Peter Kafer explores the impact of the Quaker educational system on Brown's development: "Charles. . .entered the acme of the Quaker school system, the Friends' Latin School, in June 1781. Here he studied the Quaker classics, read the Bible, and attended meeting twice a week, in conjunction with lessons in Latin and Greek, mathematics, English literature, and geography" (46).[7] Brown's formal schooling offered a springboard to more expansive explorations in European literatures and the Classics. From an early age, he was an avid and varied reader. According to Harry R. Warfel, Brown

> read through the encyclopedia; he held memberships in libraries; and he acquired a large personal library. Milton early became a favorite poet; Shakespeare was systematically reread;

[7] Kafer describes how Brown developed a mode of thinking that separated him from the ideological constrictions of the Quaker meeting: "Having lived his childhood in Revolutionary Philadelphia, Charles Brown did not feel and think like an orthodox Quaker. In fact, as the future would reveal, he didn't feel and think like anyone else, period" (49).

> and the current magazines and newspapers were conned with scholarly care. Robert Proud taught him to cherish the Latin of Cicero; he learned French alone, and at the age of thirty he studied German. (9)

As noted by Lisa West, "Proud...was a distinguished scholar, notable for penning the prodigious volume *The History of Pennsylvania* in 1797. Though a Quaker, Proud was well versed in both the classics and the sciences" (11; Cowie 315–17).

In the most reductive sense, his direct aesthetic influences, especially during his apprenticeship years from 1787 through 1797, include his response to, and his reformation of, the popular eighteenth-century tradition of epistolary narrative, especially as reflected in Samuel Richardson's *Pamela* and Jean Jacques Rousseau's *Heloise*, a text Brown frequently mentioned in letters and clearly emulates when he copiously wrote to Joseph Bringhurst, Jr. and William Wood Wilkins during the spring of 1792. Brown was especially drawn to such innovative figures as Mary Wollstonecraft, William Godwin, and Robert Bage (Warfel 17; Kafer 70–71, Christopherson 4–5) and to the seminal work of Gothic intrigue, Ann Radcliffe's *The Mysteries of Udolpho.* Bill Christopherson's study of Brown's life and work concentrates on his reconfiguration of Gothic materials in shaping a foundational body of essentially American fictions (xi). Kafer and Robert S. Levine elucidate Brown's relation to British and Continental traditions of Gothic narrative. Kafer argues that Brown possesses "the requisite Gothic imagination to sense the dark histories already weighing down on the American republic" (xxi; see Weinstock). Levine associates Brown's maturation as a distinctly American novelist as part of a vibrant, transatlantic process—one that was animated by the agency of Godwin's *Caleb Williams* and other works by European intellectuals, who focused on political movements that advanced revolution:

> Godwin clearly was a literary conduit for Brown, linking him to Continental representations and concerns about the French Revolution. Brown's early and continued interest in

> Enlightenment thinkers like Condorcet and Volney instructed him on the progressive possibilities of the new ideas. *Caleb Williams* dramatized the darker, cyclical side of revolution and the concomitant anxieties of displacement and constant revolutionary change. ("Arthur Mervyn's Revolutions" 146)

As Levine's emphasis on the forces underlying social mutability suggests, Brown's recurrent dramatization of extreme forms of personal and political unrest finds issue in a kind of ideational doubleness that becomes manifest in the boundary-breaking tendencies of his imagination. For example, while remarking on Brown's disaffiliation with many aspects of mainstream Quakerism, Kafer examines William Godwin's *An Enquiry Concerning Political Justice* and describes how Godwin's political philosophy extolling the primacy of individual "rights" and conscience and his argumentative resistance to the "contracts" that shape civil government "was in profound accord with the historical experiences, and cultural values, of Pennsylvania's Quakers" (71).[8] Essentially, Brown's wide-ranging affinities during his lengthy literary apprenticeship put him outside the purview of any distinct political party or rigid ideological affiliation, whether Federalist or Republican. The beleaguered, uncertain plight of individuals, caught within "mazy paths," was his paramount subject (*W* 1).

Toward the Creation of an Authorial Self

With the weight of his family's social expectations upon him, with the example of iconic (and iconoclastic) literary progenitors inspiring him, with the pursuit of his legal studies challenging and vexing him, Brown continued to discover that the physical and emotional experience of writing was a refuge, a self-justifying pleasure, and a restorative,

---

[8] See Kafer for his extended discussion of Brown's "anti-Godwin" strain (132–66). As Battistini argues, "[T]he Quaker element is impossible to isolate from...[Brown's] later Woldwinite reading and the Friendly Club" (319).

therapeutic activity that was emotionally re-creative and aesthetically self-formative—one that frequently found issue in expansive, epistolary experiments. What impelled these aspects of Brown's nascent literary agenda, especially as expressed in his conflation of epistolary forms and Gothic modalities, was his seemingly indefatigable commitment to the *physicality* of composition—the very activity of writing itself. In his teen years, this elemental attribute provided a cathartic outlet for his love of letters—letters in the encompassing public sense of Belles Lettres as well as those performative epistles that he effusively generated for the edification, amusement, and provocation of his closed circle of friends, most notably Bringhurst and Wilkins.[9] It was within and through the energies of a highly supportive literary cohort that Brown tried his authorial hand at a number of proto-fictional experiments that provided opportunities not only for Brown to construct exploratory theories regarding compositional aesthetics, but also to expand the reach of his own narrative voice beyond autobiographical statement *toward* the creation of highly fluid, eminently adaptable, fictionalized authorial personae. His literary apprenticeship was a wayward period marked by false starts, misdirection, career indecisions and revisions, as well as by his commitment to a number of notable projects that displayed his incremental progress toward professional authorship. His obsessive dedication to the physical activity of writing emerges through a multitude of contextualized dramatic occasions, most notably as this nascent authorial persona develops in response to competitive pressures imposed by peers, most notably fellow members of the Belles Lettres Club; through the short-lived prospect of becoming a publishing serial essayist; and via epistolary experiments with a closed circle of correspondents. The spontaneous, exhilarating experience of writing was for

[9] West summarizes some of the influences that inform Brown's epistolary endeavors: "These letters frequently employ dramatic language and invented dialogue. Rousseau and Richardson are his most obvious touchstones in these experiments, but he also draws heavily on Pope, William Shakespeare, French Enlightenment writers, Johann Wolfgang von Goethe, and other influences" (15).

Brown a form of self-empowerment and self-validation—a way to assert and express the permanence of his fleeting thoughts, a form of narrative self-making that became actualized through the construction of a projected double-self. The production of a text under hand forged a palpable artifact that voiced the protean fluidity of the thinking mind, but that also constituted a private display of what publication—words commodified in print—could eventually become.

Indeed, in willing himself to become a writer, Brown channeled the full range of his life-influences into the transformative enterprise of creating an inchoate authorial self, what he describes in a letter as his "other self" (*L* 13, emphasis in original), a writerly avatar who appears within his emergent texts as an independent voice—sometimes identified as "C.B.B." or Edward Stanton, or Julius Brownlow. The genesis and slow evolution of these authorial personae appear within various apprenticeship pieces and generate the elements that inform Brown's originating experiments in narrative self-making. In his letters to Bringhurst and Wilkins, Brown often employs this voice to interpolate a number of mini-narratives that frequently displaced Brown himself as well as his quotidian setting—his room in Philadelphia, for example—and replaced his immediate circumstances with a narrative voice speaking from an imagined, exotic locale like London, Switzerland, or France. As these varied materials attest, the most elemental force driving Brown's development as a writer became his insistent preoccupation with exploring how the protean configurations of the authorial voice could achieve textual presence as a projected double of the authorial mind.

My purpose in this foundational investigation is to explore selective literary materials that give shape and substance to Brown's long creative foreground. These materials include Brown's precocious, and prescient, address to the Belles Lettres Club; the first two "Rhapsodist" essays; Brown's explosive 1791–92 letters to Bringhurst and Wilkins; and the "Henrietta Letters." Of greatest significance are the serial letters of spring 1792 that complement, and perhaps impel, Brown's momentous revision of his "Henrietta Letters" at about the same time. Here he developed and refined an ability to write within the epistolary voice of a highly accomplished, daring, sometimes transgressive literary lady. The "Henrietta Letters" made possible Brown's eventual creation of Mrs. Carter in *Alcuin*, Clara in *Wieland*, Constantia Dudley in *Ormond*, and Achsa Fielding in *Arthur Mervyn*. His revision of the "Henrietta" materials constitutes a pivotal, transformative event that consolidated the gains he made in earlier compositional ventures, especially his 1787 address to the Belles Lettres Club and his truncated series of "Rhapsodist" essays. This procreant period in Brown's life established a strong foundation for the growth and emergence of his authorial self. This embryonic process looked forward to, and made possible, the completion of his literary apprenticeship in late 1797 and early 1798 as Brown prepared to publish *Sky-Walk*, while also planning for the publication of *Alcuin* and "The Man at Home" in the early months of 1798.

First Formulations

Throughout his childhood and teenage years, Brown not only immersed himself in reading but was obsessed with the physicality of writing. Dunlap reports that Brown "composed and transcribed letters and even copied into his journal the epistles he received from his correspondents. This severe tax upon his time was intended for improvement both in thinking and writing, and as a record of that improvement."[10] Begun in his youth, Brown's lifelong habit of "journalizing"

[10] Dunlap frequently condenses materials from Allen's biography, while retaining some of the original writing. For example, Allen writes, "After the day was spent in the office of Mr. Wilcox, [Brown] retired to his chamber and recorded in his journal all the incidents which in that space of time had fallen under his notice, with his observations on each. Here he likewise transcribed all the letters he received from, and all the letters he addressed to his correspondents, accompanied with his own comments. This formed at that period the apex of his ambition, and from this employment he was never drawn but with manifest reluctance. The benefit which he proposed to derive from this severe tax upon his time was, to make his page the record

(Dunlap, *The Life*, I, 15) suggests that even the seemingly tedious act of copying received texts, rather than being a mind-numbing, mechanical activity, could become a form of autodidactic instruction, a self-enforced discipline, nothing less than the most elemental form of imitation. If one's mind becomes engaged in the scrivener's task at hand, one comes to live within the tropes and rhythms of the transcribed, epistolary voice. Anyone who has copied long passages from written texts—for example, *Hamlet*, *Paradise Lost*, or *Moby-Dick*—realizes how much one can learn, both consciously and unconsciously, from what might seem an exercise in drudgery. Brown apparently enjoyed this tactile, literally hands-on form of appropriation.

Like "intellectual labour itself," the activity of writing embodied for Brown "a species of recreation" (Dunlap, *The Life*, I, 12).[11] He thus became imbued with a passion for new creation, for the transformational energies that coincided with intellectual discovery. In his journal, for example, Brown reveals a youthful preoccupation with the nature of taxonomy and epistemology. In one entry prompted by a request he made of John Davidson, a member of the Belles Lettres Club, Brown himself goes on to present a disquisition on "*the relation, dependance, and connection of the several parts of knowledge*." This precocious, post-Cartesian epistemological inquiry on "[m]ind and matter" as "the two grand divisions of science" (Dunlap, *The Life*, I, 18, emphasis in original) leads him to classify ways in which "man" is both an "animal" as well as a higher-order, cognitive being—a creature of "apprehension, reason, and will" (Dunlap, *The Life*, I, 19). Here

---

of his own mind, to mark his various stages of improvement from time to time, to acquire a promptitude in his narrative of facts, and a graceful style of writing" (12–13).

[11] Dunlap echoes Allen's description of Brown's ingrained pursuit of "intellectual revelry": "In this state of intellectual revelry, by diversifying his studies and pursuits he gave to each a character of novelty; and illustrated and confirmed by his example one important moral fact, that a change of studies answers all the purposes of relaxation, better than inaction.... [T]he same species of exercise became alternately labour and relaxation" (11).

Brown attempts to define basic ideational complexes within the fevered activity of composition. Indeed, he often uses his apprentice pieces to work his way through abstruse, intellectual problems. What matters here is not so much the content of what he argues—original or otherwise—as the fearless, intrepid intellectual vigor impelling the inquiry.

In 1787, when Brown was sixteen, he became a member of the Belles Lettres Club, a society founded for the purpose of providing a forum for young, ambitious, competitive, upwardly mobile intellectuals to pursue a self-help regimen within a supportive, yet challenging, communal environment. The society's avowed purpose was for members to develop skills "in composition and eloquence" (Dunlap, *The Life*, I, 16). They occasionally met at the home of Benjamin Franklin. In a journal entry, Brown mentions "the meeting at Franklin's" (qtd. in Dunlap, *The Life*, I, 18). As Gilmore observes, "Multiple lines connect the nation's first 'canonical' novelist to the self-made Philadelphia printer who delighted in novels and adopted a female persona in his earliest publication. Like Franklin's *Autobiography*, Brown's fictions declare themselves to be acts of writing and hence products of print culture in contrast to the oral modes that previously held sway in America" ("Charles Brocken Brown" 644). One can easily imagine that the aged, semi-retired printer, inventor, scientist, author, and nation-builder recognized in these young men a nostalgic reflection of his own experience in 1727 when at the age of twenty-one he helped to create the Junto club, his own set of upwardly mobile wranglers, who met weekly for "mutual Improvement" (Franklin 47).[12] More importantly,

[12] Brown's first known publication turned into a fiasco. He wrote a poem honoring Benjamin Franklin, but when it was published on February 26, 1789 in *The State Gazette of North Carolina*, George Washington's name was printed in place of Franklin's. Brown was not amused: "The blundering printer. . .from his zeal or his ignorance, or perhaps from both, substituted the name of Washington. Washington therefore stands arrayed in awkward colours.... Every word of this clumsy panegyric was a direct slander upon Washington, and so it was regarded at the time" (qtd. in Dunlap, *The Life*, I, 17–18). For the text of the poem, see Warfel 32–33. See Axelrod

Franklin would have seen in the Belles Lettres Club not simply a reminder of his own pilgrimage into the realm of public discourse, but a hopeful harbinger of the country's future. This sort of literary community intrinsically celebrated the possibilities of individual intellectual development within the companionate framework of impassioned debate—a veritable template that brings together the energies of self-making with the attempt to realize the collective imperatives of practical, socially useful, Republican communitarian ideals, a process that directly prefigured, and may have made possible, his later membership in the New York Friendly Club (Waterman, *Republic of Intellect* 4). In the Belles Lettres Club were "several young men of brilliant talents, amiable dispositions and ardent minds, who, though all of characters very distinct from [Brown's], excited his emulation and called into action his mental powers" (Dunlap, *The Life*, I, 15). Brown's friends and associates established the supportive environment wherein he could express and revise his arguments, speculations, and compositions. His cohort, as it were, rescued him from—or provided an antidote to—an innate tendency towards moody insularity. His early years of reading and writing and the fluidity acquired through an assiduous writing habit came together with his developing intellect and passion for public self-expression. This process culminated with his address on the purpose of the Belles Lettres Club—the first major textual marker reflecting Brown's development as a writer.

These centuries later, this address remains a remarkable achievement for a sixteen-year-old, especially for its sophisticated ideas, its self-assured enthusiasm, and its audacious authority of statement. Brown's address marries the compositional process to the complementary experience of public performance. The text was prepared for oral delivery with the avowed purpose of charting the group's collective path. In ways that Brown may or may not have intended, the text serves as a highly personalized prolegomenon in which he feels his way into

---

for an extended discussion of Franklin and Brown 148–56. See Kafer's discussion of the Belles Lettres Club 49–51.

pressing issues that reflect those intellectual and aesthetic forces beginning to shape his vocational aspirations. In writing more presciently than he likely knew, he sketches a self-reflexive manifesto defining the embryonic configuration of his emergent, authorial self. He articulates how the writer can best be understood in performative terms. Indeed, Brown explicitly describes his impending literary career as a form of histrionic activity. He speaks of himself as one "destined to begin the career of literary improvement, and to enter immediately upon that theatre which to others still remains in distant and imperfect prospect" (Dunlap, *The Life*, I, 21). Brown figures himself as a literary pioneer preparing to set foot on the public stage. Within this brief, self-dramatizing proto-fiction, he indicates that narrative self-making constitutes a public, theatrical act. The written page becomes analogous to a metaphorical stage. He connects this dramaturgic process with the power of improvisation and role-playing. Upon entering the "theatre," Brown "gives his imagination full liberty to range without controul through the whole circle of human knowledge, in the belief that whatever calls for the exertion of his mental faculties is already within his reach, and may reasonably be appropriated to his own use. He confides in prospects which present an endless gradation of improvement" (Dunlap, *The Life*, I, 22). In sketching the contours of an independent, proto-romantic artist, Brown delineates an incipient instance of his later habit of using histrionic tropes to evoke the power of role-playing as it becomes enacted within the encompassing sphere of public—that is, *politicized*—performance. Throughout his mature work, his insistent use of words like "theatre," "prompt," and "author" would in time delineate how authorship possesses a fundamental capacity for shaping in positive and negative ways the unstable social world. In using the third-person pronoun to describe his own artistic agenda (and by extension the purpose of the society), he objectifies how this developing authorial self has a pioneering role to play within the cultural politics of the time. The poetics of narrative self-making leads to the adumbration of a self-liberating aesthetic agenda.

Brown's status as proto-Romantic writer emerges as this unfolding educational process derives its power and direction not so much from rationality or reason as from the daemonic influence of the "fancy": Brown writes of "those who find an interest in yielding to the persuasions of fancy, even in opposition to the sober dictates of their judgment" (Dunlap, *The Life*, I, 22). At this juncture, where the power of "fancy" threatens to usurp the office of "judgment," Brown presents a prototype of those incendiary figures of power, who in his four major novels seek to dominate their respective social world. In describing "a being of superior power and capacity" whose "habits and disposition... [and] faculties have attained their full vigour" (Dunlap I, 23), Brown anticipates the creation of such transgressive figures as Carwin, Ludloe, and especially the utopic and diabolical aspects of Ormond's divided personality. Even though admitting that "dreams of absolute perfection, can be realized only in another world," Brown nevertheless claims that "success...will be commensurate to the ideas of perfection." By appropriating the notion that experience must be rooted in the ethereal, nebulous realm of idealization, Brown demonstrates how the aspirant Romantic artist might be tempered by exigence, yet still recognize the complex qualification that *only* the most "exalted" ideas will likely produce "exalted" results (Dunlap, *The Life*, I, 23).

Without question, Brown's predilection here favors the agency of the fancy over the dictates of reason or judgment. As he proceeds in the address, he briefly rejects the balance between fancy and reason and asserts the primacy—even the sovereignty—of fancy in the creative process. Reason's voice, as it were, becomes drowned out by intoxicating imaginative excesses. In noting that "we are soon...to step forth upon the theatre of life, supported only by our own talents and address," Brown celebrates the "bewitching charms" of Belles Lettres and describes how "they become regardless of the voice of reason, and are totally immersed in the soothing pleasures of intoxicated fancy. The enthusiasm of poetry is no less strong and violent than that of religion; they flow in separate channels, but are derived from the self same fountain" (Dunlap, *The Life*, I, 25). By fusing the energies of literary creation and religious rapture, Brown displaces (at least temporarily) any reliance upon the ostensibly complementary office of reason. It seems to be a breakthrough idea for Brown that the sensational experience of art and religion generates from the unseen realm of inspiration—inspired by the Muse, infused by the indwelling of Divine Grace, or imbued with the sanctifying power of the Quaker Inner Light—and creates a passionate species of revelation that is capable of overwhelming—and then transforming—this nascent Romantic self. In the case of these extreme lovers of letters, they reject "the noise and clamour of the forum" and "fly to solitude and silence, to musing, and to contemplation, frequenters of the shade, and accustomed to indulge the airy flights of a fancy vigorous from use, and bold from the absence of constraint, they are equally governed by imaginary inspiration" (Dunlap, *The Life*, I, 25).

Such a premise can be powerful and dangerous. While driving the energies of literary creation, this principle can also shape the absolutizing, self-justifying mindset of Theodore Wieland—a man who accepts as phenomenologically efficacious the putative experience of a Deific visitation (*W* 167–68). Early in his writing life, Brown establishes how human subjectivity—that core element of revolutionary, Romantic consciousness—and one's interior pursuit of ultimate forms of validation constitute the explosive ground on which transactions of the most "exalted" kind can occur and thereby be justified as *real* by the very subjective energies empowering these exaltations, whether aesthetic or religious, in the first place (Dunlap, *The Life*, I, 23).

In describing the procreant agency of the fancy, Brown attempts to stipulate how literary creation happens. He not only speaks to his colleagues in the Belles Lettres Club; he not only attempts to develop working notes toward a credo that will impel the members of this Junto along the rutted path of "literary improvement" (Dunlap, *The Life*, I, 21); but more importantly, he self-reflexively speaks *to*, and *about*, his own newly formulated credo. Out of the very activity of writing and delivered within the histrionic performance of a discursive speech act, Brown voices a prelude, so to speak, that conjures the inviting shape and direction that a literary future might take.

Given Brown's vocational attraction to a literary life and his early preoccupation with utopian schemes and political self-empowerment, it may be tempting to view his ongoing legal studies as little more than an encumbrance, a steadfastly tedious expense of energy that merely appeased his family with the promise of social standing and financial compensation, all in the cause of thwarting his life's central purpose. The record suggests otherwise. From the time he composed and delivered the Belles Lettres address until 1793 when he gave up his legal apprenticeship, Brown remained committed to both endeavors.[13] For six years, day by day, he went to work in Alexander Wilcocks's law office, where he studied, learned, and did his job. As Kafer explains, "During this time he registered his desire for intellectual fellowship by joining a law club, whose members debated and analyzed and issued legal decisions on hypothetical cases" (49). After his workday ended, he wrote in the evening. His later strident, mocking denunciations of the legal profession should not lead one to read backward and conclude that life in Wilcocks's office was purgatorial misery. He did not wallow within a torturous state of frustrated animosity. Instead, like many young people, he pursued what amounted to a double major. As he did so, the large issue of how exactly he would live his life remained an open question. The various attributes of both professions created a self-sustaining dialectic. The evidence clearly suggests that he not only adapted himself to the dictates of the legal world, but that he excelled in this endeavor. Between 1788 and 1793—a long time in anyone's

---

[13]Brown did not end his legal apprenticeship with a loud and defiant shout proclaiming his liberation. His tendency was to emit ambiguous intimations in letters that suggested that he may prefer not to become a lawyer. He was moving on from the law as early as 1793, but he comes back to the issue in later letters. His April 19, 1795 and his September 1, 1796 letters to his brother James made it clear that he was finished with a career in law. See *L* 290–91 and *L* 363–64, respectively.

book—Brown did not spend his days agonizing over which alternative would be the road not taken. The issue was how best to reconcile the demands of both offices—the life of a man of letters and the life of a practicing attorney—all the while performing due diligence to the responsibilities and enticements of both apprenticeships. The formal structures of his legal work might even have facilitated his slow growth as a writer.

Brown excelled as a student of the law. Alive and well in both worlds, he became adept at the craft (or art) of multi-tasking. As his later aptitude for composing a number of fictional narratives while simultaneously engaged in editorial work and essay/review writing indicates, Brown was able to compartmentalize his legal and literary endeavors. In retaining Paul Allen's work, Dunlap prints some sample case-studies that display Brown's talent for legal disquisition. Essentially, he was skilled at manipulating and controlling the exigencies of various compositional styles, which is to say he could modulate the dictates of diverse, rhetorical purposes by adjusting the register of his authorial voice. Brown was not only a member of the Belles Lettres Club but "[a]s [a] member of the law society, Charles was no less zealous and active [than with the Belles Lettres Club]. While president, it was part of his official duty to record his judgment on the questions debated. These records are now preserved, and they afford an honourable testimony to his sagacity, sound judgment and research. They are likewise delivered in a style of gravity, becoming a judge, and widely different from that in which he usually wrote" (Dunlap, *The Life*, I, 16; see Allen 15 and 3–39). Another way of interpreting this assessment is to suggest that Brown was able to master the *voice* of a judge. In directly transcribing Allen's words, Dunlap goes on to quote an unnamed friend, who states that Brown's legal judgment

> is delivered with more perspicuity than any of the rest, in a language destitute of all embellishment, and with peculiar nicety of detail. He was in fact…a model of the dry, grave, and judicial style of argument. Directly after he had disposed of

> this question, as appears from his journal, he gave vent to his fancy in a poetical effusion, as much distinguished by its wild and excentric brilliance, as the other composition was for its plain sobriety and gravity of style. (*The Life*, I, 16)

With remarkable agility, Brown's ability to adjust his style to the exigencies of the moment could only have benefitted his development as a writer.

"The Devious Wanderings of a Quick but Thoughtful Mind"

In his biography, Dunlap occasionally displays annoyance over Brown's questionable social skills, especially his slovenly style of dress and seeming indifference to money. As a playwright and theatrical producer, Dunlap attempted to make a living by balancing the fruits of literary creation on the scales of marketplace viability. The problem of making money was never far from Dunlap's mind and this problem could not be dissociated from an anti-art bias afflicting the early decades of the new nation. As Michael T. Gilmore observes,

> The selfless notion of authorship was strengthened by the simple reality that only the rare American book returned a profit. The few writers who wanted to be professionals earning a livelihood from art—Charles Brockden Brown, Rowson, Dunlap—ended up pursuing other careers.... Dunlap, who went bankrupt in the theater, staved off the almshouse by painting miniatures and compiling biographies and histories. ("Letters of the Early Republic" 553)

Not surprisingly, Dunlap takes a dim view of Brown's divided commitment to those serious matters of social propriety and gainful employment. Dunlap critiques Brown's first foray into print as a preening act of dereliction: "While thus ostensibly studying law, but in reality indulging himself in every freak, suggested by his love of literature and of fame, he presented himself to the world in the Columbian

Magazine, in the character of a rhapsodist" (*The Life*, I, 16–17). In fact, Brown's first publication had very little, if anything, to do with fame. Published anonymously in *The Universal Asylum, and Columbian Magazine* from August through November 1789 (*R* xiii–24), these four essays successively appeared and were signed by the letters B, R, O, and W. There never appeared a "Rhapsodist" essay ascribed to the letter N.

The appearance of these essays, however, signals neither a descent into self-indulgence, a full embrace of a literary life, nor the repudiation of his legal apprenticeship. Rather, Brown simply attempted to make the most of an inviting opportunity: he could turn out one essay per month and perhaps find himself on the path to becoming an American incarnation of Joseph Addison and Richard Steele in *The Tatler* or heir to Samuel Johnson and his *Rambler* essays. Emory Elliott situates Brown in relation to his American contemporaries: "In these essays Brown adopted the semi-narrative essay form with which Freneau, Brackenridge, and Dwight had experimented. His persona is a hermit-explorer who has spent many months alone in the Ohio wilderness, meditating on human nature" (*Revolutionary Writers* 220). Despite the "Rhapsodist" papers' short run, Brown's four essays offer irruptive performances that reflect his ability to pursue a literary sideline, all the while maintaining his daily duties in Wilcocks's office. Paying scant attention to the content of these essays, Dunlap dismisses their importance. For example, he quotes one passage in which the Rhapsodist discusses the reconciliation of solitude and sociability and uses these sentiments to support his claim that Brown temporarily rejected the "romancing vein" in favor of "real life": "That Charles thus early saw the error of indulging in this romancing vein, and perceived that it unfitted him for the conversation and duties of real life is here made evident; but that he had at this time or even much later in life, corrected the evil, was not true. He long after this period loathed the common pursuits and common topics of men, and appeared in society an eccentric, if not an isolated being" (*The Life*, I, 17). Dunlap fails to see the narrating Rhapsodist as a projected fictive persona, as Brown's first published proto-fiction, and thus as his first published embodiment of his emergent authorial self. In using a selective passage to justify a dismissive psychoanalytical summary, Dunlap steers attention away from the content of these essays and, like some others after him, is all too quick to reject the developmental significance of these essays. Although correctly recognizing these pieces as providing "hints of the novelist to come," Warfel is hamstrung by the critical axiom that Brown's skills as a novelist are best displayed through his ability to generate moralizing, high-sounding maxims (35). David Lee Clark finds that the essays "are little more than random and disjointed speculations on life in the manner of the late eighteenth century. Intrinsically they are of little value" (46). Later, Watts cogently claims that these essays "constituted a benchmark in the young man's development both as a writer and as a human being." The essays provide both a "self-portrait" and "an exercise in sublimation" (44). Kafer deftly contends that Brown's "'rhapsodizing' needs to be viewed in this broader Romantic-era context" (62)—with Wordsworth and Coleridge serving as alter-egos or counterparts (59–63).

Brown's "Rhapsodist" essays offer more than biographical, psychological, or aesthetic oddities. Essentially, they give Brown the opportunity to sketch the nascent contours of his authorial self and to present through his emergent voice a penchant for narrative self-making. Brown describes an extrinsic authorial identity that extends, even as it remains distinct from, the flesh-and-blood writer working at his desk. In creating the voice of a rhapsodist, Brown presents an Ohio narrator, who adopts a playful tone designed to engage his audience with conversational familiarity. In his careful account of "[t]he character of a rhapsodist" (*R* 5), he conflates the mind generating thoughts in the unfolding compositional present with the delineation of a distinctly identifiable authorial identity. As Allen notes, Brown sought "to make his page the record of his own mind" (12). The figure of the rhapsodist fuses improvisation—in the form of seemingly "artless and unpremeditated language"—with the dynamic, interactive appearance of an unfolding speech act (*R* 5). In blending inspiration and conversation, the rhapsodist expresses the ostensibly spontaneous nature of this authorial voice. Indeed, in the activity of writing, he wishes to be recognized as *speaking* directly to the reader:

> A rhapsodist is one who delivers the sentiments suggested by the moment in artless and unpremeditated language.... He pours forth the effusions of a sprightly fancy, and describes the devious wanderings of a quick but thoughtful mind.... [T]he rhapsodist...may be remarkable for sudden transitions in his subjects, and hasty discussions, but not for an affected singularity in his opinions, or an absurd incoherence of thought. In short he will write as he speaks, and converse with his reader not as an author, but as a man. (*R* 5)[14]

Paradoxically, the author's voice derives from his odd insistence that he will not speak as an "author." Brown's convoluted premise is that the authorial voice of the rhapsodist is somehow not fictive, that it is neither artificial nor contrived. He claims to speak "as a man"—a nebulous distinction until one recognizes that the novice author has already associated the character of an "author" with the constructed, aesthetic activities of imposture, dissimulation, and deception. Earlier in the first number, the rhapsodist declaims against the dark arts of "[f]alsehood and dissimilation" (*R* 2). At the outset, he explicitly announces that "the sincerity of my character shall be the principal characteristic of these papers" (*R* 1); he will make the whole truth his compositional province. His promise to be a candid writer, conversely,

---

[14] In a [Summer 1792] letter to Wilkins, Brown describes how his letters to his brother Joseph are actually forms of direct speech: "I have a brother, whom I am bound by innumerable ties to revere and love. I have not seen him except for a few days, these eight years. He has gained wisdom by experience, a bitter series of experiments; but though there has subsisted no personal intercourse between us for so long a time, we have talked frequently and copiously to each other by the assistance of the pen" (*L* 28).

leads him to define the very prototype of those powerful, adversarial tricksters that later populate his novels:

> Wherever I perceive the least inclination to deceive, I suspect a growing depravity of soul, that will one day be productive of the most dangerous consequences. Falsehood and dissimulation, however embellished with the softest colours, and touched by the most sparing and delicate hand, stamp an infamy upon the character hardly to be equaled by the perpetration of the blackest crimes. (*R* 2)

In broad terms, the rhapsodist anticipates, and summarily rejects, the nefarious "consequences" that will later be engendered by the likes of Carwin, Ludloe, Craig, and Welbeck. In the very strength of his denunciation, he concedes, whether purposely or not, the inherent attraction of the "double-tongued" arts of deception (*W* 1).[15] In an essay ostensibly celebrating the moral imperative of total truthfulness and self-disclosure, Brown shows that the rhapsodist's evocation of truth cannot be dissociated from its dialectical relation with falsehood and imposture. At this early point in his career, Brown reveals his elemental interest in connecting a narrator's professed truth, on the one hand, with the inherent instability of such a truth within any text, on the other. "The Rhapsodist: No. I" articulates Brown's foundational views on the tangled relationship between truth and dissimulation and points to the protean possibilities that obtain when narration assumes the fluidity associated with the spoken word. Cast within a fixed text, the

[15] In considering the place of these essays in Brown's life, Watts argues, "With 'The Rhapsodist' essays the earliest stage of Brown's life reached a highly schizoid culmination. On the one hand, by early manhood his literary definitions and goals had begun to crystallize into a coherent intellectual foundation for his career. At the same time the young writer's personal definition and selfhood had fallen into increasing incoherence and disarray" (46). The sense of fragmentation described by Watts makes the process of self-making a necessary compensatory process: Brown overcomes fears of failure as he articulates the incipient outlines of a self-generated, protean authorial self.

seemingly improvisational speech act coincides with, and is indistinguishable from, the compositional act itself. Not only will he compose his thoughts in the improvisational manner of direct speech, but he will project the illusion that his writing is at one with his speech—that is, direct, immediate, genuine, a reflection of the unvarnished truth.

"The Rhapsodist: No. I" provides an early indication that Brown saw the process of writing and its culmination in publication as an inherently ambiguous process, wherein one finds the incipient presence of a double self—one who professes truth, even as one cautions readers regarding the seductive attraction of truth's diametrical opposite. As a fiction-writer, Brown would come to create characters that project in histrionic terms a "depravity of soul" of the sort the rhapsodist decries, but he would also dramatize the ambiguous attractions of such overreaching, protean villains. It is important to see "dissimulation" and "falsehood" as synonyms for a certain kind of fictionalizing—not merely as telling lies but as lies perpetrated in the cause of constructing an active, dominating, performative self, who asserts control over the contingencies or "consequences" of social experience.[16]

When Brown turns to "The Rhapsodist: No. II," he veers away from his description of the rhapsodist's voice and the conflicted aesthetics of truth-telling toward exploring specific applications of this voice and the nature of literary creation that such a voice might engender. Early in the essay, the rhapsodist reveals that his claim in the first essay for inviolable purity of utterance becomes reconceived—in a way befitting the protean aesthetics of improvisational speech—when the rhapsodist announces "his fondness for solitude" (*R* 6). Paradoxically, within the published text wherein he purports to address his reader "as a man," he admits a deep attraction to isolation. The ostensible

[16] In the December 1, 1792 letter to Bringhurst in which Brown has again described "my other self" (178)—his authorial self—he reflects on the danger that imposture poses to the social order: "Let me put your sincerity to the test, your friendship; for without confidence and mutual sincerity, what is friendship but a confederacy of villains or a compact of imposture?" (*L* 179).

distinction between "truth" and "dissimulation" as proposed in the first essay collapses as this self-characterizing, putatively solitary voice asserts the primacy of fiction and fancy over the facts of everyday, social life. The rhapsodist "loves to converse with beings of his own creation, and every personage, and every scene, is described with a pencil dipt in the colours of imagination" (*R* 6). That is, he loves to create the very proto-fictional world that he will then inhabit. The rhapsodist uses solitude and the words emanating from the Ohio wilderness to depict the evolving nature of his protean aesthetic.

Instead of developing a character to express his views, the rhapsodist offers a series of broad-brush summaries. Most notably, he rejects the quotidian in favor of the visionary. The rhapsodic artist must fly beyond the limits of human nature and aspire to heights limited only by his imaginative scope. In this procreant moment, Brown attempts to give voice "[t]o his strong and vivid fancy": "[The rhapsodist] turns from the feast of reason and ridicule with the same unsurmountable disgust, and waits impatiently for the hour of departure, when he shall be left to the enjoyment of himself, and to the freedom of his own thoughts. It is only when alone that he exerts his faculties with vigour, and exults in the consciousness of his own existence" (*R* 6). By propounding an ideational conflation between the offices of poetry and religion, he depicts the artist as a solipsistic, sovereign maker. Rather than forging new ground, Brown recycles a long passage from his address to the Belles Lettres Club. In defining the rhapsodist in idealized terms, Brown makes calculated emendations:

> He meditates amidst the splendor of the morning with the enthusiasm of a poet; and reflects in the silence and solemnity of midnight, with a rapture bordering on devotion. The enthusiasm of religion is little different from that of poetry, and these are with great difficulty distinguished from a sublime and rational philosophy. They flow in separate channels, but it is most probably that they are derived from the self same fountain. <u>The effects, at least, of their several propensities, are</u>

> exactly similar. Abhorring equally the noise and clamour of the forum, they fly to solitude and silence, to musing and to contemplation, frequenters of the shade, and accustomed to indulge the airy flights of a fancy, vigorous from use and bold from the absence of constraint. They are equally governed by imaginary inspirations. Tired and disgusted with the world's uniformity, they turn their eyes from the insipid scene without, and seek a gayer prospect, and a visionary happiness in a world of their own creation. (*R* 8–9; Dunlap, *The Life*, I, 25; underlined words identify Brown's interpolations into the original version printed by Dunlap.)

Significantly, Brown's two major revision sites assert how the poet's rhapsodic effusions are experienced as "exactly similar" forms of sensation that provide exciting alternatives to "the world's uniformity." This religiously-inspired aesthete rejects the crowded crossroads of everydayness in favor of self-generated and self-contained singularity. The rhapsodist *asserts* that he can create a kind of idealized, prelapsarian "prospect" as well as a form of "visionary happiness." Like the good Lockean he sometimes seems to be, Brown locates the experiential foundation of art and religion within the phenomenological realm of human sensation. If the sensational "effects" of these two creative forces are "exactly similar," then poetry and religion might also derive from "exactly similar" forms of creative agency.

These fledgling, seminal essays disclose that Brown's improvisational, protean artist proclaims, rather than actualizes, the complementary offices of poetry and religion. At this early point in his career, Brown seems content with a sophisticated form of ideational play. He cheerfully retreats from further pursuit of his highest aspirations: "It is the melancholy fate of castle builders...to raise an infinite variety of imaginary structures, without once having it in their power, materials sufficient to build a single edifice upon a solid and durable foundation" (*R* 10). Here, Brown admits that he has the ideas yet no story. In time, Brown will transfigure the rhapsodic strain of his self-making artificer into a series of insurgent figures—a band of duplicitous, "double-tongued" deceivers (*W* 1), who use dissimulation, imposture, and role-playing to engage in hubristic forms of aesthetic and political empowerment.[17]

Lives in Letters: "The Excursive Imagination"

Following the demise of his four-month career as a fledgling rhapsodist, Brown continued to live within the dualistic demands of his legal and literary apprenticeships. He maintained an active, if private, writing life that found him in late 1791 and through the first five months of 1792 engaged in a highly revelatory spree of epistolary activity.[18] His explosive letters to Bringhurst and Wilkins were inscribed at approximately the time he was revising the "Henrietta Letters" wherein a fictional C.B.B. engages in an ardent, epistolary courtship with a fictional Henrietta G.[19] These letters provide a framework for examining his

[17] Boyd sees Brown's failure to continue the series as a result of his "inability to put theory into practice, and the series ends in comical awkwardness when the narrator withdraws his aesthetically adventurous voice before a hostile editorial correspondent. . ." (489).

[18] Fliegelman elucidates the broad implications of letter-writing as a genre in the eighteenth century: "The letter affirmed the importance of the individual voice....In short, the letter allowed one to reflect on his or her experience, to learn from it, and to reach out beyond the prescriptive world of the household and its roles. It enhanced the development of the self, just as the novel built around the letter asserted the claims of that self" (29). Hewitt notes, "[T]he intensity of [Brown's] devotion to the [epistolary] form is exceptional....Brown understands the familiar letter as a repository for psychological interiority....[H]is letters also reveal his understanding of identity as a product of managed and mutable performance" ("Letters" 225–6).

[19] Barnard, Hewitt, and Kamrath indicate the foundational importance of these letters to Brown's emerging artistry: "[T]hese letters were received by Bringhurst and Wilkins as inventive and often playful narrative and poetic texts that manifested Brown's artistic ambitions and reflections concerning fiction writing" (834). In the May 16, 1792 letter to Bringhurst, Brown discusses the therapeutic, peripatetic power of the imagination: "How miserable should I be were I not rescued from the tedious or distressful present, by the aid of an excursive imagination?" (*L* 79). See

sophisticated literary experimentation and theorizing (*L* 178). In highly innovative ways, Brown reconceives the modal form of the epistle by using it as a medium for depicting spontaneously generated fictions. The Brown-Bringhurst-Wilkins correspondence and the faux "Henrietta Letters" led Brown to a host of achievements that shaped the emergence of his authorial self.

In a late 1791 letter to Wilkins, Brown conflates epistolary conversation, autobiographical self-dramatization, and narrative self-making. Halfway through the letter, Brown casts his own voice as a projected narrative persona and plunges into an irruptive fictional scene. He imagines himself as a secret invader of a "literary asylum" (*L* 11)—home, one speculates, to an idealized, yet currently absent, version of Brown's own authorial self—a space filled with books, the possession of a "wondrous learned personage," who may return and catch him rooting around in his lair. Here Brown shapes the contours of a scenic, speculative proto-fiction. After they vacate the room—"We are gone"—Brown begins to apostrophize—and indict—the constricting power of "Memory! thou witch! Thou art busy to pernicious purposes" (*L* 11). In this performance, glibly staged for Wilkins' amusement and approbation, the narrator depicts himself as a type of Menelaus wrestling with the recalcitrant Proteus, seeking to subdue this "[i]mperious, stubborn and refractory" figure that is "the cause of all my Infelicity" (*L* 11). Through his own rhetorical powers, he conquers his antagonist: "But I have thee now. My eyes have long been eagerly searching, but, till this moment, thou hast Proteus-like activity. In chains of adamant thou art bound: And now will I inflict vengeance on thee" (*L* 12). By capturing and containing the elusive figure of "Memory" (*L* 11), Brown liberates his narrative voice and celebrates how the "Fancy shall assume thy vacant throne" (*L* 12). By defeating the power of memory, he transfers its "Proteus-like activity" to his own creative imagination,

---

Letters 17 and 18, both written in late May 1792 to Bringhurst, for examples of Brown's critical reflections and spontaneous creation of proto-fictions within these letters (*L* 105–15).

"That heavenly power! Source of Rapture! Mother of ten thousand nameless joys" (*L* 12).

Brown's escape from the determinate force of memory not only imports associations with the slippery, powerful shape-shifter of Homer's *Odyssey*, but more significantly, Brown appropriates the figure of Proteus as a generative paradigm of narrative self-making. The invocation of Proteus stands as a synoptic metaphor that replaces the stultifying conjurations of the past with the imaginative activity unfolding within the compositional present. The defeat and subsequent re-construction of the Proteus figure celebrate the fluid possibilities associated with free-flowing imagination. The epistolary form reveals itself as being especially adaptive to these mercurial experiments with narrative voice. As he had in the past, Brown associates the writing process with the improvisational energies of speech. The epistolary form displaces his quotidian self in favor of foregrounding the voice of a vibrant fictive persona. Later in the letter, he accentuates the distinction between "my own self" and "my other self," between his everyday person and his fictionalized persona: "If I am not permitted to write about my own self, will you suffer me to talk about my other self! What a fertile theme that would be?" (*L* 13, emphasis in original). The "other self" is no less than Brown's unfolding, authorial self—his procreant voice—as it assumes the status of an independent, if fictive, identity. This projected authorial self appears in a number of avatars—for example, in C.B.B. of the "Henrietta Letters" and in fictional alter-egos Edward Stanton and Julius Brownlow. In these letters, irruptive, protofictional scenes come into being through the agency of seemingly spontaneous, ostensibly improvisational, acts of literary conjuration.

Immediately, after advising Wilkins to "leave the disposal of the future to providence or destiny" (*L* 11), Brown depicts the literary artist's profane, self-aggrandizing attempt to replace providential design with a scene of his own invention. He takes note of the sudden change in his physical location: "Hah! By what invisible agent was the Scenery so instantaneously changed? Whither have the actors vanished? Where am I?" (*L* 11). Upon finding himself in the "Closet...[o]f some secluded and contemplative and literary person" (*L* 11), he pays homage to his own unexpressed powers of literary creation. This absent student is an inchoate projection of Brown's "<u>other</u> self," whose impending successes will soon be actualized: "The Inhabitant of this cell is indeed a whimsical and singular personage, but his character will be best discovered in his performances" (*L* 11). The content of these "performances" can only be known as the improvisational voice emerges through the wavering dictates of Brown's prolific muse. The "performances" will be a consequence of the artist's power to express himself within "this literary asylum" (*L* 11). These compositional gyrations reflect the evolving contours of Brown's proto-romantic sensibility, especially his reliance on how one's free play of mind is not restricted by the limits of space, time, and matter. As Gretchen J. Woertendyke argues, "Unlike Enlightenment historiography and, later, the realist novel, romance is utterly unmoored by verisimilitude, providing a space for experimentation and the opportunity to trace the paths of various hypotheses, back and forth in time" (156).

In an (Early or mid-1792) letter to Wilkins, Brown depicts the activity of letter-writing as an unfolding conversation with the essential purpose of using his own words to establish his correspondent's *presence* within the text. He emphasizes the artist's power to use words that dictate the content of an unfolding social scene:

> Here am I seated at my desk. With pen and all the writing implements at hand; and shall I not employ them? Yes in good sooth I will, and they shall, for the present, be devoted to the pious use of shewing my friend that his absence does not annihilate him; his local absence for he is always intellectually present, and as he stands almost single in the Writers catalogue of Friends, my soul principally converses with his kindred spirit, —Lend me your wings I pray you, tend me your wings. (*L* 21)

The narrator transfigures Wilkins' physical absence into semiotic presence and then initiates an exploratory dialogue that playfully evokes the power of the imagination. The dialogue unfolds between Brown's "soul" and Wilkins' "kindred spirit," whereby Brown asks the "kind propitious amiable gracious bountiful divinity" for the "gift" of his wings (*L* 21). The "soul" of Wilkins avers that a "spirrit can traverse half the universe within a moment" (*L* 21). The imagination is not confined by physical laws but is a sovereign force unto itself. The comic irony within this dialogue finds Brown celebrating the expansive power of literary art, even as the "kindred spirit" refuses to lend his "pinions," even for an instant. Significantly, the passage includes a redacted Miltonic allusion from the poet's invocation of the Muse in Book 7 of *Paradise Lost*. Here Brown makes a significant emendation of Milton's text. As Barnard, Hewitt, and Kamrath observe, "Whereas the Miltonic poet asks the Muse Urania to safeguard him in the 'narrower bound / Within the visible diurnal sphere,'" Brown substitutes "beyond" for "Within," altering the meaning of the line (*L* 24, Note 6). Not only does the "soul" romantically aspire to poetic excursions "beyond" any ascribed limit, but Brown's voice laments the spirit's ostensible refusal to lend his wings.[20] With its allusive, self-confident expression of compositional play, this letter reflects Brown's unequivocal love of the writing process. In playing upon the compositional instrument and expanding the reach of his "<u>other</u> self," Brown moves with ease in and out of numerous fictional personae. In signing this letter "C. B.

---

[20] The presence and example of John Milton and his poetry dominated the consciousness of pre-Romantic and Romantic writers. Milton was the artistic exemplar, who challenged his successors to emulate and surpass his greatness. In a [December 13, 1792] letter to Bringhurst, Brown writes of Milton and Francis Bacon: "Such men as these did once most certainly exist. Is there any physical impossibility that they should again exist? How is it to be known but by experiment whether Heaven has appointed us their rivals and competitors? How can it be esteemed a proof of vanity to suppose it possible for ourselves to equal them? or at least to believe that our attainment of their elevation is sufficiently doubtful to justify the attempt?" (*L* 199).

Brownlow," he displaces the autobiographical self in favor of a fictional avatar (*L* 23).

Throughout this formative period, Brown's letters to his two friends depict recurrent experiments in narrative self-making. In promulgating a number of irruptive, exploratory proto-fictions, Brown turns ostensibly personal letters into improvisational, artistic proving grounds: "My pen is the best Interpreter of my Sentiments: My pen, therefore, shall, if <u>possible</u>, weary you without its ceaseless volubility If possible! mark the vanity of that audacious '<u>IF</u>'....I will overwhelm you with a torrent of exaustless though perhaps insipid gayety" (*L* 12–13, emphasis in original). The overwrought diction suggests Brown's lurking insecurity regarding who he is and what he might become, even as the letters operate in an intrinsically salutary manner. In a letter to Bringhurst later that year—December 21, 1792—Brown makes explicit the degree to which the very act of writing operates as a form of therapy: "When I am uneasy with myself, and dissatisfied with all the world, I generally betake myself to my pen. Writing is an employment which always proves to me a source of sovereign consolation, because it forces me to think, and a rapid current of ideas washes away a thousand muddy cares and vexatious impediments" (*L* 209). Narrative self-making becomes both a form of psychological therapy and a compensatory, provisional form of self-promotion. His wavering sense of artistic self-doubt becomes (momentarily) alleviated through these epistolary excursions. The physical and psychological need for the balm of composition— "sovereign consolation"—infiltrates the deepest recesses of his being. His effusive forays and irruptive proto-fictions displace the stultifying entrapments, or "impediments," associated with everyday life.

Within these letters, Brown not only gives shape to incidental or wayward moods, but he suddenly shifts from discussing personal matters into depicting spontaneous proto-fictional performances. For example, an irruptive scenario obtrudes into Brown's May 16, 1792 (separate) letters to Wilkins and Bringhurst. After making clear to Wilkins that he will always be ready to repair any breach in their friendship, Brown plunges into the storytelling mode. His first-person narrator describes a world that comes into existence only *as* he writes: "I am now in the midst of a delightful Country, which the purity of manners and the political and domestic felicity of the Inhabitants, the fertility of the soil and the beauties of the Landscape have combined to render a paradise. Here am I immured in pleasing and inchanting solitude, banqueting on classical literature, or conversing with rural Simplicity" *(L* 70). Borrowing from Rousseau's *Heloise*, the fictionalized C.B.B. announces himself as being in love with the fourteen-year-old Jacquelette.[21] To add a supporting character, he introduces the Englishman Edward Stanton. Later that evening, Brown continues this freewheeling proto-fiction in the Bringhurst letter. The fictive narrator in the fictive scene discusses an actual letter received from the real-life Bringhurst. Once again, Brown conflates his present life with the imagined scene, which leads to a lengthy, political dialogue between the fictive C.B.B. and his fictive alter-ego Edward Stanton. The proto-fiction reaches an abrupt termination as Brown replaces a fabricated Switzerland with all-too-real Philadelphia, a transition from the magical arena of literary conjuration to the quotidian confines of his room:

> O my friend! How miserable should I be were I not rescued from the tedious or distressful present, by the aid of an excursive imagination? A long quotation in a letter is intolerable, but there is a passage in Eloisa so expressive of my sentiments and situation that I can scarcely forbear inserting it. Its

---

[21] Nye claims, "The most powerful French influence on Brown's personality and ideas...was Jean Jacques Rousseau, whose...*La Nouvelle Heloise* (which Brown probably knew under its English title of *Eloisa*) struck his generation hard" (318). Barnard, Hewitt, and Kamrath indicate that imagined scenes appear in 17 of the 45 letters Brown wrote from 1792–92 (833–34). See Brown's fictional London letter to Bringhurst (*L* 63). From Brown's apprenticeship pieces onward, one finds an insistent transatlantic dimension to his art. The concept of Europe in his early proto-fictions often transports his narrating avatars to a prime European location. See Apap and Leask for discussions of the transatlantic aspect of Brown's art.

> purpose however is to shew that the imagination is the Source of human felicity. No one was ever less calculated for the drudgery of business than myself. Science and Literature are the Idols of my soul: Love and Friendship constitute my existance. (*L* 79)

The creation of literary art, then, must be seen as an alternative, as well as an antidote, to the pedestrian affairs of everyday life. The "excursive imagination" is what drives literary invention and confers the balm of "intellectual excellence and moral beauty" (*L* 79).

Even as he admits, in the aftermath of his "excursive" flight of mind, his incapacity for the "drudgery of business," even as he shoots the gulf between his "own" voice and one of his "other" voices, Brown continues to refine the contours of his protean aesthetic. For example, in an October-November 1792 letter to Bringhurst, he summarizes a proto-romantic theory of spontaneous literary creation:

> I do not pretend to be reasoner and shall do little more, at any time, than throw upon the page the conceptions of the moment, than mingle, with capricious eagerness and copiousness, the streem of Sentiment and fancy, amuse my amiable correspondent with the air built Structures of a wild, undisciplined, intractable imagination, and whisper soft effusions of a soul that longs to mingle with a kindred spirit in his minds attentive ear. (*L* 150)

The *activity* of writing constitutes an intuitional, improvisational, unfolding performance. Brown writes to discover where his writing will take him. In effect, these letters are analogous to one-sided conversations, where questions are posed and answered: "I left Wilkins yesternight at Eleven OClock.... and spent an hour in delightful Meditation. Shall I give you a copy of my soliloquy? Will it not weary you? Yes; I know it will. I do nothing but fatigue my friends with self-interesting Narratives. I will here after be more sparing of them" (*L* 79).

The epistolary form easily accommodates the dialectical imperatives of this creative double self—this interaction between his individual, everyday person and his irruptive, fictionalized personae. Brown posits a working theory of creative symbiosis in which the private self becomes one with a fictive, narrating persona suddenly living in London or Switzerland. In the May [19], 1792 letter to Bringhurst, Brown introduces the outline of his prospective story about the twins Julius and Julietta Brownlow and insists that the character of the writer only becomes known through the details of his work. He describes how he is *present* within this persona: "The hero of my tale I distinguished by the Name of Julius Brownlow. I believe in every work of this kind, the character of the writer, such as it, really, is, or such as he imagines, or wishes it to be, may be found. I confess that at this time my ambition extended no farther than to act and speak like <u>Julius</u>" (*L* 90, emphasis in original). Brown discovers, even as he creates, the latest delineation of the authorial self. In this passage, the multiple qualifications, the involuted syntax, and cluttering commas evoke the self-entangling nature of the unfolding compositional process. As he writes, as he seeks accuracy, he becomes deluged by a swarm of explanatory particulars that attempt to address—and define—as many contingencies as possible. He goes on to state: "On the amiable Julius therefore I conferred every excellence, mental and corporeal, yet mingled with certain failings which I discovered in myself and which reduced this exalted personage to the level of probability" (*L* 90–91). The process of literary creation takes this idealized, aspirant, fictive self and imbues him with the writer's own flawed attributes. His purpose is to make this invented figure appear plausibly human. In other words, the act of story-telling establishes a kind of reciprocity between the composing authorial self and the fictionalized projection of this self. Narrative self-making implicates Brown in the construction of various symbiotic doubles. The authorial self becomes a mediating presence that links the flesh and blood author with an expanding array of fictional identities, a process that asserts, even as it validates, the ontological status of these fictional personae.

His preoccupation with articulating the aesthetic implications of this creative symbiosis appears frequently throughout the Bringhurst-Wilkins correspondence of spring 1792 and, most significantly, comes to dominate the "Henrietta Letters," especially Brown's abiding insistence that C.B.B. and Henrietta are living, breathing beings.[22] In the May [19], 1792 letter to Bringhurst, Brown presents a meta-narrative that conflates a number of aesthetic frameworks—Brown's letter-writing voice; the imagined world of his alter-ego C.B.B.; C.B.B.'s enraptured description of Henrietta; and Brown's unification with Julius Brownlow, another fictional alter-ego. The letter-writing Brown describes in summary fashion the epistolary activities and life events of Julius and twin sister Julietta; he mentions "the benevolent and hospitable case of Mr. Wentworth and his daughter," but Brown suddenly stops this summary (*L* 94, emphasis in original). His emotions overtake him with an ecstatic outburst that leads him to conflate his autobiographical self with the emerging fiction that he is in the act of creating:

> Ah! My friend! That daughter! Sophia Wentworth! With what a pen of passion did I describe her beauties! How liberally did I shower perfection on her mind and person! The Image of my Henrietta rose before me. Then did, I indeed, assume the person of My hero. Then quickly did the studious philosophical and contemplative Julius undergo a transformation, and become a tender passionate romantic lover! like myself! (*L* 94).[23]

---

[22] Kafer contends that these "Henrietta Letters" were inspired by Henrietta Chew, the daughter of eminent lawyer Benjamin, "a birthright Quaker turned Anglican," who was in legal practice with son-in-law Alexander Wilcocks (51–52).

[23] These proto-fictions offer glimpses of complexes that appear later. For example, Sophia Wentworth anticipates Sophia Courtland, *Ormond*'s narrator. The twins Julius and Julietta prefigure Brown's use of doubled characters in *Wieland*, *Stephen*

During those months, the figure of Henrietta was a dominating interest. In the May 5, 1792 letter to Bringhurst, for example, Brown coyly writes, "I will take an opportunity to shew you the specimen of an amorous correspondence, founded on truth and nature" (*L* 32). Earlier in this letter, Brown celebrates "the illumined and impassioned pages" of Rousseau's *Heloise* and mentions his own attempts to emulate "the voice of truth and nature" (*L* 32). In a letter received by Bringhurst on May 9, 1792, Brown explains: "I devote almost all my leisure to the transcription of those letters which I have already shewn you a specimen. I think I have already assured you that those letters are genuine, and I suppose you easily perceive that one of the parties in this correspondence is myself" (*L* 52). In pointing to the "genuine" nature of this epistolary fiction, Brown emphasizes not only his performative presence within the narrative but his ontological identification with the narrator. Brown thus affirms the fancy's power to simulate a more refined truth than might be available within the humdrum world of ordinary concerns. This prolific, intrepid, undisciplined, letter-writing artificer develops a voice characterized by an exalted, lyrically-charged intensity bordering on bombast. For example, in a [May 1792] letter to Wilkins, Brown generates a playful proto-fiction where "reality" as reflected in the person of Wilkins becomes displaced by an idealized vision of Henrietta. Brown's praise for the exalted woman (comically) diminishes Wilkins' status:

> My eyes are closed, my head reposes on my arm, my thoughts are scattered, my attention dissipated. I linger for a moment

---

Calvert, and *Edgar Huntly*. See Barnard, Hewitt, and Kamrath on Brown's naming of characters: "Like Lauder Ellen, Sophia Wentworth combines character names used in several other fictions by Brown. Sophia is the name of central characters in *Ormond* (1799) and in the undated but likely circa 1800 'Jessica and Sophia' narrative first printed posthumously in the [Paul] Allen biography, *The Life of Charles Brockden Brown* (c. 1811), 108–69. Wentworth is likewise the name of an important female character in *Arthur Mervyn* (1799–1800) and a secondary character in *Ormond*" (102, Note 23).

> on the verge of sleep; I just retain discernment to discover what it is that hovers over the threshold of my imagination, and is the only one of all the throng which has just retired from the penetralia that is visible. A sound reaches me that is, with difficulty, audible. Some spirit whispers in my ear the name of Wilkins, but before its last faint echoes are departed, my slumber is disturbed by that of Henrietta.... That thy image is excluded only to admit the luminous idea of a gracious beauty, with whom if thou wast acquainted thou wouldst join me in adoring *her*, and in looking with contempt or indignation on the Dolls or Lucys that daily flutter in thy sight. Those toys! Those gildings, those baubles to amuse a thoughtless hour, those eye deluders; who, when absent, are invisible. (*L* 55, emphasis in original)

Not only does the figure of Henrietta transform Wilkins' presence into rhetorical absence, but she also becomes far more tantalizing than those actual women, who "daily flutter in thy sight." The power of literary art takes precedence over women who actually walk the earth.[24] Only by being rapt within the lyrical excesses of his narrative voice does he engender the performative construct that is the "*other* self"—the C.B.B. of the "Henrietta Letters," the writerly voice who *becomes* a character within the text (*L* 13).

At work within this matrix is a self-induced form of auto-eroticism, Brown's narcissistic fascination with the fruits of his own labors, a kind of aesthetic self-love leavened with a tone of self-satirical play. As the wry reference to the fluttering "Dolls" suggests, Brown is acutely conscious of *performing* and part of the performance concerns how far

[24] The dismissive evocation of the fluttering "Dolls" does double duty as a jocular, for-your-eyes-only reference to Dorothy "Dolley" Payne Todd, the wife of attorney John Todd, under whom Wilkins served his legal apprenticeship. Prior to Dolley Payne's marriage to Todd, Brown "wrote several admiring poems" praising the woman, who later married James Madison and became First Lady Dolley Madison (Barnard, Hewitt, and Kamrath 25, Note 12).

he can extend the intensities of his diction, especially as he pens hyperbolic, "mind-irradiated" praise for Henrietta:

> Where is that superiority of understanding, that sublimity of sentiment, that sanctity of virtue, that union of grace and dignity! Where are those features, mind-irradiated, and those eyes each glance of which appears to be an emanation of divinity? Ah, my friend, in the image at which my solitary hours are employed in gazing, all those attributes and more than I can number are comprised. (*L* 55)

Although the ostensibly ideal attributes of this projected lover remain beyond the reach of language, Brown labored to depict this dialogic relationship. The "Henrietta Letters" illustrate an important chapter in Brown's development as a writer, especially through his ardent depiction of C.B.B. as a projected authorial self and through Henrietta's emergence as the first powerful female voice in Brown's fiction.

First Love: "Our Intercourse is Intellectual"

Because of Brown's enthusiastic propensity for discussing his protofictional characters as if they were flesh-and-blood beings, Clark viewed the "Henrietta Letters" as providing autobiographical evidence of a romantic relationship between Charles Brockden Brown of Philadelphia and Henrietta Golophon of Connecticut (53–55). One cannot fault Clark for using these letters in an attempt to expand the documentary record of Brown's life, especially in light of how credible it all sounds, how lifelike both voices are, and especially in view of Henrietta's plausible, matter-of-fact summary of how the great romance began:

> How perfectly do I recollect all the circumstances of the origin of our friendship? Nine months ago how should I foresee that the youth whom I observed frequently passing my window and whose habit and demeanour gave no token of his real character, would at this time have acquired all my confidence, and bound me to him in the bonds of

> indissoluble affection? I saw you often but I saw you only with indifference, untill, one morning, as you passed the window I observed you looking into it with a timid but eager curiosity. When you saw nobody you appeared disappointed, and slackened your pace to examine more attentively. But you suddenly met my eyes. You were startled, were covered with blushes and confusion.... All that day your idea haunted me incessantly. (*L* 713)[25]

Henrietta's voice has more than enough real-life timbre to take in willing believers, but from a more detached perspective, one can view this fictionalized scenario as another proto-fiction, a constructed literary moment. From a psychological perspective, Henrietta surrenders herself to initiating an uncertain, deeply felt experience, wherein actual events provide pre-texts for subsequent epistolary ruminations that magnify the range and intensity of the developing romance. The letters that pass between C.B.B. and Henrietta are ardent narratives composed in the near aftermath of what seem to have been fairly mundane direct encounters. *What happened* when they were together simply provide occasions that impel their fervent, compositional exchanges. The letters operate as projected speech acts—expansive monologues—that drive their mutually effusive, dialectical responses.

---

[25] See Hewitt for her discussion of the "Henrietta Letters," especially Rousseau's influence on the evolution of Henrietta (" Letters" 230–33). Watt discusses the attending matter of verisimilitude in relation to the epistolary form as developed in the English novel in the eighteenth century. The reality expressed by the epistolary form "is one which reveals the subjective and private orientations of the writer both towards the recipient and the people discussed, as well as the writer's own inner being.... [T]he use of the epistolary method impels the writer towards producing something that may pass for the spontaneous transcription of the subjective reactions of the protagonists to the events as they occur" (191–92). As Hewitt suggests, "What makes Brown's investment in literary letters so compelling...is that he so frequently calls attention to the mediated and performative quality of all epistolary writing" ("Letters" 229).

Brown inscribes these interactions between C.B.B. and Henrietta as a rhetorical competition—she tries to out-write him and he tries to out-write her—that allows them to explore the reaches of emotional and psychological extremity. These hyperbolic, rhetorical displays examine the nature and limits of the very aesthetic they are enacting. To this extent, the letters operate as mutually self-reflexive meta-texts that embody, even as they analyze, the very processes whereby they communicate—and dictate—who they are and what their relationship means. C.B.B.'s language experiments appear as impromptu "performances": "You have seen only those performances which were dictated by my love, which were produced at the luminous, and impassioned moment in which all my faculties were suspended in the contemplation of your charms" (*L* 679). As in the Bringhurst-Wilkins correspondence, Brown enacts an aesthetic of spontaneous address—those irruptive feelings immediately translated into highly emotional language. Indeed, the passions experienced by the fictionalized, authorial C.B.B. for the fictionalized, authorial Henrietta *create* the necessary occasion for the unfolding of their rapturous, epistolary creations. C.B.B. continues:

> Is it to be wondered at that at such a moment officious and unbidden eloquences awaited on my lips? My conceptions are often too big for words, they struggle in vain for utterance, and in the hurry and confusion which their multitude, in thronging to my pen produces, I cannot hesitate in the choice of words. Whichsoever first offer themselves, are instantly adopted. I have no liesure to reflect and weigh to chuse. I am unsolicitous of elegance or accuracy. (*L* 679)

His language is, as he observes, unprompted and unmediated; his words are incapable of communicating the ineffable content of his putatively transcendent emotions. Brown defines in nascent form the basic, and ultimately irresolvable, quandary of the Romantic writer, who recognizes that language can never adequately represent transcendent ideational or spiritual essences. While words, words, and more words cannot accurately express the unsayable, they can delineate Brown's abiding interest in exploring the protean possibilities of narrative self-making as expressed within the rapturous, rhetorical energies of intellectual and erotic foreplay.

The letters to Henrietta provide a way for C.B.B. to emerge from seclusion, for him to reject the insular world of a scholar's closet in favor of opening an intercourse with Henrietta's rich, luxuriant sensibility. Brown's axiomatic premise is that the authorial self achieves liberation and pleasure through writing: "But the passion for study was quikly supplanted by the delight which I began to take in composition, and my hand was less frequently furnished with a book than with a pen" (*L* 693). By pursuing this delightful "occupation" (*L* 697), C.B.B. affirms how his artistic principle is based on freedom of address: overwhelming sensations require immediate utterance, however inadequate, inchoate, or incoherent such utterances may be. These effusions point to how the "Henrietta Letters" constitute a lengthy paean to Brown's first love—the love of literary creation as it assumes shape within the emergent compositional present:

> Why should I review and correct what I have written? And no otherwise than by incessant revision and correction, can exactness be acquired.... I am not that despicable thing that mopes away his hour in the dusk of a library.... I deliver the Suggestions of my heart. I speak in my native character. So rapid is generally the torrent of ideas, in writing to my angel, that I cannot mark the connection and dependance, and am sometimes fearful that the abruptness of my transitions has occasioned some degree of obscurity. (*L* 679)

Even with these self-mocking insinuations, C.B.B.'s protean exploration finds its dialectical counterpart in the performative exuberance of Henrietta's own epistolary discourse. This powerful, independent female voice prefigures a host of characters that includes *Alcuin*'s Mrs. Carter, *Ormond*'s Constantia Dudley, and *Arthur Mervyn*'s Achsa

Fielding.[26] Henrietta becomes C.B.B.'s ontological and literary alter ego. Her question— "Why should Women be outstripped by men in literary pursuits?" (*L* 688)—functions less as a petition than a radical declaration of gender equality and literary independence.

Like C.B.B., Henrietta is most intent on trying out the expansive possibilities of the compositional process. She too engages in an aesthetic of improvisational address with the significant distinction that she almost always appears more reasonable, focused, mature, and self-possessed than her frequently overwrought correspondent. Henrietta knows that C.B.B.'s letters express a transgressive sensibility that counterpoints his staid conventional behavior when they are together. Letter-writing becomes C.B.B.'s cathartic vehicle for releasing his pent-up, aching sensuality. Whereas he proclaims, "Our intercourse is intellectual," he reveals that his eroticized discourse displaces, or at least defers, his desire for an active, conjugal consummation (*L* 697). When C.B.B. goes too far, Henrietta is ready to reel him back within the confines of propriety. At the beginning of Letter III, for example, she assumes a hectoring, chastising tone:

> Oh! My capricious and unaccountable friend!...How would you be induced to write in that inexcusably licentious manner?—I read it with indignation and regret, but let this be the last time, that you recall to my remembrance that epistle or the circumstances which produced it. I shall not forgive a second and equally flagrant violation of decorum. I blush for you. (*L* 682)

Such censure is actually a teasing form of play wherein her decorum masks her *own* penchant for testing the limits of propriety. Although Henrietta encounters numerous occasions where she must forgive C.B.B.'s "violent and domineering passion" (*L* 683), she does not

---

[26] These nascent explorations of a self-empowered female voice pre-date Brown's reading of Mary Wollstonecraft's *A Vindication of the Rights of Woman* (1792).

confine herself to the role of reason's constabulary disciplinarian. In fact, she invents a provocative scenario, wondering how he would respond if she suddenly rejects him:

> I will immediately leave this City and return to Connecticut. I will send you a letter, to be delivered to you after my departure, in which I will solemnly renounce all affection for you, declare, with all the virulence of female indignation, that some parts of your conduct has mortally and inexpiably offended me, and that hereafter no correspondence or connection shall subsist between us. What sayest thou? I hope thou wilt applaud the ingenuity of this contrivance. (*L* 683)

This proto-fiction attempts to incite the very sort of hyperbolic display she supposedly deplores. Following C.B.B.'s receipt of this letter, Henrietta assumes the role of semiotic dominatrix and pesters him to report what his sensations *would be* had their romance ended. Although quickly withdrawing the request, she nevertheless uses her prospective decampment to emphasize her power over him. In playing the dubious role of his soul's physician—"But the disorder must be known before it can be cured. What is thy disease my friend?" (*L* 683)—she recognizes how she enflames the very malady that exacerbates his emotional distress. The point of such badinage is to keep both parties writing at a feverish pace.

Significantly, Henrietta impulsively generates her irruptive proto-fictions in the manner of Brown's own creations within the Bringhurst-Wilkins correspondence. She too has a powerful creative unconscious: "[S]leep at length overtook me, but you still haunted my Imagination. I saw you under a thousand different shapes" (*L* 714). Henrietta recounts a series of proto-fictions designed to replace quotidian life with the seductive power of new opportunities: "At one time methought, you came to visit me in a magnificent Equipage, with a splendid Retinue. At another time that you put on a mean disguise and became a servant of the gardener, and that you threw down your spade, and discovered yourself to me, as I happened, one morning, to be walking alone in the Garden" (*L* 714).[27] Like C.B.B. and Brown himself, Henrietta becomes a protean artificer. Through her fictionalizing power, she casts her correspondent in contrastive roles of affluence and indigence—whatever form of imposture her procreant fancy feels moved to create. In spinning these truncated proto-fictions, she imbues the ephemeral products of her wayward imagination with the provocative power of textual (and sexualized) presence. Brown thus infuses the correspondence with emotional immediacy. By creating the illusion of her real-life presence, Henrietta blurs the distinction between the pedestrian world of everyday things and the realm of literary invention. This epistolary interaction documents the emergence of mutually interdependent, symbiotic selves, thereby overcoming their physical separation and asserting the illusion of shared ontological immanence. Henrietta writes:

> When are you absent from my mind? You are never absent, and, would you believe it, are most intimately present when in sleep. The Soul appears to be divested of her moral fetters, and to enjoy, the interval of freedom, in realizing the wishes of our waking hours.... Not a moment, during the Night after your visit was my spirrit separate from thine, and Methought the conversation of the Evening had not suffered interruption. (*L* 702)

Given this spiritual power, she feels she can hold him in place while she entertains some female guests. She *writes* him into being and controls his actions: "Stay thee, friend, in my closet till I return. As soon as I am disengaged I will devote another hour to this most pleasing occupation" (*L* 702). When Henrietta's friend leaves, she liberates C.B.B. from confinement: "She is gone. I will open the closet and release You" (*L* 703). For as long as Henrietta continues to write this

---

[27] This prospect anticipates Ormond's "disguise" when he surreptitiously visits the Dudley household in the role of a Black chimney sweep (*O* 133–34).

letter, C.B.B. remains within the semiotic confines she inscribes, which are no less than the limits prescribed by decorum.

When C.B.B. takes up the action in his epistolary response, however, he wrests control of Henrietta's plot. An eroticized, turbulent C.B.B. bristles at the notion that he must follow her instructions and be a safely closeted man. With pen in hand, with fancy in play, he generates an audacious fiction of sexual transgression. Since she has (in *her* fiction) already placed him in her closet, he has a warrant to *be* there. Although Henrietta thus holds her gestating narrative in abeyance, C.B.B. breaks loose and finds that her letter awakens his "lawless Imagination" and incites "the most furious passions" (*L* 707). In response, he constructs a transgressive scenario. This Romantic act of incendiary self-liberation not only inscribes his self-fashioned fiction of erotic anticipation but enacts an aesthetic form of domination. By escaping the bonds of Henrietta's narrative, C.B.B. becomes free to imagine a scenario of conjugal conquest: "Into what fatal reveries did your letter plunge my imagination! A momentary phrenzy, deadened my Intellects, and beguiled my Senses" (*L* 707). Extending the fiction of his dramatic presence, he asserts his control of the dramatic scenario she originally composed. He thus creates a reconstructed scene—cast within the exaggerated language of hyperbolic, sexual passion—that positions his fictionalized self within the closet that opens on her bedroom. The imagined scene unfolds before the reader's eyes in the dramatic present. He hears her approaching, sees her enter the bedroom, and watches her undress. Upon seeing her naked flesh, the tumescent voyeur nearly explodes:

> Far more beautiful in the careless and voluptuous elegances of a Night dress, than in the studied decencys, the splendid Neatness of the noon or evening. How does the lawn flow in wanton luxuriance about you! How dazzlingly white; How exquisitely fine its texture! How suitably adapted to the purposes of love! to shroud without obscuring your resplendent beauties, to shade without concealing that exstatic bosom.

> Could my eyes be otherwise than intoxicated with the Sight. (*L* 707–08)

After looking at her mussed bed, he leaves the closet and enters the sanctum. After she sees him, he enfolds her in his arms. As a consequence of his "rambling and unsanctified Imagination," he takes on the voice of a rapacious seducer. She is

> almost stiffled by my kisses. Your blushes but heightened the disorder of my Senses, And your struggle only augmented my impetuosity. And—O heavenly creature! when so little was wanting to compleat my phrenzy, and render me the most happy and most miserable of mankind, a word a look from you, extinguished my ardour in a moment & dissolved me in tears of shame and regret. (*L* 708)

By commanding him to stop, Henrietta arrests C.B.B.'s erotic narrative and causes him to rein in his runaway imagination. C.B.B. dissolves into an abject state of penitential self-loathing, which leads him to play a new role. In the near aftermath of Passion Interruptus, he mounts a retrospective critique of her "inauspicious power" and his performance as a prospective rake:

> What inauspicious power presided over your pencil, and induced you to describe, with such pernicious exactness, the Curtain drawn aside at Midnight, the Chamber yet illumined with the rays of the sinking moon, the beauteous sleeper awakening from a vision, in which her active imagination was filled with the idea of her friend, and rising from her Coutch. The receptacle of beauty, the assylum of love, her delicate arms and luxuriant bosom defenceless and uncovered, her dishevelled locks flowing with voluptuous profusion over her snowy shoulders, and leaning over the Side to view the gleaming west, and marks the progress of the peaceful hours. (*L* 709)

This letter celebrates her "active imagination"—the very agency that provokes the feverish display of his own "lawless Imagination" (*L* 707).

What remains most in evidence is the "voluptuous profusion" of their two-sided discourse. Indeed, Brown is the creator of the entire epistolary exchange. It is all made up, an elaborate form of literary auto-eroticism, nothing but words. There is no naked bosom, no impending act of sexual transgression. By creating both voices, by becoming both characters, Brown explores how far his language experiment can take him. Brown gleefully tests the limits of his compositional powers, especially as he describes erotically charged moments created in the service of rhetorical and imaginative independence—an independence qualified by the privately circulated, unpublished epistolary performance. Brown delights in C.B.B.'s display of rhetorical and emotional excess that prompts Henrietta's simultaneous repulsion from, and attraction to, his sensual, compositional "phrenzy" (*L* 708).

The "Henrietta Letters" constitute for Brown a literary proving ground. He used the highly-adaptable, epistolary form to exercise and extend the reach of his compositional powers. His experiment seems most successful when his amorous descriptions provide the source of an effusive, eroticized lyricism. These language-forms depict not only fragmented aspects of his emergent, authorial self, but also an exterior world redolent with self-reflexive and allusive intensities. For example, in one passage, C.B.B. connects the allure of carefully selected Miltonic texts and his love for Henrietta herself:

> This morning I repaired thither, before the east had exhibited any tokens of approaching light, with Miltons Comus Licdas and Il Penseroso in my Pocket, intending to devote the hours to those performances, and to investigate the principles of that divine philosophy which they teach, but alas! My thoughts continually wandered from the page before me, and the Image of my beauteous Harriot incessantly interposed between the poet and the critic, and intirely diverted my attention from the book. (*L* 718)

In the letter, C.B.B. prepares to present a paean to the creative possibilities inherent in place and prefigures young Carwin's formative artistic experience in the "vocal glen" in *Memoirs of Carwin the Biloquist* (*M* 235). C.B.B.'s allusions to "Lycidus" and "Il Penseroso" evoke a suggestive matrix of Miltonic materials that includes Comus as a magical artificer and melancholic associations of "Il Penseroso." Significantly, the "Image of my beauteous Harriot" displaces his interest in reading these works. In fact, he proclaims his overwhelming "inclination" to give up critical reading so that he might not be distracted from writing to her.

Throughout his apprentice pieces—his Belles Lettres Club address, his "Rhapsodist" essays, the Bringhurst-Wilkins correspondence of 1792, the culminating case of the "Henrietta Letters"—Brown's primary subject remains the procreant mind revealing itself in the very activity of writing and the consequential construction and development of the shape-shifting authorial self, this American Proteus. Given Brown's process approach to composition and the interactive nature of the dialogic epistolary exchange, given the way his entire performance delineates the irruptive emergence of spontaneous thoughts, Brown could easily have extended the C.B.B./Henrietta correspondence indefinitely. Brown, however, terminates his language experiment by making a radical change in narrative structure. The "Henrietta Letters" conclude with Brown incorporating a final dialogue between C.B.B. and Henrietta within a letter written to fellow Belles Lettres Club member John Davidson. As Hewitt argues, this letter "should not be read as a 'real' letter to Davidson—or at least not only as such—but rather as the final letter" in the "Henrietta" narrative ("Letters" 229). Brown's decision to write Davidson displaces the direct representation of Henrietta's voice in favor of C.B.B.'s retrospective reconstruction of their final face-to-face conversation. Although C.B.B. supposedly provides an accurate re-construction of Henrietta's words, he nevertheless takes sole possession of the scene and circumstances leading to their separation. Significantly, he also takes possession of her words and thereby diminishes the force and immediacy of her textualized presence.[28]

This significant modification allows Brown to have C.B.B. construct the relationship's end game on his own terms. Rather than coming into being *now*—within the procreant process of her letter writing—Henrietta's words *were* spoken during their final meeting and might have been completely lost without the restorative agency of C.B.B.'s letter to Davidson. This real-life letter to a real-life person about the fictive conversation between two fictive personages accentuates Brown strategic attempts to blur the distinction between real life and his epistolary proto-fictions. The Davidson letter frames, contains, and ostensibly validates C.B.B.'s overwhelming obsession with the power of a single "Subject" (*L* 734): "The whole world is nothing to me, and every circumstance derives its importance from its relation to her" (*L* 735). His *possession* of her remembered words within the Davidson letter alters the apparent ontological status of Henrietta's voice. She appears less as a person framing her own thoughts than as a projected aspect of Brown's fiction-making activity. Consequently, as Brown and C.B.B. become a unified voice, as the letter writer assumes authority over (and consequently controls) his lover's voice, Henrietta becomes a synecdoche of the displaced, bi-partite double that stands for one half of C.B.B.'s inchoate, authorial self. The recorded dialogue functions as a literary bridge connecting his fancy to everyday experience, transfiguring the energies of this narrative process into an assertion of romantic and artistic closure. Having exited the interactive, binary form of those dueling letters, Brown recalls the C.B.B. authorial projection back into himself and constructs a coda that assumes the shape of a formalized recapitulation. Indeed, the earlier energies governing their compositional discourse give way to a studied, stylized, even polite form of declamation. In fact, C.B.B. reports that Henrietta

[28] See Hewitt's discussion of problematic taxonomies associated with confronting the presence of nonfiction and fiction in Brown's epistolary writing ("History and Romance," 538).

commanded him to "Descend from your heroics & chain your fancy to the earth or I shall believe your phrenzy incurable" (*L* 740). In the Davidson letter, Henrietta has already gone away and C.B.B. identifies the terms by which he might "chain [his] fancy to the earth."

The conversation as recorded in the Davidson letter has a pedantic quality in its expressed concerns for their mutual health and well-being. C.B.B. and Henrietta both adopt a "moralizing disposition" (*L* 739) that counterpoints their erotic epistolary exchanges. Both voices flatten into an acceptance of everyday life. Gone is the experiential immediacy of their compositional frenzy. If their interactive, serial letters celebrate the protean power of romantic spontaneity, then this reconstructed dialogue indicates how a *formal* distance now separates them. In attempting to achieve rhetorical closure, Brown indicates that the relationship culminates (and concludes) in an idealized resolution. C.B.B. reports what Henrietta said: "From this moment we are indissolubly one" (*L* 740). Their relationship has become an ideational construct dissociated from those sexualized vitalities that animated their exchanges. Through the agency of the Davidson letter, C.B.B. and Henrietta remain locked within a golden moment. They have no existence beyond the words that have been their only reality from the beginning.

Transatlantic Affiliations

Throughout his life, Brown was fortunate in the acquisition of friends, who buoyed him emotionally, but who also provided a supportive network wherein he nurtured his talent. During his teenage years, Brown discovered authorial possibilities that derived from his epistolary exchanges with Bringhurst, Wilkins, and Davidson, among others. Brown's development as a writer and thinker was greatly enhanced through his friendship with Elihu Hubbard Smith—who Brown met in Philadelphia in 1790—and the social and intellectual milieu to which Smith gave him access. Most notably, Smith facilitated his membership in the Friendly Club of New York and Brown's friendship with Dunlap. Bryan Waterman notes, "Made up of doctors, lawyers, scientists, merchants, playwrights, poets, editors, a novelist, and a minister, the Friendly Club produced much of what we now consider the cornerstones of early American literature" (*Republic of Intellect* 1). Smith's founding of the Friendly Club was only one major achievement among many in a crowded, remarkable life. His diary offers a stunning record of a man, who seemed to be living many lives at once.[29] Prior to his tragic and untimely death by yellow fever on September 19,1798, Smith was a physician, a public man of letters, a self-proclaimed religious apostate, an Enlightenment champion of reason, a fierce advocate of political reform, and a vigorous defender of women's rights. He was Brown's confidant, advisor, sometimes literary agent, and even the self-financed, *ad hoc* publisher of *Alcuin* in book form. With his knowledge of such literary and intellectual revolutionaries as England's Mary Wollstonecraft and William Godwin as well as a host of continental writers, Smith helped Brown expand his intellectual, cultural, and aesthetic reach.

As a member of the Friendly Club, Brown conversed with gifted men and women. Waterman's *Republic of Intellect* focuses on the wide-

---

[29] There was no friend more important to Brown, or one more singularly gifted and brilliant, than Dr. Elihu Hubbard Smith. Cronin describes this extraordinary person: "Few men today would note in their diaries that they had dined with a president of the United States and fail to add even a word of comment.... [Smith] went to school to Timothy Dwight and Benjamin Rush. He debated with Hamilton, dined with Adams, collaborated with Webster, edited the works of Charles Brockden Brown and William Dunlap, and was casually acquainted with an astonishing number of senators, governors, college presidents, judges, inventors, millionaires, and poets. He himself was one of the pioneers of our literary history, although he died at the age of twenty-seven" (16). Elliott notes, "In 1790 Brown formed a new friendship that was to have a significant impact upon his intellectual development. The arrival in Philadelphia of Elihu Hubbard Smith, a medical student with literary talent and radical philosophical views, was an important stimulus for Brown (*Revolutionary Writers* 220–21). For accounts of Brown, Smith and the Friendly Club, see Waterman (*Republic of Intellect* 33–49) and Kafer 72–94. Waterman writes, "...as early as 1795 Smith projected a literary magazine called *Proteus*, an idea that would eventually be realized by his friend in 1799 as the *Monthly Magazine, and American Review*" (*Republic of Intellect* 46–47).

ranging, transformational, social, and cultural possibilities that derived from elevated conversational discourse. As Waterman explains, "[C]onversation" constituted the Friendly Club's "organizing principle" and "meant something more than mere talking; it was what made the cardinal virtue 'industry' possible" (*Republic of Intellect* 34). For Brown, interactive speech was a foundational value that impelled his protean cultural and aesthetic enterprises. To speak within an open-ended forum became the prelude as well as the impetus for civic engagement—whether via pamphlet, letters, history, prose fiction, or political theory. In Brown's case, such conversational ventures helped him develop those creative attributes that had already appeared within his various apprentice pieces. A staple of Brown's early aesthetic was the idea that the process of writing reflected the emergent qualities of speech. The axiom that to write *is* to speak informed Brown's epistolary experiments, especially as manifest in the "Henrietta Letters"—texts that reveal Brown's radicalized (pre-Wollstonecraft) views regarding the equality (and, arguably, the superiority) of women.

Through his membership in the Friendly Club, Brown became exposed to a sophisticated, free-flowing, interactive community that linked the agency of reading and writing not only with aesthetic activities, but with larger speculative issues dealing with how cultural revolution might impinge upon the formation of public policy. Brown's basic approach was to absorb and adapt writers who provoked him. According to Waterman, "The gentleman's conversation club, a principal Enlightenment form, allowed its members to enact on a miniature scale their ideal principles for public debate.... [R]eaders would converse about and judge morals and knowledge in relation to the material they voraciously read" (*Republic of Intellect* 7)—a circumstance that looks back to Brown's involvement in the Belles Lettres Club as well as his forays into judicial discourse.

Thanks to the infusion of new ideas and theories from an eclectic body of highly educated participants, the Friendly Club was not simply forging "new forms of nationalism," but was concerned with developing "the authority-making rituals of civic fraternity that constituted a transnational literary culture" (*Republic of Intellect* 9). Through the Friendly Club, Brown and other members sought to adapt radical, Eurocentric modes of literary and political discourse to more localized issues in the United States. Fredrika J. Teute contends,

> Writing under the influence of the late Enlightenment, natural science, and French revolutionary ideals, these [Friendly Club] writers elaborated a universalist faith in humans' innate equivalence and capacity to reason. Antiaristocratic and antiauthoritarian, they eschewed established political systems and promoted social change through private associations, scientific inquiry, and their intellectual productions. (152)

The philosophical heft of Brown's four major novels derives mostly from his innate characteristics as a thinker, though it is important to note that his thoughts were modified by what seems a special, synergistic affinity for, and embrace of, the works of Wollstonecraft and Godwin. When considering the complex matter of Wollstonecraft's and Godwin's individual and/or joint influence on Brown's progress as a writer, one would do well to sidestep starkly determinant claims of cause-and-effect. One can find seemingly Godwinian, or as Barnard and Shapiro suggest "Woldwinite," characteristics in Brown's work as early as his Belles Lettres Club address.[30]

---

[30] Barnard and Shapiro conflate the names Wollstonecraft and Godwin and "use the term Woldwinite to highlight . . .this group's special place among the British radical democrats of the 1790" (xviii, Note 19). Their purpose is to re-cast the seemingly single-person specificity of "Godwinism" to include the irreducible, coactive force of the Wollstonecraft-Godwin relation to one another and to the loose confederacy of kindred thinkers: "Brown's enthusiastic reception of these Woldwinite ('Anglo-Jacobin') writers—above all Mary Wollstonecraft, William Godwin, Thomas Holcroft, Robert Bage, and Thomas Paine—undergirds his entire literary project after the mid-1790s." (xviii). Barnard and Shapiro outline "this group's rejection of the prerevolutionary order and their conviction that social progress may be achieved by altering dominant ways of thinking through peaceful cultural means such as literature" (xviii; also see xviii–xx). For a discussion of the relation between Brown and

Brown's apprentice writing prepared him to engage the challenging works of a host of British intellectuals—including "Bage...Robert Southey...and feminist writers like Mary Hays, Helen Maria Williams, [and] Elizabeth Inchbadd" (Waterman, *Republic of Intellect* 97) and adapt these materials to his own purposes.

Without question, these writers incited the radicalization of Brown's ideas, especially regarding the institution of marriage, women's rights, and religious hierarchies. The amorphous consequences of these multiple resources helped shape the dialogic *Alcuin* (and Brown's ability in this text to argue both sides of a question). From this provocative literary and intellectual cohort of kindred spirits, Brown experienced a multi-sourced form of creative cross-fertilization. Less amorphously, the trenchant example of Godwin's *Caleb Williams* informed the creation of the earliest drafts of *Arthur Mervyn*, the lost *Sky-Walk*, *Wieland*, and *Ormond.* Brown's reading of *Caleb Williams* influenced his use of involuted narrative nesting, elliptical plotting with an emphasis on serendipity, accident, and coincidence, and the recurrence of significant Godwinian seed words like "imposter" (196) and "author" (104) that appear throughout Brown's novels. For example, when in *Caleb Williams* Miss Emily Melville's "distempered imagination conjured up a thousand images of violence and falsehood," (70) her unsettled condition prefigures Clara Wieland's claim that the transformed Pleyel is afflicted with a self-contorting case of "distempered imagination" (*W* 117). In Godwin's tale of obsession, mental anguish, and psychological retribution, the narrator refers to his life as "a theatre of calamity" and anticipates Clara Wieland's originating attempt to situate her epistolary narrative in the aftermath of her family's

Godwin on the matter of romance, see Woertendyke (158–60). For an analysis of Brown's relation to the writings of Wollstonecraft and Godwin, see Smith Stocker. Of particular note is her discussion of Wollstonecraft's view on marriage as well as the ways that Godwin's concept of "moral independence" informs *Alcuin* and Brown's later fiction (278–83).

catastrophic experiences (*W* 3). On at least six occasions, Caleb Williams uses the word "author" as a noun: "I busied myself in conjectures, as to who could be the author of this sort of indulgence and attention" (219). Later, he writes, "I was extremely averse to be the author of the unhappiness or the death of a human being" (319–20; also see 180, 328, and 371). For Godwin and, subsequently, for Brown, to be an "author" in the "theatre" of life is to be an originator of ideas as well as an actor. To author an event is to manipulate individuals and circumstances within a fluid social situation—a process that characterizes the machinations of Brown's various self-making tricksters. Godwin's narrator makes at least one other reference to life as a "theatre" (336) and also proclaims "Providence" a determinant force that "rules us" (347). In Brown's work, the providential view often stands in direct opposition to the philosophy and aesthetic of self-making, protean tricksters seeking to shape an unfolding social script. Certainly, regarding Brown's interest in gender politics, his celebration of the un-subjugated Henrietta could only have been complemented by his later engagement with Wollstonecraft's electrifying anatomization of social injustice and gender politics in *A Vindication of the Rights of Woman* (1792). It is an open question whether Brown responded to the Woldwinite political matrix concerning the rights of women because these writers imbued him with ideas he did not already have, or how, and to what extent, their work confirmed, validated, and triggered his exploration of materials that he inchoately expressed during his formative epistolary engagements, especially in the "Henrietta Letters."

Toward the Completion of Brown's Apprenticeship

During the few years following the completion of the "Henrietta Letters" and his decision to quit the legal profession, Brown produced a great quantity of writing—letters, journal entries, faux histories, fictions eventually completed and published, fictions in the form of fragments that were either abandoned wholesale or set aside for another day, some eventually to be exhumed and revised for book or magazine publication. In an article that appeared in 1834—twenty-four years after Brown's death and nineteen years after the publication of his biography of Brown—Dunlap transcribed portions of letters received from Brown in 1794, 1795, and 1796. In a letter dating from February 1796, Brown describes his dissatisfaction not only with a specific work under hand but with his general progress as a writer:

> After wandering through fifty pages, the experiment was sufficiently made, and the thorough consciousness that I was unfitted for the instructor's chair, that my style was feeble and diffuse, my method prolix and inaccurate, my reasoning crude and superficial, and my knowledge narrow and undigested, suddenly benumbed my fingers: I dropped the pen, and I sunk into silent and solitary meditation on the means of remedying these defects. (*L* 330)

No stranger to melancholy, Brown tended periodically to descend into what seems a form of critical self-loathing. Brown's description bears the marks of a self-regarding literary performance—the "benumbed" writer on the high wire composing beautifully balanced prose describing his disgust with writing badly. Brown indicates that his prescription for "remedying these defects" would always be more writing, although here the putatively failed project in question might have been his "Phila. Novel, so fiercely undertaken in the Autumn of 1795," a work that later became fully realized in *Arthur Mervyn* (Smith 290). Given the eventual success of *Arthur Mervyn*, it is inviting to speculate that Brown may have been referring to ur-versions of materials that are certainly "diffuse"—what scholars call Brown's Historical Sketches.

During these years, Brown worked on early versions of faux histories that were composed in 1804–05 and collected by Allen and Dunlap: "Sketches of a History of Carsol" (printed in Dunlap, *The Life*, I, 170–258) and "Sketches of a History of the Carrils and Ormes" (printed in Dunlap *The Life*, I, 262–396). In his diary entry for February 10, 1797, Smith refers to what he calls the "Carlovinga" material: "Dunlap here in the afternoon. Ch. B. Brown, in the afternoon, &

evening, till near ten. He read us, from his Journal, of Carlovinga &c" (289). Smith sat and listened to Brown read from a faux European history in 1796 as well, and he found reason to lament Brown's scattershot approach to writing, complaining of Brown's proclivity for creating fragments. In his diary entry of December 14, 1796, Smith remarks,

> A visit from Ch. B. Brown—who read me several passages from his Journal. I wish he would turn his Aloas & Astoias, his Buttiscoes and Carlovingas, to some account. He starts an idea; pursues it a little way; new ones spring up; he runs a short distance after each; meantime the original one is likely to escape intirely. (272)[31]

Despite Smith's exasperation, the relationship between the "Carlovinga" and the later faux histories have a suggestive pertinence to Brown's development as a novelist insofar as they shine a contrastive light on the nature of Brown's evolving artistry. If the "Carlovinga" materials resemble the expansive sketches printed by Dunlap, they suggest that during Brown's apprenticeship years he experimented with a third-person, transhistorical narrator, who employed summary historical exposition, a form of narration successfully realized in "Walstein's School of History," published in August and September 1799 (*R* 145–56). Brown's apprenticeship, therefore, was not only characterized by a tension between careers as a writer and lawyer, but aesthetically as he oscillated between first-person epistolary address and an expository mode of third-person, historical synopsis.

As he moved in late 1797 toward professional publication, he imbued the first-person protean mode of narrative self-making with aesthetic priority. Indeed, this mode was especially congenial to Brown's

---

[31] Dunlap concluded that the Sketches were composed after Brown's career as a published novelist ended in 1801 (Dunlap, *The Life*, I, 169). See Barnard, "*Historical Sketches*," for an explanation of their textual history and Brown's use of narrative voice. See Kamrath's analysis of the aesthetics and politics of these works (109–33).

tendency for using the *activity* of writing as a means of establishing his art as a form of open-ended discovery. In a journal entry printed by Dunlap, Brown describes his approach to writing:

> When this [Parts 3 and 4 of *Alcuin*] was finished, I commenced something in the form of a Romance. I had at first no definitive conceptions of my design. As my pen proceeded forward, my invention was tasked, and the materials that it afforded were arranged and digested.... The facility I experienced in composition, and the perception of daily progress encouraged me, and my task was finished on the last day of December. (*The Life*, I, 107)

Like Allen, Dunlap contends that the "Romance" in question was the fragmentary "Jessie" material, which explores this young woman's tenuous relationship with a mysterious man named Colden—the name Brown used in 1801 for his male protagonist in *Jane Talbot.* It also seems possible that Brown may be referring to how the completion of *Alcuin* in late September or early October 1797 paved the way for the rapid composition of *Sky-Walk* in the final months of that year. Smith copied into his diary a letter he wrote to Brown on September 16, 1797. Smith notes that Brown made a reference to a Romance that could be *Sky-Walk* or some another work:

> The account you have given me of your labours has raised in me a very lively curiosity to see their fruits. Is there no way of gratifying my desire? Can you not safely transmit the copy of this precious Romance? Send it—& make your own stipulations. It shall be returned when you please. It shall be shewn to as many & as few as you shall direct. It shall receive general, or particular criticism, or none at all, as is most agreeable. But you do not so much as inform me of the nature of this performance: whether it be something altogether new, or the continuation of some one of those plans which occasionally occupied your mind while here. Be more communicative.

> I have a similar desire to see your continuation of 'Alcuin.' In this, at least, I am not singular. Mrs. S. Johnson had read the 1st and IInd parts, & is anxious to know how all this is to end. She commends the performance, on the whole—particularly the style; thinks there is much truth delivered on either side of the debate: but is at a loss to know what is the writer's ultimate design. From what she has seen, she infers his object to be to render women satisfied with their present civil condition. I can not pretend to enlighten her. (364)

If the materials from Brown's journal and Smith's diary entries are put together, it is clear that in mid-September 1797 Brown was completing Parts 3 and 4 of *Alcuin* but also penning a Romance—possibly *Sky-Walk*, "The Man at Home," the "Jessie" manuscript, or an unknown project. In a later portion of the passage cited above, Brown states that he completed a draft of the romance on the last day of 1797 and intends to revise it for publication:

> [The Romance] was at first written in an hasty and inaccurate way. Before I can submit it to a printer, or even satisfactorily rehearse it to a friend, it must be wholly transcribed. I am at present engaged in this employment. I am afraid, as much time will be required by it, as was necessary to the original composition. I do not fear but that I shall finish my labour, barring all extraordinary accidents. (Dunlap, *The Life*, I, 107–08)

If the "required" time of composition were three months, then the projected time for revision would take Brown into March 1798, when *Sky-Walk* was announced as ready for publication. A March 27, 1798 entry in Smith's diary reads: "Recd. a letter from C. B. Brown informing me of his intended marriage, that his first novel is complete, & that he writes 'The Man at Home' in the Phila. Weekly Magazine. This magazine I sought & purchased, as least such Nos. as have come to hand—& read his pieces & several others" (433–34). Even though Dunlap identifies this work as the "Jessie" fragment, Brown writes in his journal like a purposeful man with a direct mission and leads one to affirm that *Sky-Walk* was very possibly the project that had been composed in the last three months of 1797 and revised in the first three months of 1798.

In any case, it is reasonable to conclude that by New Year's Day 1798 the literary apprenticeship of Charles Brockden Brown ended and that he was working vigorously, in his multi-tasking way, on a number of publishable projects. By the early months of 1798, Brown had completed the four parts of *Alcuin*, although only Parts 1 and 2 were destined to be published in his lifetime. He finished *Sky-Walk, or, the Man Unknown to Himself—An American Tale* and was preparing to submit it to a printer. An excerpt from this novel appeared in *The Weekly Magazine* on March 24, 1798 (*R* 135–41). Brown was writing "A Man at Home" and publishing it in magazine serial form. He also had pages from *Arthur Mervyn* finished and in progress.

The case of *Alcuin* is strange. In what seems an odd breakdown of communication, Brown was busy publishing Parts 1 and 2 in *The Weekly Magazine*, even as Smith at his own expense prepared the same material for publication in book form.[32] When he became aware of Brown's serial publication, Smith quickly let Brown know of his own efforts and asked for Parts 3 and 4. Smith had ample time to read and include Parts 3 and 4 in his plans, but for reasons unknown—possibly economic, possibly a sense of critical uncertainty regarding the value or propriety of Parts 3 and 4—Smith went ahead and saw only Parts 1 and 2 into print. Perhaps Smith did not think it wise to publish the

[32] See Arner for a discussion of issues related to the publication of *Alcuin* in magazine and book form (273–78). Also see Cowie, *Wieland* (315, note 9). In a diary entry of December, 18 1797, Smith copies material from a letter he wrote to Richard Alsop: "Now for a more serious piece of literary intelligence. I am about publishing, by subscription, a performance of our friend Charles B. Brown. Do you wish to subscribe? It is a dialogue, in the manner of the Ancients, on questions relative to the intellectual equality of the sexes. It is eloquently, & I believe inoffensively, written. When I say inoffensively, you will understand me as referring to religious prejudices. The price of each copy is 50 cents" (406).

proto-fictional materials that interrupted the dialogic interaction between Alcuin and Mrs. Carter.[33] Alcuin embarks on a lengthy descriptive excursion regarding his travels to an unspecified feminist utopia, where gender equity is the rational norm, and transforms himself into a combination of Thomas More's Raphael Hythloday, Jonathan Swift's Gulliver, and Samuel Johnson's Rasselas. This journey may well have seemed to Smith to be a distracting, if not absurd, fictive exercise imposed in a preemptive manner on the realistic conversation between Alcuin and Mrs. Carter. This inset narrative reads as an irruptive digression, a discursive fantasy that derails for a time the dialogic intensities that characterize Parts 1 and 2. Nor is it believable as a record of actual travels. Additionally, the radical sentiments espoused in *Alcuin*, Parts 1 and 2, and developed in the unpublished Parts 3 and 4, were on the verge of being eclipsed by a growing conservative backlash to issues regarding gender equity. Cathy N. Davidson recounts how Brown's radical dialogue was early lauded by the likes of Dunlap, but later renounced by Dunlap and other conservative voices:

> Thus, if *Alcuin*, Brown's earliest major work and one of the most eloquent of the late eighteenth-century American discussions on the rights of women, is important in literary history as a "first," it is equally important in social history as a "last." Brown's initial publishing venture coincided with the end of an era and the climax of discussion on the "woman question." The publication of *Alcuin* came just as Americans began to regard that whole problematic subject with increasing suspicion and to view advocates of equality with moral indignation and even contempt. ("Matter and Manner" 72)

---

[33] Kafer discusses affinities between Brown himself and the views expressed within the dialogue: "There is much of Charles Brown in the conversation between the widow Mrs. Carter and Alcuin" (95). Brown's Mrs. Carter derives from Elizabeth Carter (1717–1806), a British scholar and translator. Brown associates his character with a recognizable contemporaneous, strong woman, who does not remain within the narrow confinements of female gender roles.

Davidson's comments relate to her speculation on why a complete *Alcuin* was not published in Brown's lifetime and then not until 1971. She suggests that the disparagement heaped on Wollstonecraft on grounds of alleged moral turpitude following husband William Godwin's publication of *Memoirs* would have been reason enough for Brown and Smith to withhold further polemical discussion advocating women's rights ("Matter and Manner" 72–74).

The unfortunate case of *Sky-Walk* is even more bizarre. Like Herman Melville's *The Isle of the Cross* (1853), *Sky-Walk* suffers the ill-fated distinction of being a finished lost work, a story crafted and turned over to a printer—one that exists now only as an articulated absence, a title without a corresponding tale.[34] Dunlap simply remarks that this novel

> was never published, owing to the death of the printer, who had undertaken to publish it at his own risk. Mr. Brown being then altogether unknown to the public, and the work, nearly printed being left with executors, who did not choose to finish it and would not or could not sell the sheets for such price, as Mr. Brown's friends thought proper to offer for them. (*The Life*, I, 259)

In the diary entry of April 20, 1798, Smith celebrates the high quality of *Sky-Walk*, even as he laments the unsettled state of the literary marketplace. He indicates a desire to publish this work on his own, had he the funds:

> [William] Johnson [a lawyer and Smith's roommate] came in. I was tired of writing. He took up "Sky-Walk," & read aloud to me. Every sentence increases my admiration of this performance. Why are there any obstacles to its immediate publication? Why so little liberal curiosity in our country?

[34] For a discussion of circumstances related to Herman Melville's *The Isle of the Cross*, see Parker 136–61. Like Brown's *Sky-Walk*, Melville's *The Isle of the Cross* remains lost.

> Why such sordid doubts among our booksellers? Why have not I the property, as I have the wish, to incur myself the expence of publication (439).

No documentary evidence is available that records Brown's commentary on the disappearance of this finished novel. Nevertheless, not all was lost. Later, as Dunlap observes, Brown "incorporated parts of 'Sky Walk' into other works of imagination, as his memory retained them. In Edgar Huntley, for example, the wild district of Norwalk, had its prototype in Sky-Walk" (*The Life*, I, 259). Still, it seems Brown made no attempt to re-copy or re-construct the finished product. Apparently, Brown became reconciled to the loss of his book and moved on. With the facility to create more and better literary productions, he was in no danger of running out of ideas. The prolific, wayward nature of Brown's muse, while occasionally exasperating to Smith, turned out to be Brown's greatest resource. A dead printer could not be restored to life. For whatever tangled reasons, the manuscript was not returned to its owner, but a lost book could be reconstituted into other forms and new works could emerge from a mind teeming with situations, scenes, images, and arguments. Brown tended to seem less concerned with the finished product of his aesthetic labors than with the very activity of spinning new literary lines. Dunlap offers verbatim Allen's assessment: "The author considered all his fanciful works as mere matters of recreation and amusement. As long as his imagination was prolific in blossoms, he scattered them with the same prodigal profusion" (*The Life*, I, 261; Allen 388–89). While possibly mistaking a consciously rendered affect as a sign that Brown was not ultimately serious about his fictional work, Allen and Dunlap nevertheless accurately reflect how the "prodigal" quality of Brown's compositional life was devoted to the *process* of writing—a passion for delineating the unfolding activity of his creative imagination. By the time the *Sky-Walk* manuscript was deemed unrecoverable—at the very height of the yellow fever epidemic in New York City in August 1798—Brown was almost finished *Wieland* and had even begun composing a prequel detailing the early life of Francis Carwin, the protean, "double-tongued" anti-hero predisposed to disruptive, unsettling feats of imposture (*W* 1). On August 8, 1798 Smith reports reading "Brown's 'Carwin,' as far as he has written it, & corrected a proof of his 'Wieland.'" (460). Brown also continued working on *Arthur Mervyn* and short pieces for *The Weekly Magazine.*

Early Fruits in "Prodigal Profusion"

At the age of twenty-seven, Brown began his professional career as a publishing author with the nearly simultaneous appearance of *Alcuin*, Parts 1 and 2 and "The Man at Home," a thirteen-part serial fiction in *The Weekly Magazine* that ran from February 3, 1798 to April 28, 1798 (*R* xiii). "The Man at Home" is Brown's first published exploration of one of his essential, fictional subjects—the 1793 yellow fever epidemic in Philadelphia, a horrific period that provides narrative centers for *Ormond* and *Arthur Mervyn.*

Alcuin seems to be a natural aesthetic consequence of the dialectical energies that impelled the "Henrietta Letters," although *Alcuin* is a fictional dialogue rather than an epistolary exchange. As narrator, Alcuin is more the naïve youth than C.B.B., but Mrs. Carter constitutes a powerful reconfiguration of Henrietta's independence, self-assertion, self-possession, and rhetorical brilliance. It is difficult, if not impossible, to draw the line between Brown's highly progressive thoughts regarding gender equity, the power of liberated proto-feminist consciousness, the need for a revolution in laws and folkways governing the marriage contract, on the one hand, and a host of literary sources that may have informed and influenced his thinking, on the other. For example, as Clark notes, "It can be shown that the revolutionary spirit stirred in Brown before the appearance of the [Wollstonecraft's] [*Vindication of the*] *Rights of Woman* and [Godwin's *An Enquiry Concerning*] *Political Justice*, and that the influence of these two works upon

Brown has been overemphasized" (110).[35] There is no doubt, however, that the "Henrietta Letters" themselves are an influential antecedent of the *Alcuin* dialogue. Once again, as with the relationship between the Belles Lettres Club address and "The Rhapsodist: No. 1" essay, Brown becomes his *own* influence. Brown either remembered the following passage outright or re-read and revised it for *Alcuin*. In the "Henrietta Letters," C.B.B. writes, "Man is a progressive being. He is never stationary, but is always either returning from a certain point or leaving it behind him" (*L* 730). In *Alcuin*, Brown gives this protean concept to Alcuin's conversational partner in Part III, "The Paradise of Women" section (*A* 34). This reasonable man resembles Raphael Hythloday in More's *Utopia*: "Man is a progressive being, he is wise in proportion to the number of his ideas, and to the accuracy with which he compares and arranges them" (*A* 45).[36]

Alcuin moves well beyond the intimacy of the "Henrietta Letters"—the enclosed, self-absorbed relationship of two lovers writing obsessively to one another—toward the larger world of social forms and political debate. One cannot conceive of C.B.B. asking Henrietta,

---

[35] See Arner "Historical Essay" for a discussion of Brown's sources, especially as they relate to issues regarding women's rights (273–82). West observes that Brown's life in Philadelphia society brought him frequently into "mixed-sex circles" and that these experiences led him "to writing for a more public audience" (17). Arner addresses the danger of seeking to establish direct cause and effect among Brown's many sources ("Historical Essay" 281). Nevertheless, well-founded source studies depict how Brown adapted an expansive range of reading materials. See Edwards for a discussion of the relationship between Judith Sargent Murray's "On the Equality of the Sexes" and Wollstonecraft's *Vindication of the Rights of Woman* as they possibly related to Mrs. Carter's educational theories in *Alcuin* (281–84). Brown's purpose in *Alcuin* was to write fiction rather than autobiography. As Fleischmann notes, "Readers have often found it difficult to avoid taking the character Alcuin's views as Brown's. But most of the irony in the dialogue is at Alcuin's expense; he is an unworldly naïf, skewered by a sophisticated woman" (293).

[36] See Leask on *Alcuin* and the subject of utopias (99). Kafer identifies Brown's gender-equity utopia as reflecting a "world of Quakerly Godwinianism" (98)—one that is "part Godwin, part Society of Friends" (98–99).

as Alcuin does Mrs. Carter, if she is a "federalist" (*A* 7).[37] Indeed, *Alcuin* may be best understood as a diagnostic political fiction that details, without resolving, the pervasive, and vexed, matter of gender inequality in an ostensibly new society—one that is self-identified by an ethos of liberty cast within the framework of a newly ratified *Constitution* and its "Bill of Rights." As Elizabeth Jane Wall Hinds notes, "Writing *Alcuin* near the beginning of his career as a published writer, Brown was performing in little what his contemporary Philadelphians were discussing at large: the complementary questions of rights to liberty and property under a federal constitution and the rights of the female sex within those newly-formed political and economic constructs" (34). In describing the exploratory quality of Brown's political "sensibility," Levine argues that Brown is not confined by narrow ideologies or doctrines: "At least through the 1790s, Brown's commitment to exploring and testing a range of ideas far outweighed his limited interest in party politics. His texts reflect less a political line than a sensibility—inquiring, capacious, and anxious" (*Conspiracy and Romance* 25). In appropriating a term from Mikhail Bakhtin's interpretive lexicon, Levine views Brown "as one of the most aggressively 'dialogical' of America's early national writers" (*Conspiracy and Romance* 26).[38] Brown's purpose is not to dramatize rhapsodic effusions within an overheated epistolary exchange, but to position the youthful male intellect, this inquisitive, unpolished tyro—a poor schoolmaster, no less—in conversational relation to a mature, stable, intellectually superior woman, so that he

[37] See Justin D. Edwards on Alcuin and the Federalist Question (279–90): "Here, Carter makes it clear that Alcuin's question is insulting: she does not have the legal power to vote, so she cannot possibly pledge allegiance to a specific political theory or even a particular party" (280).

[38] See Teute on the importance of conversation in *Alcuin*: "...Brown's dialogic novel *Alcuin* posited the values of a specific kind of conversation in mixed company and of a different type of salon society.... The conversation between Alcuin and Carter conveys both the model and content of appropriate inquiry in the new nation and foregrounds the woman as the preceptor of taste and understanding for the man" (162).

might absorb, even as he flounders to critique, her radically subversive ideas regarding suffrage and marital rights. Watts argues, "Thus Alcuin, rather confusingly, makes it possible to see Brown as either radical or conservative on the question of female status, both because of the book's dialogic quality and its protagonists' shifting opinions" (62). Hinds offers the qualification that Brown's dialogue is less original or radical than may appear. Brown's purpose was more a matter of mediating between varieties of argumentative positions:

> Taking up both the moderate and radical ends of the debate, Brown's *Alcuin*, then, was a timely synopsis of the woman question rather than...a forward-looking and, therefore, radical tract by America's first professional novelist. *Alcuin* does offer, in the manner of Godwin, the specter of an extreme, radical version of the debate, illustrating as it does the possibility of absolute equality, offering up a vision of coeducation, equal property rights, political representation for women, and—most radical of all—the abolition of marriage as an institution. But this utopianism represents only one side of Brown's presentation; the debate itself turns up an alternative position, one as conservative and as viable for Brown as Godwinian radicalism. (Hinds 35)

Fritz Fleischmann suggests that Brown's attempt here is to gain a readership without alienating a sizable portion of his prospective audience: "For an author like Brown, in search of a public and a living, to write about such a charged topic as women's rights, closely associated with Wollstonecraft, necessitated a strategy that allowed a full exploration of the issues but also a modicum of ambiguity—or deniability" (289). Brown's ambiguity should be seen as a carefully calibrated strategy designed to accentuate the play of dialectical energies. The issue of women's rights, as expressed in this dialogue, became intricately bound up with the long-standing process of Brown's professionalization. In this piece especially, he was a young, emerging writer seeking to express and validate the intellectual liberation he experienced through his relation to his New York circle of friends.

Throughout the dialogue, Brown not only establishes the proto-fictional template that he develops later in the relationship between Arthur Mervyn and Achsa Fielding, but he creates a rhetorical "stage" (*A* 21)—a histrionic space—on which the repartee between Alcuin and Mrs. Carter emerges through the free exercise of intellectual discourse.[39] Mrs. Carter repeatedly challenges conventional social forms and indicts them as unenlightened constructs that violate a woman's natural rights to just treatment. She takes particular exception to social forms that countenance and sustain codes and statutes of arbitrary exclusion. As she contends, to except women from Natural Law rights would be the same as excluding "every one who had a mole on his right cheek, or whose stature did not exceed five feet six inches, who would not condemn without scruple so unjust an institution? yet, in truth, the injustice would be less than in the case of women" (*A* 29). She despises the present system of marriage. In Mrs. Carter's words,

> My objections are weighty ones. I disapprove of it, in the first place, because it renders the female a slave to the man. It enjoins and enforces submission on her part to the will of her husband. It includes a promise of implicit obedience and unalterable affection. Secondly, it leaves the woman destitute of property. Whatever she previously possesses, belongs absolutely to the man. (*A* 54–55)

In fact, Brown's purpose in having Alcuin report what he "saw and heard" (*A* 36) on his journey to the utopian "paradise of women" (*A*34)—perhaps, a proto-fictional (if ironic) template for Ormond's

---

[39] Davidson argues, "...*Alcuin* anticipates Brown's later novels and is consequently at least as noteworthy for its manner as for its matter. To begin with, the dialogue technique approximates the conversational tone and the pseudoepistolary form Brown would later employ in his fiction" ("Matter and Manner" 75). See Davidson's discussion of how Mrs. Carter anticipates Brown's strong female characters in his novels ("Matter and Manner" 77–78).

hegemonic, utopian schemes—is to make clear that the order of society is nothing other than a collection of histrionic forms that can be made and unmade. At the center of this society, as Alcuin finds it, is a theater of social equality. This utopian theater provides a counterpoint—an alternative stage—designed with the purpose of critiquing and replacing the present social order—one wherein Mrs. Carter does not have the legal right to vote. Alcuin asks his guide, "[W]hat is the condition of the female sex among you? In this evening's excursion I have met with those, whose faces and voices seemed to bespeak them women, though as far as I could discover they were distinguished by no peculiarities of manner or dress" (*A* 38). These "peculiarities" are nothing more that the mandated impositions of custom that dominate social life and dictate one's role in it. On this utopian isle, daily life becomes an expression of the actors' equity—a theater in which men and women play interchangeable parts. Alcuin continues:

> In those assemblies to which you conducted me, I did not fail to observe that whatever was the business of the hour, both sexes seemed equally engaged in it. Was the spectacle theatrical? The stage was occupied sometimes by men, sometimes by women, and sometimes by a company of each. The tenor of the drama seemed to be followed as implicitly as if custom had enacted no laws upon this subject. (*A* 38)

In the world imagined by Brown, with a little help from More's *Utopia*, the power of "custom"—the communally-received impress of determinant, social forms—does not enact oppressive laws. Essentially, society is shown to be a constellation of forms created by precedent and sanctioned by statute. Brown's histrionic metaphors—where life is a stage on which actors perform—recur in his novels and incite questions regarding the diverse ways the human world might be authored: by the power of providence; by rational and sensible people disinterestedly concerned with forging an equitable commonwealth; by patriarchal members of the Constitutional Congress; by natural forces acting through individuals; by the self-making energies of rogue opportunists, who see individuals treading the social stage as malleable entities vulnerable to the histrionic, predatory force of imposture.

In *Alcuin* Brown was feeling his way into large political and artistic questions and he was doing the same as he worked his way through the serial composition and publication of "The Man at Home"—a situational fiction in which first-person narrator Bedloe hides from penal strictures imposed by debt.[40] From an early age, Brown had a special sensitivity toward the horror of debtor's prison. In 1784, when Brown was thirteen, his father Elijah was imprisoned for debt. Kafer summarizes the career of Brown's father in the aftermath of his release: "Henceforth Elijah Brown would scrape through life as a conveyancer, a real estate broker, a copyist, picking up small commissions here and there for renting or selling other people's property and for writing up other people's official documents" (44).[41]

Having co-signed for a loan, Bedloe becomes liable for repayment after the borrower defaulted. Bedloe has the following options: he could repay the loan and render himself destitute; he could refuse to repay the loan and report to debtor's prison; or he could refuse to repay the loan and become a fugitive from justice. After deciding to hold on to his money, he goes into hiding as "a rigid recluse" in the home of Kate, his landlord (*R* 30). This premise provides a flimsy basis for Bedloe's self-generated, serial narrative, wherein the errant motions of his mind constitute nearly the entire story: "This necessity may not endure long; but meanwhile it is requisite for me to pursue some employment compatible with my restraints, from which amusement may be derived. It is for this purpose that I have taken up my pen. I have no particular object in view" (*R* 30). Lacking a specific plan, he writes for occupation

[40] Ellis identifies "Robert Morris, the great financier of the American Revolution," as the source for Brown's Bedloe (392).

[41] While seeing these fictive sketches as reflecting elements emanating from Brown's childhood experience of oppression during the Revolutionary War, Kafer delineates how Brown adapts foundational elements of his Quaker life into the materials of "Gothic 'fiction'" (104).

and diversion. Nor does he claim to have any particular sense of a public audience: "I write to myself. The pen is not, in this instance, an instrument of communication. There is no stopping, nor retarding, nor hastening the current of thought" (*R* 31). Like Brown himself, Bedloe is consumed by the physicality of writing. As with Brown's rhapsodist, Bedloe surrenders to enticements provided by the blank page and commits himself to the experience of spontaneous address. The emerging diary-account seeks to do little more than "exhibit [his] own character" as he "puts forth the energies of his mind" (*R* 32) within a "mode of careless composition" (*R* 31). While hiding from the law during the yellow fever epidemic of 1793, he confronts, and enlarges upon, the meditative consequences of self-imposed reclusion. Brown adapts the rhetoric of spontaneous address so integral to his earlier epistolary ventures to Bedloe's self-indulgent attempts to pass the time. Bedloe engages a series of subjects that are found within the humdrum dimensions of his room. With his "scrutinizing spirit," Bedloe inscribes thoughts that pass through his mind and gives substance to the unfolding present: "I am sitting here employed in this way.... It is the only exercise, as I suppose, within my reach" (*R* 40).

However limited its premise, "The Man at Home" offers a protofictional experiment that anticipates issues, scenes, and tropes Brown later develops in his novels. Joseph J. Letter remarks that this narrator "serves as a point of origin for the plots of both *Ormond* and *Arthur Mervyn*" (712). In his analysis of the relationship between Brown's allusions in "The Man at Home" and his theory of historiography, Letter explores Brown's use of such motifs as the "locked box" and its relation to enigmatic Gothic fictional forms (722). Problems associated with debtor's prison are central to *Ormond* and *Arthur Mervyn*. Similarly, Kafer links Brown's preoccupation with mystery in these sketches with more expansive imaginative possibilities inherent in Gothic narrative. "The Man at Home," as Kafer argues, "marked out the thematic parameters and rhythms of Brown's maturing imagination, as it foreshadowed his characteristic literary strategy of disguise and concealment"

(104). Problems of confinement are pressing critical complexes in *Edgar Huntly*, where the dramatic possibilities of enclosed spaces become accentuated through multiple enactments of claustrophobic forms of psychological and physical entrapment. Bedloe's preoccupation with mysteries associated with the locked box in his room offers a prototype of the more charged implications concerning Clithero Edny's closed box in *Edgar Huntly*. In considering the mysterious trunk in "The Man at Home," Christopherson wonders whether the story itself may be an analogue to this mysterious object, "a box with a false bottom, whose banal exterior camouflages an essentially American tale" (19). In this rambling proto-fiction, the locked box seems a contrivance designed to give Bedloe something to do and think about as he attempts to open it. Because anything or nothing might be inside, he has no strictures as to the scenarios he may create: "The world of conjecture is without limits. To speculate on the possible and the future, is no ineligible occupation. The invention is active to create, and the judgment busy in weighing and shaping its creations" (*R* 46).

Brown's essential subject in this open-ended, protean narrative is to dramatize how meditation—the very process of thinking—impels the creation of emergent literary forms: "On this occasion I indulge myself in picturing a thousand dramas, in which the chief actor has been the tenant of this apartment, and the chief incident, that which had produced the disentanglement or catastrophe, has been the unclosing of this trunk" (*R* 46–47). Letter argues that this narrative shows "how Brown used serial publication as a performative vehicle" (711). Additionally, Letter sees these sketches as revelatory of Brown's use of historical fiction as a foundation for the development of the romance form, as a way to conflate matters pertaining to *fact* with the transformational power of the fancy. Brown may well have taken pride and pleasure in deriving possible fictions or "dramas" virtually out of nothing. If Brown can create and publish words about a reclusive, debt-dodging fugitive in a room doing little but thinking and trying to open a locked box, what might he actually do with a compelling story—for example, the tale he encountered some years before about a man, who murdered his family at the command of an ostensibly divine voice.[42]

"The Man at Home" constitutes Brown's first published attempt to dramatize elements that pertain to the 1793 yellow fever epidemic. Scott Ellis argues that "the fever is not merely the subject of the narrative but the catalyst for thought and action following the disruption of quotidian relationships.... Disease is not merely a physiological fact but also [for Bedloe] a test of the mind" (395). Within the open form of the intrinsically digressive serial narrative, Bedloe offers some accounts that derive from "this theater of human calamity" (*R* 53). Later, in 1798, Brown will recycle the Baxter material from "The Man at Home" into *Ormond*, reprinting the earlier materials nearly verbatim: "Whether it was because this theater of human calamity was new to [Baxter], and death, in order to be viewed with his ancient unconcern, must be accompanied in the ancient manner, with halberts and tents, certain it is that Baxter was irresolute and timid in everything that respected the yellow fever" (*R* 53–54; *O* 68). Baxter's own death from yellow fever "may be quoted as an example of the force of imagination" (*R* 56; *O* 71). In "The Man at Home," the inset story of Madame De Moivre burying her dead father before the eyes of the curious neighbor Baxter constitutes a proto-fictional version of a narrative that will be an integral part of *Ormond*. In another digression, Bedloe tells the story of the schoolmaster, who pretends to possess supernatural powers. A conniving man given to "imposture" (*R* 59), he anticipates such transgressive trickster figures as Carwin, Thomas Craig, and Welbeck. These shape-shifters attempt to control the surfaces of life as if they and other people were players acting on a stage. In "The Man at Home," Brown was feeling his way toward the creation of a character

[42] Brown found his core story for *Wieland* in the materials he read either in the *New York Weekly Magazine* of 20 and 27 July 1796 or in the *Philadelphia Minerva* of 20 and 27 August 1796 detailing how James Yates of Tomhanick, New York murdered his family in December 1781 as a consequence of what he believed to be a direct divine command to do so (Cowie 323).

like Carwin, who uses words and the power of voice to alter and dominate social situations. Describing the schoolmaster, Bedloe writes, "The conversation of the evening was chiefly accidental, but converted by this skillful plotter to his own wonder-working purpose" (*R* 63)—a phrase that evokes, at least by way of echo, the title of Edward Johnson's *Wonder-Working Providence of Sion's Saviour*. This passage might offer a telling proto-fictional evocation of the self-making artificer, who attempts to contain within himself (as a prelude to usurping) the "wonder-working" power of providential determination.

Less a successful fiction than a storehouse of loosely-knit, episodic assays, "The Man at Home" holds the distinction of being Brown's first published work with a proper ending—as Bedloe, propelled by a torrent of legalese, consigns himself to debtor's prison (*R* 97–98). With all of its meandering, this piece brought Brown and his developing artistic powers squarely to the point where his career as a professional writer might begin to flourish.

2

Competing Voices: *Wieland* and the Limits of Disclosure

In Search of Readers: The Problem of a Novel Commodity

For a writer in post-colonial America in the last years of the eighteenth century, the rapidity of composition, production, and publication reflected not so much the non-bureaucratic niceties of a simple time as the exigencies of local (as opposed to mass market) publication. A writer's printer was often the publisher. The product—bound today, delivered tomorrow—would await the gentle buyer at a bookseller's shop. Promotion was not the province of a honey-combed marketing department but the author's basic problem. In another world, in Old England, perhaps, an established author might begin his work with a dedication to his patron. The artist was paid in advance and in the process of literary production. The patron's motive was not profit—he lived in a realm of economic transcendence where profit was immaterial—but the pleasure of supporting worthy artistic endeavors. Ian Watt explores how in the eighteenth century the decline of patronage in England and the rise of market-savvy booksellers facilitated the development of the novel, a process that created (in light of proliferating literacy among non-aristocratic classes) a popular literary marketplace geared toward leisured readers seeking diversionary entertainment (35–59). The transition from patron-driven literary production to a bookseller's profit-motive made the writer of fiction acutely dependent on the vagaries of popular tastes, even as writers like Daniel Defoe and Samuel Richardson were among the predominant authorial agents shaping and sustaining the public's growing appetite for this novel form of literature.

The case in Charles Brockden Brown's America was dismal. For one thing, there were no patrons.[1] Without a reading public shaped by nearly a century-long evolution of the novel genre, American novelists took their stand on highly unstable ground as author and bookseller embarked on a precarious, speculative adventure. Cathy N. Davidson summarizes this foundational premise: "[T]he model for the American book industry is not so much the diadic relationship of, in traditional capitalistic terms, the producer and the consumer, but a triadic interrelationship between the writer, the printer/publisher, and the reader" (*Revolution and the Novel* 15).[2] In this nebulous enterprise, monetary profit could only follow the successful solicitation of strangers. In the manner of such writers as William Hill Brown and Susanna Rowson, Brockden Brown had to confront a prodigious difficulty: why would a reader with other things to do—especially with the yellow fever epidemic ravaging communities in late summer 1798—consent to gamble precious money and time on so questionable a commodity as an *American* novel? A prospective reader would enter the bookseller's shop, pick up the article, and weigh its prospective educative and entertainment value in relation to its monetary cost. To overcome such obstacles facing *Wieland*, Brown prepared devious enticements.

---

[1] Watts observes, "For literary aspirants, the paramount difficulty in a growing culture of capitalism was immediate material survival. Aristocratic patronage, the mainstay of traditional European culture, was both unavailable and unacceptable in a republic" (9).

[2] See Davidson's Chapter 2, "The Book in the New Republic," for her analysis of the emergence and significance of the literary marketplace in the aftermath of the American Revolution (*Revolution* 15–37). Warfel discusses the implications of book distribution as it relates to a bookseller's geographic area: "[A]n American author in the 1790s had to depend almost entirely for income on sales within the trading area in which his books were printed" (142). Thirty years after Brown, the problem of linking authorship to a viable market economy remained (Wallace 23).

The "Double-Tongued" Capacity of Voice

Brown's epigraph and "Advertisement" to *Wieland* were designed to cast a wide net. Working in tandem to make a complex sales pitch, these prefatory materials provide an artfully duplicitous promissory note. In attempting to balance the antithetical claims of orthodoxy and rebellion, Brown juxtaposes the "forth-right journey" of the "Good" and the dubious attractions of "double-tongued" wanderers:

> From Virtue's blissful paths away
> The double-tongued are sure to stray;
> Good is a forth-right journey still,
> And mazy paths but lead to ill. (*W* 1)

The "double-tongued" voice constitutes a foundational trope that informs Brown's divided, even subversive, relationship with his audience. Moralistically inclined readers could anticipate the inevitable defeat of evil; more transgressive temperaments might anticipate—and relish—seductive diversions to be found along "mazy paths."[3] Similarly, the "Advertisement" seeks (at least ostensibly) to reconcile conflicting imperatives, articulating the terms whereby Brown hoped to advance his literary career. He associates his "American Tale" with canons of social ethics and utility: "The following Work," Brown avers, is "the first of a series of performances" designed not merely for entertainment but directed toward "the illustration of some important branches of the moral constitution of man" (*W* 3). [4] Such a claim is not made lightly. In 1798, it would be unusual to think that

---

[3] See Barnard and Shapiro for the relationship of the "double-tongued" trope to the matter of "sincerity" in *Wieland* (xx–xxiv). Faherty positions the epigraph as a telling point of departure from which flows a host of dialectically-charged moral complications: "Privileging a forthright commitment to plain speech, the poem defines virtue as self-generated by placing emphasis on the danger facing a speaker who detaches her use of language from her genuine intentions" (53).

[4] Davison discusses the conventional view of novels in early America as being expected to provide amusement and instruction (*Revolution* 72–74).

delineations of "the moral constitution" of human behavior could, or should, be separable from corresponding aesthetic aspirations. Michael T. Gilmore observes that "postrevolutionary literature" needs, at least initially, to be approached in relation to critical categories that are not primarily aesthetic: "Strictly aesthetic terms give limited access to an array of works dedicated to utility; categories drawn from outside literature have greater explanatory power" ("Letters of the Early Republic" 542). Words like the *moral*, the *useful*, and the *good* made immediate sense to readers and provide points of reference for Brown's dialectical pursuit of more expansive critical and aesthetic goals.[5]

As Brown attempts to present his work as a morally useful form of entertainment, he sidles away from conservative pieties and pitches his sensationalistic delineation of "incidents" both "extraordinary and rare." He genuflects toward the conventional as a prelude to invoking the miraculous or dramatizing the bizarre. He teases prospective reader with references to Francis Carwin's "extremely rare" powers—whatever they are—and to Theodore Wieland's unnamed psychological and criminal perversions—read on and find out. The balancing act continues with the insistence that these strange attributes will correspond to known principles of human behavior. Wieland's prospective "Transformation" will be plausible—or achieve "sufficient vindication"—as long as "history furnishes one parallel fact" (*W* 3). Brown's "one

[5] Gilmore summarizes the cultural forces that shaped the emergence of a postrevolutionary literature in the United States: "Early American literature was the product of a historical formation dominated by republicanism, communalism, and a preindustrial agrarian economy. Republicanism, the governing ideology of the revolutionary era, envisioned one's highest calling as active participation in the civic realm.... Liberalism, strongly on the rise after independence, was challenging republican assumptions and chipping away at the public-private hierarchy" ("Letters of the Early Republic" 542–43). Verhoeven's suggests that readers should "attend less to solving the vexed issue of whether Brown was 'conservative' or 'radical,' and if or when he changed his political allegiances, and more to thinking about his negotiations with eighteenth-century philosophical and historical thought, and to his place in the tradition of what has been called 'philosophical history' or, alternatively, 'the philosophical novel'—the narrative rendering of philosophical explorations" (29).

parallel fact" is James Yates' 1781 real-life slaughter of his wife and four children. Yates acted in response, he claimed, to a direct deific command (*W* 323).[6]

Far from simply advocating the "forth-right journey" of the "Good," Brown demonstrates the crafty doubleness inherent in his own words as he introduces this novel's elemental epistemological quandary about whether language can depict the unambiguous truth about anything. In fact, the epigraph and "Advertisement" reflect Brown's attempt to link legitimacy and license—legitimacy as a useful writer providing moral sustenance; license as a transgressive writer purveying sensationalistic horror. Even Brown's choice of setting reflects his "double-tongued" imperatives. The "Advertisement" establishes the narrative's historical epoch. The events take place sometime between the French and Indian War and the American Revolution, between 1756 and 1776—a placement that seems to qualify critical approaches that seek to establish what Duncan Faherty describes as "a synecdochical connection between family and emerging nation." Faherty critiques those tropisms that present "the figuration of *Wieland* as intimately linked to questions of nation formation and community consolidation after the Revolution" (49) and favors approaches that situate the novel in relation to more expansive forces. Writing in the turbulent post-revolutionary times of Federalist America, Brown

[6] See Cowie, *Wieland* 319–20 and 323–24. Cowie suggests that Brown "may well have begun thinking about the major action of his novel—Wieland's destruction of his family" as early as 1796 when he read the "Account of a Murder Committed by Mr. J[ames] Y[ates] upon His Family" (319). Warfel discusses the 1791 Yates murder in Tomhanick, New York and Brown's reading about this event as reported in the New York *Weekly Magazine* on July 20, 1796 (104). In an [October–November] 1792 letter to Bringhurst, Brown wrote, "Self-murder, or the murder of ones wife and child, are in the opinion of mankind crimes of the deepest malignity" (*L* 139). Axelrod offers an illuminating discussion regarding parallels between Yates' murders and the Abraham and Isaac typology (53–58). See Barnard and Shapiro for contemporary documents concerning the Yates murder (278–86). Kafer views Brown's attraction to adapting the Yates murder in *Wieland* as reflecting Brown's preoccupation with elements of his own "disorienting family trauma" (113).

distances his "American Tale" by three decades and displaces his own authorial presence in favor of his letter-writing narrator, Clara Wieland.[7]

This preoccupation with "double-tongued" expression in *Wieland* not only informs Brown's poetics, but it also characterizes his political sense of a new America. From this perspective, the political has less to do with the push and tug of overtly topical affairs—men mired in the committee-room grit of revolutionary manifestoes and constitutional crises. Brown's sense of the political extends beyond topical issues and includes his exploration of root structures of individual and collective experience, especially as depicted in competing hermeneutical issues regarding causality and agency. Early in *Wieland*, for example, this interest in opposing explanatory paradigms emerges with the death of the elder Wieland. If a bizarre event like the immolation of Clara's father is perceivable only through the imperfect medium of the senses, then the putative nature—or possible truth—of such an experience can only be approached through a reconstructive narrative—one that delineates what was perceived to have happened in relation to a subsequent critical process stymied by the narrator's limited access to information and the inscrutable content of the catastrophic event itself. In reconstructing the scene and shaping (and limiting) interpretive possibilities, Clara Wieland herself becomes "double-tongued": for example, her imputation of divine agency stands in diametrical opposition to her

---

[7] Christophersen sees Brown's distancing of his novel's action from his own historical moment as a deflection that allows Brown the freedom to dramatize forces alive in his own time (27). Barnard and Shapiro play down the matter of Brown's significance as a progenitor of American literature and explore the impact of transatlantic writers on Brown's syncretic aesthetic: "Few other American-produced novels so consciously recall and insert themselves within a contemporaneous internationalized literary realm" (xi). Kazajian explores the importance of situating Brown's novels within his contemporary publishing milieu: "The familiar critical narrative that positions Brown as the founder of American literature overlooks not only William Brown Hill, whose novel *The Power of Sympathy* was published in 1789, nine years before *Wieland*, but also a lengthy list of literary predecessors who raise the very question of what 'American' and 'literature' might mean" (140).

speculations regarding the (putative) naturalistic agency of spontaneous combustion. At no point in the novel is the causal mystery of the elder Wieland's death conclusively explained: his death could have resulted from an act of providence; his death could have derived from irruptive, biochemical abnormalities (*W* 19). Such hermeneutical uncertainty abounds in *Wieland* and becomes reflected as Brown insistently dramatizes elemental questions regarding being, epistemology, and agency and a host of aesthetic and political issues that generate from them. The very fact that the providential explanation appears as one alternative rather than the indisputable root cause suggests how Brown favors speculative hermeneutics over the pursuit of objective causality. In the aftermath of his apprenticeship years and his experiments with portraying multiple versions of his authorial self, Brown responds to such "double-tongued" imperatives by initiating in *Wieland* an innovative experiment with narrative self-making.

Sensation Narrative and Critical Narrative

Brown's doubleness—his strained sense of audience and purpose—finds a fitting complement in Clara Wieland's disconcerted efforts to compose her tale. By attempting to satisfy inquiries from her European correspondents, she displays the shifting imperatives that inform her epistolary performance.[8] At the outset of her narrative, Clara wrestles with the problem of how to inscribe the remembered past and thereby induct her correspondents into an authoritative engagement with the Wieland family tragedy. Her conflicted response to the problem of narrative reconstruction and present-time analysis connects her most

[8] In referring to Clara's "obsessed narrative," Davidson associates the "Gothic's unpredictable disorder" with a story-telling mode that delineates harried thoughts percolating within an unfolding present (*Revolution and the Word* 224). Auerbach discusses a number of implications associated with "the necessary duplicity of writing in the first person. Calling into question the very meaning of a 'proper identity,' the storyteller's 'I' simultaneously plays the part of anguished participant and dispassionate observer, the narrated self who acts in the past and the narrating self who retrospectively analyzes that past action in the present" (5).

intimately to aesthetic possibilities inherent within epistolary narration, especially through what Jay Fliegelman identifies as "Locke's sensationalist framework" (24). In exploring the relationship between epistolary form and "sensationalist epistemology" (26), Fliegelman maintains that "[t]he letter affirmed the importance of the individual voice.... In short, the letter allowed one to reflect on his or her experience, to learn from it, and to reach out beyond the prescriptive world of the household and its roles" (29).[9] While writing her long letter, Clara finds herself intermittently delineating both her past experiences and the sensations that accompanied them, on the one hand, as well as the emergent content of her present-time critical analysis, on the other. Clara occasionally disrupts her retrospective account to describe her perturbed emotions that undermine her efforts to continue writing. These lamentations include outraged recriminations attacking Francis Carwin. Such irruptions dissolve the illusion of an unfolding, past tense, dramatic sequence and replace it with an account of what the writer is thinking and feeling while engaged in the compositional process. The retrospective tale, therefore, assumes its true character: it does not constitute a mimetic reproduction of the past but instead embodies a self-generated, highly subjective version of the past—one that inducts the reader into experiencing how these recollected events affected her at the time they occurred. The dialectical relationship between sensation narrative and critical narrative establishes a foundational aesthetic form in *Wieland* and reflects Brown's innovative adaptations of materials from his apprenticeship years, especially his seemingly improvised proto-fictional experiments, his attempts to create an authorial self

---

[9] For a discussion of the emergence of the term "sensation," see Barton and Phegley 1–2. Apap explores Brown's debt to Godwin, the "sensational," and the generation of philosophical discourse: "[T]hough Brown shared with Godwin an interest in sensational plots, Brown's most famous works. . .used sensation as a platform from which to launch philosophical musings that rival Godwin's in depth and breadth" (24). Apap also discusses connections between English and German Gothic traditions and their impact on Brown (26).

within an emergent epistolary narrative, and the protean hermeneutics inscribed within the unfolding compositional process.

By juxtaposing Clara's past tense sensation narrative with the experiential immediacy of her present tense critical narrative, Brown dramatizes the inherent epistemological instability of his first published novel. When beginning her letter, Clara believes her life to be virtually finished: she casts herself as a battered survivor, a vestigial voice sounding from the ruins. All that remains is for her to supply the requested account, put the destruction of her life on record, and await a timely, merciful death. Clara does not indicate that she intends to withhold, or distort, the truth. Her story is elicited by trusted friends and she wants to give them a veritable account of what she experienced. It will be up to her correspondents to decide whether her account will be made available to a larger audience. Private disclosure offers a possible prelude to public performance.

At the outset of her letter, Clara is plagued by the unsettled state of her present consciousness. The extremity of her psychological distress entails an array of aesthetic consequences. She does not immediately launch a linear account of the events that culminated with her current troubles. Instead, she seeks to interpret, contain, and explain the exigencies of the past and thereby direct her reader's understanding of a tale that has yet to be told. Seemingly unaware of the inherent ambiguity of the events that will shape her narrative, she propounds a heavy-handed summation and becomes enmeshed (as she typically is) in doubleness: she predicts that her story "will exemplify the force of early impressions, and show the immeasurable evils that flow from an erroneous or imperfect discipline" (*W* 5). At first glance, this moral provides a comforting premise. The first-time reader cannot know that she is writing about her brother. Only the re-reader recognizes her contention that Theodore Wieland was corrupted by "early impressions" and how with perfect discipline, he could have resisted the ostensibly divine directive to slaughter his family. The critical reader—the re-reader, as it were—can view Clara's prospective tale in relation to what has been omitted from her moralistic platitude—essentially, Clara's knowledge of Carwin's agency as enacted through his disruptive, covert, biloquial performances. For the critical re-reader, Clara's interpretation does not begin to address the layered complexities that animate the subsequent narrative. The critical re-reader knows that Carwin was responsible for most, but not all, of the disembodied voices, some but not all of the strange events. Certainly, Carwin could not have been responsible for the mysterious death of the elder Wieland. Nor could he have staged the auditory and visual sensations reportedly experienced by Theodore Wieland, most notably his conviction that he enjoyed a direct vision of a transcendent figure he believed to be God (*W* 167–68). Ironically, Wieland's massacre of his family is itself an expression of perfect discipline and his actions derive less from "early impressions" than from an impassioned response to answered prayers. At the very least, the contingent relationship between "impressions" and "discipline" presupposes the existence of Wieland's volition, especially insofar as he demonstrates the capacity to perceive those ostensibly deific instructions, fret over them, delay their execution, and then act with self-possessed, willful, and deadly conviction. He could have rebelled against the directive and possibly come to suffer a fate similar to his father. In describing her father's frantic state of mind prior to his death, Clara writes, "A command had been laid upon him, which he had delayed to perform. He felt as if a certain period of hesitation and reluctance had been allowed him, but that this period was passed. He was no longer permitted to obey. The duty assigned to him was transferred, in consequence of his disobedience, to another, and all that remained was to endure the penalty" (*W* 12–13). Ambiguities abound. What was the command, if any? Did some deific entity order the elder Wieland to slay his family? In the aftermath of his supposed dereliction, was this "duty" then assigned to his son? These are troubling questions that the narrative excites but never answers.

At the outset, however, Clara's summary explanation undermines individual agency and validates her conviction that the universe is controlled by an inscrutable providence, the Author of the universe. Clara's interpretation conflates the determinate power of providence with the conclusive province of fate: "Fate has done its worst.... The power that governs the course of human affairs has chosen his path. The decree that ascertained the condition of my life, admits of no recal. No doubt it squares with the maxims of eternal equity. That is neither to be questioned nor denied by me. It suffices that the past is exempt from mutation" (*W* 5). But while the past *is* "exempt from mutation," the *meaning* of the past is not exempt from subjective extrapolations and dangerous misapprehensions of limited first-person narrators. Seemingly at every point, Clara's intrepid sense of rectitude is undone, or made problematical, by all that exists beyond her knowledge and control. For Brown, the subjective content of Clara's providential perspective constitutes her equivocal point of departure and reference. In no way does Brown affirm Clara's providential perspective as an efficacious interpretative paradigm. Clara's subjectivity is a given. Her sensation narrative, therefore, makes possible a critical narrative that is only ostensibly authoritative. In fact, the critical narrative is nothing more than the present-tense content of Clara's unfolding—and vacillating—speculations. In effect, Clara becomes an interpretive reader of the very tale she inscribes. Thus, the chronological account of the mystery surrounding the irruptions of disembodied voices provides the basis for Clara's inevitable failure, or inability, to report all she currently knows. Nor does Clara's story even begin to account for the multitude of events that take place outside her perceptions.

Thanks to the interpolated accounts of other (embodied) first-person narrators—Henry Pleyel, Theodore Wieland, Francis Carwin, and Thomas Cambridge—Clara's own tale frequently offers dramatic displays of ignorance and mis-perception. Indeed, her past-tense, sensation narrative often conflicts with her present-tense, critical narrative. For example, when she first mentions Carwin's name, she vilifies him (*W* 49); but when she first encountered him, she was enraptured by his "wholly new" voice (*W* 52). Carwin's degree of culpability is never resolved, although multiple opinions obtain. At various points, Clara describes him as merely human; a human with superhuman powers; a demon; and a human being who directs demons. The levelheaded Uncle Thomas Cambridge views Carwin as a bungling interloper, who may have prodded Wieland in the direction of maniacal delusion. For what it may be worth, Carwin stridently denies Clara's demonic accusations and represents himself as a well-meaning man addicted to "a species of imposture" (*W* 201).[10]

When inhabiting the compositional present—her writing time—Clara intermittently insists on providential design. It is, however, crucial that the reader never moves beyond the subjective reach of first-person narration. Clara's interpretations, then, whether delivered within her sensation or critical narratives, are not so much authoritative judgments as propositions to be tested. The many aspects of Clara's "double-tongued" account—her recurrent affirmations of human and supernatural agency, for example—dramatize Brown's preoccupation in *Wieland* with unsettling those cognitive premises that establish the basis of human authority.[11] What is crucial is not that Clara is somehow wrong or right, or that she might be confused and contradictory, even at times incoherent, all of which she sometimes is. Nor is the content, or possible rectitude or fallaciousness, of any specific interpretation a predominant concern. Indeed, the other interpolated narrators offer a multitude of explanations, no one of which answers. What

---

[10] Fliegelman argues, "Brown's novel of authority misrepresented and authority imagined is a terrifying post-French Revolutionary account of the fallibility of the human mind and, by extension, democracy itself' (239).

[11] Davidson examines the relationship between the novel form and the breakdown of authority: "For. . .men of power and prestige. . .it was a chaotic new world, and the novel, more than any other literary genre, was seen as the sign of a time when their authority was being called into question" (*Revolution* 39). Gabler-Hover examines how the Gothic offers a fit environment for the proliferation of "epistemological chaos" in *Wieland* (59). Against this strain, Gabler-Hover contends," is a "steady discourse on ethics.... [E]thics in the novel evolve in response to the fearsome power of voices, the fearsome power of language, language specifically in the sense of its rhetoricity—in its power to seduce or to persuade" (60).

remains at stake is Brown's delineation of the tenuous and flawed process of making judgments—of creating meaning—in the first place and the inherent political dangers that obtain when one elevates subjective propositions to the status of universalizing truths.

Fractured Beginnings: The Origins of "an Imperfect Tale"

Perhaps in response to her broken and enervated condition, Clara Wieland seeks to dramatize a stable point of origin and unwittingly, it seems, enacts the problematic American quest to fix a beginning.[12] As Christopher Looby contends, "Clara's narrative begins, as Franklin's *Autobiography* did, by detailing the prehistory of her family" (151). Clara initiates her narrative by moving two generations back and presenting an account of her paternal forebearers. Her summary treatment not only illustrates the failure of Old-World Europe to accommodate her father's desires, but also the failure of New World America to offer an alternative to those oppressive Eurocentric forms he carries within him and never renounces.[13]

Clara's "American Tale" begins with her grandfather's repudiation of family strictures and class values. Undeterred by "parental menaces and prohibitions," he marries the daughter of a merchant, incurs the wrath of his family, and becomes "entirely disowned and rejected" (*W* 6). After earning "a scanty subsistence" from his musical compositions, he dies "in the bloom of his life, and was quickly followed to the grave by his wife" (*W* 7). Their son does not regain his father's lost stature but suffers through an impoverished apprenticeship in London. He

---

[12] See Terence Martin for his exploration of "the protean importance of a sense of beginning in American literature and culture" (ix).

[13] Weldon sees the Wieland family as "not a model for emulation but a standard of failure" (1). For example, Weldon argues that Theodore's reading of Cicero provides an allusive context for understanding the mayhem loosed within multiple generations of the Wieland family (2–3). See Axelrod's examination of the European roots of the Wieland name (61–66).

retreats into himself and "gradually contracted a habit of morose and gloomy reflection" (*W* 7). He exercises his reflective powers through an obsession with Protestant theology, specifically the writings of a "Camissard apostle" (*W* 9).[14] He becomes a fanatical adherent to "[t]he empire of religious duty.... All levities of speech, and negligences of behaviour, were proscribed" (*W* 9). Clara's father thus internalizes a narrow, controlling vision. The expiration of his apprenticeship and a small bequest from his father-in-law reinforce a "most imperious and irresistible necessity." He discovers "his duty to disseminate the truths of the gospel among the unbelieving nations" (*W* 10).[15]

Clara's account reflects, even as it complicates, the mythos of Old World/New World emigration. The elder Wieland suffers economic and religious privation and seems to embrace New World possibility. At the same time, however, he possesses a missionary and colonizing zeal that has roots in predatory Eurocentric ideologies. As Faherty notes, "Brown's decision to ground the plot's prehistory in questions of empire, transnational capital, and mobility destabilizes readings that suggest that the concept of an isolated nation forms *Wieland*'s objective correlative" (51). Believing that his messianic fervor is authorized by

---

[14] See Barnard and Shapiro for their discussion of the elder Wieland's "enraptured" response to "a French Prophet text": "Since [the elder Wieland's] current condition as a belabored expatriate and child of disinherited and absent parents corresponds to many of the structural pressures that gave rise to the Camisard movement, the youth has good reason to be attracted by its rhetoric of personal redemption and punishment against worldly evil" (xxix). Waterman discusses the elder Wieland's "religious extremism" as it relates to the Camisards and the Albigenses (*Republic of Intellect* 81). See Kafer's discussion of Clara's father as a "spiritual seeker" (119; also 114–16). Kafer describes Brown's use of an "historical frame" (114) that associates Theodore and Clara Wieland with their father and his affiliation with the Camisard philosophies, related forms of religious extremism, and "mystic seekers" (115).

[15] See Tompkins' discussion of the impact of the European past on the Wieland family and the seemingly disjunctive and underdeveloped Louisa Conway plot (61). Rosenthal discusses the elder Wieland's theological extremism, especially his embrace of radical heresies ("The Voices" 102–05 and 122, n. 5). Bradfield contends that "Europeans never found a 'free space' in the New World because they took too many Old World stories along with them to light the way" (xiii).

God, the elder Wieland seeks to enact "what he deemed the will of heaven" (*W* 10). Originally, however, he is less than intrepid. The alleged "savage manners" of Indians dissuade him from pursuing his missionary goals. With the aid of "African slaves," the elder Wieland takes up the agrarian life. When he finally attempts the "conversion of the savage tribes," he eschews the "pleadings of parental and conjugal love" (*W* 10–11). After his missionary enterprise fails, he is not called home by family life, but by an internal prompting, presumably from God: "He desisted not till his heart was relieved from the supposed obligation to persevere" (*W* 11).

Brown casts this émigré not as Crevecoeur's optimistic "new man" (43) animated by the prospect of Agrarian self-redemption, but as one who carries the cultural seeds of European decay, specifically the hybrid fusion of exploitative missionary and colonial imperatives.[16] His journey lacks the transformational qualities typically associated with American novelty. Thus, he finds himself continuous with—rather than dissociated from—the European past. As immigrant, missionary, and slave-holding farmer, he embodies those elements that impede the creation of new forms in America. Clara's attempt to establish a stable point of familial origin is compromised by her father's identification with, and importation of, hegemonic European forms. In retaining his

[16] Tompkins argues, "Dramatizing the precariousness of Crevecoeur's 'perfect' society, the novel's plot offers a direct refutation of the Republican faith in men's capacity to govern themselves without the supports and constraints of an established social order" (49). Hsu contends, "The early chapters. . .thematize the agrarian idea that the basic unit of this expandable grid might be furnished by an independent yeoman farmer epitomized by Jefferson's ideal of self-sufficient private life at Monticello. Theodore Wieland's independent country estate at first appears a self-sufficient, infinitely reproducible unit of democratic space whose neo-classical 'temple' recalls Monticello's ideal of modesty" (31–32). According to Faherty, the matter of the elder Wieland's migration, the "ethnoscape" his experiences reflect, and his bizarre death indicate "the impossibility of disentangling the Wieland family from a wide range of circum-Atlantic influences and networks" (50). Bound within the elder Wieland's story are the entangled cultural and political landscapes of continental Europe, England, Africa, and Philadelphia—one of the cradles of the Revolution.

God-directed passion, he merely seeks a space appropriate for its full enactment. On the one hand, he may seem an heir to the fervent piety of first-generation Puritans of The Great Migration (1630), who brought to New England the righteous fire of Covenant theology and a militant colonizing zeal. On the other, the elder Wieland lacks the early Puritans' sense of vested communalism. As an extreme agent of the Protestant Reformation, the elder Wieland rejects mediatory ecclesiastical forms.[17] As sole member of his own church, "He allied himself with no sect, because he perfectly agreed with none.... He rigidly interpreted that precept which enjoins us, when we worship, to retire into solitude, and shut out every species of society" (*W* 11). To advance his theological dictates, he constructs his own prayer space, a private "temple of his Deity" (*W* 12). He claims to have received a divine mandate:

> A command had been laid upon him, which he had delayed to perform. He felt as if a certain period of hesitation and reluctance had been allowed him, but that this period was passed. He was no longer permitted to obey. The duty assigned to him was transferred, in consequence of his disobedience, to another, and all that remained was to endure the penalty. (*W* 12–13)

The ambiguous formulation associated with this ostensible "command" never specifies the actual imperative or identifies the person to

---

[17] In his conviction that he enjoys direct communication with God, the elder Wieland might be associated with such radical Antinomians as Anne Hutchinson and the American Quakers with their dedication to the agency of the Inner Light. But Hutchinson's threat to the religious homogeneity of Massachusetts Bay Colony in the early 1630s lay not so much in the specific content of her beliefs as in the threat of political subversion made manifest through her brow-beating mastery of biblical exegesis and her proselytizing fervor. Before the frowning faces of the appalled Massachusetts Bay patriarchs, Hutchinson was creating her own cult, as it were, an alternative basis for a theocratic community. Unlike Hutchinson, the elder Wieland does not hold conversations in his home. Nor is he interested in establishing a cohort of converts.

whom the task was transferred. Perhaps the elder Wieland received the same instructions as his son later claims to receive. If so, the major catastrophe of the novel—Theodore's slaughter of his family—would constitute the son's later enactment of the father's divinely-prompted, and neglected, duty. The ostensible dereliction of the father prescripts the horrific crimes of the son. Brown thereby subverts the notion that New World emigration establishes a personal and cultural point of origination. America simply contains this latest tragedy in the long-playing drama of generational succession. In refusing to enact deific commands and asserting his individual prerogative, the elder Wieland prescripts his imminent doom. In dismantling the immigrant myth of American newness, Brown dramatizes what amounts to the elder Wieland's time-bound, predestined, personal apocalypse.

As narrator, Clara cannot appropriate, and thereby cannot represent, the actual content of her father's experience and consciousness. We are left—because Clara is left—with the shreds and patches of narrative lacunae. In her attempt to depict the exigencies (and abiding mystery) of the novel's originating tragedy, Clara relates not *what happened* but a partial account of what reportedly happened. Thus, Brown distances his narrator (and her readers) from the past. In presenting this event, Clara shifts the focus from her mother's limited perspective to her maternal uncle's fragmented tale. First on the scene, Thomas Cambridge reports seeing something that "resembled a cloud impregnated with light" (*W* 17)—a light that is quickly extinguished. Upon being interrogated, the elder Wieland offers what is variously described as "an imperfect account" and "an imperfect tale." Significantly, the elder Wieland's "fancy" depicts a strange, possibly supernatural incident: "My uncle was inclined to believe that half the truth had been suppressed" (*W* 18). The elder Wieland's account can only be reconstituted as a fragment. Consequently, causes become suppositions; effects are equivocal conjectures.

Brown does not delineate an action so much as advance an epistemological quandary, which is the very essence of his *American Tale.*

Clara's attempt to ground her story in family history reveals the instability and uncertainty of her originating materials. A six-year-old child when her father died, she relies on questionable perceptions masquerading as "facts." By dramatizing how narrative omissions generate hermeneutical process, Brown conducts the reader from perceivable effects to a quest for an inscrutable cause; from an assertion of ostensible "facts" to an irresolvable entanglement with fanciful "impressions" (*W* 19). The recondite insularity of her father's mind creates an insuperable epistemological impediment. The death of the elder Wieland dramatizes the novel's central hermeneutical problem: how can one construct narrative forms capable of explaining events that are inherently unknowable and that involve ostensibly transcendent forms of agency? Clara's account is limited not only by her father's self-containment, but also by her necessary dependence on flawed testimony. In fact, the enlargement on "imperfect" testimony constitutes the essence of her narrative performance and reflects the novel's abiding insistence on the limits of disclosure. Whereas Clara never learns any more about the causes and meaning of her father's death, she nevertheless associates the unresolved mystery with her impending account of family's tragedy: "Their resemblance to recent events revived them with new force in my memory, and made me more anxious to explain them" (*W* 19).

Irruptive Voices

Following the deaths of their parents, Clara and Theodore Wieland find themselves enjoying a secure way of life that is personally reflected in the balanced relation obtaining among two sets of doubles. Theodore Wieland's marriage to Catherine Pleyel prescripts, but does not necessitate, Clara's eventual marriage to Pleyel. Their father's prayer temple becomes converted into a pleasant summer house decorated with a bust of Cicero, an icon that casts reason as a presiding household god. Masquerading as an eighteenth-century rationalist, Wieland purports to venerate Ciceronian rhetoric as a stable basis for argumentative discourse. In describing her brother, Clara notes, "He deemed it indispensable to examine the ground of his belief, to settle the relation between motives and actions, the criterion of merit, and the kinds and properties of evidence" (*W* 23). According to such premises, the studied application of reason dissipates mystery.[18]

As Brown makes resoundingly clear, one's conscious predilections do not necessarily reflect one's essence. The paradise founded on balanced relationships and enlightened discourse is only apparent. Its destruction is signaled not by these characters' conscious devotion to rational forms, but by the lurking presence of unconscious attributes that inform behavior and direct choice—a circumstance that achieves its fullest realization in *Edgar Huntly*. In *Wieland*, the fabricated social order floats precariously upon an undercurrent of destructive forces—in the very way that the Age of Reason can never be dissociated from the Age of Revolution.

The seemingly stable homestead actually contains an uneasy amalgam of contentious energies.[19] For example, along with appearing as Wieland's surrogate brother, Pleyel is also his foil. His mirthful exuberance contrasts with Wieland's grave demeanor. Though well-versed in science and literature, Wieland is (like his father) prone to gloomy rumination. Indeed, beneath the veneer of Ciceronian discourse lurks Wieland's ingrained religious fanaticism. Far from embracing Pleyel's rational Deism, Wieland is heir to a troubled Calvinist legacy: "Moral necessity, and calvinistic inspiration, were the props on which my brother thought proper to repose" (*W* 25). The word "props" evokes a resonant skein of associations, suggesting the supporting structures of

---

[18] According to Levine, "*Wieland*'s innocent temple community is imaged as a synecdochic model of the American community.... [T]he Wielands and the Pleyels, naïve Lockean utopianists, become especially vulnerable to outsiders and even tempt the machinations of a seductive plotter whose rumored association with conspirators implies a political allegory of seduction" (*Conspiracy and Romance* 29). See Leask on the failure of the Wieland utopia at Mettingen (106–11).

[19] Rombes argues, "*Wieland*, like perhaps no other novel of its time, catalogues the tension between two vastly differing ideologies, republican virtue and anarchic abandon, and the battle leaves its scars in Clara Wieland's disintegrating voice" (37).

a building and, perhaps, even movable theatrical properties. Reason functions as Pleyel's main prop: "Pleyel was the champion of intellectual liberty, and rejected all guidance but that of his reason" (*W* 25).[20] This novel's pervading experiential chaos complements—and generates from—the fragility underlying all self-constructed forms of psychological and social order: reason stands as the novel's primary shibboleth, the icon that Brown smashes and then smashes some more. Through Wieland and Pleyel, Brown discloses how ideational conflicts between Calvinism and Deism provide tenuous foundations for constructing self-reflexive systems of value. In this novel, the dissolution of such prescribed forms reflects Brown's preoccupation with dramatizing American transformation. These "props"—whether Calvinist or Deistic—promise stability but instigate chaos.

While covertly threatened by the impending onset of psychological mutability, the ostensible paradise of Mettingen is assailed by the irruption of disembodied voices.[21] These voices—first heard by Wieland—begin the process whereby his household disintegrates beneath the weight of intrusive, seemingly supernatural forces. Through the office of her sensation narrative, Clara reveals how these disembodied voices engendered mystery and dread. First time readers share these this sense of confusion. While going to the summer house to retrieve a letter, Wieland is startled to hear his wife's voice: "Stop, go no further. There is danger in your path" (*W* 33). Informed upon his return that his wife has not left Pleyel's and Clara's company, Wieland reduces all explanations to a binary opposition: "[E]ither I heard my wife's voice at the bottom of the hill, or I do not hear your voice at present" (*W*

---

[20] See Barnard and Shapiro on the relationship of the Wieland cohort to Brown's complex critique of Enlightenment philosophy (xxxiii).

[21] See Schmidt for a discussion of disembodied voices and the relation of these voices to the Enlightenment's concern with sense-based epistemology: "By the time Paine's *Age of Reason* appeared in the 1790s, natural philosophers had long been trying to detach the voice from the presence of the speaker through a series of artificial mediations" (28). See especially his section on "Working the Oracle: A History and Politics of Imposture" (82–101).

32). Other possibilities emerge. For example, Pleyel insists that Wieland is a victim of "auricular deception." Clara intimates that "a shadowy resemblance [exists] between it and my father's death" (*W* 34)—an analogue that reinforces her suspicion that providential agency might have caused their father's death.

These tensions derive from Clara decision to limit her account to what she perceived at that time. Had she said, "I know now that Carwin impetuously assumed Catherine's voice to evade detection at the summer house," she would have foreclosed most (but not all) of the narrative's subsequent dramatic and epistemological mysteries. Everything depends on the limits of disclosure. For each character, the interpretation of this seemingly inscrutable phenomenon constitutes a form of self-projection. Wieland offers a reductive binary summary; Pleyel takes refuge in rational dismissal and levity; Clara asserts the continuity between successive generations. Her chief worry—well founded—is that her brother's experience of Catherine's disembodied voice will necessitate a chain of disastrous consequences: "Yet I could not bear to think that his senses should be the victims of such delusion. It argued a diseased condition of his frame, which might show itself hereafter in more dangerous symptoms." Clara goes on to propound a paradigmatic formulation of eighteenth-century Lockean faculty psychology: "The will is the tool of the understanding, which must fashion its conclusions on the notices of sense. If the senses be depraved, it is impossible to calculate the evils that may flow from the consequent deductions of the understanding" (*W* 35). At stake is the very origin and operation of human cognition, especially insofar as sensory experience dictates how permutations of thought shape the will and become expressed in action.[22] In *Wieland*, Brown's critique of Locke dramatizes

[22] In *An Enquiry Concerning Political Justice*, Godwin analyzes the relationship of sense to understanding and action: "Impression upon our senses may act either as physical or moral causes" (52). He argues, "Sensation is of some moment in the affair. It possesses the initiative. It is that from which all the intellects with which we are acquainted date their operations. Its first effect upon mind does in the majority of

the danger inherent in dissociating one sense from one another, especially the separation of hearing from vision. The sound of disembodied voices provides evidence that is never questioned as *being* partial. The avid embrace of supernatural causality preempts any attempt to unify auditory and visual senses—a process that, if actualized, would enlarge the range of sense experience and allow one to validate the efficacy of conclusions drawn from "the notices of sense."

Clara's precise formulation regarding the relationship between the will, the understanding, and behavior encapsulates elemental forces that impel the action of the novel. She recognizes that her brother will not discount or ignore the report of his senses. While admitting that a deception is "possible" (*W* 36), he embraces conflicting, irreconcilable explanations. He attempts to contain the transcendent within the phenomenology of reason's ostensibly clarifying power. He insists, for example, that his father's death derived "from a direct and supernatural decree." Clara, however, believes that her brother's "actions and practical sentiments are linked with long and abstruse deductions from the system of divine government and the laws of our intellectual constitution. He is, in some respects, an enthusiast, but is fortified in his belief by innumerable arguments and subtilties" (*W* 35). In theory alone, then, Wieland reconciles providence, enthusiasm, and rationality. In practice, however, Wieland's precepts later give way to an all-consuming ardor: his essential predisposition toward religious fanaticism mocks, and displaces, the wavering claims of reason's integrative power.

When Wieland and Pleyel both hear the second disembodied voice, Brown verifies the credibility of Wieland's earlier experience and nullifies Pleyel's charge of "auricular deception." The second voice—again, the sound of Catherine's voice—commands that the two men not move to Lusatia because Pleyel's fiancée, the Baroness Theresa von Stolberg, has died. The voice's ostensibly authoritative quality has

---

cases precede reflection and choice" (53). See Kafer's discussion of Brown's critique of the limits of Lockean sensationalism (125–26).

personal and cultural implications. The voice seems to be concerned for the well-being of the Wieland family and Pleyel. It also has the more encompassing effect of rejecting the lure of tenuous Old World patrimonial claims. Throughout the novel, the prospect of renouncing America and returning to Europe asserts an intermittent appeal. Significantly, Carwin controls the unfolding scenario and forecloses the possibility of Wieland's pursuit of aristocratic privilege in Europe. Carwin's meddling has an aesthetic and political dimension. The very process of imposing an improvised fiction on Wieland and Pleyel constitutes the chief manifestation of Carwin's protean, American attributes. Through his biloquial powers, he creates a script that will shape the experience of his malleable dupes. At least for the moment, Carwin gets lucky. He guesses that Theresa is dead. Whereas the first voice warned Wieland away from some vague, impending danger, the second voice informs Wieland and Pleyel of a past event capable of being verified. Shortly thereafter, Theresa's death is confirmed by verbal testimony that is later countermanded. Within her sensation narrative, Clara gives full play to the possibility of supernatural visitation:

> Here were proofs of a sensible and intelligent existence, which could not be denied. Here was information obtained and imparted by means unquestionably super-human.
>
> That there are conscious beings, beside ourselves, in existence, whose modes of activity and information surpass our own, can scarcely be denied. Is there a glimpse afforded us into a world of these superior beings? (*W* 45)

Her convictions, however, are suppositions that will be tested by subsequent events and revelations. She does little more than impose a fiction of supernatural interference. The irruptive voices set the stage for the ongoing collision between two distinct forms of agency—the divine and the human. The providential perspective achieves its greatest credibility within Clara's sensation narrative. Conversely, affirmations regarding the domain of human causality belong to her critical narrative.

The very introduction of Carwin—Clara's vexed, authorial necessity to write his name—unsettles her controlled, retrospective account. In disrupting her sensation narrative, she locates herself once again within the compositional present. Her very ability to continue writing her letter looms as a daunting challenge: "Now it is that I begin to perceive the difficulty of the task which I have undertaken" (*W* 49). How can she describe him as he *seemed*, knowing what she believes as she writes? Clara inhabits a judgmental position made possible both by her experience of the preceding events and by her memory of a succeeding chain of circumstances. By articulating her "difficulty"—how to write about Carwin—she draws attention to her structural problem, specifically her disconcerted purpose in the compositional present to repress her current knowledge and report the content of her past ignorance. She must not simply withhold her limited (and partly erroneous) knowledge of Carwin's machinations, but she must delineate her misperceptions regarding Carwin's initial appearance. When asserting that "the most turbulent sensations are connected" with Carwin's name, Clara prescripts the first-time reader's reaction to him. Even though Clara has impugned Carwin's reputation, she nevertheless must repress her venomous outbursts, find a language to depict him as she then perceived him, and still do justice to what he now seems to be: "[H]ow shall I support myself, when I rush into the midst of horrors such as no heart has hitherto conceived, nor tongue related? I sicken and recoil at the prospect, and yet my irresolution is momentary" (*W* 49). In displacing her critical narrative in favor of her sensation narrative, Clara imposes on Carwin the language of authorship and theatrical performance: "Let me tear myself from contemplation of the evils of which it is but too certain that thou wast the author, and limit my view to those harmless appearances which attended thy entrance on the stage" (*W* 50).[23] In a world that Clara has already claimed is controlled by

[23] Bell views Carwin as "a teller of tales"—a literary artist who oscillates within a dialectical interplay between sincerity and duplicity and consistently embraces "artificiality and deception" (147). Similarly, Galluzzo examines the "interpenetration

Providence, Carwin emerges as an authorial and histrionic agent, a protean figure of power. With a new kind of voice—portentous and hypnotic—Carwin is intent on controlling the stage.

The Protean Self

One day, Clara hears a voice characterized by excessive artificiality coming from a person she cannot see: "Pry'thee, good girl, canst thou supply a thirsty man with a glass of buttermilk?" (*W* 51). However anachronistic these pseudo-Elizabethan words may be, Clara is enthralled: "[T]he tone," she asserts, "was wholly new." Combining "force and sweetness," these sounds possess the capacity to lure, to woe, to seduce: "The voice was not only mellifluent and clear, but the emphasis was so just, and the modulation so impassioned, that it seemed as if an heart of stone could not fail of being moved by it" (*W* 51–52). Clara's focus on Carwin's powerful, Orphean voice evokes its daemonic status as the primary aesthetic medium of narrative self-making and manipulation.[24]

Clara's experience of hearing without seeing creates an open fictive space, which she is all too ready to fill with rapturous fancies. Clara, however, fails to take note of the disturbing—indeed cautionary—implications of the scene. Shortly before hearing the "wholly new" voice, she saw a rustic man walking past and remarked on the ignorant simplicity of yeoman life.[25] When Clara goes to the door, she discovers that the seductive voice belongs to this seeming bumpkin: "My fancy had conjured up a very different image." In her imagination, she

---

of political concerns" ("Charles Brockden Brown's *Wieland*" 257). Galluzzo argues, "Brown's novel pits Carwin's insurgent aesthetic against Mettingen's kingdom of disinterest in a characteristically dialogical fashion" ("Charles Brockden Brown's *Wieland*" 258).

[24] See Bloom for his wide-ranging exploration of the relationship between daemonic forces of creation and their manifestations within the tradition of the American literary sublime.

[25] Roeger reads *Wieland* as "an agrarian nightmare" (85) wherein "the subversive threat of agrarianism" undermines class distinctions (86).

created an appropriate "form, and attitude, and garb...but this person was, in all visible respects, the reverse of this phantom" (*W* 52). Brown dramatizes the disparity between illusions created by the fiction-making "fancy" and the material facts of surface appearance—a disparity that should put Clara on guard regarding the efficacy of her assessments. She perceives that his voice and face emanate signs of inscrutability, intelligence, and power. He possesses "in the midst of haggardness, a radiance inexpressibly serene and potent, and something in the rest of his features, which it would be in vain to describe, but which served to betoken a mind of the highest order, were essential ingredients in the portrait" (*W* 53).

In falling prey to Carwin's duplicitous appeal, Clara fails to be suspicious. Her infatuation grows for this "double-tongued," inverted version of Yankee Jonathan (*W* 1).[26] Significantly, Brown complicates this stereotypical image of the optimistic, open-hearted American rustic, not only reconstructing a deceptive version of this type, but drawing attention to its carefully composed artificiality. Carwin's physical appearance is clearly a fabrication bodying forth a studied persona. As a figure of mystery, however, he cannot be dissociated from his role in subsequent events. Commenting in her present-tense critical narrative, Clara connects Carwin's mysterious "entrance" (*W* 50) with consequences suffered thereafter and still persisting: "How little did I then foresee the termination of that chain, of which this may be regarded as the first link?" (*W* 54). By imposing a determinate interpretation not yet supported by the action, she prepares the reader to distrust Carwin's appearance, even though she herself failed to do so.

---

[26] Royall Tyler's play *The Contrast* (1787) featured the wildly popular Jonathan, an innocent, countrified, straight-talking embodiment of decent, homely American values fostered by an agrarian life and patriotic ideals. Given the popularity of this play in the late eighteenth century, it is possible that Brown used Jonathan as a partial model for Carwin's masquerade. For a foundational discussion of the Yankee Jonathan figure in American literature and culture, see O'Rourke on the evolution of this figure and its relation to "masquerade" (6–7 and 1–18).

Within her sensation narrative, Clara describes how she indulged her fancy. After sketching Carwin's face, she gazes on this image for hours. By giving representational form to her intimations, she becomes the rapt, narcissistic admirer of her own creation, obsessed by this projected embodiment of her secret self. In fact, the voice and face of Carwin answer her unconscious longing for the energies of illicit romance. Rather than giving expression to more rooted, pietistic attributes of her being, Clara reveals latent, sensual desires that attract her to the narrative's central figure of protean power. Clara loves, as a prelude to resisting, her own seemingly autonomous power of psychological mutability. Behind Clara's self-seduction resides a sense that her cultural and aesthetic politics are woefully inadequate to meet the demands of new social and political possibilities. Her sketch of Carwin in no way fixes or contains him. It merely projects a representational illusion of Carwin's fixity. In creating layers of social artifice, Brown never illuminates Carwin's hidden nature, especially the contours of a mind that generate his nefarious schemes. In *Wieland*, one never gets beyond the misleading evidence of Carwin's performances. His histrionics never reflects essence, only a series of self-engendered actions and divergent interpretations.

Clara's bizarre obsession with her sketched image of Carwin also has the effect of displacing, or at least undermining, her status as the novel's center of interpretive authority: "Perhaps you will suspect that such were the first inroads of a passion incident to every female heart.... I shall not controvert the reasonableness of the suspicion, but leave you at liberty to draw, from my narrative, what conclusions you please" (*W* 54). Clara eschews her insistently determinate ways and confers hermeneutical authority on her correspondents. At stake is the disposition and meaning of her affections. Is this love, infatuation, or delusion? It is left to her readers to draw conclusions—a situation made more complicated by Clara's subsequent admission of an abiding (but barely hinted) romantic passion for Pleyel. Not only is psychological retentiveness an apparent prerequisite for social performance—the subversive, self-making, protean artist needs to control surfaces and hide his essence and intentions—but such retentiveness points to the unwitting aesthetic core of Clara's epistolary narrative. Such limits of disclosure reside at the heart of Brown's epistemological drama, especially insofar as so much of the action takes place outside the sphere of Clara's knowledge and direct participation.

Like Wieland and Pleyel, Clara becomes victimized by sensory assaults from mysterious sources. The very notion of disembodied voices involves an elemental disruption in one's normal powers of apprehension. These irruptive voices create their own psychological contingencies. Wieland ruminates; Clara concludes. At the least, the various, disembodied voices displace a sense of commonplace possibility and construct an unmediated space, an uncanny realm in which the familiar and the known become unfamiliar and unknown. How can the sound of Catherine's voice be—and not be—hers? Brown replaces the commonplace world with a sometimes enticing, sometimes frightening domain of escalating mystery. Consequently, the third irruption of disembodied voices is the most invasive, troubling, and weird. When Clara hears a conversation taking place in her locked and reportedly inaccessible closet, she is under the most intimate siege. On the one hand, Clara seems the prospective victim of a bizarre murder plot. On the other, Carwin, as Clara later discovers, is actually standing on a ladder, his head thrust through the window, creating a premeditated (rather than improvisational) scenario that he believes will test her courage. Clara hears the dialogue and reasonably concludes that "Murderers lurked in my closet. They were planning the means of my destruction" (*W* 58).

Clara's bedroom becomes another mediatory space within which Brown dramatizes the unknown reaches of her interiority, specifically the elemental, latent fear of impending disaster. Elizabeth Jane Wall Hinds explores the cultural implications of Brown's preoccupation with dramatizing the psychological impact of enclosed spaces on his characters: "Enclosures, tight spaces, room within rooms—these we might simply attribute to the gothic conventions Brown was working and reworking.... Brown's closet spaces metonymically embody a larger atmosphere more particularly American, and more historically situated, than their mere reiteration suggests. They constitute the most private of private property" (19). The closet-dialogue projects, as it were, the latent content of Clara's inner darkness. In her mind, the threat may prefigure a reenactment of those forces that led to her father's enigmatic death. The fact that Carwin stages this dialogue does not mitigate Clara's terror. The dissolution of security constitutes the novel's central recurrent horror. Such horrors, Brown reveals, do not simply involve the imposition of scary Gothic conventions on to everyday life. These horrors unquestionably exist and have their greatest manifestation within the human psyche. What does Wieland's mind lead him to destroy but his home, his wife, his children, and himself? Behaving as any sane person might but failing Carwin's ludicrous test of bravery, Clara runs away and faints at her brother's doorway. A loud voice enjoins the sleeping occupants to "hasten to succour one that is dying at your door" (*W* 59). As the reader later discovers, the biloquist is merely indulging his fondness for overheated scenarios. At present, however, this voice seems the third communication from an invisible, celestial guardian.

Carwin's manipulative performance initiates a range of consequences that exceed his original design. Indeed, one apparent consequence that Carwin does not control (but later interprets) is Clara's unsettling dream dramatizing her brother's suspected perfidious intentions:

> After various incoherences had taken their turn to occupy my fancy, I at length imagined myself walking, in the evening twilight, to my brother's habitation. A pit, methought, had been dug in the path I had taken, of which I was not aware. As I carelessly pursued my walk, I thought I saw my brother, standing at some distance before me, beckoning and calling

> me to make haste. He stood on the opposite edge of the gulph. (*W* 62)

The threat of destruction becomes associated not only with her bedroom closet but with her brother, their father's heir. In the dream, Wieland seems to be tempting Clara toward an abyss. This creation of the fancy corroborates the implications of the closet-dialogue: just as a place of apparent security now seems fraught with peril, so too does the person she trusts most seem a potential destroyer in terms that are explicitly murderous and (arguably) incestuous.[27] Significantly, the dialogue and the dream hasten the dissolution of order. Supernatural and psychological domains converge: "Images so terrific and forcible disabled me, for a time, from distinguishing between sleep and wakefulness, and withheld from me the knowledge of my actual condition" (*W* 62). In her state of half-waking, she stumbles in total darkness. Is Clara confused or has she apprehended an essential truth? Her "actual condition" is that she is sleepwalking and is arrested in her progress by Carwin's hand. He speaks with one of the voices she heard in her closest: "I leagued to murder you. I repent. Mark my bidding, and be safe.... If a syllable of what has passed escape you, your doom is sealed. Remember your father, and be faithful" (*W* 63). By commanding her to remain silent, however, this "double-tongued" voice also threatens

[27] Readers might reasonably find intimations of incestuous possibility within the Theodore Wieland/Clara Wieland relationship, intimations fueled by Clara's dream of Wieland attempting to lead her toward an abyss, a dream that might just as easily suggest a pre-cognitive account of Wieland's murderous rampage. There is also the matter of Catherine being eventually found dead in Clara's bed—a conflation, one imagines, of incest and homicide. As Hinds notes. "*Wieland* seems to foreground a barely suppressed impulse to incest, dramatized most fully in Clara's dream of her brother beckoning to her across an abyss.... Nearly a century of critics probably can't be altogether wrong" (101–02). In her account, Hinds explores the relationship of the incest motif to "the familial and economic matrix established by the position of the Wieland household within a growing market economy surrounding the Wieland's author" (104).

her life (*W*1). Brown suspends Clara between the plot secretly fashioned by Carwin and the action generated by her own unconscious.

The scene conflates the murderous dialogue, the voice heard by Wieland, the equivocal dream-image of Wieland, and the mystery surrounding her father's death. The fusion of these narrative lines promises some illuminating explanation, a means of solving past and present inscrutabilities, and it seems that such an explanation will be of supernatural origin. These emergent mysteries continue the sequence of disruptive events that Clara associates with her father's death: "[T]hese gleams were such as preluded the stroke by which he fell; the hour, perhaps, was the same—I shuddered as if I had beheld, suspended over me, the exterminating sword" (*W* 64). Even after Pleyel finds her, she does not escape the ominous implications of her dream and finds herself trapped within a hermeneutical maze: "I was almost dubious, whether the pit, into which my brother had endeavoured to entice me, and the voice that talked through the lattice, were not parts of the same dream" (*W* 64). Her conflicting intimations advance Brown's epistemological mystery. Part of her problem derives from her inability to distinguish between dream and waking. This confusion reflects her more encompassing problem of determining whether the disembodied voices actually derive from a supernatural entity, a human being, or her own fancy. Complicating matters further, her conviction of supernatural causality occasionally gives way to suspicions of more terrestrial forms of agency. The fact that the voice she hears from behind the lattice seems human leads her to wonder whether her father's death "portentous and inexplicable as it was, [may be] the consequence of human machinations" (*W* 66). This possibility does not unseat Clara's providential suspicions: it simply reveals them to be the provisional speculations they are.

When Carwin himself participates in the social life of Mettingen, Brown intensifies the hermeneutical quagmire that is *Wieland*'s central drama. Early on, Carwin seems a welcome addition to the insular community. On the one hand, he offers Clara, Theodore, and Pleyel an inscrutable surface that invites speculation but denies clarity; on the other, he entertains and mystifies them with his interpretations of the very scenes he covertly orchestrated. Thus, he becomes a riddle to be solved: even as he cunningly manipulates his dramatic persona to frustrate their investigations, he intensifies their speculations regarding the possibility of supernatural visitations.

An ardent interpreter of Carwin's persona, Clara is nevertheless a malleable dupe. Her intoxication with his voice—"Before evening I should be ushered into his presence, and listen to those tones whose magical and thrilling power I had already experienced" (*W* 68–69)—prepares her to become enmeshed within Carwin's designs. His retentiveness regarding personal matters facilitates his aptitude for serving as both an inscrutable text-to-be-read and a manipulator of his ostensible interpreters. For Carwin, surfaces do not seem be anything more than histrionic contrivances. All Clara, Theodore, and Pleyel seem to know about Carwin comes, at least early on, from his own deceptive testimony. Much of what they later discover stems from Ludloe's seemingly malicious fabrications printed in the city newspaper and believed by Pleyel to be indisputable truth. Clara's wildly inaccurate biographical summary portrays Carwin as an amalgam of conflicting identities: "Carwin was an adherent to the Romish faith, yet was an Englishman by birth, and, perhaps, a protestant by education. He had adopted Spain for his country. . .yet now was an inhabitant of this district, and disguised by the habiliments of a clown!" (*W* 69). As a hybrid figure, Carwin might well represent an inchoate, pluralistic ideal—though his pluralism undermines rather than unifies the social sphere. Within a more encompassing framework, Faherty situates Carwin in relation to "any number of global revolutionary practices," a quality that allows him to be understood "as a transnational adventurer" (56). But his actual personification of a new America does not ultimately derive from these incongruous transnational and transcultural affiliations. Carwin is not an Englishman, a Spaniard, or an Illuminati conspirator. In *Memoirs of Carwin the Biloquist*, the unfinished prequel to *Wieland*,

Carwin appears as a native of rural Pennsylvania, a son of the Lehigh Valley. His American character emerges not merely in terms of his actual, native-born status, but through his subversive, histrionic antics, especially through the power of voice and the studied manipulations of dress that enable him to fashion a variety of performative identities both at home and abroad. Thanks to the protean power of his biloquial voice, he can become, as it were, the lead player in any story. Interestingly, Carwin is not only playing the role of a Yankee Jonathan type, a rustic bumpkin who embodies a new version of an American self, but this native son ironically becomes cast as an alien. The free and open education of the Wielands have made them, in Shirley Samuels's view, particularly susceptible to chaotic disruptions from outside forces:

> In *Wieland*, that chaos is blamed on Carwin, whose intrusion has excited sexual tensions in Clara and Pleyel and an insane and murderous religious enthusiasm in Wieland. Published while the fear of contagion by the alien was at its height, the novel foments and yet tries to explain away the threat by both blaming Carwin for introducing sexuality, disorder, and violence into the Wieland family, and explaining that introduction as nothing more than an enhancement of sexual and familial tensions already present. (53)

Carwin controls (and is eventually controlled by) the wavering lines of his proliferating, narrative inventions. He teases his companions by withholding information. For example, he will not talk about why he left Spain. While possessing "that degree of earnestness which indicates sincerity," Carwin remains full of secrets about his past and present activities (*W* 71). His "incongruousness" is the visible form that projects his calculated ambiguity and keeps his interlocutors from seeing whatever truth might lurk behind his mutable masks: "He afforded us no ground on which to build even a plausible conjecture" (*W* 72). Clara nevertheless persists in her attempts to imbue Carwin's mysterious appearance with plausible explanations: "The secrecy that was observed appeared not designed to provoke or baffle the inquisitive, but was prompted by the shame, or by the prudence of guilt" (W 73). Clara supposes that Carwin is driven not by histrionic energies but a wounded psyche.

Clara's search for motive misses the point. To insist on some specific ur-cause is to infer that Carwin's persona correlates with a stable, psychological essence. She assumes that any performative act necessarily expresses some corresponding ontological truth. What impels Carwin is not "shame" or "guilt" but an abiding imperative to re-invent his performative self and reshape the social scenarios he encounters. Carwin persistently reveals himself to be a protean, self-making performer. Given Carwin's retentiveness, his interlocutors are free to create their own versions of him. For Clara, his surface features are both alluring and unsettling. Because of her penchant for supranatural explanations, she cannot help but see him in hyperbolic terms: "I could not deny my homage to the intelligence expressed in [his face], but was wholly uncertain, whether he were an object to be dreaded or adored, and whether his powers had been exerted to evil or to good" (*W* 71).

As an actor, Carwin enters the Wieland household and becomes part of their dialogic theater. Throughout these friendly conversations, he is both an object of speculation and a speculating participant. Comically enough, he hears about what he has been doing. After they discuss the disembodied voices, Carwin offers his opinions. He does not say, "I am the perpetrator of these events. Listen, and I will give you Catherine's voice. And here, Clara, you can again hear my two murderous rogues." Rather, he toys with them, endorsing both sides of the discussion. He first tries to get them to believe they were hearing deific voices and then he surreptitiously describes his own complicity. As Toni O'Shaughnessy observes, "Carwin is an author who refuses to make concessions to society and communication, who does not seem interested in the meaning his interpreters discover in his discourse, or in whether they discover any meaning there or not. He does not use his voice to communicate but to elicit an effect" (44). Carwin's "effect," in this case, is sinister: his authorial duplicity is designed to tease them, mock them, and lead them into hermeneutical mazes. Emotionally entangled in Carwin's high-sounding fictions, Clara is especially enthralled by his inventive speculations: "His fancy was eminently vigorous and prolific, and if he did not persuade us, that human beings are, sometimes, admitted to a sensible intercourse with the author of nature, he, at least, won over our inclination to the cause" (*W* 74). Knowing well that he is a human "author," Carwin gives with one hand and takes away with the other. For example, he explicitly countermands his earlier endorsement of supernatural agency. No seemingly supernatural incidents, he claims, "were perfectly exempted from the suspicion of human agency" (*W* 74).

In what seems a disinterested, speculative dialogue, Carwin actually (and unbeknown to the first-time reader) celebrates his protean artistry, implicitly placing it in competition with "the author of nature." Carwin goes on to talk about *his* ostensible experience with similar events. But instead of offering a truthful, autobiographical account, he enacts a spontaneous performance: "His narratives were constructed with so much skill, and rehearsed with so much energy, that all the effects of a dramatic exhibition were frequently produced by them." In displaying "the exquisite art of...[a] rhetorician," he casts himself as a reader rather than an author (*W* 74). He explains away precedents, though he admits that no events directly parallel the situation at Mettingen. He disingenuously wonders how the events may have happened. He tenders two explanations—apparent suppositions that are actually lies—regarding the closet dialogue. He says it was either an auditory delusion, or there were two people talking inside the closet: "A tale of this kind, related by others, he would believe, provided it was explicable upon known principles; but that such notices were actually communicated by beings of an higher order, he would believe only when his own ears were assailed in a manner which could not be otherwise accounted for" (*W* 75). In his most insidious and audacious comic assertion, Carwin invests his own auditory powers with hermeneutical authority, all the while demonstrating that one's hearing—like all the senses—is eminently capable of being deceived. In making an oblique confession, he gives away the game, although no person contained within the novel's linear timeline—neither character nor first-time reader—would know that Carwin is carefully describing his own escapades. In bringing up the possibility of mimicry, he boldly claims that it is a common attribute: "How imperfectly acquainted were we with the condition and designs of the beings that surrounded us?" (*W* 76). Carwin conflates issues regarding agency—whether God or a human being is the "author" of events—with the inherent unreliability of the senses. In celebrating his own mastery, Carwin flaunts his victims' inability to see through his wiles. He exposes the limitations of their knowledge, even as he mocks them. While continuing to control his performances, Carwin nevertheless discovers that he cannot control the contingencies deriving from them.

The "Distempered Imagination"

After Carwin weaves his net of duplicitous conjectures that describe even as they hide his machinations, Brown makes overt those mostly latent complexes that propel Clara, Pleyel, and Wieland toward psychological disintegration and experiential chaos. Clara, we discover, truly loves Pleyel. She suspects that his lingering dejection has more to do with her seeming indifference to him than with the reported death of his fiancée. On the night of Pleyel's inexplicable absence, Clara and Theodore wait for him so that they can rehearse, of all things, a closet drama. Clara now repents sending mixed signals: "Had I not demeaned myself like one indifferent to his happiness, and as having bestowed my regards upon another?" (*W* 82). Having acted as though she was infatuated with Carwin, Clara now wishes to be understood as having loved Pleyel all along. These fulminations might be dismissed as little more than post-adolescent angst, except that Clara's consternation intensifies Brown focus on dramatizing the effects of Carwin's disembodied voices and on exploring the consequences of his studied retentiveness and histrionic manipulations.[28]

Brown's abrupt accentuation of the latent love plot exploits the ominous implications of Pleyel's absence and reiterates the epistemological limitations implicit in Clara's sensation narrative: there is so much that she simply does not—and cannot—know. For example, both Carwin and Pleyel have been prying into her private papers, but Pleyel, at the very time when he is supposed to be rehearsing, is investigating Carwin. All the while, Wieland hopes that God will demand proofs of his perfect faith. From Clara's perspective, Pleyel's absence suspends her in a condition of unrelieved anxiety. Frustrated by her inability to express her love, she is also tortured by morbid fears regarding Pleyel's safety. In his investigations of Carwin, Pleyel finds his suspicions confirmed: he discovers and fully believes what seem to be malicious falsehoods fabricated by Ludloe, Carwin's former mentor and current adversary. Frequently in *Wieland*, a putative truth does little more than mask another lie.

Pleyel's absence allows Brown to construct the contrived plot sequence—a thoroughly improbable skein of coincidences—that culminates with his characters losing control of their lives. Clara's fears regarding Pleyel coincide with Carwin's literal emergence from her bedroom closet. It is a momentous shift: Carwin becomes an overt rather than covert actor. What follows is a farcical series of deceptive contingencies that lead Clara and Pleyel into behaving in ways that are starkly antithetical to what each has hitherto seemed to be. Clara finds herself cast by Pleyel as the most profligate of women; the rational Pleyel becomes the impassioned dupe of his senses. Off stage, as it were, a most horrific drama unfolds within Theodore's psyche.

As Clara waits in her bedroom for Pleyel's return, Carwin hides trapped in her closet. Having earlier snooped into her private papers,

---

[28] Rombes sees the revelation of Clara's love for Pleyel as a decisive turning point in the novel: "This is a crucial moment in Clara's narrative, for she can no longer effectively cloak herself in republican virtue" (40).

he delights in his status as voyeuristic observer of her inner life. When Clara decides to enter the closet and retrieve her father's manuscript, she tries the lock and cannot budge it. She concludes that "some being was concealed within, whose purposes were evil" (*W* 84). Ensnared as she is by Carwin's spun lies—his biloquial fictions—and unable to see beyond them, she believes she is pursued by a superhuman antagonist and protected by a supernatural guardian. She finds solace in recalling her guarantee of safety in "every place but the recess in the bank." Upon touching the doorknob, Clara hears a "shriek so terrible. . .it acted on my nerves like an edge of steel." From behind her roar the words, "Hold! Hold!" (*W* 85). This "mysterious monitor" speaks in the same voice that "had terminated my dream in the summer-house" (*W* 86). That the voice spoke within her dream and now speaks from behind her ear argues for its supernatural qualities. The senses, once again, offer unstable foundations for establishing epistemological certainty. If the voice had come from a human being, then this person would have been seen: "The shock which the sound produced was still felt in every part of my frame.... But that I had heard it, was not more true than that the being who uttered it was stationed at my right ear; yet my attendant was invisible" (*W* 85). This illusion of the senses convinces her that her protective "monitor" is an emissary from God. Clara delivers the novel's clearest rendering of what providential agency is: "He to whom all parts of time are equally present, whom no contingency approaches, was the author of that spell which now seized upon me" (*W* 87). Her description of Providence accentuates His status as "author" of events. The idea of God as "author" of this unfolding moment justifies her impulse to open the closet door.

Brown brings Clara's providential fiction into irresolvable collision with Carwin's self-fashioned performance, his domain of slapdash artistry—a spontaneous theater that imposes the subversive artificer's tenuous control over the emergent events of Clara's life. Carwin is trying to scare Clara into running away so that he may enact his own escape, leaving, as he later confesses, "wonder and fear behind me" (*W*

209). This stratagem backfires. Her intimation of divine presence emboldens her. With the door open, Carwin must conjure some means to contend with his embarrassing predicament. The truth will not do. Art (or artifice) always provides Carwin a dubious refuge: his art gives him a means to interfere; it offers a means of self-invention. In this instance, his performance precipitates unforeseen contingencies.

The primary complication is that Carwin advances Clara's conviction of providential design. In one way, Clara's discovery of Carwin provides an initial justification for her livid, defamatory introduction of him. By any measure, Carwin has egregiously violated her. Rather than admitting the truth—that he was snooping into her papers—Carwin extends the plot he started with his shriek and the warning to "Hold!" Once caught, Carwin improvises with the purpose of controlling the passing moment, which is nothing less than his histrionic domain. Paradoxically, his freedom to make a new version of himself implicates him in a heated sex plot, casting himself as a prospective ravisher. Once assuming such a role, he limits subsequent options. Previously, he has remained in hiding; now, he projects his voices and analyzes its implications without, however, admitting his own agency. In questioning Clara about the protective voice—the voice of her supposed invisible guardian—Carwin affirms Clara's convictions regarding supernatural intervention: "Whoever he was, he hast done you an important service.... That sound was beyond the compass of human organs.... He is my eternal foe; the baffler of my best concerted schemes. Twice have you been saved by his accursed interposition. But for him I should long ere now have borne away the spoils of your honor" (*W* 89–90). Carwin casts himself as a prospective rapist thwarted by the beneficent presence of a divine agent. Both author and actor, Carwin spontaneously composes the very scene he enacts. By appropriating the providential plot, Carwin ironically celebrates the power of human self-making, even as he necessitates his own banishment: "I must doom myself to endless exile" (*W* 92).

Indeed, there is always more to Carwin's machinations than meet Clara's eyes and ears. Numerous actions are taking place outside the range of Clara's perceptions and therefore beyond the range of her sensation narrative. Shortly after his departure from Clara's house, Carwin goes into the woods and mimics her voice. An astounded Pleyel hears and believes auricular testimony that Clara is Carwin's depraved paramour. Carwin sets a trap wherein sensation plays havoc with the fragile dispositions of reason. As Leigh Eric Schmidt makes clear, the auditory sense invites not only misapprehension but chaos: "Associated in complex ways with learning, the passions, credulity, ecstasy, and Christian proclamation, hearing possessed an ambiguous, unstable power that made its careful management especially urgent" (7). Carwin's malicious, auditory performance alters Pleyel's life and spawns a host of unintended consequences. While in Clara's room, Carwin could control the fiction he creates. Once Carwin leaves, Clara is free to interpret subsequent experience any way she sees fit. Carwin's playacting with Clara and Pleyel establishes the experiential basis on which each character evaluates subsequent situations. Thus, Carwin's aesthetic manipulations set the stage for a farcical series of misadventures. Clara believes that Carwin is the prospective rapist he described himself as being; Pleyel believes that Clara is the fallen woman whose voice he heard in the dark woods.

Infected by Carwin's fictions, Clara and Pleyel make poor choices. For example, when Clara hears footsteps on the stairs, she fears that Carwin is returning to ravish her, although it is actually Pleyel approaching to discover if she is in her bedroom. After locking the door, Clara remains silent. She never suspects Pleyel's presence, not even when the figure withdraws, enters the "room...usually occupied by Pleyel," and slams the door (*W* 99). For his part, Pleyel has already concluded that Clara is the woman he heard speaking in the forest but did not see. After hearing nothing further for some minutes, Clara looks out the window and sees Carwin "standing on the edge of the bank" (*W* 100). Even now, Clara never suspects that Pleyel has returned. Within her sensation narrative, Clara depicts her drama of misconception: "My conjecture then had been right. Carwin has softly opened the door, descended the stairs, and issued forth" (*W* 100). Clara slips quietly down the stairs and locks the front door. Pleyel did not hear her go down, but he hears her coming back up. In this matter, Brown exploits the histrionic exigencies of staging—with his characters performing, both wittingly and unwittingly, as actors and audience in a drama that appears to be raw, real life but is actually the result of imposed contrivances. Carwin, for example, appears to be confessing a truth, but he is actually constructing a series of fictions. He painted himself as a profligate rake and later casts Clara as his corrupt lover. After hearing Carwin's imitation of Clara's voice, Pleyel consigns her to the role of "fallen" woman (*W* 103). For Brown, however, the fall being dramatized derives not from sexual transgressions but from perceptual mayhem.

From Carwin's performance springs a spiral of misapprehensions. According to Clara, Pleyel's behavior derives from his disappointment at having been jilted. At this point, Clara does not know that Pleyel construed the sound of her voice in the forest as proof of her licentiousness. In this jangled world, all competing plots are based on fabrications, which in turn generate new scenarios and new evidence for subsequent interpretations and actions. Clara, for example, cannot escape her conceptual premises. In one odd formulation, she replaces God as universal "author" with Carwin as an omnipotent artificer: "[T]hy form is a combination of steely fibres and organs of exquisite ductility and boundless compass, actuated by an intelligence gifted with infinite endowments, and comprehending all knowledge" (*W* 114). In *Wieland*, Brown dramatizes that the providential plot, while possibly possessing validity, remains a human construct, a supreme fiction of universal coherence.

At stake is the protean nature of narrative representation. Events are directly perceivable only through the agency of human sensation and then refashioned through a narrator's reconstruction. For example, when Clara goes to Pleyel in hopes of vindicating herself, she seeks a way to make her outlandish (but true) story repudiate the efficacy of Pleyel's reasonable but erroneous conclusions that were based "on the notices of sense" (*W* 35). She must "plead the cause of my innocence, against witnesses the most explicit and unerring, of those which support the fabric of human knowledge" (*W* 114). Because he is sure he heard Clara's lascivious speech, she must be guilty. Her tears signify remorse; her words denote penitence. Here is life, Brown suggests, and life is theater, a series of roles that careen without direction. Clara can do little more than assert the fallacy of Pleyel's premises: "My offenses exist only in your own distempered imagination" (*W* 117).[29]

Oddly, Pleyel—hitherto the rationalist and skeptic—now becomes the antithesis of what he believed himself to be. As himself an American Proteus—one of many in *Wieland*—Pleyel adopts as an explanatory trope the providential perspective, complete with a firm faith in a divinely-directed teleology: "An inscrutable providence has fashioned thee for some end. Thou wilt live, no doubt, to fulfil the purposes of thy maker, if he repent not his workmanship, and send not his vengeance to exterminate thee, ere the measure of thy days be full. Surely nothing in the shape of man can vie with thee!" (*W* 118). This transformation reveals Pleyel to be an especially unsavory embodiment of hermeneutical self-righteousness. Pleyel's earlier rationalism turns out to be thin, ideational cover for latent Puritanism. To Pleyel, Carwin has "witchcraft" in him: "I have disguised, but could never stifle the conviction, that his eyes and voice had a witchcraft in them, which rendered him truly formidable" (*W* 124). Pleyel has not simply lost his grip on reason; he has assumed the cultural mantel of reason's

[29] In *Caleb Williams*, Godwin describes Emily Melville's descent into psychological disarray: "When a momentary oblivion stole upon her senses, her distempered imagination conjured up a thousand images of violence and falsehood, she saw herself in the hands of her determined enemies, who did not hesitate by the most daring treachery to complete her ruin" (70). Clara uses a version of this trope: "My distempered fancy fashioned to itself no distinguishable image" (*W* 195).

ideological opposite. Again, the protean process of narrative self-making facilitates those transformations that shape this *American Tale*. The many instances of "transformation" in *Wieland* correspond to David Kazanjian's notion of flashpoint: "'Flashpoint'. . .refers to the process by which someone or something emerges or bursts into action or being, not out of nothing but transformed from one form to another" (27). These flashpoint moments disfigure an individual's personal and social ground of being.

"Do You Know the Author?"

Clara's discovery of Catherine's corpse extricates the narrative from its farcical entanglements, its near-misses, and improbable coincidences. Up to this point, most major problems have derived from the surreptitious exploits of Carwin. That profusion of disembodied voices; those erroneous conclusions; these suppositions of depravity and criminality—it was all talk. The possibility of murder, rape, and turmoil lurked in the air, but it was limited to a sense of impending destruction, closeted and contained, possibly artifice or delusion. However cyclonic the swirl of dread and consternation, Carwin had it in his power to restore a semblance of normality with a simple demonstration of his biloquial art.

As Brown dismantles the Wieland world, words can only fail to describe the involutions of agitated minds in crisis. Shortly before presenting her discovery of Catherine's corpse, Clara returns to the compositional present, thereby disrupting the reader's experience of the unfolding action, again calling attention to how the dramatic world was—and is—a construct of Clara's retrospective intelligence. Beset and befuddled, she grapples with the inherent incapacity of language:

> Alas! my heart droops, and my fingers are enervated; my ideas are vivid, but my language is faint; now know I what it is to entertain incommunicable sentiments. The chain of subsequent incidents is drawn through my mind, and being linked

> with those which forewent, by turns rouse up agonies and sink me into hopelessness.
>
> Yet I will persist to the end. My narrative may be invaded by inaccuracy and confusion; but if I live no longer, I will, at least, live to complete it. What but ambiguities, abruptnesses, and dark transitions, can be expected from the historian who is, at the same time, the sufferer of these disasters? (*W* 147)

What she apprehended *then* cannot be depicted *now*.

In *Wieland*'s concluding episodes, Brown critiques the possibilities and limitations of first-person narration, especially a narrator's inability to escape the benighted dimensions of one's subjectivity. Clara, for example, frequently unmakes determinations already made. For example, on her way up the stairs, shortly before finding Catherine's body, she glimpses a face that suddenly appears and disappears—it turns out to be Carwin's face—as she hears a voice shout, "*hold! hold!*" The shock to her nerves is "real. Whether the spectacle which I beheld existed in my fancy or without, might be doubted" (*W* 147, emphasis in original). What was perceived as having occurred may not have happened. Nevertheless, she contends, "This face was well suited to a being whose performances exceeded the standard of humanity." Whatever the experience was—hallucinatory or not—it impinged on her senses and incited a conflicted hermeneutical response. She concludes, "Be the face human or not, the intimation was imparted from above" (*W* 148). After insisting on the divinely ordained nature of this ostensible event, she discounts the very efficacy of her insistence:

> I cannot delineate the motives that led me on. I now speak as if no remnant of doubt existed in my mind as to the supernal origin of these sounds; but this is owing to the imperfection of my language, for I only mean that the belief was more permanent, and visited more frequently my sober meditations than its opposite. (148)

The very phrase, "more permanent," rather than conferring a sense of immutability, makes relative her attempt to achieve fixity of statement. What she means by "more permanent" is that her conviction of "supernal" visitation was *not* permanent, that it was part of a matrix of confused speculation.

As the plot unravels, as action displaces prefiguration, Brown presents a series of confessions that, paradoxically, accentuate rather than elucidate the novel's central mystery. Rombes argues that "the novel becomes the locus of a struggle over narrative control, as competing narratives vie to be heard amid a whirlwind of differing voices" (38).[30] If Brown's America—with Carwin as its exemplar—constitutes a protean, political sphere engendered through the transformational theatrics of narrative self-making, then the dangers of this emergent state become manifest in the proliferation of contradictory postulants and aberrant actions. In a frenzied diatribe, the once-rational Pleyel evokes witchcraft, predestination, and Providence (*W* 118 and 124). In confronting her transfigured brother, Clara experiences cognitive dissonance. Even when Wieland appears in her bedroom with an exultant "new expression" (*W* 152) and clearly announces his intention to award her "[d]eliverance from mortal fetters," Clara does not suspect him of being Catherine's murderer (*W* 154).

Catherine's murder intensifies Brown's preoccupation with the authorship of events. Thomas Cambridge re-enters the novel as a circumspect, judgmental presence, who attempts to distinguish between what seems and what is. After awakening from her swoon, she asks her uncle what has been done about "punishing the author of this unheard-of devastation." He responds, "The author!...Do you know the author?" (*W* 160). He reports that Carwin was *not* the author, that "[h]is

[30] Rombes links the anarchistic energy of competing, disintegrated voices to Mikhail Bakhtin's theories regarding dialogic form within the novel: "In these various voices lie what Bakhtin would call the novel's ideologies.... A particular language in a novel is always a particular way of viewing the world, one that strives for social significance" (38).

agency is...a mystery still unsolved.... Have I not said. . .that the performance was another's? Carwin, perhaps, or heaven, or insanity, prompted the murderer; but Carwin is unknown. The actual performer has, long since, been called to judgment and convicted" (*W* 161). The insistent evocation of authorship and histrionics accentuates the aesthetic involutions of Brown's narrative and the degree to which actions in life become *authored* in a manner analogous to the creation of words in a text.

This notion of authorship has extensive implications regarding world view and individual agency. To explore this matter, Brown dramatizes two climactic acts of narrative self-making: Wieland's courtroom testimony and Carwin's confession to Clara. In these inset narratives, Wieland attempts to speak with the voice of deific authority, whereas Carwin casts himself as a chastened manipulator driven by addictive impulses.

Wieland's confession to the court dramatizes the danger of absolutizing one's vision. Despite having committed many horrific murders, Theodore insists on "the soundness of his integrity, and the unchangeableness of his principles" (*W* 164). Believing himself incapable of error, he continues to enact his putatively God-directed plot. Brown imbues Wieland's self-assurance with a host of collateral theological contexts. Wieland embodies an extreme example of how the Protestant Reformation positions the single individual alone before God, a repetition, as it were, of his own father's obsessive theological solitude. As Bryan Waterman notes, "In *Wieland*, Brown offered memorable illustrations of just how dangerous religious voices could be" (*Republic of Intellect* 56).[31] Eschewing the Calvinist/Puritan suspicion of religious

[31] As Waterman argues, part of the agenda driving the American Enlightenment, and the Friendly Club, was the imperative to displace religion as the central force of society: "Once we recognize that what most united the club's inner circle—Smith, Brown, Dunlap, and [William] Johnson in particular—was not an antipathy toward Jacobins or Jeffersonians but a shared derision of established Christianity, we can begin to recognize ways in which this skepticism fuels Brown's *Wieland* and haunts his entire novelist career in significant ways.... *Wieland*. . .stands not as a

enthusiasm, Wieland is totally consumed by God. Unlike his Calvinist forbearers, Wieland abjures the Bible as the contractual, black-letter articulation of God's covenant. Wieland not only believes that divine revelation is on-going, but that the will of God can be personally communicated—a position shared by Antinomians ranging from Ann Hutchinson to the Quakers. At the level of action, Wieland personalizes and exaggerates the Abraham-Isaac typology. His "blissful privilege of direct communication with thee, and of listening to the audible enunciation of thy pleasure" takes the reader to the heart of the matter (*W* 167). Schmidt identifies Wieland's desire to hear God speak as a refutation of Locke's emphasis on reason: "In a Lockean framework in which reason is the ever vigilant judge over religious experiences of immediate inspiration, God's silence is both assumed and desired" (29). It is not only unreasonable but impious for Wieland to wish that God speak directly to him.

Ultimately, Wieland's "direct communication" not only reveals the Deity to be the author of life—"[t]he author of my being" (*W* 166)—but Wieland's experience of God's voice associates him more intimately with his father's mysterious demise and creates the possibility—never refuted; never affirmed—that the elder Wieland may have been punished for refusing to enact a divine directive, perhaps the slaughter of his family. Significantly, Wieland testifies that his experience was not merely auditory but visual and sentient: "It was the element of heaven that flowed around."[32] He claims that he saw some manifestation of Divine Being but "is forbidden to describe what I saw: Words, indeed, would be wanting to the task. The lineaments of that

---

warning cry against the breakdown of civic authority but as a dramatic illustration of the reasons that religious voices should be suspect sources of knowledge" (*Republic of Intellect* 77).

[32] Schmidt argues that during the Enlightenment a hierarchy emerged regarding the ranking of the senses—one that placed vision at the apex of human perception (16–19). On matters related to Wieland's belief that he heard God speak, see Schmidt's chapter, "Sound Christians," where he explores the relation of Protestant Evangelism to the direct experience of the divine voice (38–77).

being, whose veil was now lifted, and whose visage beamed upon my sight, no hues of pencil or of language can pourtray" (*W* 167–68). In this extreme circumstance, Wieland confronted the implacability of choice and he chose murder. In order to be at one with his version of God, however, he had to empty himself *of* himself and surrender whatever made him a responsible, socialized being.

This moment of divine communication is analogous to what Terence Martin describes as a mystic's entrance into an "Abyss": "In entering the Abyss one leaves behind the limiting awareness of self and becomes imbued with a pure sense of the eternal. One cannot, of course, sustain such an experience; it takes place only at the instant in which the finite meets the infinite" (63). Such an experience must remain interior and self-contained. The mystic's union with God becomes apprehended as a polymorphic event fusing the sensual and the cognitive. Wieland's tragic error is that he insists on expressing the *sense* of bliss not by prayer or worship but by performing many murders. Despite his affiliation with what Clara identifies as "calvinistic inspiration" (*W* 25), Wieland warps certain Calvinist premises regarding God's sovereignty:

> [Calvin] demanded that [his disciples] contemplate, with steady, unblinking resolution, the absolute, incomprehensible, and transcendent sovereignty of God; he required men to stare fixedly and without relief into the very center of the blazing sun of glory. God is not to be understood but to be adored. This supreme and awful essence can never be delineated in such a way that He seems even momentarily to take on any shape, contour, or feature recognizable in the terms of human discourse, nor may His activities be subjected to the laws of human reason or natural plausibility" (Perry Miller 51).

Wieland errs insofar as he ties adoration to a conviction that he could apprehend, or understand, and then act upon God's commands as delivered solely to him. Wieland thus negates Calvin's premise that the human mind is inherently inadequate to penetrate the mysteries of ontotheology: "It is of the essence of this theology that God, the force, the power, the life of the universe, remains to men hidden, unknowable, unpredictable.... He cannot be approached directly; man cannot stand face to face with Him" (Perry Miller 51–52). Wieland's strident, self-assured, self-isolating confession displaces the legitimacy of all social forms. He uses this act of narrative self-making to dissociate himself from his "[i]mpious and rash" judges. In fact, he derides them as "usurp[ing] the prerogatives of your Maker! to set up your bounded views and halting reason, as the measure of truth!" (*W* 176). In the name of speaking with divine authority, Wieland discounts the efficacy of open-ended human discourse.

When Carwin once again appears in Clara's bedroom—the novel's central stage—he offers his confession—a speech-act that succeeds in dissolving some of the differences between what the first-time reader and the re-reader know. Seemingly shocked by Clara's vituperation—her claim that he possesses "a malice monstrous and infernal" (*W* 195)—Carwin responds with the novel's most self-revealing understatement: "I think I know the extent of my offences. I have acted, but my actions have possibly effected more than I designed.... I come to repair the evil of which my rashness was the cause, and to prevent more evil. I come to confess my errors" (*W* 195–96). Readers on the hunt for a full explanation will be tempted to receive Carwin's confession as the climactic moment of illumination and resolution. Seemingly unaware of Wieland's murders, Carwin proclaims, "Perhaps I have but faint conceptions of the evils which my infatuation has produced; but what remains I will perform. It was *my voice* that you heard! It was *my face* that you saw!" (*W* 197, emphasis in original).

The problem is that Carwin's description of his "double-tongued" antics does not explain everything (*W* 1). He explains the voices heard by Wieland, Pleyel, and Clara. He explains the closet voices and Pleyel's reasons for believing in Clara's profligacy, but Carwin does not explain the voices prompting Wieland to kill. Nevertheless, Clara tries to blame Carwin for the murders: "But if Carwin's were the thrilling voice and the fiery visage I had heard and seen, then was he the prompter of my brother, and the author of these dismal outrages." (*W* 197). Carwin responds, "I am not this villain; I have slain no one; I have prompted none to slay; I have handled a tool of wonderful efficacy without malignant intentions, but without caution" (*W* 198).[33] At this point, certainly, Carwin could be lying, or he could be telling the truth. Either way, Brown emphasizes the histrionic premise of the entire narrative. As paradigmatic artist-in-life, the biloquist is the most overt practitioner of this elemental human activity. Unlike Clara and Pleyel, Carwin is aware that one's voice is a "tool." Compulsively drawn to the exercise of his art, Carwin becomes paradoxically trapped by the freeplay of his antic manipulations. As artist and audience, he is both sole performer and solitary witness. His "passion for mystery, and a species of imposture" led him frequently to stage improvisational interruptions of life, with the result being a kind of aesthetic autoeroticism: "I cannot convey to you an adequate idea of the kind of gratification I derived from these exploits; yet I meditated nothing. My views were bounded to the passing moment, and commonly suggested by the momentary exigence" (*W* 201). As both performer and audience, Carwin marries his capacity to counterfeit voices to the "exigence" of the moment. He uses this improvisational art to exercise power and domination: he can change his own appearance; he can reconfigure the consciousness of another person; he can enjoy his mastery: "To deceive [Pleyel] would be the sweetest triumph I have ever enjoyed" (*W* 210).

Nevertheless, Carwin's confession, while resolving some mysteries, excites new problems: it is itself a tale of miscalculation. Repeatedly, he recounts his failures to control dramatic surfaces. After the

[33] Schmidt identifies ventriloquism in the eighteenth century as "a tangible way of thinking about oracular religion as rooted in illusion.... In performative practice, the ventriloquist's art also shifted the focus of learned attention from the divine struggle over the soul to the protean malleability of personal identity, the fears and attractions of imposture, and the sheer pleasures of amusement" (136).

closeted murder-dialogue causes Clara to fear for her life, Carwin claims to have "felt the deepest regret at this unlooked-for consequence of my scheme" (*W* 202). Carwin's confession actually dramatizes the *limitations* of authorial and histrionic forms of agency, the artist's ability to interrupt but seldom to direct (and control) the unfolding affairs of life. Pervading Carwin's confession is his insistent sense of failure, his rueful admission of being disrupted by "exigence so abrupt and so little foreseen" (*W* 214). The irresistible, addictive power of Carwin's craft continually overwhelms him: "[Y]et had I not rashly set in motion a machine, over whose progress I had no controul, and which experience had shewn me was infinite in power?" (*W* 215–16). By engaging in these histrionic acts, the self-making artificer might purport to displace providential power, but in practice he does little more than transform himself into a self-entangling author of misrule.

3

Imposture and Subversion: *Memoirs of Carwin the Biloquist*

The New American Artist as a Young Man

While still at work on the later pages of *Wieland; or The Transformation: An American Tale* (1798), Charles Brockden Brown began composing *Memoirs of Carwin the Biloquist.* On August 8, 1798, Dr. Elihu Hubbard Smith noted in his diary: "Read Brown's 'Carwin,' as far as he has written it, & corrected a proof of his 'Wieland'" (460). With the yellow fever epidemic raging about him, the intrepid novelist finished *Wieland* by early September, began the lengthy but unfinished *Memoirs of Stephen Calvert,* and stopped working on *Memoirs of Carwin,* probably before the end of September.[1] Over the next seven years, he occasionally returned to *Memoirs of Carwin* and pushed the narrative forward. Beginning in November 1803, he intermittently serialized the tale in *Literary Magazine and American Register.* In a July 4, 1804 letter to future brother-in-law John Blair Linn regarding the June

[1] See Cowie for a discussion of matters related to the genesis and publication of *Memoirs of Carwin* (335–36). For Brown's experiences with the yellow fever epidemic in New York during August and September 1798, see Dunlap, *The Life* 2: 3–11: "But in 1798, Charles, by remaining in New York until too late to fly, either with safety or propriety, was made an inmate of the disease, beheld it in its most horrid forms, and saw expiring, the victims of its irresistible power, men as much distinguished for their talents and acquirements as for every virtue which can dignify our nature" (2: 3). See Waterman's discussion of Brown's strained circumstances during this life-threatening, but crucial time in his fiction-writing career (*Republic of Intellect* 1–7). Waterman describes the dreadful situation: "Those with means fled into the countryside; those who remained died by the dozen, especially in crowded waterfront neighborhoods, where streets that reeked of garbage and spoiled goods served as the seat of commerce and as home to thousands of immigrants and other urban poor" (*Republic of Intellect* 2). On September 19, 1798 came the death of Elihu Hubbard Smith, whose loss to Brown in personal and professional terms cannot be overstated.

issue of *Literary Magazine*, Brown laments that he has run out of material: "The manuscript of Carwin is exhausted, and it was impossible to piece the thread and continue it in due season for that number" (*L* 622). Nevertheless, he later extended the story's irresolute life for two more installments, concluding mid-scene in the March 1805 issue.[2]

It is certainly possible that Brown's work on *Arthur Mervyn* before August 1798 provided the impetus for portraying Carwin's teenage years in the Lehigh Valley. Indeed, the early lives of Arthur Mervyn and Francis Carwin have close affinities: both youths are second sons, who need to leave a patriarchal world limited by the tenets of primogeniture and other family complications. *Memoirs of Carwin* not only has associations with the evolving novel, but the earlier pages of this fascinating fragment—pages no doubt written in August 1798—find Brown exploring foundational aesthetic complexes that inform his fitful attempts to express the emergent contours of an American poetics and politics of self-making. *Memoirs of Carwin*, then, should not merely be viewed as an abortive addendum to *Wieland*, as an interesting beginning to a truncated prequel, or as a convenient lode of materials for Brown to mine and expand in response to his later incessant need for magazine copy. Instead, through the youthful figure of Carwin, Brown depicts how the nascent American artist's suffocating and repressed relationship with his patrimonial heritage provides the impetus for discovering (and literally internalizing) revolutionary, transformative, and subversive powers inherent in nature's hidden forms.

Brown's approach to creating an American tale, however, cannot be dissociated from his insistent concern with establishing his art

---

[2] The fact that Brown composed *Memoirs of Carwin* near the beginning and after the end of his career as a publishing novelist presents unusual problems concerning this work's genesis, composition, and contextualization. In their edition of *Wieland*, Barnard and Shapiro print "*Memoirs of Carwin* in the serialized form in which it originally appeared, rather than in the continuous form that editors began to adopt after Brown's death. The installment numbers before each segment are our addition" (xlvii).

within transatlantic contexts.[3] In the early pages of the *Memoirs*, Carwin's gradual, covert self-empowerment achieves expression not only through the agency of natural, local, and American forces but also through an allusive matrix connecting John Milton's *A Mask* with William Shakespeare's *The Tempest.* First produced as Brown was entering his greatest period of writerly achievement, *Memoirs of Carwin* constitutes a work of aesthetic self-definition—a self-reflexive meta-narrative—wherein Brown portrays Carwin's halting, and ultimately ineffectual, attempts to transform a poetics of imposture into a politics of subversion. This chapter focuses on one dimension of Brown's complex creative life during the pivotal months of August and September 1798 when he was finishing *Wieland* in consultation with fellow members of the New York Friendly Club (Waterman, *Republic of Intellect* 4–7), working on *Arthur Mervyn*, surviving the devastation of the yellow fever epidemic, all the while attempting to give the protean biloquist of *Wieland* a plausible and provocative past for his already written future. In establishing Carwin's experiential foreground, Brown reveals how Carwin develops an aesthetics of self-fashioned empowerment only to remain trapped within recurrent conditions of social dependency.

---

[3] See Barnard and Shapiro for a discussion of Brown's transatlantic affinities (xvii–xx). Axelrod notes, "Brown's fiction was wrought between two forces—the eastward pull of the Old World past...and the westering lure of the New World future" (xix). Apap focuses on the transnational dimensions of Brown's artistry, exploring the relationship between William Godwin and Brown, especially in response to the issue of Carwin's moral responsibility in *Wieland* (27–28). Giles views Brown's affinity with "the Federalist point of view" as an inherent critique of American exceptionalism: "[R]ather than a benign belief in American exceptionalism, which would assume the new nation was exempt from...old European quarrels, the Federalists preferred to appropriate and continue the logic of the British Empire, as exemplified by their activities on the Caribbean frontier and by their design of the Alien and Sedition Acts of 1798 to circumscribe the political influence of German and Irish immigrants" (30). Leask explores Brown's integration of Irish revolutionary utopias and Gothic contexts.

Recreating Carwin

Brown's decision to begin *Memoirs of Carwin* derived from his growing fascination with this conflicted and wily artificer and a desire to see what he could make of a tale about his early life. Brown was also looking ahead for money to be made in the uncertain event of *Wieland*'s economic success. The impetus for a prequel may have been sparked late in *Wieland* by Carwin's announced intention to leave the Wieland homestead and assume the task of authorship. During his lengthy confession to Clara Wieland, Carwin explains why he attempted to arrange a bizarre late-night rendezvous at her house: he claims he was worried that she would believe Ludloe's planted newspaper tale summarizing Carwin's alleged Old World criminality. After his attempt "to repair the evil of which my rashness was the cause" (*W* 196), Carwin outlines his intention "to seek some retreat in the wilderness, inaccessible to your inquiry and to the malice of my foe, where I might henceforth employ myself in composing a faithful narrative of my actions" (*W* 212). Carwin's ostensibly "faithful narrative" about the nature and extent his earlier duplicity is prefaced by a moralistic summation that complicates rather than explicates the subsequent tale. Carwin promises that his tale would teach "a lesson to mankind on the evils of credulity on the one hand, and of imposture on the other" (*W* 212).

A putatively true story coming from the mouth and pen of a practiced fiction-maker, manipulator, and role-player is necessarily fraught with problematic hermeneutical and aesthetic implications. From one perspective, Carwin's confession and the prospect of a "faithful narrative" detailing "the evils of credulity...and...imposture" actually unsettle his claims to authority and accentuate the epistemological quandary animating *Wieland.* His confession reveals just how deceitful and perfidious he was. As Christopher Apap argues, "Carwin's experiment with ventriloquism has disastrous results: he ruins Clara's reputation as a virtuous woman...and...precipitates Wieland's psychotic break" (27). Given such a destructive history, how likely is it, one wonders, that Carwin would suddenly abjure the protean process of self-making to tread the pedestrian plains of truth? As *Wieland* insistently delineates, the *truth*, as Carwin confesses it (and as Clara, Henry Pleyel, and Theodore Wieland profess it), amounts to little more than the errant, insistently dubious content of personal testimony. From another perspective, Carwin's willful exposure of his biloquial art makes credible his admission of remorse and repentance. In revealing the artistic means by which his machinations succeeded, he supplies those very materials that make Clara's narrative a benighted exercise in misapprehension. At the least, his confession eclipses her abiding belief in the beneficent, providential offices of her ostensible supernatural protector. In any case, Brown provides no exit from this web of self-justifying explanations. The world of *Wieland* constitutes a domain of competing, misinformed first-person narratives: at every juncture, certainty crumbles and social identity emerges as a tenuous, self-divided construct.[4]

In *Wieland*, Carwin's ambiguous status as a self-professed, (putatively) truthful storyteller not only excites epistemological concerns regarding the efficacy of individual testimony. It also shares the problem afflicting every dénouement of every mystery story ever told—the solution is far less profound than those tantalizing mysteries it purports to resolve.[5] Prior to Carwin's confession, the tale's accumulating power resided in the unfolding dramatization of increasingly suspenseful and threatening mysteries. The first-time reader wanders in a labyrinth, led down twisting paths that baffle, amaze, and disconcert. The enigmatic, disembodied voices hold every promise of being supernatural. At its most provocative, Clara's narrative conjures the possibility that human

[4] Roeger examines the matter of social identity as it pertains to pervasive class conflicts informing both *Wieland* and *Memoirs of Carwin* (87).

[5] Near the outset of his study on the analytic detective story, Irwin writes, "If the writer does his work properly, if he succeeds in building up a sense of the mysterious, of some dark secret or intricately knotted problem, then he has to face the fact that there exists no hidden truth or guilty knowledge whose revelation will not seem anticlimactic compared to an antecedent sense of mystery and the infinite speculative possibilities it permits" (2).

beings might become privy to the voices of spiritual agents, perhaps even the voice of God Himself.[6] Carwin's confession—his ostensible attempt at personal vindication and moral reconciliation—necessarily deflates the agitated energies that have driven the tale. Clara's speculations regarding a host of supernatural agents are mostly countermanded by Carwin's determinant tale of his bungling manipulations. Terribly enough, explication tames. It reduces apprehension, elucidates details, and defuses tension. As Carwin describes how he "handled a tool of wonderful efficacy without malignant intentions, but without caution" (W 198), he simplifies much of the preceding narrative into a comprehendible form. Effect finds cause. The mysterious is demythologized, if not made ludicrous: as noted earlier, one need merely imagine the spectacle of Carwin standing on a ladder, his head thrust inside the small window of Clara's closet, and enacting the dueling voices that play out his "double-tongued" murder scenario (*W* 1).

If Brown's decision to have Carwin write his *Memoirs* was inspired by Brown's growing fascination with Carwin and by an attending desire to *create* Carwin's past, then his decision to suspend composition in mid-to-late September might have at least partially derived from his impatience with the aesthetic limitations imposed by the necessity of having Carwin tell his own tale. For Brown to make Carwin the narrator (and protagonist) of his own story is to continue the self-deflating, even demythologizing, tendency initiated in Carwin's confession in *Wieland.* In seeking to present the unvarnished essence of his character, Carwin must locate himself as a social being with a discernible

[6] The issue of whether the voices are natural or supernatural has bearing on the matter of genre. Can the events afflicting the Wieland household be confined within the aesthetic conventions associated with realism or do these events require that Brown extend the narrative's boundaries to include a romance world where the strange, the liminal, and even the supernatural are accepted as experientially efficacious? It is generally recognized that Brown uses Gothic materials to establish the nascent contours of an American romance form developed later by Poe, Hawthorne, and Melville—a genre that often fuses elements of the natural and the supernatural into a hybrid form.

history and this account necessitates his intimate acquaintance with his reader. In the *Memoirs* as in *Wieland*, Carwin's capacity to manipulate dramatic circumstances generates from his ability to keep his biloquial talent secret.[7] Consequently the very narrative structure of this work restricts Carwin's ability to hide in the dark and operate as a mysterious figure of power. Throughout the *Memoirs*, Carwin's subversion—his putative status as a surreptitious, manipulative agent—exists mostly as a matter of potential.

Not only does Carwin's first-person point of view impede Brown's ability to develop dramatic possibilities, but the presentation of Carwin's pre-Mettingen life constrains Brown to the logical necessity of connecting the neophyte Carwin with the more devious figure already inscribed in *Wieland*. Brown might well have been frustrated by having to construct a plausible, cohesive past for the already-lived future. In any case, to write this particular story, Brown had to simplify Carwin. No longer the antic, mysterious, portentous artificer of *Wieland*, Carwin becomes recast as a naïf, a frustrated young man estranged from his father and brother, at odds with his constraining agrarian existence, and hungering for an expansive intellectual and imaginative life.

Novelty as Covert Insurrection

The basic dramatic situation of *Memoirs of Carwin* offers a redaction of materials from *Arthur Mervyn* already being published in serial form.[8] As second sons, Arthur Mervyn and Francis Carwin must endure a restrained life on their fathers' farms; both love their deceased

---

[7] In discussing how secrecy inhabits a central focus within Brown's novels, Downes explores "the obsession with secrecy in post-revolutionary American politics and, in particular, the function of secrecy in the production of the new constitutional citizen" (90).

[8] See Grabo for a discussion of the necessarily speculative compositional history of *Arthur Mervyn* and for details concerning its early serialization in the Philadelphia *Weekly Magazine* ("Historical Essay" 450–54): "By 16 June [1798] the first chapter of *Arthur Mervyn* was carried in number 20 of the *Weekly Magazine*, to be succeeded by a chapter a week for the next four weeks, Chapter 5 appearing on 14 July" (452).

mothers and are emotionally estranged from their fathers. In these two young males, Brown creates protean American youths, who associate their respective separations from their fathers with a peripatetic imperative that exposes them to expansive opportunities for travel and adventure. Jay Fliegelman argues, "Rational pedagogy took up with a vengeance the cause of 'second sons' against the institution of primogeniture...which not only inequitably distributed the parental estate, but all too often inequitably divided parental affection and thus forced the second son into the prodigality for which he is blamed in Christ's parable" (52).[9] Regarding Mervyn and Carwin, both fathers are disagreeable men and neither deserves the son's affection; both sons do not become prodigal so much as indigent, ostensibly innocent exiles, who have just cause to reject the patriarchal world. While retaining a spiritual bond with a deceased mother, these sons attempt to cut themselves loose from familial history and responsibility. They try to forge new identities out of the vagaries of experience and the protean exigencies of self-making.

As an additional point of reference regarding the cultural significance of second sons, the originating circumstances of *Memoirs of Carwin* anticipate by more than thirty years Nathaniel Hawthorne's classic dramatization of how Robin Molineux's conflicted (and ironically self-deflating) initiation into the unknown world encapsulates and critiques the collective psychology and ideology of a nation emerging from Colonial rule.[10] Unlike Robin, whose journey is sanctioned by a loving

---

[9] Kazajian note, "The first few pages of *Memoirs of Carwin* foreground the ethical and aesthetic framework of this national allegory, as Carwin is placed at the very threshold of a passage from the old morality and lifestyle of his father to the new possibilities held out by signs of enlightened modernity: books, experimentation, knowledge" (148). Van Leeuwen explores Carwin's anti-patriarchal attributes in relation to "Hermetic philosophy, and utopian idealism" (1).

[10] This brief mention of these parallel tales is not meant to insist on Brown's influence on a young Nathaniel Hawthorne, although direct influence is certainly possible insofar as Hawthorne knew and admired Brown's work and even bestowed on him a retired place of honor in his "Hall of Fantasy": "In an obscure and shadowy

father, Carwin's prospective journey to Philadelphia is frustrated by a dictatorial, oppressive, ignorant, and angry father. The elder Carwin remains antagonistic toward his second son's desire for independence and self-actualization. Emotionally alienated from his father and brother, Carwin despises the agrarian life as a dull, static, stultifying existence: "My eldest brother seemed fitted by nature for the employment to which he was destined. His wishes never led him astray from the hay-stack and the furrow. His ideas never ranged beyond the sphere of his vision, or suggested the possibility that to-morrow could differ from to-day" (*M* 232). Carwin rejects the agrarian myth of the good life as little more than an enervating form of mind-numbing entrapment. His complaint, however, is less an attack on the drudgery of farm labor *per se* than a repudiation of the mental constriction ostensibly coincident with such a life.[11]

Carwin's new pilgrim's progress, as it were, purports to be intellectual and imaginative: "My thirst of knowledge was augmented in proportion as it was supplied with gratification. The more I heard or read, the more restless and unconquerable my curiosity became. My senses were perpetually alive to novelty, my fancy teemed with visions of the future, and my attention fastened upon every thing mysterious or unknown" (*M* 232). His sense of independence, like his budding iconoclasm, is self-contained. His bid for intellectual freedom remains at odds with his condition of social dependency. Obsessed with

niche was reposited the bust of our countryman, the author of Arthur Mervyn" (174). For a discussion of the Brown-Hawthorne connection, see Kafer (198–200). Kafer makes a strong case for Brown's direct influence on Hawthorne's creation of "My Kinsman, Major Molineux," contending that Hawthorne "was most definitely thinking about 'the author of Arthur Mervyn' when he wrote his great early short story, 'My Kinsman, Major Molineux,' for it is patently patterned after the very novel that qualified Brown, in Hawthorne's eyes, for the 'Hall of Fantasy'" (199). See Colacurcio's discussion of the ironic, political, and mythic dimensions of Hawthorne's classic story (130–53).

[11] See Roeger's discussion of Carwin and the figure of "an Articulate Farmer" and its relationship to class subversion in *Wieland* and *Memoirs of Carwin* (92–100).

"novelty," Carwin seeks to inhabit an imaginary sphere of expansive consciousness that is alien to his brother's unthinking acceptance of dull repetition and threatening to his father's repressive intentions to "keep [Carwin] within these limits" (*M* 232). In longing for a creative sphere of protean consciousness, an idea-realm inimical to familial servitude, Carwin enacts an idiosyncratic, ideational form of rebellion. He opposes his father's authority, but he does so neither through a ritual of violence nor a call to arms. Rather, he naively wishes to move beyond socially confining (and therefore historically rooted and ideologically bound) contexts. The key words that describe Carwin's critique of home life—*novelty, fancy, visions, future, mysterious, unknown*—suggest the prospective aesthetic attributes of this son's impending liberation into the realm of romance.[12] Carwin's internal sense of rebellion provides a dialectical alternative to, rather than an overt displacement of, Old World patrimonial forms.

Consequently, Brown associates Carwin's father not only with European models of genealogical succession but with a highly diluted, parodic version of Calvinism. Carwin describes his father not as a Royalist in the mode of Major Molineux but as a latter-day Puritan. Ironically, the elder Carwin's brand of Calvinism is little more than anti-intellectual fulmination. Deeply disturbed by his son's love of books, the elder Carwin "has often lamented, with tears, what he called my incorrigible depravity, and encouraged himself to perseverance by the notion of the ruin that would inevitably overtake me if I were allowed to persist in my present career" (*M* 233). The son's "depravity" and the father's "perseverance" ironically echo classic Calvinist complexes describing the dissociation of a reprobate from the elect. Evoked in this

---

[12] Levine examines the performative dimension of the American romance: "The urgency of the American romancer's performative art...has its sources not only in critical and philosophical concerns but in social ones as well; for it is precisely the need to convert limitation into power—and the accompanying concern about the experimental provisionality of creation—that links romance to America" (*Conspiracy and Romance* 3).

heavy-handed, parodic passage is the Calvinist creed of total depravity, an absolute alienation from God—the primary consequence of Adam's fall—as well as the perseverance of the saints, an indication of the stalwart passage of the elect as they proceed toward salvation.[13] The elder Carwin's argument with his son, however, derives not from doctrine but from a kind of know-nothing narcissism: the father is angry that his son does not want to be as ignorant as he. The dissociation between the allusive, highly charged language of "depravity" and "perseverance" and the elder Carwin's blatant anti-intellectual bias signals the collapse of the Calvinist-Puritan mindset into mere authoritarianism. Carwin's father may echo the rhetoric of his Calvinist forebearers, but he has none of their respect for the power of mind. Brown's ironic evocation of classic Calvinist tropes reflects the stultification afflicting a dying tradition that is inimical to the protean power of self-making. In divorcing himself from his father, Carwin rejects the patriarchal prejudice against "novelty," "fancy," and mystery. He rejects conventional religion in favor of transgressive ideational and aesthetic possibility.

Unlike the riotous, anarchic, late-night, tar-and-feathering merrymakers of Hawthorne's exemplary tale, Carwin does not attempt to assert his will at the expense of his father's physical well-being. Carwin is not interested in patricide, fratricide, or symbolic regicide. What he longs for is an alternative sphere of intellection and action. Thus, he pursues a strategy not of overt confrontation but of cunning evasion. He becomes not Thomas Paine but an artful dodger: "[His father] could not outroot my darling propensity. I exerted all my powers to elude his watchfulness." To avoid corporal punishment, Carwin "was incessantly employed in the invention of stratagems and the execution of expedients" (*M* 232). This form of clandestine activity does not directly undermine his father's authority, but Carwin's progression

[13] See Calvin's treatise describing the foundations of protestant theology. See especially Book Two wherein Calvin explores the relation between self-knowledge and the fall of Adam and the transmission of original sin throughout human history (1:241–55).

toward self-actualization begins, as Paul Downes notes, with "an act of filial disobedience" (105). Essentially Carwin rejects his father's power over him. In retaining his "darling propensity"—his capacity to read, think, and invent—he nevertheless must find a way to translate his expanding intellectual powers into dramatic action.

Nature's Hidden Forms

In the *Memoirs*, Brown develops Carwin's inchoate and self-contained rebellion through Carwin's acquisition of a potentially subversive form of self-expression and social control. Brown retains the public image of Carwin as a dutiful son, all the while developing his private capacity for enacting a disruptive form of creative agency. Brown dramatizes the emergence of Carwin's secret life through his discovery and cultivation of biloquial powers.

In his fourteenth year, Carwin "ascertained [his] future destiny" (*M* 233). In seeking a shortcut home, he happens upon "a narrow pass." This domain of "solitude and darkness" does not elicit "sensible" or physical dangers but "violent apprehensions" of a spectral, supernatural kind (*M* 234). To mitigate the Gothic terrors associated with this "gloomy recess," Carwin yells "as loud as organs of unusual compass and vigour would enable me. I uttered the words which chanced to occur to me, and repeated in the shrill tones of a Mohock savage…'Cow! cow! come home! home.'"[14] When he reaches a difficult point of passage, he suspends his chant until he can safely deliver it

[14] See Hsu for his examination of this crucial scene "where the vocal intrusion that distorts democratic space is linked to disorderly Native American sounds" (41). In discussing this scene, Hsu identifies Carwin's "vocal experiments" as "embodied performances of spatial dislocation" (46). See White's discussion of Brown's use of geography (50). See Downes' discussion of the relationship between Carwin's "secret voice" and the dynamics of revolution (106–08). Axelrod argues that "Carwin discovers in the wilderness a hitherto unknown elementary—radical and primitive—aspect of himself" (90). Schmidt suggests that Brown may have been influenced by the eighteenth-century auditory experiments of Joannes Baptiste de La Chapelle (143–57).

again. Following this attempt, he hears "the same cry from the point of a rock some hundred feet behind me; the same words, with equal distinctness and deliberation, and in the same tone, appeared to be spoken." He originally thinks that a human being imitated his voice. After hearing the strains repeated four more times from different directions "with little abatement of its original distinctiveness and force" (*M* 234), Carwin realizes that he has discovered "an echo of an extraordinary kind." He thus stumbles upon the turning point of his life. He no longer fears the consequences of his father's anger. Instead, he surrenders himself to the lure of nature's novelty, exhausting "my lungs and my invention in new clamours.... I seized the first opportunity of again visiting this recess, and repeating my amusement; time, and incessant repetition, could scarcely lessen its charms or exhaust the variety produced by new tones and new positions" (*M* 235). This access to "new tones" creates the entryway into Carwin's highly problematic future, even as this discovery positions his emergent American voice in relation and opposition to indigenous voices within the agrarian, colonial sphere, especially as he internalizes these natural sounds in the voice of a "Mohock savage." According to David Kazanjian, Carwin stands as a "figure of articulation [who] indexes the emergence of imperial citizenship in early America" (13). Carwin's initiation experience in the "vocal glen" fuses aesthetic, natural, and cultural contexts and constitutes what Kazanjian theorizes as a "flashpoint" wherein Carwin's transformational "process" can be understood "less as a breaking out of chaos than as a material transformation with powerful effects" (27). The most significant "material" consequence of this moment of discovery is Carwin's development of his biloquial art of "imposture" that he eventually seeks to express in subversive ways.

In this scene, Brown dramatizes a spontaneous form of natural theater in which the human voice harmonizes with the intricacies of topography. Here, nature replicates human speech, even allowing these vocal sounds not merely to be doubled but quintupled. By releasing pent-up energies, Carwin entertains himself. In more complex ways, his voice assumes an existence independent of his direct exertions. What he hears repeated with virtually undiminished volume is, and is not, his voice. In experiencing the pleasure of being both performer and audience, he discovers in this mode of theatrical play a self-liberating alternative to—and a temporary refuge from—the rigid demands of familial servitude. His experience of "novelty" and independence derives from an aesthetic expansion of the self, the translation of voice into artifice. This "vocal glen" constitutes Carwin's aesthetic and liminal space (*M* 235). Isolated from fellow human beings, surrounded by a frightening wilderness, he literally discovers a force—constrained by physical laws—that fulfills the deepest longing of his being. The "vocal glen" furnishes a dramatic sphere wherein Carwin releases his latent imaginative power, an internal predisposition that he has already defined as an unsettling craving for novelty, fancy, and mystery. This power becomes initially manifest when he listens to reverberations of his voice, although it later becomes expressed through his ability to control and transfigure these elements in the cause of manipulating other people and reconstituting the social scene. Through this power, Carwin creates multiple projections of his vocalizing self. The creation of disembodied voices constitutes for Brown an essential paradigm of narrative self-making.

Carwin's status as artificer derives from his appropriation of energies latent within this unusual, if not unique, landscape. He initiates a process whereby he internalizes, controls, and replicates acoustical properties of the "vocal glen." This symbiosis between voice and topography establishes a synergy that coalesces with Carwin's burgeoning sense of creative and intellectual independence, especially as he awakens to the possibilities of applying these natural forms of artistry within social situations. Significantly, Carwin's biloquial art cannot be dissociated from Brown's oblique celebration of specific transatlantic literary sources that accentuate the aesthetic agency animating Carwin's putatively subversive agenda. Indeed, Brown's deft use of allusions illuminates the disruptive, revolutionary politics informing Carwin's prospective growth as a performative artist. The subversive implications of Carwin's emerging powers not only derive from the impress of natural forces within a wild American landscape but also become manifest through the direct evocation of magical, self-defining literary figures drawn from Milton's 1634 poem about Comus first published as *A Mask Presented at Ludlow Castle* and from Shakespeare's *The Tempest.*[15]

Carwin's episodic narrative repeatedly recasts the conflict between the second son's strained dependency on parental figures and the prospective liberation that might attend the social enactment of his newly discovered and virtually untested powers. Only at night can Carwin indulge his secret passion for going alone into nature, for reading, and for developing his biloquial art. On one of his midnight rambles, Carwin writes, "I posted first to my vocal glen, and thence scrambling up a neighbouring steep, which overlooked a wide extent of this romantic country, gave myself up to contemplation, and the perusal of Milton's Comus" (*M* 235). Throughout his career, Brown associated his aspiration for literary greatness with the example of John Milton. Years earlier, in the "Henrietta Letters," Brown's narrator C.B.B. offers a prototype of Carwin's great awakening, combining landscape description and self-portraiture with the purpose of establishing a conflict between the allure of carefully selected Miltonic texts and his love for Henrietta herself:

> This morning I repaired thither, before the east had exhibited any tokens of approaching light, with Miltons Comus Licdas and Il Penseroso in my Pocket, intending to devote the hours to those performances, and to investigate the principles of

[15] Milton never published *A Mask* under the title *Comus*. The poem was first performed in 1634 and published in 1637 and 1645, on both occasions retaining its original title: "It seems to have been given the un-Miltonic title of *Comus* first by Dr. John Dalton when he printed it as *Comus, A Mask, Now Adapted to the Stage*, in 1738" (Hughes 86, note 1). The present discussion retains the poem's title as Milton intended it.

> that divine philosophy which they teach, but alas! My thoughts continually wandered from the page before me, and the Image of my beauteous Harriot incessantly interposed between the poet and the critic, and intirely diverted my attention from the book.... I at length forbore my unavailing struggles, and hastily returned determined no longer to withstand my inclination, and, as you were personally inaccessible, to spend the day in writing to you. (*L* 718)

This passage places C.B.B. (and Brown) in company with a host of Romantic writers—John Keats, in particular—who, while inspired, also felt oppressed and overshadowed by Milton's literary achievements. In the letter, C.B.B. anticipates Carwin's discovery of the creative possibilities inherent in place. Like C.B.B., Carwin is drawn to Comus, a subversive artist figure who combines Orphean powers and lascivious sensual desires.[16] In *Wieland*, Carwin's sexualized attributes become fully realized as he uses his voice, natural charms, and physical sensuality not only to seduce Clara's servant Judith but also to threaten the person and reputation of Clara herself.

In the *Memoirs*, the allusion to Milton's *Mask* offers a rich array of intertextual parallels that associate Carwin's reading with artistic self-empowerment and the possibility of political subversion. Milton's poem validates Carwin's formative attempt at artistic self-dramatization, while also pointing to Comus himself as a paradigm of Carwin's own antic, disruptive, and seemingly magical energies. As magician, demigod, outlaw, as subversive artificer, Comus has contempt for the conventional Puritan world and reflects Brown's insistence in *Wieland*

[16] In a December 1792 letter to Bringhurst, Brown contends that individuals can become "acquainted with the force and extent of their own faculties...only by experiment.... No spectale is to me more deplorable than a vigorous understanding neglected and uncultivated" (*L* 198–99). Only through such an inductive process might young writers attempt to emulate, and even surpass, the achievements of Milton and Francis Bacon: "Such men as these did once most certainly exist. Is there any physical impossibility that they should again exist? How is it to be known but by experiment whether Heaven has appointed us their rivals and competitors?" (*L* 199).

on placing the manipulative Carwin in direct opposition to divine agency. By having Carwin read Milton in the "vocal glen," Brown associates Comus' magical powers with Carwin's disciplined ability to fuse his voice with nature's extraordinary echo. Such magic is a metaphor for the transformational power of art—an art that is performative and manipulative, and even political in that it is later used as an instrument of social control. Carwin is not about to take up Comus' "*Charming Rod*" (Milton 92, emphasis in original) or "bare wand" (line 614), but in *Wieland* and his *Memoirs*, he certainly uses his voice not only to perpetrate illusion and but also to generate actions that enthrall, mystify, seduce and, possibly, even corrupt.

A brief rehearsal of elements central to Milton's *Mask* will suggest the applicability of Brown's intertextual evocations. The direct allusion signals Brown's attempt to incorporate and transfigure salient aspects of the Miltonic paradigm. In this work, Milton brings Christian and Pagan forces into collision. The attendant Spirit descends from a "mansion…where those immortal shapes / Of bright aereal Spirits live insphere'd / In Regions mild of calm and serene Air" (lines 2–4) and lands in "the perplex't path of this drear Wood, / The nodding horror of whose shady brows / Threats the forlorn and wandr'ring Passenger" (lines 37–39). The Spirit arrives with the mission of protecting the lost Lady from the "mighty Art" of Comus (line 63). Son of Bacchus and Circe, Comus looms as a disruptive demigod, a chaotic, mighty figure, whose potions transform a "weary Traveller" (line 64) into a lower life-form: "[T]heir human count'nance, / Th' express resemblance of the gods, is chang'd / Into some brutish form of Wolf, or Bear" (lines 68–70). Milton thus dramatizes a conflict between pure, innocent virtue and corrupting, sensual pleasures. More significantly, Comus embodies the histrionic perversion of the divine, creative office. A sorcerer "[d]eep skill'd in all his mother's witcheries" (line 523), he uses his voice to generate illusion:

> Thus I hurl

> My dazzling Spells into the spongy air,
> Of Power to cheat the eye with blear illusion,
> And give it false presentiments. (lines 153–56)

This relationship between voice, illusion, and transformation unites Comus and Carwin as disruptive figures of power.

Whereas in Milton's poem the transcendent realm is figured as a stable, unassailable domain, in Brown's fiction the very existence of the transcendent realm remains an open question, with options ranging from the Christian orthodoxy of Clara Wieland to Ormond's self-deifying claim to "something like Omniscience" (*O* 116).[17] Brown's figures of human power—Carwin and Ormond, in particular—set themselves in opposition to Providence and they do so by assuming suprahuman forms of identity and self-expression. In his reading of Milton's poem, Carwin might well have recognized not only the magical properties inherent in Comus' voice, but also the deceiver's ability to control the sublunary world. As the paradigmatic antic-artificer, then, Comus is associated with insurrection. He causes permutations in the natural order; he imposes disfiguration on his victims; he threatens to defile an embodiment of idealized, female virtue. By importing Milton's *Mask* into his narrative, Brown accentuates Carwin's emerging status as a potentially subversive artist, a man at home in nature and at odds with orthodox authority. The question remains, however, as to whether the youthful Carwin can translate the subversive energies inherent in his aesthetic experimentations into politically charged actions.

[17] In using artistic means to control contingency, Ormond (like Carwin) is engrossed by the pursuit of power: "He was delighted with the power [imposture] conferred. It enabled him to gain access, as if by supernatural means, to the privacy of others, and baffle their profoundest contrivances to hide themselves from his view. It flattered him with the possession of something like Omniscience. It was besides an art, in which, as in others, every accession of skill, was a source of new gratification" (*O* 116).

Imposture and Subversion

Carwin's reading of Milton's *Mask* may well inform his inspired decision to apply the power of nature's hidden forms in a novel fashion: "Could I not so dispose my organs as to make my voice appear at a distance?" (*M* 235). No longer does Carwin merely take delight in projecting his voice through this strange, acoustical phenomenon: he now wishes to internalize the glen's inherent aesthetic attributes. He passes beyond "speculation" to "experiment": "I learned to accommodate my voice to all the varieties of distance and directions." His ability "to talk from a distance"—this seemingly magical attribute—associates his artistry with the direct imitation of natural forms. He proceeds from a premise that celebrates—even absolutizes—the power of will to develop latent physical attributes: "It cannot be denied that this faculty is wonderful and rare, but when we consider the possible modifications of muscular motion, how few of these are usually exerted, how imperfectly they are subjected to the will, and yet that the will is capable of being rendered unlimited and absolute, will not our wonder cease?" (*M* 236). In pursuing the "unlimited and absolute," in pursuing what amounts to a policy of romantic insurgency, Carwin promulgates a thesis that invests individual will with the ability to counter the supreme fiction of providential order. By dramatizing the process whereby an artist becomes his own muse, Brown casts the emerging artificer as a figure of self-generated, procreant power. The artist-in-life assumes this very office of structuring the moment, but only in reference to some hidden self-aggrandizing purpose. As Brown dramatizes most fully in *Ormond*, such a view presupposes the rejection of all forms of philosophical idealism as well as any transcendent theological system that sets a postulated superstructure above the exigencies of the passing phenomenological moment. Early in his life, Carwin internalizes the power of nature; later in life, when wreaking havoc at the Wieland homestead, he uses his biloquial powers to impel his acts of "imposture," frequently assuming the voices of putatively supernatural beings (*W* 212).

Significantly Brown's protean figures like Carwin (and Ormond and Welbeck in *Arthur Mervyn*) do not create their art through texts or in the theater. Instead, their medium of conscious manipulation is social life: they are driven to impose their wills on others by surreptitiously constructing a histrionic domain. Carwin's breakthrough emerges with his recognition that his biloquial art, in order to be most powerful, must undergo a telling modification:

> There remained but one thing to render this instrument as powerful in my hands as it was capable of being. From my childhood, I was remarkably skilful at imitation. There were few voices whether of men or birds or beasts which I could not imitate with success. To add my ancient, to my newly acquired skill, to talk from a distance, and at the same time, in the accents of another, was the object of my endeavours, and this object after a certain number of trials, I finally obtained. (*M* 236)

Just as he absorbs the attributes of the "vocal glen," so too does he subsume the voices of other people. As *Wieland* demonstrates, the biloquial artist engages in "imposture" and thereby attempts to become the "author" of events (*W* 216). In the *Memoirs*, Carwin reports on the nascent process whereby he seeks to impose the hidden fiction-making artist's will on unsuspecting victims. The key issue for young Carwin is whether he can adapt his private powers in public situations and use these powers to challenge and subvert familial and social forms of authority.

Throughout the *Memoirs*, Carwin's grandiose theories and diminutive achievements stand in ironic relation to his seemingly inescapable condition of social dependency. Despite his newfound power, Carwin remains tentative and uncertain regarding its uses. At one point, he plans to manipulate his father's superstitions: "I frequently asked myself whether a scheme favourable to my views might not be built upon these foundations" (*M* 237). He intends to imitate his late mother's voice—a voice he hopes will convince the elder Carwin to allow his second son to leave home. Carwin, however, has qualms about perpetrating a potentially blasphemous act. He views his impending performance as a usurpation of the divine office and even describes a universe controlled by a jealous and watchful Jehovah-figure prone to outrage and vengeance: "To imitate the voice of the dead, to counterfeit a commission from heaven, bore the aspect of presumption and impiety. It seemed an offence which could not fail to draw after it the vengeance of the deity" (*M* 237). Nevertheless, Carwin rationalizes this fear and plans to proceed with his experiment. After entering his sleeping father's chamber, Carwin interprets the violent storm outside as a special providence, a divine message addressed specifically to him: "Heaven seemed to be present and to disapprove my work; I listened to the thunder and the wind, as to the stern voice of this disapprobation" (*M* 238).[18] Does he become overtly transgressive and assume his mother's posthumous voice? Or does he accept the intimation of divine censure and remain silent? By whatever means—God or chance—lightning strikes the barn; his father awakens; Carwin never makes his choice. Crucially, Brown structures the moment to focus attention on Carwin's interpretive oscillations. His response is appropriately "double-tongued" (*W* 1). Speaking for both sides of the question, Carwin rejects and affirms the possibility of divine intervention:

> It was, doubtless, absurd to imagine any connexion between this portentous scene and the purpose that I had meditated, yet a belief of this connexion, though wavering and obscure, lurked in my mind; something more than a coincidence merely casual, appeared to have subsisted between my situation, at my father's bed side, and the flash that darted through

[18] See Barnard and Shapiro for their discussion of how Milton's "Thunder heard remote" phrase from *Paradise Lost* affects this context (238, note 13). This scene accentuates Brown's recurrent practice of critiquing religious forms. As Waterman notes, "*Wieland* argues against the utility—and for the dangers—of faith in divine intervention, and offers pointed parodies of Calvinist Christianity and Quakerism alike in its illustrations" (*Republic of Intellect* 83).

> the window and diverted me from my design. It palsied my courage, and strengthened my conviction, that my scheme was criminal. (*M* 239)

Brown sets up—but does not dramatize—a collision between Carwin's subversive desires and the ostensible imperatives of providential design. Carwin even comes close to affirming the conventional Puritan mode of reading events as emblems. There remains a connection between Carwin living at home in his father's house and his lingering attachment to the providential view. He has not yet jettisoned conventional religious formalism—the vestigial force of which animates his father's debased Calvinistic rhetoric. Brown is careful here to depict a world of immutable hierarchy. Carwin's intention to assume his late mother's voice is stifled by the possibility—never discounted—that a sovereign God does indeed speak through the language of natural force. Carwin's "courage" is "palsied" by nothing less than the imposing possibility of divine retribution. Given the opportunity, Carwin fails to step beyond the circumscribed limits of orthodoxy and resorts to that most diminutive form of fiction-making—the basic lie. When his father awakens and asks his son what he is doing in the room, Carwin claims to have come to tell him about lightning striking the barn. By impersonating the behavior of a dutiful son, Carwin indicates the complex process whereby he *fails* in the *Memoirs* to emerge as the protean artificer he later becomes in *Wieland.*

Ironically, Carwin retains his hidden powers, but he remains ineffectual in his attempts to dramatize them within the social sphere. Intimations of subversion dissolve when the elder Carwin suddenly permits his son to leave home. While living with his aunt in Philadelphia, he exchanges "[d]etested labour...for luxurious idleness" and spends three years reflecting "on the use to which [his "biloquial faculty"] might be applied." Once again, his elevated self-image— "I was actuated by ambition. I was delighted to possess superior power"—contrasts with his diminutive achievements. Essentially, he trivializes his talent as he performs little tricks or parlor games.[19] He is unconcerned with "consequences. I sported frequently with the apprehensions of my associates, and threw out a bait for their wonder, and supplied them with occasions for the structure of theories" (*M* 240). His first successes are negligible affairs—explicitly theatrical, mildly entertaining, and minimally disruptive. These performances evoke conversational wonder and discursive sallies. At one point, Carwin performs a dog trick. He creates the illusion that his dog Damon understands English and responds correctly to verbal commands: "His actions being thus chiefly regulated by gestures…it was easy to produce a belief that the animal's knowledge was much greater than in truth, it was" (*M* 241). As circumstances require, Carwin fashions proof of the dog's sagacity and sustains the illusion of Damon's rational and interactive abilities.

Even with such diminutive capers, Carwin manages to infuse everyday encounters with a seeming prodigy that in turn inspires conversational flights. At one point, his playful manipulations lead to a discussion "on the subject of invisible beings. From the speculations of philosophers we proceeded to the creations of the poet." The company wonders whether Shakespeare was being realistic in his "delineations of aerial beings" (*M* 242). That is, does Shakespeare present chimeras or does he imitate on stage the actual existence of preternatural beings? Carwin wishes to demonstrate that spiritual beings actually exist. By employing his biloquial powers, he conjures the voice of Ariel from *The Tempest* (5.i.89–92) and creates the illusion that a part of the play occurs in the living moment. Carwin graduates, so to speak, from performing dog tricks to staging a seemingly supernatural event. The lines uttered by Ariel— "In the Cowslip's bell I lie, / On the Bat's back I do fly" (*M* 242)—celebrate his liberation from Prospero's domination, but like Carwin's "*thunder heard remote*" allusion to *Paradise Lost* (238, emphasis in original), this quotation is ironic and points not to

[19] Axelrod connects young Carwin's "impish, parlor trick" with the more dire, invasive and consequential "'murderous dialogue' counterfeited for Clara" (88).

Carwin's empowerment but to his ongoing thralldom.[20] As Hsuan L. Hsu notes, "By impersonating Ariel...Carwin again assumes the voice of a dominated native" (48).[21]

Carwin's problem throughout the *Memoirs* is that he develops an aesthetic ideology of self-empowerment only to remain caught within recurrent conditions of social dependency. A few days later, Carwin meets Ludloe, a keen perceiver capable of interpreting duplicitous surfaces. Having witnessed the Ariel performance, Ludloe was not gulled: "I was somewhat startled when [Ludloe] expressed his belief, that the performer of this mystic strain was one of the company then present, who exerted, for this end, a faculty not commonly possessed." While claiming not to know the identity of the perpetrator, Ludloe "expatiated with great profoundness and fertility of ideas, on the uses to which a faculty like this might be employed. No more powerful engine, he said, could be conceived, by which the ignorant and credulous might be moulded to our purposes; managed by a man of ordinary talents, it would open for him the straightest and surest avenues to wealth and power" (*M* 244). As Nigel Leask observes, "Ludloe rapidly offers himself as Prospero to Carwin's Ariel" (102). In claiming that the capacity to feign Ariel's voice constitutes a "powerful engine," which, if extended, might even lead one to usurp the divine order, Ludloe maintains that human artifice can simulate the appearance of providential purpose and thereby manipulate the behavior of duped religionists:

> Men, he said, believed in the existence and energy of invisible powers, and in the duty of discovering and conforming to their will. This will was supposed to be sometimes made known to them through the medium of their senses. A voice coming from a quarter where no attendant form could be

---

[20] See Bernard and Shapiro for their discussion of these materials (238, note 13 and 242, note 18).

[21] Kazajian explores Brown's dramatization of the colonial implications of this allusive matrix: "*Memoirs of Carwin* turns the echo of 'a Mohock savage' into Ariel." Kazajian also sees this narrative as "a cautionary tale of modernity's excesses" (165).

> seen would, in most cases, be ascribed to supernal agency, and a command imposed on them, in this manner, would be obeyed with religious scrupulousness. (*M* 244–45)

In wishing to appropriate the appearance of divine agency, Ludloe describes a pragmatic program of desacralization, the purpose of which is to reduce transcendent possibility to self-serving, manipulative purposes. In rejecting the very existence of the transcendent realm, Ludloe perceives all human actions in histrionic terms. His demythologizing of providential possibility coincides with the reconfiguration of life as a "theatre" and human society as a stage on which witting actors and deluded fools strut. After Carwin tentatively wonders how he might be useful, Ludloe replies, "If you are qualified to act a part in the theatre of life, step forth; but you are not qualified" (*M* 250). In this figuration, Brown evokes the conventional world-as-stage motif, expanding it into a warrant for self-generated and self-justifying political action. Ironically, at the very point at which he exercises subversive power, Carwin finds himself on the verge of following an overbearing mentor with dubious intentions. In identifying the unsettling split that exists between Ludloe's philosophies and performative ethos, Anthony Galluzzo describes him as "a seeming exponent of Godwinian utopianism who is also an oppressive opportunist" ("Brown, the Illuminati, and the Public Sphere" 342). In fact, rather than using his powers for purposes of self-liberation, Carwin winds up being swayed by vaporous enticements. In becoming Ludloe's ward, Carwin embarks on an ambiguous apprenticeship that may include his potential initiation into a conspiratorial band very much like the Illuminati.[22] In his halting way,

[22] Summarizing Carwin's relation to Ludloe, who first appears as Carwin's nemesis in *Wieland*, Barnard and Shapiro describe possible sources for Brown's adaptation of the Ludlow name (*M* 244, note 21). Concerning the genesis and composition of the *Memoirs*, Dunlap supplies vital evidence. In the September 14, 1798 entry in his *Diary*, Dunlap identifies the extent of Brown's progress in composing Carwin's story: "Afternoon read C B Browns beginning for the life of Carwin—as far as he has gone he has done well: he has taken up the schemes of the Illuminati" (338–39). In installment VI printed as such in the Barnard and Shapiro edition, Ludloe discusses his membership in a sect that

as their relationship develops, Carwin refuses to surrender himself completely to Ludloe's wishes. The very fact that Carwin withholds from everyone (especially Ludloe) the secret of his remarkable aptitude makes possible, and may even accentuate, his subversive inclinations. To expose his talent to Ludloe would have the effect of disempowering himself.

Despite the complications introduced by Ludloe's presence, Carwin's Ariel performance reinforces potentially self-liberating intertextual resonances first stirred by Carwin's reading of Milton's *Mask*. Brown's choice of Damon for the dog's name conjures a resonant doubleness that reinforces Carwin's attraction to figures and myths that are classical rather than Christian. Damon, of course, suggests the faithful friend of Pythias, though Brown may possibly mean to evoke the notion of "daemon," a word that appears early in *Wieland* as "the Daemon of Socrates" (*W* 48) and later in *Memoirs of Carwin* (*M* 261).[23] In *Wieland* Clara associates Carwin with satanic guile and artful tales. More to the point in the *Memoirs*, the concept of the "daemon" calls attention to the creative force, a spiritually procreant other self, one's own muse, a figure related to the disruptive, magical Comus. In the citation from *Wieland* just mentioned, Brown clearly evokes Socrates' discussion of his own daemon—his creative other—in the *Symposium*. The same matrix that associates Comus and Damon/daemon includes

---

resembles the Illuminati (*M* 258–61). By mid-September 1798, Brown at least reached this point. See Justin D. Edwards and his discussion linking The Friendly Club and the Carwin-Ludloe relationship (292–99). Levine associates the figure of Ludloe with the Illuminati conspiracy as it roiled public consciousness in the late 1790s (*Conspiracy and Romance* 17–24). By the time Brown came back to composing *Memoirs of Carwin* for magazine publication in 1803, he had finished *Ormond* and *Arthur Mervyn*. Thus, his further development of Ludloe's character in the later *Memoirs of Carwin* materials published serially in the *Literary Magazine and American Register* between 1803 and 1805 should be critically examined in relation to Brown's presentation of such figures as Ormond and Welbeck. See Galluzzo for his discussion of connections between Ludloe, Ormond, and the Illuminati (342).

[23] See Bloom for an expansive discussion of the daemon and its relation to the tradition of the American sublime.

Ariel, Prospero's enslaved (and finally liberated) magical spirit. In *The Tempest*, Ariel constitutes the living embodiment of the creative principle. Prospero—perhaps one of Milton's sources for Comus—is a consummate artist figure (Hughes 87). He controls the elements; he controls the spirit world; he controls the social world of impending human villainy.

Through such expansive allusive associations, Brown reinforces Carwin's creative attributes, although he leaves undeveloped the histrionic implications that might obtain if Carwin were to combine the power of Prospero and Comus with the transformational energies of a creative daemon and a liberated Ariel. Within this allusive cluster, Brown conflates subversive and magical figures that locate Carwin's models not in the social context of colonial America, but in a transnational, transhistorical literary world characterized by magic and manipulation. Carwin's problem—never overcome in his *Memoirs*—is to marry his artistic capacity for manipulation and self-making to his ongoing life within a social and political realm wherein he remains a dependent player.

Fragmented Forms and the Irresolute Lure of Literary Creation

Brown was a mercurial literary performer. He spent his authorial apprenticeship and novel-writing years skipping from project to project, producing an impressive body of finished work as well as a sometimes-baffling array of fragmented pieces. *Memoirs of Stephen Calvert*, for example, is a nearly finished novel that explores cultural collisions between old world and new world contexts as well as complex psychological doublings associated with the Calvert twins. After writing more than two hundred pages, Brown left this story in a bewildering state of compositional arrest. Did he run out of ideas? Did he decide he did not like the work? Did he become immersed in the next great project? Did he care? With at least some exasperation, Elihu Hubbard Smith identifies this tendency as a foundational attribute of Brown's authorial identity. It is pertinent here to recall Smith's diary entry of December 14, 1796, where he complains of Brown's wayward compositional practices: "He starts an idea; pursues it a little way; new ones spring up; he runs a short distance after each; meantime the original one is likely to escape intirely" (272).

The same predilection for unfinished business emerged in the composition of the *Memoirs*. After casting Carwin as a protean figure who finds the key to aesthetic and political power through the internalization of nature's hidden forms, after depicting Carwin as a second son who pursues a transformative, self-made American identity outside the social strictures of primogeniture, and after traveling to Philadelphia where he played biloquial tricks and met the enigmatic Ludloe, Brown suspended composition shortly after the publication of *Wieland* and did not resume work on this prequel until he saw it as a source for magazine copy in autumn of 1803. In late September 1798, momentous matters of life and death intruded. In the near aftermath of *Wieland*'s publication, the yellow fever wreaked havoc in Brown's life. Tragically, on September 19, 1798, this disease killed Smith—this brilliant physician and extraordinary man of letters. Soon, Brown himself became infected and fell ill. Subsequently, he moved to the more healthful environs of Perth Amboy, New Jersey, where he recuperated at the home of friend and biographer William Dunlap (Warfel 123). Brown's illness was likely instrumental in his decision to put Carwin's story aside, but in any case, his work on the *Memoirs* had reached a creative impasse. Brown appeared unable to move beyond dramatizing varying episodic demonstrations detailing Carwin's experiences of social confinement. His bids for power and freedom brought little more than recurrent encounters with dependency and stultification. Brown left Carwin suspended between enduring tensions that impelled his attempts at self-reformation and competing imperatives that governed his relation to his father and his wavering notions of God. In fact, Carwin finds that the predominating impress of social status gives the lie to self-making and transmutes it into its simulacrum.

Whereas Brown no doubt had concerns about where the Carwin story was going, it is clear that he did not run out of material. Rather, while convalescing, he seems to have redirected his imaginative energies and responded to a surfeit of inviting narrative possibilities that could not be contained within the narrowing perimeters of Carwin's tale. Perhaps he thought the entangled tribulations of a disaffected youth seeking his place in the world could best be developed in the evolving, elliptical tale of *Arthur Mervyn*. More importantly, Brown's exploration of Carwin's ambiguous relationship with the conspiratorial Ludloe seems to have marked a decisive turning point. Without question, Ludloe constitutes a prototype for the mysterious Ormond and his nefarious power games. It is plausible to think that Brown's development of Ludloe's character in the "Ariel" episode created the impetus for Brown to cast the story of a powerful shape-shifter within a narrative frame that would not be confined to Carwin's already written future. Perhaps, by leaving Carwin behind, Brown saw in this new work exciting opportunities for pursuing his growing interest in the poetics and politics of imposture and subversion, especially insofar as confidence trickster Thomas Craig—a diminutive reconfiguration of Carwin—and cosmopolitan, self-deifying Ormond come into conflict with the pure and upright Constantia Dudley and her inept father. In a December 20, 1798 letter to his brother Armitt, Brown summarized the rushed composition of the new novel that took up the final three months of this packed, transformational year:

> Some time since I bargained with the publisher of Wieland for a new performance, part of which only was written, and the publication commencing immediately, I was obliged to apply with the utmost diligence to the pen, in order to keep pace with the press.... I call my book Ormond, or the Secret Witness. I hope to finish the writing and the publication together before new-year's day, when I shall have a breathing spell. (*L* 442)

In this "new performance," Brown gave narrator Sophia Courtland the formidable mission of telling Constantia's tale, while pursuing the daunting task of rendering "a just delineation of the character of Ormond" (*O* 111).

4

Toward a Supreme Fiction: *Ormond; or, The Secret Witness*

A Theater of Imposture

In the prefatory epistle to her "history of Constantia Dudley," Sophia Courtland warns German correspondent I. E. Rosenberg to expect from her true-to-life, personal narrative neither "unity of design" nor "that harmonious congruity and luminous amplification, which might justly be displayed in a tale flowing merely from invention" (*O* 3). The premise here is that a fictional narrative possesses controlled focus, a modulated arrangement that depicts an ordered, coherent, but decidedly constructed (and therefore artificial) world. On the contrary, a record of life—autobiography, biography, history—can be little more than a halting gathering of pieces: in presenting the archival strands of experience woven into narrative form, the historian can do little more than render a muddled inclusiveness. According to Sophia's premise, fiction is notable for its perfected polish, history for its unsightly fragmentation.[1]

Ironically, such "unity of design" and "harmonious congruity" precisely describe the methodology used by inveterate trickster Thomas Craig in forging his "circumstantial and consistent" account of his life. His story presents the basic paradigm of the American immigrant saga:

---

[1] As Kamrath's study documents, Brown was a sophisticated theorist of the relationship between history and romance, between narratives depicting factual and/or faux historical events and narratives depicting imagined materials. Brown's representation of Sophia as a historian—one who doubles as an inventive romancer—points to the on-going synergy that Brown delineates in his reflections on history and romance. See Kamrath's discussion of Brown's essay on "The Difference between History and Romance," which appeared in *The Monthly Magazine and American Review* in April 1800 (85–88).

an Old-World origin in Yorkshire, England; a large, honest, stable family; a yearning for "independant subsistence" in the New World. In using a fiction to authenticate his fabricated identity, Craig meticulously establishes an appearance of "veracity...liable to no doubt." With little ado and much confidence, Stephen Dudley believes Craig's story and hires him. Having arrived in a fluid society amplified by a steady influx of strangers, Craig need only reconcile his constructed account with his subsequent actions. For over two years, he lives within the articulated confines of his cover story, performing his duties with "probity" and "fidelity" (*O* 8). To provide ongoing evidence of his rectitude, Craig engages in "a punctual correspondence with his family, and confided to his patron, not only copies of all the letters which he himself wrote, but those which, from time to time, he received" (*O* 9). His employer becomes unwittingly enmeshed in this textualized, self-generated, and self-referential web-work of lies as he witnesses the epistolary display of interacting, fictionalized lives. From this perspective, Dudley believes he can more fully measure Craig's actions in relation to testimonials regarding his sterling character. After reposing more and more confidence in Craig, Dudley finally offers his seemingly "faithful servant" a business partnership: "[Craig] professed unbounded gratitude, considered all that he had done as amply rewarded by the pleasure of performance, and as being nothing more than was prescribed by his duty" (*O* 10). In this language lurks a teasing "double-tongued" duplicity that associates Craig's ostensible dedication with his actual perfidy (*W* 1). What Dudley does not yet suspect is that he himself has become less a judgmental arbiter than an unwitting dupe within Craig's elaborate, dramatic charade.[2]

Thomas Craig and his story are too good to be true. The "harmonious congruity" of his account points to its status as a fiction and facilitates his criminal successes as a fiction-maker loose in life. He

---

[2] Stern contends that Craig's "criminal self-authorization...and mysterious business dealings...presage a future where the lure of the marketplace supplants familial and communal bonds" (194).

"profess[es] unbounded gratitude" for the opportunity to fleece Dudley, while reveling internally in his "performance"—his nearly flawless management of surfaces. He transfigures his immediate social world—his life, the lives of the Dudleys—into a theater of "imposture" in which Craig is author, director, actor, and audience (*O*12). In *Ormond*, as in *Wieland* and *Memoirs of Carwin*, the word "imposture" recurrently signifies a specific, dramatic act of feigned self-representation; but it goes beyond the contingencies of any particular charade and functions as an informing trope that synoptically evokes an entire theatrical process. As reflected most powerfully in the figure of Carwin, imposture facilitates one's capacity to transform the affairs of life into artifice. Brown begins *Ormond* with a demonstration of how Craig's "stability and integrity" are a consequence of his carefully constructed campaign (*O* 9). His performative feats go well beyond the youthful Carwin's slapdash, episodic wiles in the *Memoirs* and come to assume the encompassing dimensions of a *gestalt* dedicated to the arts of narrative self-making. Craig does not simply play a role. Over five long years, he lives the life of a fabricated person, assiduously creating corroborating, documentary evidence that testifies to the existence of a mother, brother, and sister back in Merry Old England. In this theater of life, Craig practices "the most atrocious arts" (*O* 20). His life operates as a double plot, with his overt role hiding the insidious machinations of his covert constructions. The very surfaces of everyday life provide raw materials for the perfidious manipulations of this protean self; the assumed character *is* Thomas Craig's life.

In Brown's world, a corollary to how a social milieu can be methodically constructed is the alacrity with which it can be thoroughly deconstructed. No matter how carefully Craig controls appearances, he occasionally has cause to leave town. *Ormond* insistently dramatizes the province as well as the limitations of narrative self-making when used as a tool for social theater. The seemingly accidental impingement of contingency or chance—in this case, a letter ostensibly dictated by Craig's illiterate, real-life mother in New Hampshire—exposes, disrupts, and destroys the artifices of social invention—in this case, both the faithful life-story of Thomas Craig as well as the apparent prosperity of Mr. Dudley. Even when Dudley achieves sufficient insight to realize he is watching Craig lie, he can do nothing to keep himself and his daughter from plunging into abject poverty. His imposture exposed, Thomas Craig simply exits the stage.

The opening movement of Brown's expansive novel reveals how the fragility of social constructs makes possible the predatory power of narrative self-making.[3] To underscore this point, Brown has the suddenly impoverished Dudley take a job as a writer in a law office. Brown does not so much dramatize the exigencies of Dudley's destitute state as provide an occasion for Brown—through Sophia, his narrator—to express contempt for the practice of law and by extension precedent, legal forms, and a matrix of exasperating societal constructs:

> He was perpetually encumbered with the rubbish of law, and waded with laborious steps through its endless tautologies, its impertinent circuities, its lying assertions, and hateful artifices.... It was one tedious round of scrawling and jargon; a tissue made up of the shreds and remnants of barbarous

[3] The sprawling reach of *Ormond* has stirred divided assessments among scholars. Watts disparages the work as "a rather wooden novel of ideas.... [driven by] the carrot of melodrama, [and] the stick of didactic intellectualism" (89). Nye relates the eclecticism of this text to the variety of Brown's fictional sources: "The most popular varieties of fiction available to Brown as models were the sentimental romance of Samuel Richardson; the Gothic tale of Walpole, Radcliffe, and Lewis; and the 'novel of purpose' favored by contemporary social and political activists in England and Europe" (313). In summarizing the relationship between the text's politics and aesthetics, Levine contends, "All of Brown's major romances develop connections between social and narrative uncertainty, all express concern about individual and social vulnerability, and all draw on themes and images of conspiracy" (*Conspiracy and Romance* 17). Stern argues, "Brown's abiding subject is the unraveling of sympathetic relations, the betrayal of fraternity: strategically assuming the female voice in several of his major novels, and particularly, in *Ormond*, he imagines a polity beset by epidemic disease, where brotherhood, masculinity, and affect itself are perilous liabilities" (183).

> antiquity, polluted with the rust of ages, and patched by the stupidity of modern workmen, into new deformity. (*O* 20)

For Brown himself, authorship provided an alternative to (and an escape from) the legal profession. In this passage, animated as it is with spirited rancor, Brown seems to commandeer his narrator's province and release what seems an autobiographically resonant, yet simplified and invidious, account of his own experiences. More importantly, this passage offers a collective view, castigating the artifices of law as flimsy, perverted, and degraded—an accumulation that bespeaks the encumbering dross of history itself. If society is an amalgam of contrived forms, then the legal constructs sustaining it provide little more than a porous foundation. The virulence of this attack is directed not against the ideal of law but against the *language* of law—especially how its ragtag eclecticism, convoluted rhetoric, and pernicious choplogic obstruct the application of any informing ideal. Legal forms are both a source and reflection of life's instability. One difference between the artifice of law and the artifice of narrative self-making is that law relies, at least putatively, on precedent—this accumulation of outmoded judgments—whereas narrative self-making is associated with the arch fluidity of speech, with novelty, with imposture—usually actualized through the fabrication of a seemingly whole imposter-self springing into a performative mode thanks to the fertilizing vitality of words, words, words. In fact, as Craig's adept but imperfect scripting of his relation to Dudley's world reveals, social stability can become dependent on the devious machinations of the protean imagination: the artist-figure set loose in life is impelled by the errant imperative to mold the lives of other people to serve his selfish, rapacious purposes. With ease, Craig creates the delusive *appearances* of personal history replete with seemingly authentic documentary evidence: "The history of the Wakefield family, specious and complicated as it was, was entirely fictitious. The letters had been forged, and the correspondence supported by [Craig's] own dexterity" (*O* 16). With his faux life-story a product of narrative invention, Craig embodies American novelty—with the product of his authorial gambit being the fictive profile of a credible acting self. Craig—like Carwin—exemplifies the transformative energies, indeed the destructive volatilities, of nascent, inchoate American selfhood. Robert S. Levine examines Craig's confidence game within the context of Brown's "conspiratorial discourse" and his "own very real concerns about the authority, stability and, in the largest possible sense, vulnerability of the new republic" (*Conspiracy and Romance* 31). Levine connects the private plight of the Dudley family to public problems inherent in America's emerging market economy: "That an economic marketplace governed by laissez-faire individualism should become a proving ground for hoaxes, frauds, and counterfeitings of identity and currency is an important working premise of much early American fiction and, more generally, Anglo-American literature from the sixteenth century on" (*Conspiracy and Romance* 32–33).

At the outset of *Ormond*, Brown highlights the problematical practice of reposing confidence in the stability of identity, fortune, legal language, and the theater of social life. Brown thus establishes one critical element of this novel's informing dialectic. Narrative self-making is only possible within a world characterized by individual freedom, shifting appearances, and undefined potential.[4] The unfolding present constitutes the inchoate medium out of which future forms might emerge. Narrative self-making intrinsically belies—or at least disputes—the coherence and teleological insistence of the providential plot. In fact, the machinations of the protean self establish perspectives from which one might recognize the competing presence of alternative modes of causality. As the arrival of a letter from Craig's biological mother suggests, events may simply derive from chance or one can

[4] Within his study of the confidence man in American literature, Lindberg offers trenchant observations on "the basis" of Brown's fictional world: "Dubious impressions are, in fact, the basis of Charles Brockden Brown's fiction. Over and over his characters have to 'solve' appearances. His narratives are contrived to emphasize ambiguities, and what is given seems always to admit of wrong constructions" (98–99). See Blair and Hill for their exploration of confidence tricksters as American types (46–52).

interpret the letter's arrival as itself a providentially-ordained event. When Dudley's sudden blindness follows the collapse of his fortune, one might interpret this outcome as accidental bad luck, an idiomatic physiological event, a stress-induced malady, or a divinely-imposed, Job-like affliction. Indeed, Dudley's suffering can even be understood as having typological significance: his trial-by-blindness might signal providence's scourge, or test, of a sinful fool. On the contrary, if one espouses belief in a world ruled by arbitrary accident, then the protean shape-shifter stands as an ambiguous, self-serving figure out to impose his own meaning—his own order—upon emergent chaos. When cast in opposition to the argumentative framework supporting the existence of a providential universe, however, the protean fiction-maker stands as a romantic usurper, who competes with God to become the author of events. Of particular import in *Ormond* is the open competition that exists between these possible, if competing, claims. Whether one's supreme, explanatory fiction concerns the power of self-making, the chance-driven irruption of accidental contingencies, or the determinate force of providential design, the particular contours of any specific *explanatory* narrative remain a human construct. What emerges in *Ormond*, then, is a dialectic among alternative possibilities—a dialectic managed by a human narrator (herself the invention of a human author)—a dialectic that is itself directed by the recurrent imposition of aesthetic and theatrical tropes.[5] Dudley's sudden poverty offers a case in point. He feels that he is reduced to being a pathetic object of public scrutiny: "He could not endure to exhibit this reverse of fortune in the same theatre which had witnessed his prosperity" (*O* 19). Even in describing Dudley's misfortune, Sophia Courtland evokes the dominant trope of performance and spectatorship.

Against the machinations of the protean self, in opposition to the possibility that the world is either a theater of malicious tricksterism or the domain of arbitrary chance, stands the rock-solid consistency of

---

[5] Scheick presents a ranging exploration of those competing forces that unsettle Sophia Courtland's epistemological pursuits (138).

Dudley's daughter. Her name looms as the most obvious expression of her fixed standards. Constantia, or Constance, Dudley embodies the possibility that ontology and behavior can be grounded in immutable standards: "She had learned to square her conduct, in a considerable degree, not by the hasty impulses of inclination, but by the dictates of truth. She yielded nothing to caprice or passion" (*O* 21). Like the American protean self, Constantia views life as an unfolding tableau. But her status as circumspect *arbiter* of truth and falsehood—rather than as manipulative performer—is inseparable from her enactment of a determinate, hermeneutical process that relies on her ability to read one's words and surface form as precise reflections of one's essence. In evaluating other people, she "was ever busy in interpreting the language of features and looks. Her sphere of observation had been narrow, but her habits of examining, comparing and deducing, had thoroughly exhausted that sphere.... She delighted to investigate the human countenance, and treasured up numberless conclusions as to the coincidence between mental and external qualities" (*O* 76–77). Although unable to have seen through Craig's five-year-long "countenance" of lies, she nevertheless believes that one's performance expresses the nature of one's being. For Constantia, then, life in its individual and collective manifestations constitutes an ordered story and a sign of the unflagging agency of an immutable truth.[6]

In *Ormond*, how one views and pursues marriage provides an index to understanding a character's identity as well as reflecting the nature of one's supreme, explanatory fiction. Marriage constitutes the novel's primary social form: does one see marriage as creating an essentialist union among companionate souls or as a contrivance that

---

[6] Waterman argues that "*Ormond* emerged directly from a nexus of Friendly Club discussions of education, gender, religion, and politeness. It tests—and ultimately vindicates—many of the club's foundational tenets, in particular its members' confidence in the efficacy of women's education and improvement" (*Republic of Intellect* 118). See Waterman's discussion of gender politics and the impress of Godwinian thought (*Republic of Intellect* 116–29).

facilitates the subjugation of another person? Marriage might offer a way to double the self in a divinely-ordained, spiritual union with the deepest qualities of another person's soul, or marriage might serve to ensnare the woman into a debilitating state of abject servitude.[7] Constantia's firm belief in marriage as a holy union stands in radical opposition to Ormond's view of marriage as a destructive power game.

Unlike Ormond, Constantia celebrates marriage neither as a consequence of accidental juxtaposition nor as a rapacious power play. In her pragmatic estimate, marriage operates as a stable construct, "a contract to endure for life." Before she would agree to marry, Constantia has every intention of *knowing* her husband: "To form this connection in extreme youth, before time had unfolded and modelled the characters of the parties, was, in her opinion, a proof of pernicious and opprobrious temerity" (*O* 21). She seeks in a prospective husband "that permanence of character, which can flow only from the progress of time and knowledge" (*O* 22). For Constantia, the progression of time inevitably leads one toward the revelation of those elements that constitute "permanence of character." In her view, behavior must coincide with essence. Her jettisoned, unnamed suitor, however, embodies the wavering nature of the all-too-human. Even after he deserts her shortly after her father suffers economic misfortune, Constantia does not waste her tears: "He had exhibited less constancy and virtue than her heart had taught her to expect" (*O* 23). Clearly, this belief in essence functions as the ideational center around which revolve the machinations of such shape-shifters as Craig and Ormond.

Parallel Tales, Competing Fictions

The plot of *Ormond* lurches to the arrhythmia of sudden reversal occasionally succeeded by surprising benefaction. The interplay of

---

[7] See Davidson for her discussion of marriage and the literary contexts most available to women in the late eighteenth century (*Revolution and the Word* 122). See Horne for a discussion of marriage as a "companionate model" in the eighteenth century (1).

misfortune becoming displaced by good fortune, and vice versa, reflects not merely the episodic agitations of melodramatic excess but also provides a way to concretize the narrative's elemental hermeneutical problem: how does one derive from life's seemingly bizarre and unpredictable transformations a workable explanatory paradigm, or possibly, even the contours of a supreme fiction? In *Ormond*, Brown dramatizes the competition between conflicting, even irreconcilable, explanatory narratives. As her family circumstances become increasingly dire, Constantia remains unfailingly optimistic in her anticipation of impending beneficence: "[H]er knowledge of the vicissitudes to which human life is subject, taught her to rely upon the occurrence of some fortunate, though unforeseen event" (*O* 30). In Constantia's world view, existence has form, direction, and purpose. Her great expectations encourage her and assume the psychological force of inevitability.

Constantia's ingrained sense of being a favored player within the plot of providential design becomes most fully dramatized as Brown places her within a horrific scene of mass death. Although economically and emotionally tasked, she nurses the victims of the yellow fever epidemic and remains uninfected. An angel of mercy and compassion, she travels through miasmal quarters and assists afflicted and dying people. Constantia remains steadfast, even as the epidemic reflects a socially encompassing and lethal version of life's inconstancy. Bill Christophersen views the plague as a foundational symbolic device and motif: "The yellow fever, then, an abstract symbol of 'evil, political and physical,' as well as a literal motif, signifies various spheres of action or emotion—sexual, political, and perhaps even aesthetic...that...pose a threat to the health of the individual and society" (66). Similarly, Nicholas E. Miller explores how the novel's focus on the yellow fever epidemic brings together "a political and a biological valence" that becomes expressed in the contingencies deriving from the intersections of "contagion, conspiracy, and crisis" (66).[8] In *Ormond*, Brown's

---

[8] Nicholas E. Miller argues, "Written against the backdrop of revolutions in both France and Saint-Domingue, *Ormond* became a sprawling narrative of

recurrent subject concerns the impingement of catastrophe upon individuals and his exploration of the consequences springing from these horrid visitations. Repeatedly, the narrative gives voice and aesthetic form to the very worst of life's afflictions. For example, Mr. Baxter's death seems particularly horrendous: "His muscular force now exhausted itself in ghastly contortions, and the house resounded with his ravings" (*O* 61).

As narrator, Sophia Courtland uses theatrical tropes to present these gruesome materials. When the epidemic first appears, the morbidly depressed Mr. Dudley expects that "[t]he tragedies of Marseilles and Messina will be reacted on this stage" (*O* 36). For Dudley, history affords a mirror of the emerging present. His sense of how the plot of life works reflects not providential progression but cyclical recurrence. The "stage" image functions as a figure of speech, even as it gives focus to the narrator's dramatic arrangement of incident. When visiting Sarah Baxter to ascertain the cause and extent of the family's troubles, for example, Constantia becomes Sarah's audience as she recounts the events leading to her husband's death. Constantia's concern for the Baxters' well-being parallels ill-fated Mr. Baxter's concern for Monrose and his daughter Ursula. In Sarah's story—recast from "The Man at Home"— Mr. Baxter appears driven by compassion and curiosity. From his position as a secret witness, he watches "this theatre of human calamity" (*O* 68). As Ursula buries her deceased father, Baxter's "blood ran cold at this spectacle" (*O* 69). Brown depicts this moment within a series of nested narrative frames replete with multiple audiences: Sophia Courtland reports on Constantia's account of having listened to Sarah's story of her husband watching a daughter bury her father. The theater motif not only contains horror within a series of aesthetic frames and makes explicit the dramatic content of this event, but it also

---

conspiracy and contagion, an experiment in deconstructing the bonds that hold us together as a society" (66). Ellis explores the economic crisis that derived from the yellow fever epidemic as it informs *Ormond* and, more expansively, *Arthur Mervyn* (387–90).

creates dire consequences that exacerbate the calamitous plot. Baxter himself comes to have a horrid part to play. He catches yellow fever, possibly from his proximity to the deceased Mr. Monrose or even perhaps from "the force of imagination" (*O* 71)—seemingly, a kind of psychosomatic or self-induced condition deriving from his alarming experience as witness of what he takes to be the daughter's extreme suffering.

It is ironic that Ursula Monrose, speaking later as the powerful warrior Martinette de Beauvais, gives an alternative version of her emotional state: "The rueful pictures of my distress and weakness, which were given by Baxter, existed only in his own fancy" (*O* 210). Martinette's redaction underscores the self-generated theatricality of Baxter's twice-told tale. The fact that Ursula later claims only to have *appeared* to be distressed accentuates both the constructed nature of all human stories and the degree to which surface appearances may be at odds with the truth of one's affective condition. Despite his empathetic misreading of Ursula's feelings, Baxter suffers an appalling death and transforms "Sarah's house…[into] a theatre of suffering" (*O* 61). Impervious to the latent doubleness of this inset narrative, Constantia attempts (and ultimately fails) to wrest from Sarah Baxter's account a determinate interpretation. After listening to Sarah's tale, Constantia identifies with Ursula Monrose:

> Such were the facts circumstantially communicated by Sarah. They afforded to Constance a theme of ardent meditation. The similitude between her own destiny and that of this unhappy exile, could not fail to be observed. Immersed in poverty, friendless, burthened with the maintenance and nurture of her father, their circumstances were nearly parallel. The catastrophe of her tale, was the subject of endless but unsatisfactory conjecture. (*O* 72)

This inset narrative seems to provide a mirror of her condition and casts Ursula as a sympathetic embodiment of her own life story. This parallelism suggests not a narcissistic projection of her latent, or unconscious, desire for identification; instead, it offers a more socially cohesive manifestation of how two people might have mutually self-reflecting life-experiences. Constantia imagines that she too will soon be burying a father. She also has an innate sense that Ursula might be a companionate soul: "Perhaps there was a coincidence of taste as well as fortunes between them" (*O* 72). Constantia's abiding imperative is to defeat the forces of chaos and negativism and to find herself among a community of like-minded women.

The plot of *Ormond* hinges on some arresting coincidences—most notably, the discovery that Martinette Beauvais is, or was, Ursula Monrose; the fact that Martinette is Ormond's sister; and the unlikely contingencies that lead to the reunification of Constantia Dudley and Sophia Courtland.[9] In these circumstances, Constantia attempts to undo some of the horrors deriving from her family's destitution. For example, she tries to recover her father's pawned lute. In this venture, she makes her winding way to Martinette. Constantia also attempts to reacquire Sophia's miniature portrait, an item pawned by landlord McCrea.[10] Constantia's pursuit leads her to a drawing room where she happens to hear Sophia singing from the next room the same lyric she had sung when they parted. In both cases, Constantia recovers far more than she intended: she seeks lost objects and finds lost persons—individuals bonded to her in essential ways. Both discoveries dramatize the stabilizing power of unwavering female friendship and may even suggest that behind such unlikely coincidences lurks the possibility of divine intention and the supreme fiction of providential purpose.

Upon encountering Martinette Beauvais, Constantia is awed by this remarkable person, a figure of tremendous power, a new kind of

---

[9] See Grabo on the place of coincidence in Brown's fiction: "Coincidence...may sometimes strike us as a trivial annoyance, but it may also function as the foundation of the stories themselves" (*The Coincidental Art* x).

[10] See Boyd for a discussion of Constantia's miniature portrait of Sophia (496–98). The portrait is "really about establishing Sophia's narrative authority, her position as a family intimate, and her own social and class position" (Boyd 496).

woman. Constantia once again finds herself listening to a personal narrative. In adolescence, Martinette was enmeshed with a protean figure. Her protector Madame de Leyva "was perpetually assuming new forms" (*O* 203). Martinette emerges as a resourceful cosmopolite—a student, a soldier, a raconteur. Hers is a tale "particularly distinguished by female enterprize and heroism." Martinette becomes a counterpart and counterpoint to brother Ormond and his roving cosmopolite attributes. Ormond's tales "had carried [Constantia] beyond the Mississippi, and into the deserts of Siberia.... Her new friend had led her back to the civilized world, and pourtrayed the other half of the species" (*O* 205). As Nicholas E. Miller observes, "Both Ormond and Martinette offer freethinking, cosmopolitan contrasts to the virtuous republicanism of Constantia" (63). Whereas Martinette possesses Ormond's combative characteristics, she is not predatory and does not wish to possess Constantia.[11] Rather, when Martinette becomes Constantia's soul-mate, she fulfills Constantia's earlier desire to be at one with Ursula Monrose. Similarly, the song Sophia and Constantia sung before their separation, and which Constantia hears Sophia singing in the next room, is "connected with the image of a being like herself" (*O* 187). The discovery of the companionate double celebrates the existence of shared essence. As Julia Stern notes, "...if compassion in the postrevolutionary period is not to be found between brothers, fathers, and surrogate daughters, where does it reside? The answer, in *Ormond*, lies in the bond of sisterhood, in both female homosociality and romantic love between women" (204). To find oneself in the being of another argues for the possibility of an ideal unity that transcends the uncertain ways of a changeable world. For Constantia, essence and stability underlie the multiple forms of contingency. Such a state of unification continues to infuse and strengthen her despite her persistent entanglements with duplicitous types like Craig and Ormond. Martinette not only actualizes the latent power of Constantia Dudley, but

[11] See Levine for an alternative reading of Martinette. He argues that her character becomes "increasingly monstrous" (*Conspiracy and Romance* 51; 50–53).

she also prefigured this power when operating within the "theatre" of European politics. Martinette constitutes a grotesquely enlarged version of Constantia Dudley—one who takes heroic action not to the dismal, dark corners of a plague-ridden city, but to the battle-stage of European revolution.[12]

Sophia's inset narrative recounting her own life story is not the clumsy, gratuitous appendage it might seem to be, but a simplified figuration of *Ormond*'s main action. The conflict between Constantia and Craig becomes replicated in Sophia's tortured relation with her mother, seemingly a prostitute who "laboured for years to obtain the controul of my person and actions; to snatch me from a peaceful and chaste assylum, and detain me in her own house" (*O* 225). The attempt to possess and control another person's being constitutes a high crime in Brown's novels as it later does in the moral histories dramatized by his descendent romancer, Nathaniel Hawthorne. Sophia's mother appears as a diminutive version of Ormond, a cousin-germane to Craig. Having "left New-York, which had long been the theatre of her vices," she becomes an inveterate role-player: "She delighted to assume all parts, and personate the most opposite characters. She now resolved to carry a new name and the mask of virtue, into scenes hitherto unvisited" (*O* 226). Sophia's mother is to Sophia what Madame de Leyva is to the young Martinette. The lost-as-found plot defeats—or gives the lie to—the notion of life as a succession of mere accidents and chance collisions. Repeatedly in *Ormond*, as these coincidences proliferate, sudden order bursts from the swirl of apparent randomness. In commenting on this remarkable reunification, Sophia describes what might be little more than chance or contingency as the surprising realization of a predestined design:

[12] Fleischmann argues, "The critical discussion of how to sort the different models of womanhood in *Ormond*—the beautiful but dependent Helena, the rational and resourceful Constantia, the exotic Marinette, proponent of revolutionary violence, and the sentimentally savvy Sophia, the narrator—also circles around the question of Brown's gender politics—and of his politics in general" (296).

> On how slender threads does our destiny hang! Had not a momentary impulse tempted me to sing my favorite ditty to the harpsichord, to beguile the short interval...I should have speeded to New-York, have embarked for Europe, and been eternally severed from my friend, whom I believed to have died in phrenzy and beggary, but who was alive and affluent, and who sought me with a diligence, scarcely inferior to my own. We imagined ourselves severed from each other, by death or by impassable seas, but, at the moment when our hopes had sunk to the lowest ebb, a mysterious destiny conducted our footsteps to the same spot. (*O* 249–50)

The assertion of "a mysterious destiny" presupposes the insistent unfolding of a benevolent master-plot. The lost-as-found scenario links Constantia, Martinette, and Sophia, especially as their past experiences of fragmentation and disarray become reconceived through parallel tales of unification and self-actualization. Individual pursuits culminate in putatively preordained resolutions. From one perspective, one might see Brown indulging in a stock melodramatic device. Even so, such a device may well reflect the possible impingement of an informing power that transcends, even as it controls, the dynamics of human intention. On the earthly plane, human beings can do little more than recognize the evidence of surprising restorations and then interpret their meanings as they will.

The assertion of a determinate order—with the attending insinuation that life is controlled by the contours of an occasionally glimpsed supreme fiction of providential design that can be cast within the trope of "a mysterious destiny"—becomes apprehensible within a text via the operation of a retrospective, narrative intelligence. Such unifications and surprising resolutions offer not proof but merely hermeneutic speculations regarding the possibility of providential design. Such conjectures provide countertexts to the self-generated, self-making activity of Brown's wily fiction-makers and protean performers. Significantly, Brown does not privilege the notion of a providential fiction over the machinations of self-making or the vagaries of chance. Instead, these perspectives offer competing explanations of the unfolding human drama. After the epidemic, which brought much horror, a theatrical troop comes to town and people flock to see it:

> Such is the motly and ambiguous condition of human society, such is the complexity of all effects from what cause soever they spring, that none can tell whether this destructive pestilence was, on the whole, productive of most pain or most pleasure. Those who had been sick and had recovered, found, in this circumstance, a source of exultation. Others made haste, by new marriages, to supply the place of wives, husbands, and children, whom the scarcely extinguished pestilence had swept away. (*O* 73)

Here, the affective dichotomy of "pain" and "pleasure" displaces any inquiry into the meaning of the epidemic. Despite this passage's brutal insensitivity—its all-too-easy erasure of individual and communal tragedy—Brown unsettles the notion that the epidemic brought nothing but catastrophe. New life emerges in the hollows left by the dead. Is the advent of new possibilities a matter of instinct, randomness, or design? None can tell for certain what the master-plot is; the narrative structure of life-as-lived in a complex society can only be delineated through an expanding array of competing accounts. Brown's narrative emphasizes that an overriding sense of ambiguity is an unavoidable concomitant to "all effects from what cause soever they spring." At every point, Brown depicts the protean flux of life as a dialectical theater of ultimately irreconcilable, but intermittently valid, alternatives.

The Divine Will and the Protean Self

By positing an explanatory narrative that stipulates how the hand of God operates in time, human beings create the hermeneutical bridge that gives narrative shape to one's desire to identify and then comprehend acts of divine volition. Consequently, Brown's dramatization of this elemental conflict between providence and self-making has everything to do with emergent intensities of human experience—once lived and now reconstructed—and very little to do with a library full of theological tomes debating the intricacies of freedom, necessity, Original Sin, infant damnation, and so on. Brown is not writing a philosophical tract like David Hume's "Of the Standard of Taste" or a theological exegesis like Jonathan Edwards' *Freedom of the Will.* Instead, Brown dramatizes the conflicted plight of human beings, who apply distinct hermeneutical principles in the attempt to explain and comprehend the meaning of their lives. By embracing the concept of providence, Constantia Dudley believes that her life and all phenomena conform to a master-plot that expresses the workings of a transcendent, Divine Will. On the contrary, self-making of the sort practiced by Craig negates the claim that such a supreme fiction exists and instead celebrates the agency of the protean self—the maker of novelty—as the determinate intelligence guiding whatever becomes dramatized in the theater of life. Brown's *Ormond* presents multiple versions of how private, public, and cosmological domains interact; or to put it more precisely, how individuals *formulate* the relationship obtaining among these domains and then *apply* these constructs to elucidate the meaning of interactive personal relationships. Brown's characters insistently construct multiple, conflicting formulations in the attempt to posit a supreme, clarifying fiction. Aesthetic questions, then, emerge as hermeneutical issues before they become actualized as political, or social, problems. In *Ormond* especially, the politics of experience concerns not a referenced smattering of topical issues regarding governmental processes or public policy so much as a consideration of the essential foundations on which private and public affairs might be enacted.

Brown approaches the dramatization of such issues from the perspective of human action and (literally) from the point of view of human narration. For example, Constantia's unwavering faith in providential design does not in any way undermine her stalwart sense of herself as a volitional agent. Whether she recognizes it or not, her notion of providence is—indeed, has to be—faith-based and suppositional, a conceptual paradigm that seeks to tie an individual's story to a cohesive cosmic drama created and sustained by divine intention and agency. As a story generated by human beings who theorize the reality of operative transcendent ideals and who aspire to explain the unspeakable grandeur of God, the providential view appears as one version of a supreme, clarifying fiction. Within the unfolding dialectic of *Ormond*, narrative self-making, conversely, repudiates the concept of divine essence in favor of a non-transcendent concentration and expression of personal power often effected through the dynamics of imposture. If the concept of providence situates the acting self in relation to suppositions regarding God's authorial will, then the protean artificer eschews the primacy of an essential, immutable, ontologically stable and divinely ordained private self, rejects the existence of any transcendent entity, and celebrates as a supreme fiction the histrionic enactments that impel human forms of self-determination. In categorically rejecting the existence of a divine master-plot, the aesthetics of narrative self-making position the protean self as the defining force within hitherto un-determined contingencies erupting in the theater of life. Providence and self-making, then, generate alternative interpretive possibilities regarding individual, social, political, and theological experience.

What infuses the powerful juxtaposition and collision of such contrastive complexes remains the adjudicating power of human consciousness, mostly notably, in this case, the mind of narrator Sophia Courtland. As Sophia indicates, Constantia's belief in spiritual essence makes it possible to project the existence of an integrated sodality of related persons. One's belief in ontological synthesis has a cognate manifestation in one's belief in transcendent ideals. The concept of providence, then, becomes the form, or story, within which Constantia (and Sophia) attempt to unify the relationship between visible and invisible domains of experience. They attempt thereby to comprehend, even as they promulgate, a pattern that links past, present, and future. Of crucial concern for Constantia, therefore, is her desire to maintain the divinely authorized power of personal freedom, that is, her capacity to perform good works as she exercises the power of will and self-determination—the very attributes that Craig and Ormond attempt to commandeer. Brown presents the unity between Constantia, Martinette, and Sophia in order to actualize and celebrate a feminized, social sphere of mutuality, respect, and devotion—the very elements that marriage should—but usually does not—supply. In *Ormond*, marriage is essentially a corrupted institution, a domain characterized by pernicious and suffocating male hegemony. When Mr. Dudley's troubles begin, Constantia's first suitor abandons her. Later, Constantia is courted by Balfour, a man of wealth but of pedestrian personal attributes. She sees him not only as unworthy but as a potential jailor: "Marriage would annihilate this power [of economic self-determination]. Henceforth she would be bereft even of personal freedom. So far from possessing property, she herself would become the property of another" (*O* 84). Like Mrs. Carter in *Alcuin*, Constantia insists on her right to self-determination; she asserts a willful desire to live according to her own ideal dictates. Later, in trying to help Ormond's mistress—the weak, beautiful, and befuddled Helena Cleaves—Constantia tries to convince Ormond to treat her with justice, or at least to elevate her from the degraded status of a concubine to the less diminutive status of wife. By bringing her full powers to bear on Helena's cause, Constantia succeeds only in inciting Ormond's sexual desire to possess her by any means whatsoever. Constantia insists on retaining her power of self-actualization, which becomes expressed through her ability to care for her father and herself. If she is ever to marry, she will settle for nothing less than a marriage of souls. She will find in a man the kind of ontological unity she shares with Marinette and Sophia. This desire to take care of her father leads her to encounter Craig and, through Craig, the formidable figure of Ormond.

After discovering the whereabouts of Craig—is it by chance or design? —Constantia must decide how to proceed. She wants Craig to restore her father to some measure of financial stability: "Craig was indebted to her farther. He had defrauded him by the most atrocious and illicit arts. On either account he was liable to prosecution, but her heart rejected the thought of being the author of injury to any man" (*O* 91). Like the word "imposture," the word "author" possesses a range of resonant associations in Brown's major novels. The term denotes a perpetrator or a doer, one who initiates, designs, and executes an action, but the status of author also invests the individual with the power of creation. To author an action emphasizes one's inventive characteristics and imperatives, especially insofar as one might pervert this power by imposing one's will on another person's life without the victim's knowledge or consent. When one becomes the author of an action, one creates contingencies and consequences that make decisive impacts on individuals and more encompassing social situations. Upon refusing to seek legal redress from Craig, upon refusing to become, at least in her mind, "the author of injury," she unwittingly fabricates an image of Craig founded entirely on her desires and, in doing so, creates a false premise that impels her to appeal to what she supposes is his "humanity": "He was not divested of the last remains of humanity. It was impossible that he should not relent at the picture of those distresses of which he was the author." Constantia reveals her tendency to advance a fictionalized supposition, which she invests with certainty. Casting Craig as audience and herself as narrator, she intends to put before him "the picture...of which he was the author" (*O* 92).

Brown's daunting narrative challenge is to dramatize Constantia's conjectures regarding Craig, even while indicating their intrinsic fallaciousness. In a way that might trouble those readers (of the Henry James persuasion) who prefer consistency in point of view, Brown has Sophia render the inner workings of Craig's unfolding consciousness. Within the novel, such an irruptive shift in point of view seems to defy those premises that establish Sophia's epistemological authority: she can depict Constantia's interior world with such credibility because she knows her so well, even though an implicit premise circumscribing the authority of any conventional first-person narrator must be the ineffable content of any other person's subjectivity. Sophia's sudden display of narrative omniscience may simply be Brown's makeshift contrivance, a clumsy response to the perceived dramatic necessity of revealing the unmediated activity of Craig's conspiratorial intelligence. In temporarily expanding Sophia's narrative reach toward omniscience, in transgressing the limits of disclosure so meticulously maintained up to this point, Brown juxtaposes the unfolding activity of two subjectivities. In sacrificing the epistemological mystery associated with the question of what Craig might here be thinking, Brown presents the central ideational opposition of the novel. Sophia delineates Craig's mental machinations as he authors the contours of ensuing circumstances. In the process, Craig overtly eschews ethical and moral imperatives. In an interior monologue prompted by Craig's position as surreptitious reader of Constantia's letter, he recognizes her idealism and ridicules her embrace of moral absolutes:

> I know this girl: When her heart is once set upon a thing, all the devils will not turn her out of her way. She promises silence.... I know she'll do what she promises. That was always her grand failing. How the little witch talks! Just the dreamer she ever was! Justice! Compassion! Stupid fool! One would think she'd learned something of the world by this time. (*O* 96–97)

Brown dramatizes two contradictory views of experience—each view demanding specific authorial imperatives. Constantia's belief in absolute "Justice," for example, presupposes the reality of a fixed, transcendent order, the very basis that allows her to promulgate her supreme fiction. Craig's mockery of "Compassion" rejects the efficacy of human empathy, altruism, and benevolence in favor of the predatory force of power politics. In presenting the world as a savage place, Craig articulates a brutal, Hobbesian mantra that justifies his dismissal of ethical paradigms. Craig empowers himself to operate as the author of events. To keep Constantia from "obstruct[ing] his present schemes," Craig tenders "the gratuitous gift of fifty dollars." She goes home happy, mollified. The first-time reader is nothing short of puzzled: even though this act "sat uneasily upon his avarice," one wonders how Craig could perform such an office (*O* 97). The money, we later learn, is counterfeit—a circumstance that authors more trouble for Mr. Dudley. To counterfeit legal tender is to create the illusion of monetary substance. In a raw sense, Craig transforms a worthless, theatrical prop into an apparently authenticated note of exchange. The bogus currency comes to operate as its own fiction set loose in Constantia's life. Craig's fictions proliferate from his wily, improvisational intelligence and he designs these fictions to meet and defeat potentially hostile exigencies.

Ormond himself first appears on the novel's "stage" as an ambiguous figure. His association with Craig leads Constantia to ponder a central question: "Who was this Ormond? she enquired of herself as she went along: whence originated, and of what nature is the connection between him and Craig? Are they united by union of designs and sympathy of character, or is this stranger a new subject on whom Craig is practicing his arts?" (*O* 94–95). By again embracing omniscience as she brings the reader into Ormond's mind, Sophia seeks (at least, provisionally) to answer this question. In her estimate, he first seems to be a reader of surfaces: "On leaving Mr. Ormond's house, Constance was met by that gentleman. He saw her as she came out, and was charmed with the simplicity of her appearance. On entering, he interrogated the servant as to the business that brought her thither" (*O* 98). Brown's expansion of his narrator's limits of disclosure reflects an unstable hold on point of view, a tenuousness that reinforces the novel's underlying dramatization of epistemic uncertainty. Of greater interest than Brown's violations of consistency in point of view is his strategic need to bring into the novel the interior workings of Ormond's mind. Once Sophia begins to delineate Ormond's thoughts, she reveals the alacrity with which he seeks to make Constantia an object of his defining intelligence. Ormond must, in fact, *read* her through the very narrative promulgated by Craig. Ormond confronts Craig regarding his business with Constantia and Craig obliges by presenting a "story": "Craig had not expected this address, but it only precipitated the execution of a design that he had formed. Being aware of this or similar accidents, he had constructed and related on a previous occasion to Ormond, a story suitable to his purpose" (*O* 98). He relies on an earlier fabrication—his invention of a brother, his evil double, the fictive projection of Craig's past betrayals. Half a century before the term entered American discourse, Brown depicts the figure of the American Confidence Man, who relies on a mask of innocent sincerity and the power of story to create the contours of a believable social surface: "Craig was one of the most plausible of men. His character was a standing proof of the vanity of physiognomy. There were few men who could refuse their confidence to his open and ingenuous aspect" (*O* 99). Gary Lindberg could be describing Craig: "The confidence man is a manipulator or contriver who creates an inner effect, an impression, an experience of confidence, that surpasses the grounds for it. In short, a confidence man *makes belief*" (7, emphasis in original). Craig's power derives from his ability to extract "confidence" from his auditors and his undoing derives from his self-consuming, pathological addiction to "habits of imposture":

> To this circumstance, perhaps, he owed his ruin. His temptations to deceive were stronger than what are incident to most other men. Deception was so easy a task, that the difficulty lay, not in infusing false opinions respecting him, but in preventing them from being spontaneously imbibed. He contracted habits of imposture imperceptibly. In proportion as he deviated from the practice of truth, he discerned the necessity of extending and systematizing his efforts, and of augmenting the original benignity and attractiveness of his looks, by studied additions. The further he proceeded, the more difficult it was to return. Experience and habit added

> daily to his speciousness, till at length, the world perhaps might have been searched in vain for his competitor. (*O* 99)

Craig's incorrigible compulsion for social manipulation entraps him. The demands of synthesizing his "studied additions" trap him within untidy plot lines. Like Carwin, this artist-in-life becomes a victim of his own game of imposture. Craig not only fabricates the tale of a fictional brother but makes "various additions to it, serving to aggravate the heinousness of his guilt. This arose partly from policy, and partly from the habit of lying, which was prompted by a fertile invention, and rendered inveterate by incessant exercise" (*O* 99–100). In Craig's spun yarn, Constantia was seduced by the fictive brother. Drawing on his "skill in chirographical imitation," Craig even forges letters in Constantia's handwriting, which "sufficiently attested her dishonor." The unwitting audience to Craig's performance, Ormond discerns the divergence in "spirit" between the letters actually written by Constantia and Craig's malevolent fabrications (*O* 100).

Unlike Craig, Ormond is no low trickster. Sophia distinguishes Ormond's deep purposes from Craig's superficial intrigues. Ormond intentionally tries to tender monetary relief to the Dudley family. He gives Craig one hundred dollars to pass on to them, although there is no evidence to indicate the money reaches its supposed destination. In conferring his "benefits," Ormond characteristically wishes "to conceal the author" (*O* 100). So begins Ormond's attraction to, and pursuit of, Constantia Dudley. She initially appeals to him as a problem of interpretation. In pondering the forged note from Craig, he wonders, "Might not this girl mix a little imposture with her truth? Who knows her temptations to hypocrisy? It might have been a present from another quarter, and accompanied with no very honorable conditions. Exquisite wretch! Those whom honesty will not let live, must be knaves. Such is the alternative offered by the wisdom of society" (*O* 110). By seeing duplicity where there is none, he succeeds in projecting on her a version of himself, which he narcissistically wishes to possess.

Upon viewing her as an "[e]xquisite wretch," he imbues Constantia with his own capacity for duplicity. Ormond could not be more wrong.

The Problem of Narrative Authority

Chapter XII marks a decisive turning point. Craig fades from view and Ormond assumes dramatic centrality. As a prelude to her engagement with this daunting figure, Sophia disrupts her retrospective narrative, positions herself in the compositional present, and echoes the form of spontaneous address characteristic of Clara Wieland's critical narrative: "I know no task more arduous than a just delineation of the character of Ormond" (*O* 111). This interlude leads Sophia to ponder the very nature of narration. Of all of Brown's first-person narrators, Sophia Cortland seems the most agile and protean. Like her recent embrace of apparent omniscience, her overt, self-referential intrusion into the text draws attention to the constructed nature of this—and any—story.[13] The impending "delineation" of Ormond's "character" will only occur after her expansive investigation, although she is retentive regarding the extent or nature of her inquiries. In her prefatory note "To I. E. Rosenberg," Sophia refuses "to unfold *all* the means by which I gained a knowledge of his actions; but these means, though singularly fortunate and accurate, could not be unerring and compleat" (*O* 3, emphasis in original). This formulation offers assurance, even as it takes it away. She asserts that her narrative has validity, although it does not offer unqualified accuracy. This principle of distortion, as it were, is innate, an intrinsic concomitant to the inherent subjectivity of any conventional first-person narrator. Sophia's remarks on the problematic

---

[13] As Nicholas E. Miller argues, "Recent scholarship has…tended to focus on the value of *Ormond* as an experimental and radical novel, one capable of destabilizing definitions of gender and genre." One could add here that this novel assertively destabilizes conventional confinements that would limit the oscillations of Sophia's point of view. Miller explores how the collapse of conventional taxonomies informs Brown's radicalized aesthetic (65).

nature of any psychological exploration cannot be dissociated from speculations regarding the novelist's degree of epistemological authority:

> To scrutinize and ascertain our own principles are abundantly difficult. To exhibit these principles to the world with absolute sincerity, can scarcely be expected. We are prompted to conceal and to feign by a thousand motives; but truly to pourtray the motives, and relate the actions of another, appears utterly impossible. The attempt, however, if made with fidelity and diligence, is not without its use. (*O* 111)

The difficulty of sounding one's own depths makes axiomatic the inscrutability of the other: indeed, the very nature of being—its recessive quality, its mysterious involutions—necessitates the epistemological uncertainty of any first-person narrative. But what follows from such an admission is, paradoxically, the very imperative that prompts Sophia to speak or to write, that emboldens her attempt to promulgate a valid fiction. The inscrutable mystery of Ormond's inner life impels Sophia's open-ended quest to give shape to a version of his "character" that possesses "fidelity" but not completeness.

By accentuating the constructed nature and inevitable limitations of Sophia's account, Brown mounts a sophisticated idea-play on the dynamics of biography and autobiography. In Sophia's meta-commentary, one finds the suggestion that any attempt at biographical "delineation" cannot be dissociated from the voice constructing the narrative—the very narrative that claims to lack the polish of fiction—all the while this intrepid voice insists on depicting the ragged edges of life. Indeed, Brown's *fiction* is that he is not writing, and we are not reading, a fiction. His imaginative premise is that we are approaching actual lives, that we are locked in real-life entanglements. While unable "truly to pourtray the motives, and relate the actions of another," Sophia nevertheless asserts that the act of "representation...may yet be considerably exempt from error" (*O* 111). Sophia believes her combination of "fidelity and diligence" anchors her claim to a qualified form of narrative authority. "Fidelity" entails one's belief in the truth of something extrinsic to the self, whereas the "use" to which the story may be put relates to the domain of social interaction and social utility. Both premises presuppose an order that exists outside the self.

In the process of having Sophia make such fine distinctions, Brown evokes essential attributes that underlie the providential view, especially the conviction that a pervasive form of coherent intentionality animates the seeming vagaries of human experience. On the contrary, the aesthetics of self-making presuppose that those extrinsic phenomena lack purposeful order and merely provide raw materials for the artistic manipulations and power plays dedicated to the cause of constructing a self-determined, social theater. In the simplest case, to lack "fidelity" is to become Craig. As a subversive, predatory confidence trickster, Craig dupes his victims into believing in the efficacy of his inventions. Ormond, as we shall see, takes the confidence game to a more sophisticated level. With the focused conviction of a psychopath, he has no sense of "fidelity" to any standard external to himself. His purposes are always narrowly self-serving. In fact, he insists on absolutizing his own will in the process of attempting to dominate others. Ormond's rhetoric is not only self-serving but self-deifying. Sophia's narrative, on the contrary, is animated by intensive self-reflexivity, a humble desire to call attention to the very limits of her own conflicted discourse. She examines—and makes her audience conscious of—the problematic premises that inform her artifice. What is true to life is the intrinsic limitation of any conventional first-person narrative; what is false to life—what is invention or supposition—is any "delineation" that pretends to complete omniscience. Her claim to "fidelity" grounds her effort to translate Ormond's interiority into a valid verbal approximation. In retrospect, then, as part of the reader's unfolding experience, Sophia's expansion of her first-person narrative perspective *toward* the expression of an apparent omniscience becomes reconceived as a dramatic supposition—a rhetorical construct based on an unspecified body of incomplete, though putatively credible evidence. By eclipsing the expectation of total revelation, she translates her ostensibly true life "biography" into a mediatory space, which thereby creates a hierarchical sense of incremental possibility: that is, one version of truth can prove to be more accurate than another: "To comprehend the whole truth, with regard to the character and conduct of another, may be denied to any human being, but different observers will have, in their pictures, a greater or less portion of this truth. No representation will be wholly false, and some though not perfectly, may yet be considerably exempt from error" (*O* 111).[14] This passage makes and unmakes claims to knowledge. It creates the impression of fixity, but it dissolves into an amorphous pool of subjunctives and qualifications. Sophia, however, does make possible her incremental accession toward a mediate, plausible (though intrinsically suppositious) understanding of Ormond's character, locating the narrator's province not in the rigid determinations of unquestionable fact, but in the indeterminate, though informed, possibilities of her speculative intelligence. Thus, Sophia wittingly exposes her forays into the minds of Constantia and Ormond as fictions fabricated via "means…singularly fortunate and accurate" (*O* 3). She summarizes her responsibilities as a narrator: "My knowledge is far from being absolute, but I am conscious of a kind of duty, first to my friend, and secondly to mankind, to impart the knowledge I possess" (*O* 111).

Nevertheless, even after having Sophia promulgate this theory of narrative delineation, Brown is not relegating story-telling to a vortex of merely fanciful subjectivities. Rather, he is experimenting with competing ways of telling the story, even as he has his narrator entangle herself in the very difficulties on which she speculates. Sophia's attempts to articulate her narrative principles prefigure what we might see as metafictional ruminations or as a deconstructive un-making of putatively fixed constructs, but she is most involved in formulating a

[14] See Brown's "Walstein's School of History" (*R* 145–56) for an exploration of theoretical concerns regarding the nature of narrative disclosure in history and romance.

good faith effort to warn the reader about the inherent limitations of what she asserts as her provisional, yet valid, interpretations of things to come. Sophia's artistic self-consciousness, then, has the added benefit of reflecting Brown's refined capacity to mount an implicit critique of his own authorial activities. One does well to keep in mind Sophia's admission in her preface that she is writing not a fiction but a biographical or historical account of real people and actual lives. Writing out a limited version of life's encompassing and uncontainable reality momentarily stabilizes the self and makes accessible a partial account of the mystery of psychological interiority. Provisional authority—the only kind possible within human narrative—emerges paradoxically through the admission of one's inability to achieve omniscience and in the revelation that the appearance, or assertion, of omniscience is in itself no more than a rhetorical supposition and self-generated tactic.

Sophia's meditation on the possibilities and limitations of truth-telling highlights the ethical and moral implications involved in any attempt to penetrate and illuminate the mystery of another person's subjectivity. This is to say that Sophia wishes, from a basic moral and ethical perspective, to distance herself from the manipulations and machinations that characterize Ormond and his increasingly malevolent intentions. With the emerging centrality of Ormond, Brown adjusts Sophia's narrative focus. She moves from depicting Craig's confidence game toward a high-stakes metaphysical engagement with the process and consequences of Ormond's attempt to impose his hegemonic designs on others.

In presenting Ormond, Sophia attempts to keep things relatively simple. She will not "communicate a knowledge of his schemes.... I shall merely explain the maxims by which he was accustomed to regulate his private deportment" (*O* 112). Unlike Craig, who is not only a confidence trickster but a compulsive, sociopathic liar, Ormond is no mere predatory villain. In the figure of Ormond, Brown elevates narrative self-making to the level of a self-conscious and self-deifying metaphysic. What he pursues is not anything as base as money: Ormond has more money, it seems, than anyone else in the novel. In fact, he freely shares his wealth and often does so through acts of anonymous philanthropy. Having put the quest for money aside, Ormond pursues absolute psychological dominion over other people's lives and thus embodies the conspiratorial possibility of some dark hegemonic force—particularly regarding his association with an international conspiracy like the Illuminati—descending upon individuals and by extension the larger community.[15] In this novel, Brown dramatizes the ethical and moral implications of achieving—and then abusing—access to another person's subjectivity, the very process and consequences of imposing one's fictions on another person's life. The emerging force of Ormond's domination is made possible—and is indeed preceded—by his self-deifying rhetoric. In making his foundational arguments, Ormond imposes reductive definitions and thereby seeks to contain such encompassing entities as "mankind" and "nature" within a self-validating verbal matrix. Ormond sees human beings as cogs in the godless domain of mechanism. In "the abstract" sense, these individuals "were… impelled, by the breath of accident, in a right or a wrong road, but whatever direction they should receive, it was the property of their nature to persist in it." He views human beings as caught in a necessitated, undeviating form of inertia. Once an action becomes originated, one is impelled by mechanical consequences and prefabricated, maleficent contingencies. Ormond's view of this "social machine" is also characterized by a

> mortal poison [that] pervaded the whole system by means of which every thing received was converted into bane and purulence.... The principles of the social machine must be

[15] As with Ludloe in *Memoirs of Carwin,* Ormond has associations with the Illuminati conspirators: "Brown himself was fascinated with the Illuminati, and they figure in several of his works, including *Ormond* and *Arthur Mervyn.* But especially useful here is the way in which the hysteria surrounding the Illuminati highlights Federalist attempts to answer the question: who is the alien?" (Gardner 436). See Levine's analysis of the Illuminati conspiracy (*Conspiracy and Romance* 17–44).

> rectified, before men can be beneficially active.... Man...was part of a machine, and as such had not power to withhold his agency.... Whether he went forward, or stood still, whether his motives were malignant, or kind, or indifferent, the mass of evil was equally and necessarily augmented. (*O* 112).

From this bizarre, anomalous mix of social determinism and assumptions of universal depravity, Ormond rescues the possible efficacy of "virtue and duty," but only at the individual or personal level. Such attributes can only be self-serving, never altruistic: "[V]irtue and duty were terms without a meaning, but they require us to promote our own happiness and not the happiness of others" (*O* 112–13). By these means, he exempts himself from participating in the mechanistic, social continuum. Ormond's unspoken premise is that he places himself outside the intricacies that characterize his fatalistic system. In fact, he defines himself as a prime mover rather than a dependent participant. His "principles" describe a world view that disempowers the mass of humankind, while exempting himself from suffering a similar form of enervation (*O* 113).

This fusion of determinism and depravity creates the metaphysical basis against which Ormond empowers his solipsistic sense of the "good." Once he asserts that "the happiness of others" is unattainable, he justifies—and licenses—the pursuit of "his own good" (*O* 112–13). At the root of his sophisticated, rhetorical diminution of "mankind" is what Sophia identifies as a disparity between Ormond's words and deeds. Like even diminutive confidence tricksters, Ormond celebrates his "sincerity.... He affected to conceal nothing" (*O* 114). As Sophia suggests, "no one was more impenetrable than Ormond, though no one's real character seemed more easily discerned" (*O* 116). Given such a radical disparity between "his real and assumed characters" (*O* 117), his earnest profession of "sincerity" constitutes the rhetorical means whereby Ormond hides his intentions. He conceals through his very insistence that he has nothing to conceal. Ormond's "sincerity" is a self-congratulatory aesthetic: it reflects *affect* rather than essence. As

Levine makes clear, Sophia's analysis of Ormond has encompassing political implications that bear not only on questions concerning how Brown may or may not be speaking through Sophia but also regarding whether Sophia may, at least intermittently, serve as another embodiment of Brown's authorial self: "It seems likely, then, that Brown structured Sophia's narrative to convey his own distrust of the Federalists' countersubversive tactics during a time when, under the duress of the Alien and Sedition Laws, a more direct attack would have left him vulnerable to the charge of high misdemeanor" (*Conspiracy and Romance* 41).

In sketching the contours of Ormond's character, Sophia casts herself as audience and adjudicator. She presents his "maxims" (*O* 112) as a prelude to critiquing them: "In listening to his discourse, no one's claim to sincerity appeared less questionable. A somewhat different conclusion would be suggested by a survey of his actions" (*O* 114–15). Thus, Sophia introduces Ormond's histrionic attributes: "In early youth he discovered in himself a remarkable facility in imitating the voice and gestures of others. His memory was eminently retentive, and these qualities would have rendered his career, in the theatrical profession, illustrious, had not his condition raised him above it" (*O* 115). In outlining Ormond's acting ability, Sophia reconstructs—and enlarges on—those very attributes that Brown uses to delineate Carwin's character. Ormond can assume any role: he can be a shape-shifter, an American Proteus, whose elemental conviction is that people and social forms are constructed and therefore susceptible to imitation and imposture. Like Carwin, Ormond uses artistic forms to control life. Once, in seeking to redress an undefined wrong, he "assumed a borrowed character and guise, and performed his part with so much skill as fully to accomplish his design" (*O* 115). It is not such histrionic actions, however, that distinguish Ormond from a miscreant like Craig. Craig's obsession with imposture never permits him to establish a self-protective distance. He succeeds in hurting others, but only as a prelude to victimizing himself: as Constantia points out, Craig "always persisted till he made himself the dupe of his own artifices" (*O* 150). What distinguishes Ormond from Craig is Ormond's reflexivity, self-control, and self-awareness—his critical recognition of how "those powers...are so liable to be abused." Seemingly describing the self-defeating tricksterism of Craig, Sophia indicates that a "subtlety much inferior to Ormond's would suffice to recommend this mode of action." Mere "necessity" is sufficient to draw one to committing acts of imposture (*O* 115). Ormond, however, is moved by "other considerations." What Ormond wants to possess is not another person's money or material property, but the very interiority that Sophia views as fundamentally ineffable. Ormond wishes to penetrate an individual's "privacy," an especially depraved form of transgression that amounts to an unauthorized assault on one's essential identity. In using artistic means to control contingency, Ormond pursues power:

> He was delighted with the power [that imposture] conferred. It enabled him to gain access, as if by supernatural means, to the privacy of others, and baffle their profoundest contrivances to hide themselves from his view. It flattered him with the possession of something like Omniscience. It was besides an art, in which, as in others, every accession of skill, was a source of new gratification. Compared with this the performance of the actor is the sport of children. This profession he was accustomed to treat with merciless ridicule, and no doubt, some of his contempt arose from a secret comparison, between the theatrical species of imitation and his own. He blended in his own person the functions of poet and actor, and his dramas were not fictitious but real. The end that he proposed was not the amusement of a playhouse mob. His were scenes in which hope and fear exercised a genuine influence, and in which was maintained that resemblance to truth, so audaciously and grossly violated on the stage. (*O* 116)

In this way, the unscrupulous artist-in-life becomes a secret witness or a calculating, manipulative voyeur. In order to discover the means whereby he can influence the Dudley family with "beneficent acts," Ormond disguises himself as a black chimneysweep:

> He resolved, without hesitation, to supply their wants. This he performed in a manner truly characteristic. There was a method of gaining access to families, and marking them in their unguarded attitudes more easy and effectual than any other.... The disguise, also, was of the most impenetrable kind.... It was the most entire and grotesque metamorphosis imaginable. It was stepping from the highest to the lowest rank in society, and shifting himself into a form, as remote from his own, as those recorded by Ovid. (*O* 133–34)

His transformation, like Carwin's in *Wieland*, reflects Ormond's most American attribute. Again, like Carwin, Ormond operates as an American Proteus. In using his body for a kind of performance art, in revealing himself to be an inveterate shape-shifter, he accentuates the dynamic fluidity of social forms. The apparent difference between the "highest" and "lowest" is merely a matter of histrionic enactment. Indeed, the world as theater is not simply Ormond's most characteristic and self-reflexive trope: it is his animating principle that impels his conquests and creates the medium through which others become unwitting participants in his schemes. Once in the Dudley home, hidden within his masquerade, he "viewed every thing with the accuracy of an artist, and carried away with him a catalogue of every thing visible" (*O* 135). In taking over the Dudley family debts, he appears to be altruistic. Actually, however, he is propping himself up to be a determinant force in their lives.

A major consequence of Ormond's accession to the Dudley household emerges as Constantia and Ormond become rival discussants regarding his abusive treatment of Helena Cleves. As Ormond's concubine, Helena is a woman characterized by physical beauty and diminutive intellect. With unabashed insistence, Ormond degrades her. He sees—and uses—Helena "merely as an object charming to the senses" (*O* 120). Ormond "wanted instruments and not partakers of his authority" (*O* 128). A defenseless innocent, "artless and ingenuous," Helena is easy prey. Part of her victimization resides in her loss of self-possession and self-containment: "[Ormond] was her divinity to whom every sentiment was visible.... [I]t was the same thing to speak and to think in his presence" (*O* 125). Her status as sexual plaything follows from his usurpation of her inner life, his insistence on his own hegemonic preeminence. Ormond asserts the priority of male dominance as the central feature of his misogynist gender politics: "To make her wise it would be requisite to change her sex. He had forgotten that his pupil was a female, and her capacity therefore limited by nature" (*O* 129). She is—or through his offices becomes—the living embodiment of form without substance, merely ornamental, a vessel to be filled.

Appalled by Helena's debasement, Constantia becomes a judgmental reader of Ormond's schemes: "What unauthorised conceptions of matrimonial and political equality did he entertain! He had fashioned his treatment of Helena on sullen and ferocious principles. Yet he was able, it seemed, to mould her, by means of them, nearly into the creature that he wished" (*O* 140). Constantia Dudley embodies a reconfiguration of *Alcuin*'s Mrs. Carter, a protective and liberated female mind released from the confinements of drawing room dialectics and completely capable of confronting an adversary worthy of her attention. In defense of Helena, Constantia proclaims, "The intercourse must cease" (*O* 141). Helena's predicament focuses the terms of the contest taking place between Ormond and Constantia, specifically regarding the issue of marriage. In *Ormond*, marriage offers the context for either a loving union of companionate mutuality, the prospective ideal espoused by Constantia; or marriage constitutes an abusive compact sustained by dominating male egotism, the insidious goal of Ormond. Constantia insists that Ormond and Helena must marry and that, once married, Ormond should attempt "to rectify deliberate errors and change his course by the change of his principles" (*O* 146). Rather than trying to control Helena, Constantia attempts to assist her toward having a companionate (instead of a subservient) relationship with Ormond.

Rather than convincing Ormond to treat Helena with justice, Constantia succeeds in drawing Ormond's predatory gaze to herself. Ormond finds their spirited arguments charming. Indeed, these dialogues resonate for him with the power of sensual stimulation: "Constantia delighted her companion by the facility with which she entered into his meaning, the sagacity she displayed in drawing out his hints, circumscribing his conjectures, and thwarting or qualifying his maxims. The scene was generally replete with ardour and contention, and yet the impression left on the mind of Ormond was full of harmony" (158). For Constantia, their dialogues genuinely concern the adjudication, and possible rectification, of Helena's humiliating predicament. For Ormond, these discussions mask his predatory sub-text. Ormond expects to dominate Constantia and is surprised, even stimulated, by her rhetorical prowess. He responds by perceiving her, mistakenly, as a version of himself: "Her discourse tended to rouse him from his lethargy, to furnish him with powerful excitements, and the time spent in her company, seemed like a doubling of existence" (*O* 158). Significantly, he perceives her ability to reason as possessing "a manlike energy" (*O* 159). Constantia, however, is not anything like Ormond. His narcissistic projection blinds him to the fact that her immutable essence will dictate her behavior. Ormond rejects Helena as a desirable object and proceeds to offer Constantia his hand in marriage. He dangles before her the lure of obtaining complete access to the intricacies of his own being. He claims that he will tender himself as an object to be dominated: "And now, say truly, are you willing to accept Ormond with all his faults? Who but yourself could be mistress of all the springs of my soul?...Is there no part of me in which you discover your own likeness?" (*O* 166–67). Ormond merely enacts the rhetorical form he believes will ensnare Constantia. What motivates Ormond is the desire to possess—rather than merely subjugate—this putative equal: "He entertained little doubt of his ultimate success with Constance" (*O* 168–69).

Helena's suicide makes way for the drama attending Ormond's focused pursuit of Constantia. His sense of life as theater and his nihilistic predilections lead him to view Helena's death as nothing more than "[a] piteous spectacle! But what else, on an ampler scale, is the universe? Nature is a theatre of suffering. What corner is unvisited by calamity and pain...Thou has done my work for me" (*O* 171). Brown uses Helena's death to reconstruct the social scene. Helena leaves Constantia her worldly goods. Her death and bequest resolve the economic hardships that hitherto impelled the plot and thus clear the way for the climactic power play between Ormond and Constantia.

"This Spectacle of Death"

The fact that Ormond, in his narcissism, misreads Constantia as a version of himself informs his ironic and ultimately self-defeating quest to undermine and then destroy this (grossly mistaken) sense of mutuality. In this mission, he remains steadfast in his use of histrionic methods, specifically through subliminal forms of manipulation:

> Ormond aspired to nothing more ardently than to hold the reins of opinion. To exercise absolute power over the conduct of others, not by constraining their limbs, or by exacting obedience to his authority, but in a way of which his subjects should be scarcely conscious. He desired that his guidance should controul their steps, but that his agency, when most effectual, should be least suspected. (*O* 177)

Having become for the Dudley family "the authour of extensive benefits" (*O* 176), Ormond feels that he now has the right "to govern the thoughts of Constantia, or to regulate her condition" (*O* 177). He wishes that she become, like Helena, a personification of his desire. He intends not only to manipulate Constantia's thoughts, but to eradicate her independence: "The person and affections of this woman, were the objects sought by him, and which it was the dearest purpose of his existence to gain. This was his supreme good." The key issue here is that he seeks histrionic control over her being: "Constance was to be obtained by any means" (*O* 178). He would marry her if he must, but "only when every expedient was exhausted, for reconciling her to a compact of a different kind" (*O* 178–79). In order to make his way, Ormond "prescribed to himself, a path suited to the character of this lady.... [I]f he were unable to effect a change in her creed, he was determined to adopt a system of imposture. To assume the guise of a convert to her doctrines, and appear as devout as herself in his notions of the sanctity of marriage" (*O* 179).

Ormond does not realize that Constantia mounts a penetrating, critical examination of him that constitutes its own form of empowerment. In attempting to distinguish between public form and private essence, she accepts as a given Ormond's capacity for imposture. As with her earlier suitor Balfour, she relies on time's passage to expose the truth of Ormond's inner self. A more astute reader of character than Ormond is willing to admit, Constantia begins with the premise that "Ormond was imperfectly known." Her knowledge of him "flowed chiefly from his own lips, and was therefore unattended with certainty. What portion of deceit or disguise was mixed with his conversation, could be known, only by witnessing his actions with her own eyes, and comparing his testimony with that of others" (*O* 181). Casting herself as spectator, investigator, and judge, she has faith that her observations and research will culminate in what Sophia calls a "just delineation of the character of Ormond" (*O* 111). Constantia is in exactly the same position as the narrator, although Constantia does not share Sophia's belief in the intrinsic inscrutability of the other.

One might, at this point, wonder why Ormond has become so malevolent, such a monstrosity. On the one hand, his antagonistic stance seems partially dictated by Brown's desire to wrench the plot toward a highly-pitched (and sexualized) confrontational climax. More significantly, Ormond's emerging malevolence seems a consequence of his expanding desire for enacting "something like Omniscience" (*O* 116). With overt insistence, Ormond goes beyond the confines of his implied politicized association with the subversive Illuminati and casts himself as the determinant force in a universe he finds bereft of providential order: "The universe was to him, a series of events, connected by an undesigning and inscrutable necessity, and an assemblage of forms, to which no beginning or end can be conceived" (*O* 180). Ormond does away with any cosmology of origin or ending, substituting a never-ending, non-transcendent unfolding of brute, mechanical processes that actually anticipates some of the material assumptions regarding force that later inform the philosophical and scientific foundations of American literary naturalism.[16] The histrionic, power-obsessed Ormond intends to subvert this "inscrutable necessity" or what he later identifies as "Fate" (*O* 254). Through the self-enabling power of rhetorical declamation, he identifies himself with omniscience: "What do I know? Every thing. Not a tittle has escaped me. Thy letter is superfluous: I know its contents before they are written" (*O* 256). Reminiscent of Ludloe's claims to omniscience in *Memoirs of Carwin*, Ormond attempts to scare Constantia by foretelling a future of irrevocable horror. According to Ormond, what *will* happen to Constantia already *has*: "Shall I warn thee of the danger that awaits thee? For what end? To elude it, is impossible.... Foresight, that enables not to shun, only pre-creates the evil.... Though future, it knows not the empire of contingency. An inexorable and immutable decree enjoins it" (*O* 258). This convoluted utterance offers either a proposition to be examined or testimony to a life already scripted and predetermined. Ormond insists on his capacity for determining teleological certainty. Later, when confronting Constantia over the corpse of the recently murdered Craig, Ormond proclaims himself the enactor of his own prophecy: "Have you forgotten, said Ormond, what past at our last interview? The evil that I then predicted is at hand. Perhaps, you were

---

[16] See Ronald E. Martin for a discussion of the philosophical, scientific, and literary dimensions associated with "force" in the late nineteenth century.

incredulous: You accounted me a madman or deceiver: Now I am come to witness the fulfillment of my words, and the completion of your destiny. To rescue you, I have not come: That is not within the compass of human powers" (*O* 274). Ormond casts his life in the form of a script that he promulgates, first, as immutable, and, then, as a matter for his own execution. Within his self-generated, self-authorized master-fiction, he describes himself as the prime mover of events. After rejecting the existence of providence, he injects himself into the very void that his rhetoric ostensibly created. He figures himself as both a transcendent consciousness and a dramatic performer. Even Sophia contemplates the possibility that Ormond possesses supernatural status:

> Meanings, of which she and her friend alone were conscious, were discovered by Ormond, through some other medium than words: Yet that was impossible: A being, unendowed with preternatural attributes, could gain the information which this man possessed, only by the exertion of his senses.
>
> All human precautions had been used, to baffle the attempts of any secret witness.... All had been retirement, secrecy and silence. (*O* 260)

Ormond has either successfully projected himself into a transcendent realm or he has assumed this status via rhetorical assertions and hidden spectatorship, which coincided with an unusual, yet putatively explicable, means of accessing such hidden knowledge.

By either actually possessing or merely proclaiming an *a priori* apprehension of Constantia's unformulated thoughts, Ormond celebrates his power to collapse the distance separating one human subject from another. The repudiation of Constantia's right to psychological privacy reflects his desire to possess her subjectivity and turn her into an object only he can enjoy. Ormond has already blackmailed Craig into murdering Mr. Dudley. Ormond later murdered Craig. His self-proclaimed accession to transcendent status imbues him, so he believes, with the right and power to kill people and justify these murders according to the very exigencies that impel his purposes. Upon identifying himself as "the authour of [her father's] fate" (276), Ormond asserts a kind of deific rectitude: "My motive was benevolent: My deed conferred a benefit. I gave him sight and took away his life, from motives equally wise" (*O* 280). He construes Constantia as a co-conspirator: "My happiness and your's, depended on your concurrence with my wishes. Your father's life was an obstacle to your concurrence. For killing him, therefore, I may claim your gratitude. His death was a due and disinterested offering, at the altar of your felicity and mine" (*O* 281).

Ormond associates his will with fate and the narrative's final movement tests the efficacy of this supreme fiction—that is, his attempts to actualize his assertions of deific status. Life is his theater, and he casts himself as the dominant author and actor. For Ormond, marriage has always been a conceptual prop that he uses to advance his inmost desires. Just as he controlled the physical and psychological being of Helena, so too does Ormond seek to possess Constantia sexually and he intends to do so by raping her. He tells Constantia, "I have come hither to possess myself of all that I now crave" (*O* 282). He would even violate her corpse: "Living or dead, the prize that I have in view shall be mine" (*O* 285). Acting in self-defense, Constantia takes her knife, stabs Ormond to death, and eradicates his fiction of deific status.

In dramatizing *Ormond*'s conclusion, Brown emphasizes the narrative's dialectical intensities and histrionic framework. In confirming that the novel form is an inherently unstable medium, Brown opts for earthly consciousness and narrative indeterminacy as (ironic) staples in an epistemologically open-ended and, perhaps, inexplicable world—complexes that achieve their apotheosis in *Arthur Mervyn; or, Memoirs of the Year 1793*.

5

Arthur and the Ambiguities: *Arthur Mervyn, or Memoirs of the Year 1793 First and Second Parts*

Moral Exemplification and the Arts of Ambiguity

After Dr. Stevens discovers the homeless, disabled, and wasted Arthur Mervyn propped against a wall, he consults with his wife as to whether this indigent stranger might be taken into their home or "consent to be carried" to the hospital (*AM* 6). Cognizant of the "mortal stenches" (*AM* 173), the unspeakable squalor and contagion awaiting the stranger there, Eliza Stevens replies, "[T]alk not of hospitals." Despite the palpable threat posed by housing a randomly encountered feverish victim of the "reigning malady" (*AM* 6), the deadly yellow fever epidemic ravaging Philadelphia in 1793, the Stevenses open their doors and enact those "lessons of justice and humanity" that Charles Brockden Brown in his "Preface" associates with the ethical purpose of his "humble narrative."[1] As in earlier prefaces, Brown pays overt homage to the conventional notion that the novelist—this "moral observer" (*AM* 3)—valorizes literary art as a vehicle of moral exemplification: "He that depicts, in lively colours, the evils of disease and poverty, performs an eminent service to the sufferers, by calling forth benevolence in those who are able to afford relief, and he who pourtrays examples of disinterestedness and intrepidity, confers on virtue the notoriety and homage that are due to it, and rouses in the spectators, the spirit of salutary emulation" (*AM* 3). Given this premise, it follows that Mrs.

[1] See Grabo, "Historical Note," for an account of the 1793 yellow fever epidemic in Philadelphia (447–49). Also see Ellis. Grabo summarizes the genesis and serialization of this novel between June 16, 1798 and August 23, 1798 as well as the relationship between the novel's two parts (450–62).

Stevens would expect that subsequent "consequences" will reflect the unfolding power and purpose of providential design: "Let us take the poor unfortunate wretch into our protection and care, and leave the consequences to Heaven" (*AM* 6). Her faith in Providence complements and augments her charitable ethos. Her position presupposes a fixed value system characterized by the determinate power of transcendent authority, with the attending conviction that this sovereign God acts as the author of experience. Like his wife, Dr. Stevens performs the offices of a Good Samaritan. Serving as the first narrator in this frame tale, Dr. Stevens enacts his benevolent design and allows Arthur Mervyn to recuperate and present his lengthy, elliptical story.

Rather than circumscribing the purpose of his novel, however, Brown uses the profession of moral didacticism in the "Preface" to afford a stable point of departure and reference, one that remains associated with the virtue espoused by the Stevens. This un-ambiguous perspective provides the novel's moral and ethical center around which circulate multiple ambiguities attending Arthur Mervyn and his insistent, often problematic, attempts to discover and shape his various, sometimes discordant, performative identities. It is possible that Brown's depiction of disinterested benevolence as a core concept in *Arthur Mervyn* owes much to William Godwin's extended 1793 analysis of this complex in *An Enquiry Concerning Political Justice*:

> The system of disinterested benevolence proves to us, that it is possible to be virtuous, and not merely talk of virtue...and that, when we call upon mankind to divest themselves of selfish and personal consideration, we call upon them for something they are able to practice. An idea like this reconciles us to our species; teaches us to regard with enlightened admiration the men who have appeared to lose the feeling of their personal existence in the pursuit of general advantage; and gives us reason to expect, that...they will proceed more and more to consolidate their private judgment and their

> individual will with abstract justice and the unmixed approbation of general happiness. (359–60)

At issue is whether Brown applies this foundational concept of eighteenth-century social theory with the same steadfast "approbation" as suggested by Godwin. At the critical center of this novel resides the open-ended question of whether Mervyn's various ambiguities of thought, word, and deed create an interpretive framework that dramatize not so much the fusion of abstract theory and social practice regarding disinterested benevolence as those conflicted circumstances wherein Mervyn's thoughts, words, and deeds might be seen as sincere and ironic simultaneously—with either position serving as a dialectical counterpoint affirming the interpretive validity of its opposite. In fact, Godwin could very easily be describing Mervyn's pervasive doubleness: "If men of virtue be frequently misinterpreted or misunderstood, this is in a great degree to be ascribed to the imperfection of their virtue and the errors of their conduct" (368).[2]

"The Figure of a Man.... Disabled by Sickness"

In the *First Part*, Mervyn tries to explain disturbing allegations levied by Dr. Stevens' friend Wortley that accuse Mervyn of complicity in

[2] A subject of much philosophical inquiry in the eighteenth century, disinterested benevolence was a core concept in Jonathan Edwards' *The Nature of True Virtue* (1755), which Elihu Hubbard Smith read on December 30–31, 1796 (*Diary* 279). It is hard to imagine that Smith and Brown would not have discussed the emotional, social, and theological implications of benevolence with or without reference to Edwards. Fliegelman argues, "[T]he fast and the thanksgiving sermons of the postwar period are full of attempts at reconciling the self-interested nature of patriotism with the Christian ethic of disinterested benevolence. That ethic declared all sin and depravity the result of selfishness and limited love. It insisted that to love being in general was the truest way of loving God, the ultimate principle of being" (228). For Brown, the proving ground for the exercise of benevolence is not patriotism but the histrionic implications deriving from one's totalizing embrace of altruistic forms of self-making. Benevolence, then, becomes manifest in Brown's attempt to dramatize how the ambiguous imperatives embraced by Mervyn might offer a paradigm of a newfound social order.

criminal schemes perpetrated by Thomas Welbeck, the novel's preeminent, self-making trickster. Within Stevens' encompassing narrative, Mervyn—himself a case study in ambiguity—gradually reveals how he came to be found in such a destitute condition, a circumstance that requires him to explain his problematic association with Welbeck. What ultimately appears to be true or false will have everything to do with the credibility and ethos of each respective narrator, a particularly significant issue for Mervyn at the outset of the *Second Part*. Essentially, the *First Part* presents a reconstruction of Mervyn's evolution as tyro actor. A second son like Carwin, he leaves home and travels toward the moment where he constructs his social identity. Mervyn's task is to fill in the events that constitute his version of the past so that Stevens might render an informed judgment regarding Wortley's hectoring claims against him.[3]

In this novel, Brown largely eschews the epistolary form to create a multilayered mock-oral narrative that possesses an intrinsically protean form.[4] Mervyn's tale emerges through his dramatically rendered speech act. His lengthy monologues are improvisational performances that bring the reader directly into Mervyn's re-lived, orally reconstituted experiences. Mervyn's purpose is to lead his auditors to a full understanding of how Stevens found him confined within a kind of tableau portrait, "the figure of a man.... disabled by sickness" (*AM* 5). The completion of this dialogue between Stevens and Mervyn in the

---

[3] Elliott explores the problematic contours of Mervyn's character, his contradictions and narrative distortions, and examines the issue of whether he figures as an American Adam or an inveterate trickster. See 234–65.

[4] See Blair and Hill for their discussion of how oral discourse can become transfigured into a narrative "framework": "Oral sources, possibly, and oral influences, certainly, are indicated when 'a framework' pictures a storyteller spinning his yarn and an audience listening, while within this framework a narrative is quoted directly. The same shaping forces are indicated, though less clearly, when the author omits the framework but quotes the narrative in the words of a vernacular raconteur. The resulting narrative might be called 'a mock oral tale.' Both the story enclosed in a frame and the mock oral tale constantly imitate common speech" (30).

First Part eventually positions Brown to dramatize the consequences of Mervyn's subsequent reentry into the larger social world. Toward the end of the *Second Part*, Mervyn's narrative is no longer contained within the frame of Dr. Stevens' telling. As an expression of his expanding sense of purpose and self-empowerment, Mervyn takes over the story-telling role when he agrees to "carry on thy thread" within his own epistolary account (*AM* 354). As these permutations of narrative perspective suggest, the ground of authority never moves beyond rhetorical enactments of limited first-person narrators.[5] For example, near the beginning of the novel, Stevens invites Mervyn to tell his tale and exonerate himself. Stevens insists that Mervyn's ethical responsibility is to reject the promise of secrecy made to Welbeck. Mervyn agrees that he has a "duty to repair [Welbeck's injury to Wortley] to the utmost of [his] power." Mervyn realizes that he can maintain Stevens' "good opinion only by a candid deportment" (*AM* 15). Brown places Mervyn's tale somewhere between the Stevens' unwavering association of moral actions that align with the dispensations of providence, on the one hand, and Welbeck's histrionic attempts to engage in manipulation and imposture, on the other. Throughout the novel, the protean contours of Arthur Mervyn's identity—expressed through recurrent attempts at narrative self-making—oscillate between the twin extremes of altruistic beneficence and insidious manipulation. Whereas substantial arguments can be mustered regarding the validity of both positions, certainty never obtains.

A Man without a Plot

With the world all before him, Mervyn leaves his fractured home and marches forth essentially bereft: he carries a scant supply of money, a bundle of clothes, iconic memories of his dead mother, and a self-

[5] Davidson sees in Brown's delineation of Mervyn a proto-modern approach to depicting character: "Brown posits an intriguingly modern concept of personality, an awareness of fragmentation—the mutable, indeterminate, changeling self" (*Revolution and the Word* 253).

portrait of the late Clavering.[6] While possessing few resources and no prospects, this naïf journeys in the optimistic spirit of new world discovery: "I must build a name and a fortune for myself" (*AM* 25). After swiftly losing what little he has, he confronts a condition of experiential openness out of which the novel incrementally emerges.[7] In this destitute state, lacking preconceptions or plans, he finds himself dependent upon the consequences of accidental events. In Mervyn's story, Brown combines the capricious contingencies of the picaresque narrative with the psychological and emotional focus of an episodic action-adventure story.[8] In becoming the paradoxical sum of his incremental losses, he is open to transformational possibility: "The novelty which environed every object was, therefore, nearly absolute.... I reached the market-house, and entering it, indulged myself in new delight and new wonder" (*AM* 27–28). At this point, Brown's subject *is* newness itself, the emergent novelty of irruptive experience. Having lost everything,

---

[6] See Fliegelman on Ben Franklin and the personal and cultural implications that attend one's attempt to break from a father's control (107–13). Axelrod describes analogies between Mervyn's life and Benjamin Franklin (142–44). Christophersen summarizes the critical tradition that sees Mervyn as possessing "a prototypical American identity" (90).

[7] Kafer interprets young Mervyn and his departure from home as a fictional figuration of Brown's father Elijah and the ways in which he "had profoundly embodied the country/city dichotomy...in the late 1750s" (138).

[8] Davidson notes that "the picaresque continually blurs oppositions into ambiguities. It is even tempting to argue that the often confusing (and often confined) cosmology of the picaresque more nearly represented the mentality of many late eighteenth-century Americans than did the eloquent delineations of republican ideology argued by the Founding Fathers and their most vociferous opponents" (*Revolution and the Word* 153; also see 163–65). The picaresque is an appropriate form for reconstructing Mervyn's rambling, wayward encounters with its focus on his interactions with members of the non-elite classes and his predicaments that seem disconnected to any preconceived purpose.

Mervyn retains nothing but the inchoate self that is ready for the next new experience.[9]

Because of such a ground-clearing process, Mervyn becomes a man without a plot. He lacks a directed sense of social identity and experiential purpose. His reconstructed account of the events that lead him over five days to the point where he is rescued by the Stevens indicates how Mervyn passively accepts the circumstances, the designs, the artifices, and the manipulations that the random vagaries of life impose upon him. Once he has parted with his money and small bundle of possessions, he does not so much *act*. Instead, he is *acted upon* and finds himself enmeshed within a web-work of epistemological and teleological mystery. For example, while mulling a return to the agrarian life recently forsaken, Mervyn encounters an affable young man, who seems to befriend the penniless naïf. This smooth-talking stranger pays for Mervyn's dinner and invites the homeless youth to share his room for the night. Brown has brought Mervyn to the point of experiential openness. Anything might happen, or not. The novel depicts the unfolding script that bit by bit shapes the emergent social self. Through this charming stranger, identified later as Wallace, an object of Mervyn's pursuit in the *Second Part*, Brown places Mervyn on a pathway that leads him to explore indeterminate, dramatic situations. The stranger unlocks the door and says, "This...is my room: Permit me to welcome you into it" (*AM* 34). Mervyn's simple purpose—to sleep in this ostensibly kind gentleman's room—inducts him an amorphous array of possible plot lines. As Mervyn later discovers, the fiction-making Wallace claims to have entrapped the youth for ill-conceived purposes of jest. Brown, however, uses this episodic set-piece as a passageway into larger issues dominating the novel, especially as reflected in Brown's preoccupation with exploring the contingent costs of self-fashioned performances.

---

[9] See Terence Martin for his discussion of how the possibilities of America are often depicted in terms of negative catalogues—that is, though a listing of what is not there (3).

Wallace takes Mervyn into a luxurious house that becomes for Mervyn a Gothic projection of darkness and uncertainty. The house reflects a microcosmic image of the strange, protean world that implicitly contrasts with the Stevenses' stable world view and its counterpart in providential order. Despite wondering ineffectually "upon the possible designs of this person" (*AM* 33), Mervyn surrenders his volition. In the dark room, he has no idea what the next moment will bring. There can be no order, no form, and no direction until something happens. Thus, Brown presents an incubating period of anxious expectation. Plot possibilities proliferate. As Mervyn stands in the room, the stranger leaves with the announced purpose of getting another light. Wallace, however, turns out the light and does not return. In fact, upon departing, he locks the door, no doubt to heighten impending complications. Mervyn thus becomes a pawn in a scenario that impels him toward serendipitous encounters. Within this inchoate episode, Mervyn hears a sound from the bed and wonders: "Where, said I, will this adventure terminate?" (*AM* 35). He knows that he is careening along an undefined path. He even imagines that his "adventure" will become the source of future narrative recitations when the facts of the present will seem a fanciful, fabulous fiction: "When this night is remembered, how like a vision will it appear! If I tell the tale by a kitchen fire, my veracity will be disputed. I shall be ranked with the story tellers of Shirauz and Bagdad" (*AM* 35). His conjectures are interrupted when he hears a sound in the room that might have been a groan from "a sleeping man" (*AM* 36). He worries about the "consequence" of being detected there and questions the motives of his "conductor." In one breath, he concludes: "No doubt I had been the victim of malicious artifice" (*AM* 35). Shortly thereafter, he ponders: "Was his imposture a jestful or a wicked one?" (*AM* 36). He then thinks that the sleeper might be a woman, though it turns out to be an infant. Subsequently, a husband and wife enter the room. Tormented, huddled in the closet, Mervyn worries about what might soon happen to him. A profusion of subjunctives qualifies his verbs:

> I cannot describe the mixture of dread and of shame which glowed in my veins. The light in which such a visitant would be probably regarded by a woman's fears, the precipitate alarms that might be given, the injury which I might unknowingly inflict or undeservedly suffer, threw my thoughts into painful confusion. My presence might pollute a spotless reputation or furnish fuel to jealousy. (*AM* 36)

It might and it might not. The future has yet to happen. Mervyn becomes a pawn of circumstances set into motion by a diminutive trickster, whose arbitrarily engendered plot unfolds without apparent direction. Any number of possibilities might derive from these unscripted events. Indeed, the man without a plot ruminates over some conceivable scenarios: "I pictured to myself their entrance and my own detection. I could imagine no consequence that was not disastrous and horrible.... I waited impatiently for some token by which I might be governed" (*AM* 37). One possibility is that he will be trapped within a design directed by a divine agent: "I put up prayers to my deity that he would deliver me from these toils. What a condition was mine! Immersed in palpable darkness! shut up in this unknown recess! lurking like a robber!" (*AM* 37–38). From a societal perspective, what he will *be*, or how he will achieve definition, depends on how his presence in the closet will be interpreted. Should he simply announce that he is there? Will he be able escape undetected or will he be exposed *in flagrante*, as it were, and accused of robbery or even conspiracy to commit a sex crime?

Hiding in the closet, shoes off, Mervyn becomes a secret witness to a complex interaction between Thetford and his wife. The woman, who recently lost her baby, is not the mother of the infant in the room, although Thetford may be the child's father with the possible plan of insinuating this baby into his wife's affections as a replacement child. Mervyn overhears the couple discussing a prospective scheme that will involve defrauding a man, presumably Welbeck, of thirty thousand dollars. He listens to this fragmented conversation and tries to understand the meaning of these events. As he listens, he realizes that fiction-making is a process diametrically opposed to providential order: "How baseless are the structures of falsehood, which we build in opposition to the system of eternal nature" (*AM* 39). Mervyn's speculation accentuates the intrinsic epistemological uncertainty of human behavior and story-telling. In fact, the novel explores whether "structures of falsehood"—human constructs in general as well as those narrative falsehoods we call fictions—might somehow provide a basis for a non-transcendent ethical structure.

At this point, however, this issue gets little more than glancing attention as Mervyn, bereft of his shoes, manages to escape undetected from the closet, the room, and the house. Mervyn immediately treats his closet experience as a subject for hermeneutical conjecture: "I seated myself on the ground and reviewed the scenes through which I had just passed." He conjures a series of alternative actions: "I began to think that my industry had been misemployed. Suppose I had met the person on his first entrance into his chamber? Was the truth so utterly wild as not to have found credit?" (*AM* 45). In this passage, Mervyn becomes a critical reader of his own experience. Having achieved a temporal distance from the event, he considers what Thetford and his wife might think when they discover his abandoned shoes. In his reflections, Mervyn transfigures himself into both imaginative artist and rapt audience: "Now that I was safe I could not help smiling at the picture which my fancy drew of their anxiety and wonder" (*AM* 45–46).

"The Folly of Precipitate Inferences"

With this episode concluded without embarrassing consequences, Mervyn by chance meets Thomas Welbeck—a man Warner Berthoff describes as a "Byronic forger" (64) and "conscienceless criminal" (65)—and finds himself within the grip of the novel's most powerful fiction-maker. Welbeck joins Carwin, Ludloe, Craig, and Ormond as "double-tongued" (*W* 1) protean figures addicted to "imposture" (*AM*

58)—duplicitous men who view the social world as a stage and other people as dupes in their soon-to-be enacted scripts.[10]

A homeless tyro, Mervyn has no sense of the future other than a vague desire to return to the country. In response to this impasse, Mervyn solicits an apparently well-to-do stranger for a loan: "[Welbeck] looked at me and started" (*AM* 48). Whereas Mervyn perceives a potential benefactor, Welbeck sees a young man resembling the late Vincentio Lodi, Jr., the deceased brother of Welbeck's mistress, Clemenza Lodi, who Mervyn mistakenly imagines to be Welbeck's daughter.[11] In recognizing a host of dramatic possibilities, Welbeck takes Mervyn to a well-stocked bedroom closet and offers him a new identity: "Here is everything your nakedness requires." Mervyn is all too ready to embrace

> this instantaneous transfiguration.... Appearances are wonderfully influenced by dress.... I could scarcely forbear looking back to see whether the image in the glass, so well proportioned, so gallant, and so graceful, did not belong to another. I could scarcely recognize any lineaments of my own.... Twenty minutes ago, said I, I was traversing that path a barefoot beggar; now am I thus.... Some magic that disdains the cumbrousness of nature's progress, has wrought this change. (*AM* 51).

Welbeck authors the "lineaments" of Mervyn's new performative self that he will try to direct toward his own crafty ends. Inducting Mervyn into a gestating plot, Welbeck hires him as a copyist for the yet-to-be

---

[10] See Kafer's discussion of a possible source for Welbeck in John Swanwick, an alleged swindler with failed political ambitions (88–92). Kafer sees Swanwick as "a 'Proteus,' whose own tragic and bitter end, with its acute financial embarrassment and bankruptcy in 1797 and death in July 1798 as a victim of the yellow fever, adumbrated the fictional end of Welbeck in 1793 in Philadelphia" (91).

[11] See Boyd's discussion of Clavering's self-portrait and her discussion of Mervyn's resemblance to Clavering and Vincentio Lodi (498–99).

disclosed transcription of a manuscript purloined from the deceased Lodi.

A prospective pawn in Welbeck's game, Mervyn can view Welbeck's exterior self but cannot comprehend those machinations lurking behind the mask: "[Welbeck's] features were fraught with a meaning which I was eager to interpret but unable." Mervyn can only continue to marvel at the extremity of his surface metamorphosis: "I have read of transitions effected by magic.... but I am certain that no transition was ever conceived more marvellous and more beyond the reach of foresight, than that which I had just experienced" (*AM* 53). Mervyn wonders about Welbeck's purpose as Welbeck tells him that "[n]ext week we will enter on the task for which I designed you" (*AM* 56). Characteristically, Mervyn resorts to conjecture to explain, and thus normalize, Welbeck's schemes. In the context of Mervyn's ruminations regarding whether Welbeck will adopt him and in light of his delusion that he might marry Welbeck's ostensible daughter (but actual mistress), Mervyn reveals a lurking skeptical strain as he recognizes how even legal, familial identity might lack efficacy: "Identity itself frequently depends upon a casual likeness or an old nurse's imposture" (*AM* 57–58). As one of Brown's recurrent seed words, "imposture" sums up the fiction-making process, especially insofar as testimony, or assertion, whether grounded in fact or plausibility, supplies the shaky premise for the constructed, histrionic domain of human society. Indeed, social identity itself often constitutes one of this novel's "structures of falsehood" (*AM* 39). In this light, Jane Tomkins views the protean Welbeck as a figure of huge political importance: "Welbeck is the arch-subverter of the social currency; he is a seducer—both of women and of men...he is a counterfeiter...and he is a liar.... Welbeck attacks the social system at its base by subverting the means by which it reproduces itself, sustains itself, and communicates with itself" (75).

Central to Welbeck's nefarious designs and to Mervyn's newly fabricated social identity is Welbeck's insistence that Mervyn maintain "silence to all but himself, on the subject of my birth and early adventures" (*AM* 62). Consequently, Mervyn finds himself uncertain of what Welbeck intends. Pleased to have escaped his un-housed condition, Mervyn nevertheless resists the strident terms underlying Welbeck's stipulations. The imperious Welbeck stands as nothing less than author and director of Mervyn's mystery plot: "To act under the guidance of another, and to wander in the dark, ignorant whither my path tended, and what effects might flow from my agency was a new and irksome situation" (*AM* 63). What is most "irksome" is that Mervyn is now an actor in a plot for which he has no script. Locked in the present, Mervyn does not understand why Welbeck wants him to say nothing about his past, but it seems clear that Welbeck intends to invent for Mervyn a European backstory that links Mervyn and the late Clavering—a fictive confluence that will inform Welbeck's intent to defraud the wealthy Mrs. Wentworth, who once nursed Clavering and is desirous of information regarding his disappearance. She therefore seems a potential mark in Welbeck's confidence game.

What is notable about Mervyn's role in Welbeck's mysterious plot is that he quickly deviates from Welbeck's instructions. Mervyn is on the way to becoming a new figure in Brown's fiction—one who not only operates as a subversive artificer and a self-making inventor of plots, but one who also espouses and claims to enact a philosophy of benevolence. He behaves neither as a predatory opportunist nor a self-professed agent of providential purpose. Mervyn begins a process that will lead him toward expressing how benevolent forms of narrative self-making might be founded on non-transcendent principles. Brown directs the narrative to where Mervyn's assertions of goodwill and altruism drive the action. In carrying a letter to Mrs. Wentworth, for example, Mervyn is supposed to leave it with a servant and then depart. A series of irruptive contingencies lead Mervyn to reject the dictates of Welbeck's plot:

> I remembered the directions that were given, but construed them in a manner different, perhaps, from Welbeck's expectations or wishes.... He had permitted, rather than enjoined,

> me to dispense with seeing the lady, and this permission I conceived to be dictated merely by regard to my convenience. It was incumbent on me, therefore, to take some pains to deliver the script into her own hands. (*AM* 63–64)

In performing a rhetorically agile semantic deconstruction of Welbeck's directive, Mervyn creates a warrant for acting freely and thus superseding his commands. Once inside the house, Mervyn is shocked to find the lost self-portrait of Clavering on Mrs. Wentworth's mantle. This discovery initiates Mervyn's counterplot designed to keep his actual relationship with Clavering secret. In remaining an actor *within* the Welbeck plot, Mervyn not only retains control of his character and hidden past but also develops a critical posture toward Welbeck's machinations: "I began to form conjectures as to the nature of the scheme to which my suppression of the truth was to be thus made subservient. It seemed as if I were walking in the dark and might rush into snares or drop into pits before I was aware of my danger" (*AM* 70).

Mervyn's skepticism allows him to maintain his own purposes, even as he shows himself to be a willing player in the unfolding scheme of imposture. When Welbeck takes Mervyn to visit Wortley, for example, Mervyn perceives "with the utmost astonishment" the degree to which Welbeck fashions a "change in his deportment" (*AM* 73). Welbeck's usual sullenness gives way to a vibrant display of conversational evanescence. Mervyn reveals Welbeck to be a shape-shifter, an American Proteus, who plays a role that points to how one's acting self need not connect to one's essential self. Welbeck's "vivacity" constitutes a staged performance designed to enact some larger, as yet undefined, purpose (*AM* 73). What such a purpose may be, thanks to the limitations of Mervyn's first-person retrospective sensation narrative, remains outside the purview of Mervyn's discourse. To engage the complex, double-layered question, "Who and what was Welbeck?" (*AM* 71), is to venture into a speculative maze. "Who" refers to hidden ontological properties, those recessed attributes of his being that drive his predatory connivances. "What" evokes the inherent problem of reading surfaces that are in themselves contrived figurations spawned by this inscrutable, authorial intelligence.

The Welbeck plot explodes after Mervyn accidently sees Welbeck coming out of Clemenza Lodi's bedroom. Looking at her with new eyes, Mervyn observes what seem to be "marks of pregnancy." Mervyn repeatedly finds himself meditating on inscrutable incidents and cryptic inferences. His wavering sensations and judgments lead to vexing conclusions, which in turn incite new rounds of vacillating sensations and judgments. For example, regarding the bedroom exit, Mervyn concludes, "The depravity of Welbeck was inferred from it. The charms of this angelic woman were tarnished and withered." His suspicion that Welbeck has committed incest with a woman who may be his daughter— "the blackest and most stupendous of all crimes"—reflects "ideas [that] were necessarily transient" (*AM* 76). He generates another countertext, the notion that Clemenza may have been recently widowed: "By this new train of ideas I was somewhat comforted. I saw the folly of precipitate inferences, and the injustice of my atrocious imputations, and acquired some degree of patience in my present state of uncertainty" (*AM* 77). Even as Mervyn finds himself a benighted player in Welbeck's evolving scenario, he constructs and deconstructs hermeneutical forays that bring him not clarity, but only grounds for further conjecture.

Within the Confines of Welbeck's Plot

After deciding to inform Welbeck of his suspicions that Thetford is scheming after Welbeck's money— "To detect and to counterwork this plot was obviously my duty" (*AM* 78)—Mervyn assumes one of his roles—the obliging busybody. When trying to locate Welbeck, Mervyn is interrupted by "the discharge of a pistol" (*AM* 83). Again, Mervyn becomes entangled in a sequence of events he neither controls nor understands. Believing that Welbeck committed suicide, Mervyn enters Welbeck's room and finds him watching the convulsive death of

Captain Amos Watson. After Welbeck appears abstracted, then "tranquil" and finally "solemn," he speaks to his shocked witness:

> Mervyn, said he, you comprehend not this scene. Your youth and inexperience make you a stranger to a deceitful and flagitious world. You know me not. It is time that this ignorance should vanish. The knowledge of me and of my actions may be of use to you. It may teach you to avoid the shoals on which my virtue and peace have been wrecked. (*AM* 85)

The suddenly moralistic Welbeck views Mervyn as possessing "a rectitude and firmness worthy to be trusted" (*AM* 85) and he extracts a promise—later broken—that Mervyn will not repeat Welbeck's story. Ironically, a master-deceiver like Welbeck asserts his belief that his autobiographical narrative will be of some "use" to the naïf on the dangers of following Welbeck's perfidious example. Like Brown in the "Preface," Welbeck claims to believe that a story can be useful as a force of moral exemplification. The fact that Mervyn later recounts Welbeck's inset narrative violates Mervyn's promise to keep silent, but Mervyn's primary audience is Dr. Stevens, who convinced Mervyn of the ethical priority associated with revealing his full knowledge of Welbeck and his schemes. Welbeck takes Mervyn into his confidence and professes to present the unvarnished truth of the essential self lurking behind the protean mask.

In claiming to be the orphaned son of a Liverpool trader, Welbeck assumes the identity of another New World immigrant, but he carries with him the tendency to "dissimulation and falsehood" that undermined the stability of his and other lives while he was still in England (*AM* 86). As with the elder Wieland, the immigrant does not come to America as a blank slate or a prelapsarian, Adamic figure. Rather, he embodies (and extends) the corruption coincident with his European past. In his confession, Welbeck paints himself as a rogue, a villain, and a liar. With his "incurable depravity" (*AM* 87), he seduced the sister of Amos Watson, the American captain who had befriended him and provided his New World passage. Welbeck indulged in "customary sophistries" and pursued "a scheme of—*forgery!*" (*AM* 88, emphasis in original). He refused to work at an honest job. Destitute and without a future, bent on committing suicide, he happened on a person, who told him about a dying young man in need of someone capable of speaking French. In an uncharacteristic display of kindness, which may be self-serving opportunism, Welbeck took care of Vincentio Lodi, Jr. Prior to Lodi's death, Welbeck was charged to deliver Lodi's money and his father's manuscript to his sister Clemenza. In a characteristic display of criminality, Welbeck used these monetary and textual materials to construct a plausible social fiction: "There was no difficulty in persuading the world that Welbeck was a personage of opulence and rank.... My sudden appearance on the stage, my stately reserve, my splendid habitation and my circumspect deportment were sufficient to intitle me to homage" (*AM* 95). Given the inherent fluidity of social forms, his well-constructed appearance assumed the semblance of authenticity. Money provided Welbeck with the necessary means, or props, to create credible social fictions. Along with stealing Lodi's money, Welbeck impregnated Clemenza and had every intention to publish the elder Lodi's memoir and pocket the profits. Welbeck, however, invited reversal: he invested the Lodi fortune in a speculative trading venture that went awry when privateers confiscated ship and cargo.

An evil manipulator, Welbeck used his knack for larceny, storytelling, and narrative self-making to entangle others in his fabricated plots. When Watson appeared with the purpose of exacting vengeance, Welbeck asserted that he feared not death but the humiliation and public exposure that would attend the collapse of his social fiction. Speaking of Watson, Welbeck says, "I dreaded not his violence. The death that he might be prompted to inflict, was no object of aversion. It was poverty and disgrace, the detection of my crimes, the looks and voice of malediction and upbraiding, from which my cowardice shrunk" (*AM* 103). Prior to fulfilling his ostensible intent to commit suicide, he encountered Watson, who proposes a duel. Supposedly, Watson fired upon Welbeck and missed. Welbeck (implausibly) contends he did not aim his gun, but the "negligently raised" weapon happened to discharge and "my blind and random shot took place in his heart" (*AM* 106).

Mervyn becomes both an actor within Welbeck's spun plots and a victim of Welbeck's fictionalizing intelligence. He remains ensnared within Welbeck's artful tale and seductive promises. Characteristically, Mervyn continues to be knotted in a maze of contingencies that he does not create and does not understand. Nevertheless, Mervyn accepts the Welbeck plot as the form his new life will take. Welbeck requires two things of Mervyn—help burying Watson's body and passage by boat across the Delaware River. In viewing his relationship with Mervyn in histrionic terms, Welbeck gives Mervyn the chance to refuse: "If you chuse to fly from this scene, to withdraw yourself from what you may conceive to be a theatre of guilt or peril, the avenues are open; retire unmolested and in silence" (*AM* 107). Mervyn's options are either to remain within the Welbeck plot and become a potential accomplice to overt criminal activity or to exit Welbeck's plot and assume a voiceless role.

For Mervyn, performance—either retrospective or impending, concluded or yet to be enacted—cannot be dissociated from the hermeneutical process that performance inevitably engenders. Like Clara Wieland, Mervyn continually interprets the unfolding present. Within the sensation narrative, what he *does* cannot be dissociated from what he ponders. Under Brown's hand, the novel form grows out of emergent events: indeed, serendipity establishes the groundwork for Mervyn's induction into a kind of inchoate hypertext of experiential possibility. Actions lead to consequences and consequences excite the fluidity of thought. Novel events both precipitate and impel the self-generating force of Mervyn's fancy.

Mervyn helps Welbeck wrap Watson's corpse in a rug. They carry their burden into a bleak, subterranean underworld. Those "darksome and murky recesses" anticipate the claustrophobic, suffocating interiors of Edgar Allan Poe's Gothic tales. Welbeck and Mervyn drop the corpse within "a small and remote cell.... The narrow cell in which we stood, its rudely fashioned walls and arches, destitute of communication with the external air, and its palpable dark scarcely penetrated by the rays of a solitary candle, added to the silence which was deep and universal, produced an impression on my fancy which no time will obliterate" (*AM* 109). Repeatedly, Mervyn calls attention to the power of his fancy, the generative creative activity of his interpretative imagination: "Perhaps my imagination was distempered by terror. The incident which I am going to relate may appear to have existed only in my fancy" (*AM* 109–10). Mervyn looks at Watson and perceives "a convulsive motion in the eye-lids." Mervyn calls attention not so much to an extrinsic event—sudden movement in a presumed corpse—but to the indeterminate nature of the perceived event, the possibility that it only exists within his "distempered" imagination. The focus remains on Mervyn's addled subjectivity. Ambiguity becomes an ineluctable fact, an inescapable condition that excites hermeneutical conjecture. Was Watson's oxymoronic "languid but wild" glance an actual phenomenon, or was it a delusion of Mervyn's senses (*AM* 110)? As Robert Miles observes, "Brown's American Gothic breathes within the claustrophobic space between the hope of blessing and the fear of curse. Live burial is the master trope of the Gothic. In Brown, the trope is inflected with the uncertain struggle of Enlightenment itself" (413).

The indeterminate nature of this moment is never resolved. If Watson still breathes, he does not breathe for long. He is soon interred until Welbeck later digs him up to pilfer his money belt. In this scene, Brown focuses on Mervyn's psychological sensations. For example, after smacking his nose and bleeding profusely, Mervyn contemplates a prospective role. The "accusing stains" constitute another enveloping layer of serendipitous, narrative confinement and leads Mervyn to recognize that he may be seen as a criminal: "What effects will my appearance produce on the spectator! Terrified by phantoms and stained with blood shall I not exhibit the tokens of a maniac as well as an assassin?" (*AM* 111). The reality—Mervyn is innocent of murder—might be superseded by the credible yet false image of Mervyn *as* a maniac and murderer: "I am innocent, but my tale however circumstantial or true, will scarcely suffice for my vindication. My flight will be construed into a proof of incontestable guilt" (*AM* 112).

This fearsome prospect never materializes. Mervyn finds his way back to the burial site and watches as Welbeck "finished the task" of interring Watson. At this point, Welbeck surprisingly gives Mervyn Watson's "pocket-book, saying it...might contain something serviceable to the living." Mervyn is charged to "make what use of it [he] thought proper." Unbeknown to Mervyn, Welbeck turns over the Watson materials that will impel Mervyn to pursue a significant portion of the action of the *Second Part.* Now, however, Mervyn remains captive: "[D]riven, by a sort of mechanical impulse, in his foot-steps" (*AM* 113), lacking his own sense of volition, Mervyn longs to author, or invent, the text of his own experiences: "I had acted long enough a servile and mechanical part; and been guided by blind and foreign impulses. It was time to lay aside my fetters, and demand to know whither the path tended in which I was importuned to walk." This resolution marks a turning point. Welbeck proposes an end to their relation but first needs Mervyn to navigate a river crossing. They will part on the New Jersey shore of the Delaware River and Welbeck will "leave [Mervyn] to [his] destiny" (*AM* 114). Once on the river, Mervyn considers how "novelty"—the serendipitous creation of new plot forms—does little more than evoke "a state of suspense and wonder" (*AM* 115).

Welbeck makes one more interruptive act. Rather than completing his passage, he leaps into the water and appears to have drowned. Welbeck's control over Mervyn seems to end at this juncture. When he wonders, "What was the fate reserved for me?" he is actually asking the wrong question (*AM* 118). With Welbeck (temporarily) out of his life, Mervyn will assert his own capacity for narrative self-making. By assuming authorial control over the *creation* of his fate, in seeking his future in whatever haphazard manner, he will find that fate has less to do with the determinations of some supernatural force and more to do with *his* attempts to shape the accidents and contingencies of his life into a series of self-authorized designs—ones that will become manifest in the performance of ostensibly benevolent acts.[12] The question remains, however, whether Mervyn's pursuit of benevolence constitutes an authentic embrace of disinterested virtue or the histrionic expression of protean transfigurations.

Mervyn's benevolence, disinterested or otherwise, actual or feigned, cannot be dissociated from ambiguities associated with his character and his motives. Is he a fool, knave, or hero? Or does he embody some shifting amalgam of these conflicting attributes? On the one hand, Jane Tomkins notes the difficulty of finding stable hermeneutical ground: "We are always rushing off with this hero on half-formed quests that lead down unfamiliar streets, only to find that we've been there before, faced the same faces, been surprised by the same events" (63). She also argues that Brown's ultimate purpose is to have Mervyn "confer moral benefit" (67). Emory Elliott, on the contrary, discusses the doubleness inherent in Mervyn's character and actions: "*Arthur Mervyn* is neither a depiction of virtue rewarded, nor a study of unscrupulous deviousness, but is an anatomy of social and psychological survival" ("Narrative Unity" 160). Elliot's position offers less a

[12] Well before he began writing this novel, Brown discusses the matter of benevolence in his [October-November 1792] letter to Joseph Bringhurst, Jr. Here, Brown provides a close analysis of benevolence as an attribute of being and as a form of social action:

> Benevolence is the desire of rendering others happy. Beneficence is the act of conferring happiness. Pity or compassion is a sympathy or fellow-feeling with those that are afflicted.... Benevolence necessarily implies pity. He that wishes to relieve the miseryble, which is the proper definition of a benevolent man, must previously be sencible of Pity for their distresses. (151, emphasis in original).

This concept, especially as regards the relationship between theory and practice, resides at the core of Brown's reflections on the social contract.

conclusion than a point of departure for the materials explored in this chapter, especially insofar as Mervyn's professed intentions become manifest in his equivocal rhetoric and ambiguous actions.

"This Theatre of Death"

With his curiosity regarding Mervyn's relation to Welbeck "appeased," Dr. Stevens invites the sick young man to explain those "inducements and events" whereby Mervyn "was reconducted to the city and led to the spot where I first met with him." Through his emergent speech act, Mervyn continues his retrospective sensation narrative. Under Brown's hand, the novel moves on from various accidents that established grounds for the proliferation of linked contingencies toward another new beginning. With Welbeck having disappeared into the Delaware River and presumably drowned, Mervyn once again becomes a man without a plot. Seeking relief and solace in rustication, he wanders away from the city with the intention of trusting to chance: "My purpose was to stop at the first farm-house, and seek employment as a day-labourer" (*AM* 122). He has the good fortune to encounter the kind Mr. Hadwin and his daughters, Susan and Eliza: "The manners of this family, quiet, artless, and cordial, the occupations allotted me, the land by which the dwelling was surrounded, its pure airs, romantic walks, and exhaustless fertility, constituted a powerful contrast to the scenes which I had left behind, and were congenial with every dictate of my understanding and every sentiment that glowed in my heart" (*AM* 123). Mervyn immediately sees Mr. Hadwin as a surrogate father and the Hadwin sisters as possible, if convenient, love interests. With Susan in love with Wallace, Mervyn fixes his attentions on the younger sister: Mervyn's "romantic and untutored disposition" leads him to conjure an infatuated longing for Eliza Hadwin (*AM* 124).

Given various impediments to pursuing "a secret marriage," among them the Hadwins' Quaker heritage, Mervyn feels the need "to fix my thoughts upon a different object" and decides to translate the Lodi manuscript (*AM* 125). During his labors, he discovers banknotes glued within adjacent manuscript leaves in the amount of twenty thousand dollars. Once again, he finds himself responding to disturbing and mysterious circumstances that derive from his association with Welbeck. Mervyn considers ethical issues attending the discovery of this fortune:

> But what, said I, is my title to this money? By retaining it, shall I not be as culpable as Welbeck? It came into his possession as it came into mine, without a crime; but my knowledge of the true proprietor is equally certain, and the claims of the unfortunate stranger are as valid as ever.... The lady must be sought and the money be restored to her. (*AM* 128)

In resolving to counteract the Welbeck mode of vicious, predatory self-aggrandizement, Mervyn asserts that his actions will be founded on principles of altruism, equity, and justice. Following his acquisition of money, Mervyn no longer languishes as a pawn in Welbeck's schemes.

Mervyn's chance encounter with the Hadwin family will shape his pivotal actions. He will attempt to act out imperatives of benevolence and risk his well-being for the benefit of others. He will seek Susan's missing lover in the plague-stricken city as a prelude to bringing justice to Clemenza Lodi. In the process, he will author unwelcome consequences. Nevertheless, Mervyn's philosophy of benevolence establishes the foundation out of which he seems to construct ethical and aesthetic imperatives. The nature of Mervyn's identity and his reconfiguration of the power of self-making depend on the social feasibility of enacting non-transcendent forms of moral and ethical behavior, even though his sometimes bungling, sometimes officious, energies undermine seemingly altruistic designs.

Mervyn's attempts at self-direction are impeded by the novel's major social force, the yellow fever epidemic of 1793, a catastrophe that shatters all pretentions to individual control and communal order.[13]

---

[13] Levine discusses the social context of the novel: "*Arthur Mervyn* is about a particular post-revolutionary moment in which revolution is a blow to the

With intrepid fortitude, he plunges into the disease-stricken city. Mervyn's essential problem shifts from his confused entanglement within the devious plots of an arch trickster to his wayward, impetuous attempts to establish order within a social domain plunged into anarchy: "The city, we were told, was involved in confusion and panick, for a pestilential disease had begun its destructive progress" (*AM* 128–29). The epidemic undermines all social and natural bonds:

> The usual occupations and amusements of life were at an end. Terror had exterminated all the sentiments of nature. Wives were deserted by husbands, and children by parents. Some had shut themselves in their houses, and debarred themselves from all communication with the rest of mankind.... Men were seized by this disease in the streets; passengers fled from them; entrance into their own dwellings was denied to them; they perished in the public ways. (*AM* 129)

Mervyn responds to this overwhelming force by embarking on two quests: he will travel to the city to find Wallace; he will attempt to restore Clemenza Lodi's fortune. Finding Wallace clarifies the mystery of who tricked him into languishing in the Thetford closet. The pursuit of Lodi, extended into the *Second Part*, constitutes Mervyn's central moral imperative. Upon pursuing these ends in the city, Mervyn encounters a phantasmagoria of death and turmoil, a world replete with wraith-like wanderers and crass corpse collectors. "What's wanted?" asks one of these hearse-men. "Any body dead?" (*AM* 140).

---

imagination, an unexpected disorienting shock, an unforeseen upheaval that makes a mockery of stabilizing controls and simple cause-effect schematizations" ("Arthur's Mervyn's Revolutions" 145). For Berthoff, Brown's representation of "upheaval" has a specifically urban cast, especially as Mervyn makes his way through "Brown's nightmare metropolis" in the time of plague (61). See Axelrod's for a discussion of this urban hell (142–43). Waterman positions this novel in relation to the emergence of "fever fiction" (*Republic of Intellect* 190; also 189–230). Davidson sees the yellow fever materials as creating a nexus between aesthetics and politics (*Revolution and the Word* 219).

With the stable domain of pre-plague Philadelphia in tatters, Mervyn discovers an aspect of experiential anarchy that agitates conscious and unconscious realms. The human artificer must always contend with layers of phenomenological and psychological complication that operate beyond anyone's control. In the plague-stricken chaos of urban life, art and plot-forms are fragile constructs that prescribe the often-truncated enactments of personal volition. After Mervyn suffers a random mugging by a sick man and gets knocked unconscious, he drifts into a surreal state. His dream-sense of being "fettered" combines with the sensation of being lifted by "two grim and gigantic figures," who are preparing to hurl him into a "bottomless gulf" (*AM 148*). This dream figuratively distills what is actually happening. Two corpse-collectors, assuming he is dead, are busy bringing closure to the Mervyn narrative. As he awakens, one man prepares to drive nails into his coffin lid.

In his search for Wallace, Mervyn is helped by two seemingly saint-like men. The Quaker Estwick embodies principles of "benignity" and benevolence (*AM* 149) and Medlicote "possessed so much fortitude and virtue" (*AM* 161). Each man reflects a prospective character paradigm for Mervyn, whose newfound social imperatives will attempt to combine performance, role-playing, and self-making with plots that are grounded in principles of altruism and benevolence. As a social performer, however, Mervyn remains a tyro prone to injudicious choices. For example, Mervyn made the mistake of leaving the Hadwin homestead without telling anyone of his intent to find Wallace. Consequently, Mr. Hadwin makes the ill-fated decision to search for his surrogate son. As Mervyn remarks, "Ignorant of the part I had acted, he had rushed into the jaws of this pest, and endangered a life unspeakably valuable to his children and friends.... [M]y wretched policy had led me into this clandestine path. Secrecy may seldom be a crime. A virtuous intention may produce it; but surely it is always erroneous and pernicious" (*AM* 162). By constructing his self-authorized plot based on secrecy, this well-meaning yet inept neophyte causes Hadwin to contract the disease that kills him and Susan. Mervyn's second mistake is to tell Hadwin that Wallace is dead, a piece of misinformation that destroys Susan's shaky, mental balance.

The point is not so much that Mervyn makes poor decisions that lead to unfortunate outcomes. More significantly, the artist-in-life, Brown emphasizes, has difficulty controlling contingencies that derive from misinformed, naïve, or pernicious attempts to author experience. At this stage of the narrative, Mervyn attempts to order the affairs of life. While unsuccessful in controlling consequences, he nevertheless seems to be effective in actualizing his self-proclaimed purpose: to countermand the machinations of Welbeck and find a just way to dispose of the Lodi fortune. In the process, Mervyn himself becomes ill and finds himself on the front steps of Welbeck's house: "The incident was unexpected. It led my reflections into a new train" (*AM* 181). These two sentences encapsulate the creative principle that drives the novel: seemingly accidental or arbitrary events establish the impetus for subsequent actions as well as inviting subjects for speculation. Mervyn finds an open window and enters. With the purpose of dispersing the Lodi fortune in a socially beneficial manner, he intends to find pen and paper so he can write a note and send the money to the city's chief magistrate: "I could not conceive any more beneficial application of this property, than to the service of the indigent, at this season of multiplied distress" (*AM* 183). Welbeck, however, comes between Mervyn and the execution of this "design" (*AM* 184). From behind locked doors, the protean Welbeck, "restored to life" (*AM* 191), employs the counterfeited voice of a man named Covill in hopes of encouraging Mervyn to go away. With his "same devotion to imposture," Welbeck reveals that life is nothing more than one theatrical act after the next. Welbeck's purpose in returning from his immersion in the Delaware River was to retrieve the Lodi manuscript and appropriate the enclosed bank bills. Unbeknown to Welbeck, Mervyn has the money, and plans "to hide this truth: but my understanding had been taught...to question the justice, and deny the usefulness of secrecy in any case. My principles were true; my motives were pure" (*AM* 199–200).

Welbeck's assertion that these bills are forgeries collides with Mervyn's bizarre attempt to ground his action on principles of right conduct. Mervyn believes Welbeck's fabrication and convinces himself that "[t]he destruction of these bills was the loudest injunction of my duty." Acting not for vengeance but (ostensibly) to protect Welbeck, Mervyn expresses his concern that Welbeck will be imprisoned for passing counterfeit currency. His benevolent intentions counteract Welbeck's wily fiction. When Mervyn burns genuine bank notes, Welbeck suffers defeat through the ironic success of what he describes as "so gross an artifice" (*AM* 210). At this climactic moment, Mervyn falls prey to Welbeck's fiction, even while using this fabrication to assert his own power to *author* the affairs of life. Mervyn's ostensible purity of character not only embodies the novel's predominant ethical antithesis to Welbeck, but Mervyn's problematic claims to innocence impel his histrionic efforts to counteract the power of the pernicious fiction-making trickster.

It must not be forgotten that this entire novel—in fact, the fictional worlds of Brown's four major novels—dramatizes the dialectical proliferation of conflicting first-person voices. For every text, there seems to be a countertext. For example, Carwin's confession to Clara competes with Theodore Wieland's courtroom confession for the right to determine the true meaning of events. In the same contrastive spirit, Dr. Stevens' conviction of Mervyn's rectitude becomes assailed early in the *Second Part* by strident, antagonistic accusations. Wortley "suspected that Mervyn was a wily imposter; that he had been trained in the arts of fraud, under an accomplished teacher; that the tale which he had told me, was a tissue of ingenious and plausible lies" (*AM* 226). At the outset of the *Second Part*, Mervyn has gone to Malverton to find out what has become of the Hadwin family. In Mervyn's absence, Stevens not only listens to Wortley's allegations, but he recognizes that there are limits neither to "the bounds of fraud" nor "the combinations of fancy" (*AM* 229).

In a world populated by actors, authors, imposters, scamps, and charlatans, Stevens finds that his steadfast confidence in Mervyn's virtue is challenged by a profusion of disputative voices. Not only does Wortley describe his unyielding convictions regarding Mervyn's alleged perfidy, but Stevens also speaks to one of Mervyn's former neighbors and hears a radically different version of Mervyn's life story: Mrs. Althorpe charges that Mervyn was in cahoots with Betty Lawrence, the scheming milkmaid who married and defrauded Mervyn's father. By asserting that "a criminal intimacy" (*AM* 230) of a sexual sort existed between Arthur and Betty, Mrs. Althorpe presents an alternative narrative, a competing fiction. She attempts to dispel Dr. Stevens' belief in Mervyn's purity of character and purpose. As Hinds observes, "[I]t is Arthur's word against public opinion, with no clear evidence on either side" (83). Wortley makes a more strenuous case, but as Dr. Stevens notes, Wortley's alleged facts turn out to be little more than distorted interpretations of Mervyn's relationship to Clavering and misconceptions regarding Mervyn's interview with Mrs. Wentworth. Wortley claims that Mervyn was Welbeck's accomplice in trying to defraud Mrs. Wentworth, asserting falsely that Mervyn pretended he had recently returned from Europe and testified to Clavering's death there. Wishing to install Clemenza Lodi as the future heir of Mrs. Wentworth, Welbeck ordered Mervyn not to mention his own past—a past that already had established how Mervyn and his mother took care of Clavering on his deathbed. Mervyn retained Clavering's self-portrait as proof of this connection. By speaking to Mrs. Wentworth, however, Mervyn had already stepped out of the role dictated by Welbeck. What Wortley describes as factual evidence of Mervyn's conspiratorial relation to Welbeck actually corroborates Mervyn's earlier descriptions of his discomfort regarding Welbeck's orders. Although Stevens' confidence in Mervyn "is shaken," he does not immediately give credence to Wortley's views. Instead, he finds that his wife is "[t]he only one qualified to divide with me these cares" (*AM* 251). The central question regarding Mervyn's credibility turns on Stevens' knowledge of Mervyn's account of the death and burial of Watson. From Wortley, Stevens knows that Watson wore a money belt containing bank notes worth ten thousand pounds sterling that belong to a family named Maurice. Stevens believes he must find this "lost treasure" and return it to the now destitute, rightful owners. Stevens wishes not only to dispose of the money, but to clear Watson's name, now tainted by the reasonable assumption that the dead man had absconded with these funds. Because of justifiable fears regarding charges of possible criminal complicity in Watson's disappearance, Stevens does not believe he can simply exhume Watson's remains. He must find Mervyn and thereby establish foundational testimony regarding the nature of Watson's death: "The story which he told to me he must tell to the world" (*AM* 252).

Mervyn sends an unsigned note to Stevens requesting that he "*come immediately to the Debtors' Apartments in Prune Street*" (*AM* 253, emphasis in original). The accumulating mysteries, the unexplained contingencies, the unsettling suspicions of Stevens—these issues await explication when Stevens enters debtors' prison and finds Mervyn visiting the ailing and incarcerated Welbeck. Stevens very quickly seeks "an explanation of the scene that I had witnessed. How became you once more the companion of Welbeck? Why did you not inform me by letter of your arrival at Malverton, and of what occurred during your absence? What is the fate of Mr. Hadwin and of Wallace?" (*AM* 260). Brown makes clear his elemental artistic premise: any past experience can only be reconstituted through narrative and any narrative inevitably generates a host of competing interpretations. Indeed, the novel world of *Arthur Mervyn* emerges through the energies of hermeneutical proliferation. In this unfolding epistemological mystery, Truth has no extrinsic referent, though some putative truths slowly come to light through the process of interpretive analysis. Mervyn, for example, is imperturbable when he hears of Mrs. Althorpe's accusatory tale. With an unflappable demeanor—is he genuinely virtuous or a well-schooled performer? —Mervyn explains that his neighbors can only respond to what they see: in his view, Mrs. Althorpe's narrative, however erroneous, reflects an entrenched moral purpose, however misinformed: "It was not me whom they hated and despised. It was the phantom that passed under my name, which existed only in their imagination, and which was worthy of all their scorn and all their enmity" (*AM* 340). Given their premises, he contends that reasonable, if mistaken, conclusions will likely follow.

In this novel, one continually confronts the entangled skein of multiple narratives. At the outset of the novel, Mervyn tells the lengthy tale of how he came to be found sitting against a wall in a sickly condition. Later, Mervyn returns from Malverton and launches an elaborate account of what he experienced during his separation from Stevens. Indeed, Stevens recognizes that Mervyn's extensive account in the *First Part* possesses "all the force of novelty" (*AM* 219)—the creative power of engendered newness. Mervyn's various narrative reconstructions of his past culminate in his attempts to live out a self-generated plot founded on the ethos of benevolence and altruism. It has become his most successful role.

The Author of Resolution

As Mervyn again takes up the narrative, he presents himself not as a passive, naïve dupe, who in the *First Part* was tricked by Wallace and made-over by Welbeck. Instead, Mervyn critiques himself as possessing "a precipitate temper. I chuse my path suddenly, and pursue it with impetuous expedition" (*AM* 271). He feels empowered by the confluence of multiple altruistic purposes. As he remarks, "The past was without remedy; but the future was, in some degree, within our power to create and to fashion" (*AM* 266). He wishes to rescue Clemenza Lodi from what appears to be Mrs. Villars' house of prostitution. He would like to bring Clemenza to the Hadwin home but first must seek their permission along with discovering Wallace's fate. When Mervyn arrives in Malverton, he discovers the family in a ruinous state—Mr. Hadwin dead from yellow fever; Susan mentally deranged by grief, mortally ill, and spiraling toward an early grave. In the turbid wake of these catastrophes, Mervyn takes it upon himself to make sure that Eliza Hadwin will have a safe and stable home life. He even begins to wonder whether his affection for her should culminate in marriage.

These prospective plots, which propel the exterior action of the novel, establish a series of epistemological dilemmas that re-assert the problem and possibility that Arthur Mervyn is no more than an improvisational, protean play-actor for whom the concept of benevolence operates as his chief prop and tactic. Regarding the possibility of marriage with the teenage Eliza, Mervyn finds himself stymied by the inherent instability of human identity: "Could I rely upon the permanence of her equanimity and her docility to my instructions? What qualities might not time unfold?" (*AM* 292). Assuming his own superiority, he views marriage in terms of a plot that *he* will construct, but he worries that she may achieve independence of spirit, purpose, and action—and, in effect, come to inscribe and actualize a competing plot. Fearing that she will change in ways that he will neither control nor condone, he believes that he has a right to direct her life, a notion that irritates the willful Eliza. Wanting more than subsistence, she disputes Mervyn's conventional view of a woman's place: "Me, you think poor, weak, and contemptible; fit for nothing but to spin and churn. Provided I exist, am screened from the weather, have enough to eat and drink, you are satisfied. As to strengthening my mind and enlarging my knowledge, these things are valuable to you, but on me they are thrown away. I deserve not the gift" (*AM* 296). As this remarkable speech indicates, Eliza does not wish to be a diminutive player in the script created by the misogynistic Mervyn. To be married is to be locked within "a contract awful and irrevocable." As Mervyn sees it, marriage combines the force of "fate" with an inscribed immutability that precludes the power of dissolution. What would happen if he marries Eliza and later meets a woman "who more nearly approached that standard of ideal excellence which poets and romancers had exhibited to my view?" (*AM* 297). He sees marriage through conjured literary forms that promise "ideal" resolutions to life's conflicted tensions.

In response to Eliza Hadwin's reservations, Mervyn decides against marrying her. His alleged purpose is to find felicity within a marriage where his partner complements his essential self. This sort of fusion actually reflects one view of what marriage should ultimately be—the culminating social plot that not only integrates one's inner and outer being, but that allows the self to be doubled through union with a companionate partner. Mervyn seeks to acquire "happiness" not only through the enactment of altruistic and benevolent behavior, but also through his ability to match the interior aspect of his being with a person most reflective of those romanticized ideals of love: "I was conscious that my happiness depended not on the revolutions of nature or the caprice of man. All without was, indeed, vicissitude and uncertainty; but within my bosom was a centre not to be shaken or removed" (*AM* 312). This very "centre" impels Mervyn's various attempts to resolve these vicissitudes. Most notably, his search for an ideal spouse will eventually unite his "centre" with a woman, who (he imagines) will be psychologically complementary and socially compatible—and, of course, have a lot more money than Eliza Hadwin. Mervyn never ceases to embody an ambiguous "double-tongued" aspect that adheres to his various social identities (*W* 1).

In the meantime, Mervyn's impetuous desire to perform beneficent deeds leads him to act without sufficient knowledge: "Our good purposes must hurry to performance, whether our knowledge be greater or less" (*AM* 323). His plots, therefore, tend to become slapdash improvisations sanctioned and driven by a burgeoning messianic compulsion: "O that I were rich enough to provide food for the hungry, shelter for the housless, and raiment for the naked" (*AM* 326). This grandiose (yet comically deflating) self-image leads him to presumptive and overbearing impositions. For example, he travels to Madame Villars' house and forces his way in to see the distraught Clemenza Lodi. There he witnesses her tragic inability to relieve her dying infant.

Consumed by depression, Clemenza wants nothing to do with Mervyn. He confronts the limits of his attempts to do good deeds in "a world of revolution and perils" (*AM* 332). Mervyn's messianic complex comes without complementary deific powers or even the power of money—the primary agent that facilitates the construction of social forms. For example, Welbeck only needed sufficient funds from Lodi to construct social props that lent credence to his self-generated fiction of opulence. Mervyn constructs his fictions and generates his plot on the uncertain foundation of an altruistic, elevated self-image, even as his histrionic activities frequently incite mayhem. In the wake of his failure to help Clemenza leave Madam Villars' house, for example, he confronts an enraged woman who shoots at him, wounding him slightly. Mervyn describes the difficulty of constructing plots, or "the means," that express his exalted intentions. In the immediate aftermath of his wounding, he announces: "I am incapable of any purpose that is not beneficent; but, in the means that I use and in the evidence on which I proceed, I am liable to a thousand mistakes" (*AM* 330). Mervyn's professed, well-meaning compulsions lead him to act without the ability to control contingencies—hence his enactment of a "thousand mistakes." It is perhaps comical that an obtuse Welbeck, on the brink of death, can do little more than view Mervyn as "the maker of my poverty and of all the evils which it has since engendered.... Execrable fool! you are the author of the scene that you describe, and of horrors without number and name" (*AM* 337). An ardent misreader, Welbeck can do little more than indulge in overheated rhetorical declamations. The next day, with death imminent, Welbeck seems unmindful of his recent allegations. Instead, in a surprising display of deathbed rectitude, Welbeck wishes to set matters right and desires in particular that Mervyn find a way to rescue Clemenza Lodi. He also wants Mervyn to restore the money he extracted from Watson's corpse and make restitution to Watson's wife and the Maurice family.

The deathbed version of Welbeck constructs the agenda that informs Mervyn's attempt to enact the art of benevolence and thereby arrange other people's lives.[14] Earlier, when he goes to see Mrs. Wentworth and plays the part of Clemenza Lodi's savior, he fails. Mrs. Wentworth wants nothing to do with Welbeck's prostitute. In fact, to the worldly, reasonable Mrs. Wentworth, Mervyn's "language and ideas are those of a lunatic" (*AM* 362). When Mervyn travels to Baltimore to see Mrs. Maurice and restore her fortune, he encounters hostility, threat, and denunciation. In seeing himself as the bearer of money, and therefore as a prospective author of resolution, he is enamored by his own sense of empowerment, a belief in his capacity to prescript and direct the outcome of events. He finds, however, that the objects of his "fancy"—the creations of his procreant imagination—are not realized. In his long letter to Dr. Stevens, Mervyn describes his experience with Mrs. Maurice:

> The scene before me was the unpleasing reverse of all that my fancy, while coming hither, had foreboded. I expected to find virtuous indigence and sorrow lifted, by my means, to affluence and exultation. I expected to witness the tears of gratitude and the caresses of affection. What had I found? Nothing but sordidness, stupidity, and illiberal suspicion. (*AM* 382)

Brown's artist-in-life again discovers the intractable limits of his own sovereignty. Nevertheless, within the sweep of this expansive, entangled narrative, Mervyn has gone from being an indigent outcast and a man without a plot to acting like a confident, forceful authorial agent seeming to promulgate good works. While failing with Mrs. Maurice, he succeeds with Mrs. Watson and daughter Fanny Maurice. Mervyn discovers a deepening appreciation for social interaction: "In the intercourse of ingenious and sympathetic minds, I found a pleasure which I had not previously conceived" (*AM* 391). In fact, he encounters the

[14] Hinds notes, "Needy as he is, Arthur Mervyn is not primarily defined by need, but rather by desire.... The characters most in need are the women of *Arthur Mervyn*, who time and again function as tests for Arthur's benevolence" (87–88).

basis of a new kind of domestic narrative and a renewed belief in his power to shape the lives of others. What Mervyn seeks for himself and his putative beneficiaries is "my own happiness and that of those who were within the sphere of my influence" (*AM* 394). Mervyn thus casts himself as the agent of adjustment, adjudication, and order. Having begun his journey as an outcast from his patrimonial home armed with little more than a clutch of idealistic notions, he has grown to embrace—and articulate—his own sense of power and purpose: "[E]very day added strength to the assurance that I was no insignificant and worthless being; that I was destined to be *something* in this scene of existence, and might sometime lay claim to the gratitude and homage of my fellow-men." As a possible anti-type to Carwin, Ormond, and Welbeck, Mervyn claims to use fiction-making not to fuel addictive or narcissistic imperatives, but to establish non-transcendent structures "formed on purpose for the gratification of social intercourse. To love and to be loved; to exchange hearts, and mingle sentiment with all the virtuous and amiable, whom my good fortune had placed within the circuit of my knowledge, I always esteemed my highest enjoyment and my chief duty" (*AM* 396).

The novel moves toward its long-awaited conclusion as Mervyn shifts his attention from establishing the happiness "of those who were within the sphere of my influence" to establishing the form that his own future will assume (*AM* 394)—a conclusion that can be interpreted as either genuinely celebratory or ludicrously parodic. The widowed Mrs. Achsa Fielding, whom he met during his visit to Madame Villars' house, displaces Eliza Hadwin in Mervyn's affections and ostensibly embodies the epitome of womanly virtue, or at least he paints her as such. Mrs. Fielding has a complex history that includes a marriage, a wayward (and eventually murdered) husband, and a child left to be raised by English in-laws. As an émigré, Mrs. Fielding constitutes a personified version of American novelty: new possibilities rise from the wreck that is the past. The ravages of her past haunt her memory, even as they strengthen her character in ways that will help her forge a productive future: "I have come into a scene and society so new, I have had so many claims made upon my ingenuity and fortitude, that my mind has been diverted in some degree from former sorrows" (*AM* 425). Indeed, she becomes an educative force in Mervyn's life, even to the extent of determining the shape-shifting qualities of his acting self: "As to me, I was wax in her hand. Without design and without effort, I was always of that form she wished me to assume" (*AM* 428). The fact that Mervyn originally (and bizarrely) interprets this older woman as "my good mamma" (*AM* 407) and later as his "lost mamma" (*AM* 429) causes him to misread her prospective place in his life.[15]

In order to continue this ambiguous act of narrative self-making, Mervyn must surrender his psychosexual confusion and retrograde notions in favor of a future-facing identification of Mrs. Fielding as his self-empowered wife. Through the auspices of a kind of dialogic epithalamion, Dr. Stevens hopes to lead Mervyn out of his state of frenzied disquietude. Stevens perceives Mervyn's looming future in terms of a "drama" that will lead to harmonious resolution, a balanced finale: "[S]uspenses and doubts" will find their complement in an eventual "joyous certainty" (*AM* 435). Stevens directs Mervyn through extreme emotional turbulence that even includes sleepwalking episodes—an evocation of events that roil *Edgar Huntly*. In his dream state, order dissolves into imagistic spasms that threaten to deconstruct the forms sanctioned by his conscious ego: "It was certainly a temporary loss of reason; nothing less than madness could lead into such devious tracts, drag me down to so hopeless, helpless, panickful a depth, and drag me down so suddenly; lay waste, as at a signal, all my flourishing structures, and reduce them in a moment to a scene of confusion and horror" (*AM* 441). Mervyn must overcome these distressing irruptions spawned within his unconscious.

---

[15] Person explores the problematic implications of what may be Mervyn's oedipal desires (34). See Watts' discussion of Achsa Fielding and attending Oedipal implications, 114–15. For a discussion of Mervyn's enigmatic relationship to Achsa Fielding, see Elliott, *Revolutionary Writers*, 260–65.

Essentially, these "flourishing structures" include those controlling fictions that create order and purpose at the individual, familial, and societal levels. As his novels attest, Brown remains acutely aware that these self-made fictions can be suddenly, easily, demolished by the relentless force of an epidemic or challenged by the debilitating energies of a nightmare. Oddly enough, Mervyn views his prospective confession to Mrs. Fielding regarding his desires for marriage as nothing less than an impending force, "the sealing and ratification of my doom" (*AM* 441). When she accepts him as her prospective husband, she potentially displaces the unsettling notion that she is his "lost mamma" in favor of a future-facing embrace of protean possibility and joyous resolution.

By the end of the novel, Mervyn has completely usurped Stevens' role as narrator. His story is now being written *to* Stevens in the epistolary mode. The reader has caught up to Mervyn's unfolding compositional present as he is completing the book narrated variously by Stevens and himself. Regarding his temporary separation from Achsa Fielding, his writing serves "to allay those tumults which [their] necessary separation produces" (*AM* 445). During the time between his engagement and his marriage, Mervyn will conclude the compositional process by simply laying down the pen and awaiting the consummation of the new-life story that will, he imagines, "complete our felicity" (*AM* 446). Nevertheless, a sense of interpretive doubleness lingers. In preparing to experience what he believes might constitute a fully realized existence, he may be doing nothing more than indulging his latest spasm of wishful thinking.

6

American Novelty: *Edgar Huntly; or, Memoirs of a Sleep-Walker*

Novelty and American Literary Independence

At the outset of his fourth published novel, Charles Brockden Brown's brief prefatory address "To the Public" regarding his "new performance" (*EH* 3) echoes nascent post-Revolution demands for a culturally-specific body of national literature that expresses the life and times of the new republic. According to Michael T. Gilmore, calls for a native American literature began as early as 1775 and "increased in frequency and volume after the signing of the Treaty of Paris." Gilmore identifies Noah Webster and Philip Freneau as pioneer-advocates for "[c]ultural nationalism" (548). Emory Elliott points to an entrenched anti-art bias that undermined this venture:

> For the writers, the prospects for success were...radically altered by the Revolution. At first, as the war ended, the familiar call for American letters was given a new republican emphasis, and the literary activity of the early 1780s suggests that optimism prevailed.... However, just as the clergy had begun to experience resistance by the mid-1780s, so too the writers discovered that the promise of prosperity for the arts was very short-lived. Patriotic American poems were left unbought in the bookstores, magazines began to fold after only a few issues, and critics grew impatient and condemned American literary works as weak imitations of English or classical models or as unpolished products of the forest. (*Revolutionary Writers* 45)[1]

[1] Brown sounds a note that culminates four to six decades later in aesthetic manifestoes by Ralph Waldo Emerson's "The American Scholar," Herman Melville's

In step with wavering, contemporary interest in cultural nationalism and well before Emerson in 1837 rejects "the sere remains of foreign harvests" in favor of "a new age" of national literary creativity, Brown proclaims his desire to distance himself from European influence (83–84).[2] Whereas "America has opened new views to the naturalist and politician," it has not adequately "furnished themes to the moral painter." Put another way, the American fiction writer—this "moral painter"—has done little more than reconstitute novelistic conventions imported from Europe, recycling such putatively stale "materials" as "[p]uerile superstition and exploded manners; Gothic castles and chimeras" (*EH* 3).[3] Furthermore, Brown's lament regarding the

---

"Hawthorne and His Mosses," and Walt Whitman's "Preface" to the 1855 edition of *Leaves of Grass*. Levine explores the entangled matter associated with Brown, early American literary nationalism, and what he calls "the contingencies of empire.... Charles Brockden Brown sought to understand racial and national identities in all of their complexity, and national identities in all of their complexity, and he challenged a number of orthodoxies that we tend to associate with a traditionally optative U.S. literary nationalism" (*Dislocating Race and Nation* 22).

[2] Wallace takes a dim view of the notion that Brown and his generation of writers were successful in establishing an American literature that built upon, and transfigured, European literary forms into new amalgams: "Royall Tyler, Charles Brockden Brown, John Neal, and a host of others called for an indigenous American fiction and designed programs for it, but the very redundancy of their demands and the fact that each tended to see himself as the sole true exemplar of an American school serve as an acknowledgement that English models dominated" (2–3).

[3] Berthold argues that the phrase "'American gothic' unduly emphasizes European artistic forms over American realities.... Specifically, in *Edgar Huntly* the gothic merges with an early local color tradition in an interfusion of genres that should modify that accepted sense of the gothic in a way that might be regarded as peculiarly 'American' but also as generic in origin, not just nationalistic" ("Desacralizing the American Gothic" 128). Brown's views regarding the success of American literary art forms are long-standing and assume a saturnine cast as early as his November 28, 1794 letter to Dunlap: "It used to be a favourite maxim with me that the genius of a poet should be sacred to the glory of his country; how far this rule can be reduced to practice by an American bard; how far he can prudently observe it, and what success has crowned the efforts of those, who, in their compositions, have shown that they have not been unmindful of it, is perhaps not worth the inquiry" (*L* 287). Brown's

contemporary state of Belles Lettres seems to ignore the accumulating evidence of his own indefatigable efforts at fiction-making as well as the groundbreaking work of such contemporaries as William Hill Brown and Susanna Rowson. Indeed, the creation of an "American Tale" has been both subject and consequence of his endeavors in *Wieland*, *Memoirs of Carwin*, *Ormond*, and *Arthur Mervyn*. What appears most overtly *American* in *Wieland*, for example, includes the delineation of new world locales, political associations, and reformulations of the Gothic, what Dennis Berthold sees as Brown's tendency to modify traditional or stereotypical depictions of gothic terror as part of a process that "orients his hero to geographical and eventually psychological reality" ("Desacralizing the American Gothic" 130). What appears most American also includes Brown's innovative representations of the shifting, mercurial Carwin, a protean fiction-maker, this foundational American type, who competes with God as the author of experience. Carwin not only uses everyday life as his improvisational theater but repeatedly enlists unwitting persons as characters in a plot that he (both successfully and unsuccessfully) authors. Such self-consciously histrionic artificers as Carwin, Ludloe, Craig, Ormond, and Welbeck become makers and directors of social forms. One implication of such dangerous and disruptive experiments with imposture and manipulation suggests that the structures controlling individual identity and the political arena might come to possess a terrifying fluidity, a preoccupation that animates Brown's achievements in *Wieland*, *Ormond*, and *Arthur Mervyn* and constitutes a powerful motif in the geographical, aesthetic, and psychological reaches of *Edgar Huntly*, a work that signals the end of his quest for literary greatness.

---

call for a national literature in the preface to *Edgar Huntly* has complex antecedents and is not the work of a naïve, patriotic optimist.

Edgar Huntly's Authorial Self

In *Edgar Huntly; or, Memoirs of a Sleep-Walker*, Brown seeks to exploit what he calls "new springs of action, and new motives to curiosity" and thereby advance his attempt to construct another new "performance" (*EH* 3).[4] To effect this purpose, he enlists the epistolary form not as a record of conventional social manners celebrated, flaunted, or satirized, but as an investigative device designed to reflexively delineate the fragile state and cognitive limitations of Edgar Huntly's conscious mind and volition. This orientation accentuates the open-ended, exploratory nature of Brown's psychological and hermeneutical focus. At the outset of the novel, Huntly lives in the aftermath of "suspence" and "tremors" incited by the harrowing, violent experiences he recently survived (*EH* 5). As he writes this letter, he is also living in the aftermath of his failures to enact, like Arthur Mervyn, the art of benevolence. He is aware of how completely he failed to lead the deranged, erratic sleepwalker Clithero Edny away from his self-destructive mental pathologies. In writing to his fiancée Mary Waldegrave, Huntly attempts to establish a psychological state of "repose" that will permit him to "comply with [her] request" and write the promised account. His past experiences have created "perturbations" that must be "sufficiently stilled" before his compositional process can ensue. He needs to achieve a point of balance whereby his traumatic adventures and "headlong energies" can be translated into words. He needs, in short, to construct an operative authorial self. So far, he has not been able to disconnect his mind from the muddled present or deflect his attention from distressing apprehensions regarding "futurity." If he waits too long, he will lose his "remembrance of these events. In proportion as I gain power over words, shall I lose dominion over sentiments" (*EH* 5). This quandary, as he describes it, implies that the activity of writing involves an inveterate form of risk-taking.[5] If he writes too soon, he will be consumed by

[4] For the compositional history of *Edgar Huntly*, see Krause, "Historical Essay," 298–303.

[5] Axelrod speculates on the connection between Brown and Huntly as it relates to the expression of Brown's authorial identity within this work (16).

emotional chaos. If he waits too long, he will dull the edge of his recollections. Like Clara Wieland (and C.B.B. of the "Henrietta Letters"), Huntly locates himself within the compositional present. Like Clara (and Sophia Courtland), he sees the impending narrative as an arduous, but necessary (and possibly exhausting) task. As with Clara, Huntly's emerging voice reveals the fragile state of his psyche.

The novel as a whole contains four letters—Huntly's very long letter to Mary Waldegrave composed over weeks; two brief letters from Huntly to his mentor Sarsefield regarding Huntly's ill-advised attempt to forge a reconciliation between Edny and the former Euphemia Lorimer, now Sarsefield's wife; and a brief letter from Sarsefield to Huntly chastising him for his many bungling failures. In his letter to Mary, Huntly presents his evolving, highly conflicted, frequently misguided, and misunderstood depictions of his physical and psychological experiences. Brown dramatizes the vacillating track of Huntly's protean consciousness, the inchoate revelations of a constructed authorial self that he believes he knows and controls, even as he demonstrates how this putatively stable self is repeatedly challenged, undermined, and reinvented by the uncontrolled activities of his autonomous (and irruptive) unconscious mind.[6] At the center of Huntly's compositional process resides his preoccupation with inscribing for Mary a sensation narrative of the sort that Clara Wieland wrote for her correspondents. Within this narrative, Huntly depicts the past not as he sees and understands it while currently writing, but as he felt and understood his experiences when they occurred. He sets out to create a narrative that

---

[6] Rebhorn sees Brown's concerns with conscious and unconscious states as depicted in *Edgar Huntly* not in terms of binary domination—the Cartesian model of "a mind-over-body ontology" (444)—but as an intentional intermingling and conflation of mind-body ontologies with an emphasis in the second half of the novel on dramatizing a "mind-in-body" paradigm (462). Rebhorn's essay historicizes Brown's exploration of consciousness with reference to how mind-body relationships explored by David Hartley and Benjamin Rush are essentially ironized before giving way to "a fully realized form of embodied consciousness" (447) that is rooted in the "mind-in-body" theories espoused by Erasmus Darwin and Joseph Priestley (447–52).

will be an authentic reconstruction of his recollected (and reconstituted) past. Huntly specifically attempts to use this letter to create with Mary a companionate sense of participatory communion. His great wish is that, as she reads his words, she will live within the *sense* of his past experiences: "Thou wilt catch from my story every horror and every sympathy which it paints. Thou wilt shudder with my foreboding and dissolve with my tears.... thou wilt share in all my tasks and all my dangers" (*EH* 6). The world of his reconceived narrative will thus emerge in the form that Huntly claims to have experienced it, usually without interjected, present-tense commentary. Indeed, Huntly's sensation narrative has very few instances of him delivering the kind of present-time critical narrative that Clara Wieland frequently uses to interrupt and interpret the materials of her recollected experiences. Huntly keeps his reader within the state of confused uncertainty that characterized the psychological disorientation through which he lived and which he now attempts to detail. Huntly's letter, then, becomes a form of re-enactment for the teller and a form of direct experience for the reader. The sensation narrative not only depicts what he felt then, but it allows writer and reader to be affective participants in the emerging drama of his recollected past. His epistolary art, therefore, becomes a social venture rather than an isolated activity; or rather the isolated activity of composing the letter becomes reconceived when read as a co-dependent, companionate activity. Consequently, Mary Waldegrave becomes the reader's surrogate. By inducting these readers into the experiential context of Huntly's reconstructed life, Brown allows the mysteries that baffle and ensnare Huntly to unfold as an emergent, seemingly present-tense psychodrama. Like Mary, the reader descends into the text and inhabits the perplexing dimensions of Huntly's past world.

At the center of the novel's recollected action resides Huntly's ostensible attempt to solve the mystery surrounding the seemingly unmotivated murder of Mary's brother and Huntly's best friend, who was gunned down beneath an elm tree. As Sydney J. Krause argues, the elm operates as a synoptic, figural place that unifies an array of plot and cultural significations: The elm tree

> is the crucial landmark from which action springs and nexus of the collision and divergence of major plot lines (murder, guilt, pursuit, sleepwalking, and Indian warfare)—this great Elm functions as a psychological magnet on Huntly and Edny.... The tree...evokes a cumulative significance beyond itself by historical linkage with a comparably central image in the founders of Pennsylvania and, specifically, Philadelphia—heart of the nation to be. Namely, it evokes the long honored symbolism of the legendary "Treaty Elm," under which, tradition has it, William Penn, on arriving in the land of his "Holy Experiment" in the fall of 1682, negotiated a treaty of friendship at Shackamaxon (Kensington) with the Lenni Lenape. ("Penn's Elm" 464)[7]

Similarly, Andy Doolen observes, "The Elm is a melancholy monument to the Quaker founder's desire for peace and friendship, which the subsequent history of frontier violence and land grabs had destroyed" (354). The mystery of Waldegrave's death—and the attending historical and cultural associations stirred by the location of the murder, a reflection of the very kind of social realism that Berthold associates with Brown's reconfiguration of the Gothic—brings Huntly into contact with the strange, tormented Clithero Edny. He is the sleepwalker Huntly sees digging frantically at the spot where Waldegrave was murdered. In this novel, two obsessions converge within the same experiential pursuit. Huntly's quest for Waldegrave's killer leads him to consider Edny as the only likely suspect. In his compulsion to solve the mystery, Huntly originally believes that to discover "the author of this guilt" (*EH* 7) would be to enact the will of God:

[7] Waterman sees Waldegrave as a ghost image of Elihu Hubbard Smith and reflects Brown's quandary over whether to publish Smith's memoirs (*Republic of Intellect* 85–91). Axelrod explores ambiguities regarding Waldegrave's presence and absence within the novel (170–72).

"Methought that...to forbear inquiry or withhold punishment was to violate my duty to my God and to mankind" (*EH* 8).

Driven by this self-authorized, divine mandate, Huntly witnesses the wild figure digging beneath the elm tree and embraces the uncertain premise that any murderer will return to the crime scene. He concludes that this frenzied individual "was connected with the fate of Waldegrave, it led to a disclosure of the author of that fate" (*EH* 10). As Matthew Rebhorn notes, "[Huntly] is nevertheless a bad detective. That is, as much as the title character loves to ruminate about who killed Waldegrave, Brown likewise reveals at every turn the uselessness of this kind of rational inquiry" (454). Huntly's mistaken conviction—which relies on a number of false premises—engenders his misguided belief that he can become a redemptive force in rehabilitating the unhinged man. Huntly interprets Edny's sleepwalking as presumptive evidence that he is suffering guilt for his putative crime. As Brown makes clear in his prefatory note, sleepwalking is one of those "new springs of action" that will amuse and instruct his reader. He also (dubiously) claims that it is "one of the most common and most wonderful diseases or affections of the human frame" (*EH* 3). To Huntly, sleepwalkers are liberated from the confinements of the conscious mind: "The thoughts, which considerations of safety enables them to suppress or disguise during wakefulness, operate without impediment, and exhibit their genuine effects, when the notices of sense are partly excluded, and they are shut out from a knowledge of their intire condition" (*EH* 13). Sleepwalking becomes a manifestation of how the "mind-in-body" can operate outside of a "mind-over-body" cognitive paradigm: "Brown pushes his reader to encounter and compare the mind-over-body ontology and the radical potentialities of a mind-in-body model of consciousness"—with the un-conscious sleepwalker completely dissociated from the power of rational agency (Rebhorn 453). Enmeshed within a "fantastic drama" (*EH* 14), Edny becomes "the subject of [Huntly's] scrutiny. I was to gain all the knowledge, respecting him, which those with whom he lived...could impart" (*EH* 15). His desire to appropriate the truth of Edny's outer and inner lives leads Huntly to convince himself of his "generous purpose [that] will surely excuse me from descending to artifices" (*EH* 17).

Descend into "artifices" he most certainly does. This "generous purpose" impels his naïve, altruistic attempt to impose a benevolent design on this fractured man. In tracking and losing his quarry in the "rugged, picturesque and wild" domain of Norwalk (*EH* 19), Huntly remains convinced of Edny's guilt, but he does not know his motives or "inducements.... I see proofs of that remorse which must ever be attendant on guilt" (*EH* 32). Huntly traps himself within his own presumptions. His sense of divine mission is no more than an egotistical, self-justifying supposition. Nevertheless, the problem, as he seems to recognize, is that he falls far short of omniscience: "Were futurity laid open to my view, and events, with their consequences unfolded, I might see reason to embrace the assassin as my best friend" (*EH* 32). Even though only God in His providence can perceive the infinite expanse of "futurity," Huntly feels himself impelled to forgive Edny for the alleged murder and thereby "emulate a father's clemency, and restore this unhappy man to purity, and to peace" (*EH* 33)—a fictive, self-generated imperative that will drive Huntly's conscious relation with Edny, even as his own experiences with sleepwalking later demonstrate the limitations of his egotistical assumptions regarding his own attributes, the limitations of his powers of rational discernment, and the inherent fragility of his constructed social self. The progress of this novel dismantles Huntly's immature, self-aggrandizing notions regarding his self-proclaimed God-like and paternalistic attributes and dramatizes the dangers that attend the misguided, rational supposition that he can save Edny from his psychological compulsions. What Huntly believes is true of Clithero Edny—that he is Waldegrave's murderer—has nothing to do with what motivates both the wild Irishman's emigration to the new world and those peripatetic agitations that impel his conscious and unconscious behaviors.

The Clithero Edny Narrative: "Smitten with Excess of Thought"

Edny's extended, inset narrative—a mock-oral tale told to Huntly and now reconstructed within his letter to Mary Waldegrave—consumes approximately twenty percent of the novel—an indication of the importance Brown attaches to Edny's countertext, especially as it conflates a particularly troubling form of narrative self-making with a self-authorizing fiction of supernatural warrant. Edny's autobiographical narrative sets out to refute Huntly's accusations of "inferences" that help fabricate "a tissue of destructive errors" (*EH* 35–36). Edny quickly accepts his extreme depravity, but he ambiguously claims to be guilty of crimes more enormous than Waldegrave's murder. In detailing how as an indigent Irish boy he was taken in and raised by the altruistic and angelic Mrs. Lorimer—another agent intrepidly seeking to actualize a philosophy of benevolence—Edny delineates the chasmal distance between his efficient, affable social self, which leads him to act as Mrs. Lorimer's major domo and surrogate son, on the one hand, and his conflicted, disordered psychological compulsions, which culminate with his impending attempt to murder Mrs. Lorimer in her sleep, on the other.[8]

At the outset of his narrative, Edny prescripts the meaning of his story. He asserts that his prospective happiness was annihilated by "the daemon that controuled" and purportedly entangled him in a pernicious master-narrative (*EH* 36). Edny believes that this malevolent controller usurped his will and dictated his actions. The existence of this diabolical entity never receives extrinsic validation and appears only as a postulated fiction resembling the putatively deific voice that orders Theodore Wieland to commit multiple murders. Both Wieland and Edny claim direct communication with supernatural beings. Both believe they must square their actions according to exacting terms

[8] See Leask for a discussion of Brown's interest in Irish radicalism and its relation to Clithero (108–09).

stipulated by their (alleged) supernatural prompters. Edny associates his compulsive imperatives to kill with the directorial power of this infernal agent. The notion of a beneficent Providence has no place within the master-narrative wherein Edny believes himself trapped. Just as Theodore Wieland's God-obsession continues as a psychologically self-contained experience erupting only at the time appointed for the divinely-ordained acts of sacrificial slaughter, so too does Edny's demonic obsession remain hidden beneath his social facade until he feels driven to enact what he believes is a predestined design.[9]

Mrs. Lorimer is both the object of Edny's reverence and his intended sacrificial victim. Like Arthur Mervyn, she attempts to become the "author" of social benevolence. She was "[a]lways in search of occasions for doing good, always meditating scenes of happiness, of which she was the author" (41). In Brown's work, to "author" an action is to use one's conscious volition to originate an event within the public sphere. As a dominant trope, authorship becomes reflective of deep literary, political, and cultural foundations that expose the elemental issue of who, or what, forges the unfolding drama of human existence. Are people and events directed by God, by demons, by human will, by accident, or some combination thereof?

Mrs. Lorimer's evil twin Arthur Wiatte emerges as her behavioral and ontological opposite: "He exceeded in depravity all that has been imputed to the arch-foe of mankind.... He seemed to relish no food but pure unadulterated evil. He rejoiced in proportion to the depth of that distress of which he was the author" (*EH* 46). Wiatte operates as another authorial agent. Out of malice, he attempts to obstruct his sister from executing her benevolent designs. Years earlier, he thwarted her marriage to Sarsefield, her true love, a man who responded to this disappointment by emigrating to America, where he became Huntly's

[9] Grabo argues that the presence of the daemonic, demonic double inhabits the center of Brown's fiction (*The Coincidental Art* 170–75).

friend and mentor.[10] A more crass, cynical, and malevolent version of Ludloe and Ormond, Wiatte rejects "[l]ove and friendship...as groundless and chimerical.... [T]o bereave [his sister] of the good...was the most effectual means of rendering her miserable" (*EH* 46–47). After Wiatte's psychopathic criminality leads him to be convicted, transported, and seemingly (but not actually) killed in transit, Mrs. Lorimer asserts her power of benevolence and adopts Clarice, Wiatte's neglected, bastard daughter. After falling in love with Clarice, Edny becomes convinced of his own social inferiority and believes that any display of romantic love would betray the trust Mrs. Lorimer has in him. As a harbinger of twisted, emotional conniptions to come, he plans to quit her service, though he will speak neither of his "design" (*EH* 53) nor his "motives" (*EH* 54). Mrs. Lorimer, however, sees through "his scheme" (*EH* 56). Rejecting the premise that class distinctions should separate lovers, Mrs. Lorimer attempts to facilitate the marriage of Clithero and Clarice.

The prospective romantic resolution that would bring concord out of discord disintegrates when the self-contained fiction dominating Edny's inner life takes control of the social stage. From this perspective, his "flowing fortunes...were destined to ebb with unspeakably greater rapidity, and to leave [him], in a moment, stranded and wrecked" (*EH* 58). In speaking frequently of destiny and fate, Edny accentuates how questions regarding agency—whether concerning a single event or a more expansive, unfolding set of linked contingencies—provide the epistemic basis that informs and propels the hermeneutic process. He has no doubt that he is the victim of a supernatural power capable of manipulating his behavior and thereby dominating the social scene. He believes that his destruction was predestined by a seemingly perverse version of providential agency: "Why was not some intimation afforded me of the snares that lay in my path? In the train laid for my

[10] See Grabo on the coincidences in *Edgar Huntly*: ". . .Sarcefield's coincidental role as mentor to both Clithero and Edgar blatantly confesses Brown's failure to resist self-parody" (*The Coincidental Art* 62).

destruction, the agent had so skillfully contrived that my security was not molested by the faintest omen" (*EH* 59). In his warped mind, Edny construes postulated absence as a form of directorial presence.

What precipitates the collapse of Edny's social world is Wiatte's surprising "reappearance on the stage" as well as Sarsefield's return. Edny refuses to see these events as coincidental and instead claims that "there lurked, under those appearances, a tremendous significance, which human sagacity could not uncover" (*EH* 68). His paranoid theories always reveal more about his character than they do about the entity he interprets. Repeatedly, he objectifies, and indeed, absolutizes, his own subjective assertions—to the detriment of all concerned. Even when caught in a morally un-ambiguous situation, even when Wiatte attacks Edny in the dark and Edny shoots Wiatte in an indisputable act of self-defense, Edny makes determinate, but spurious, judgments about the alleged supernatural causes of Wiatte's death. He believes that Wiatte's slaying proceeded from "the theme of design. It must spring from laborious circumvention and deep laid stratagems." According to Edny, the demon artificer has taken over his entire being. Not only is he "impelled by an unconscious necessity," but he also becomes the self-conscious prisoner of his own mind: "Now my liberty...was at an end. I was fettered, confounded, smitten with excess of thought, and laid prostrate with wonder!" (*EH* 74). Tormented by the notion that he was controlled by a demonic force, he nevertheless retains the contradictory belief that he is completely culpable for his ostensibly coerced actions. As Huntly later remarks, "It must at least be said that [Edny's] will was not concerned in this transaction. He acted in obedience to an impulse which he could not controul, nor resist. Shall we impute guilt where there is no design?...Shall we deem ourselves criminal because we do not share the attributes of deity?" (*EH* 91–92).

Ironically, Edny's elaborate artifice of self-making creates a perverted fiction of supernatural determinism. Usually reflecting one's freedom to shape one's emergent performance, self-making here becomes contorted into a rigidly configured version of fate. Edny authors the very master-narrative that he believes is immutably predetermined. Paradoxically, freedom of mind leads to his confinement within the very forms his fancy creates. As Edny notes, "Conjecture deepened into certainty" (*EH* 78). From fallacious, self-justifying premises flow fallacious, self-justifying consequences. By personifying a diminutive version of Theodore Wieland, Edny lacks the sublime (if inherently dubious) conviction that his prospective murders are sanctioned by the direct command of a sovereign deity. Added to Edny's burden is his realization that Mrs. Lorimer also believes herself enmeshed within a malevolent plot. Convinced that the springs of her life are tied to the life of her evil twin, she believes their lives are inextricably co-dependent: when he dies, she must die.

Within the Clithero Edny inset narrative, Brown diminishes providential purpose and the concept of a benevolent, universal design into little more than destructive, mental pathologies. As Huntly notes, Edny's actions are not directed by supernatural forces, but by his willful obedience to the terms dictated by Mrs. Lorimer's own prediction: "In how many cases may it be said, as in this, that the prediction was the cause of its own fulfillment?" (*EH* 92). Through reductive thinking, Edny invents, and enacts, the terms of a rigid form of causality and thus becomes the artificer of his own fate. Since he was responsible for the death of Wiatte and since the death of Wiatte must issue in the death of Mrs. Lorimer, ergo, he must kill Mrs. Lorimer and complete the predestined design: "The period of terrible fulfillment has arrived. The same blow that bereaved *him* of life, has likewise ratified her doom" (*EH* 77, emphasis in original). Tragically, Edny cannot construct a critical perspective in distinction to his pathological self-justifications. Indeed, this narrowly determinant fiction derives its power from unconscious predilections intensified by the master narrative of diabolical agency. Brown depicts here another version of what Clara Wieland calls the "distempered imagination" (*W* 117)—a phrase that recurs in *Edgar Huntly* (164; a "distempered fancy" 228, 285).

Ironically, through his sick imagination, Edny eventually blames his prospective murder of Mrs. Lorimer solely on a malign, supernatural force: "My doom was ratified by powers which no human energies can counterwork.... Was it I that hurried to the deed? No. It was the daemon that possessed me. My limbs were guided to the bloody office by a power foreign and superior to mine" (*EH* 83). The power that impels his "bloody office" is the self-authorizing agency of his unconstrained, fiction-making imagination. The daemon here stands as both a fiendish expression of evil and a procreant force of dramatic enactment.

When Edny sneaks into Mrs. Lorimer's bedroom to find out if she has died as an empathetic consequence of her twin brother's death, he originally feels relieved upon seeing a living, sleeping form lying in peaceful repose. Soon, however, "[t]he madness...began now to make sensible approaches on my understanding" (*EH* 82). He raises a knife to kill the sleeper, but his hand is arrested. At first, he believes that a special act of divine providence restrained him. Actually, Mrs. Lorimer's hand impedes him from killing Clarice, who is asleep in Mrs. Lorimer's bed. Edny oscillates between a murderous compulsion to enact "a mysterious destiny" and the restraint imposed by the protective action of Mrs. Lorimer, "this beneficent interposer." He attempts to explain why he came to kill the woman, who was "the author" of his "benefits" (*EH* 85). He tells Mrs. Lorimer that he killed her brother and has "hastened hither, to perpetrate the same crime upon you]" (*EH* 86). He gives no mitigating details. Believing that her life will end with her brother's death, locked within a steadfast belief in the determinant power of fate, she exclaims, "Then is the omen fulfilled! Then am I undone! Lost forever!" When she collapses to the floor "pallid and breathless," Edny assumes that she is dead: "Thus was every omen of mischief and misery fulfilled" (*EH* 87). Subsequently, Edny remains unaware that Mrs. Lorimer survived her syncope. Tortured by his ignorance and convinced of the efficacy of his interpretation, Edny attempts to flee from his past, but he cannot escape the torturous confines of his mind. Near the end of his lengthy, inset narrative, he describes how his "perturbed sleep" expresses the roiling compulsions of the unconscious mind: "No wonder that sleep cannot soothe miseries like mine: that I am alike infested by memory in wakefulness and slumber. Yet I was anew distressed at the discovery that my thoughts found their way to my lips, without my being conscious of it, and that my steps wandered forth unknowingly and without the guidance of my will" (*EH* 89).

As Huntly soon discovers, there is more to the operations of his own psyche than the dictates of his conscious, authorial mind.[11] Like Edny, Huntly will come to see how his own words and actions operate independently of his will. In *Edgar Huntly*, Brown dramatizes how self-making is not simply a conscious, authorial process enacting the dictates of the protean self, but it can also be a frightening, irruptive force propelled by the autonomous unconscious mind.

"Incessant Novelty": An Ontological and Epistemological Inquiry

Following Clithero Edny's inset narrative, Edgar Huntly presents himself as an interpretive reader of this tale. At first, his "judgement was, for a time, sunk into imbecility and confusion." Subsequently, he seeks a hermeneutical posture that will enable him to proceed with "a deliberate and methodical inspection" (*EH* 91). This attempt to understand Edny derives from Huntly's informing benevolent purpose, an intrepid, zealous desire to save him from madness and death and restore him to a balanced life within a social community. Through Huntly's commitment to a philosophy of benevolence, Brown fuses what may appear to be competing imperatives—the need for individual, therapeutic self-recovery and self-development, on the one hand, and the need for a program of social responsibility that advances the common good, on the other. These very concerns reside at the heart of

[11] Rebhorn argues, "Even when Huntly is not 'reading' Clithero, Brown points out the deficiencies of intellectualism as a means of reading the world" (455).

contending political philosophies that characterize late eighteenth-century thought. Jay Fliegelman sees this apparent opposition as the source of a new synergy:

> In his study of the influence of Common Sense philosophy on Jefferson's political philosophy, Garry Wills...stressed the importance of recognizing a fundamental opposition in eighteenth-century thought between the Lockean insistence on the primacy of the individual, reason, and self-interest and, on the other hand, the Scottish insistence on the primacy of the social bond, affections, and disinterested benevolence....[T]he opposition is much less absolute than Wills suggests.... Both philosophies combined...to force a revolutionary rethinking of the relationship of individual and family, and, by extension, of obligation and personal liberty; of the progress of the soul and the progress of society. (25–26)

In his attempt to integrate individual and societal imperatives, Huntly expresses this kind of "revolutionary rethinking": for example, his application of benevolence would be salutary for Edny as a person as well as beneficial to the social sphere that may be undermined, or threatened, by the actions of a deranged Edny. By pursuing the art of benevolence, by seeking to fuse personal and communal imperatives, Huntly intends to author the future course of Edny's life.

While noble and altruistic (if not presumptuous and manipulative), Huntly's mission indicates more about the naiveté of his own predilections than it does about the implacable extremity of Edny's troubled condition and circumstances. Counting himself among the class of "dispassionate observers," Huntly initiates a drama of ontological and epistemological inquiry, an interrogation that explores "those limitations which nature has imposed upon human faculties" (*EH* 92). This pursuit includes his conscious attempt to know the truth of Edny's inner being as well as Huntly's unwitting revelations regarding the limitations of his own powers of rational discernment. For example, in seeking to exonerate Edny, Huntly propounds a sophistical theory of radical subjectivity that implicitly rejects the existence of extrinsic moral categories: "Proofs of a just intention are all that are requisite to exempt us from blame" (92). This spurious notion is especially peculiar given Edny's fervent insistence on his own criminality and the diabolical forces putatively controlling him. In light of Edny's revulsion over his own self-alleged, moral turpitude, Huntly's theory seems particularly vapid and obtuse—another failure of rational discernment of the sort examined within Rebhorn's discussion of competing ontologies. What drives Huntly is a self-defeating insistence that the world must conform to his understanding of it—a situation that casts him as Brown's least successful self-making artificer. In identifying a possible cause for Huntly's inept misreading, Christopher Stampone suggests that Huntly misses the larger cultural implications of Edny's status not simply as an irredeemable, murderous lunatic, but also as a cultural stereotype of the savage Irish, a cognate version of the stereotypical, savage Indian: "Clithero is an Irish savage in his home country *before* he comes to America, thereby remapping race thinking in the text. Edgar tries but fails to civilize the Irish savage Clithero in an attempt to demonstrate American exceptionalism's triumph over English imperialism as represented by Mrs. Euphemia Lorimer" (415, emphasis in original). Whereas "Brown very carefully demarcates the difference between the Irish and the Indian in this novel" (Stamphone 430), he nevertheless reveals that no allocation of benevolence, disinterested or otherwise, will be sufficient to cure, or alleviate, the threats embodied within these savage entities: "Brown...is the first American literary author to examine the consequences of savage invasions against American civilization from both inside, by Indians, and outside its borders, by Irishmen, in the same text" (Stamphone 437–38). Essentially, Huntly launches a reclamation project that is doomed to fail—a circumstance that leads Huntly into the wilderness, where he experiences *within himself* the shocking, ontological irruption of these culturally encoded modes of savagery that have been lying dormant within his own divided, American self. The irruption of unconscious forces within

Huntly dramatizes the cognitive limitations of what Rebhorn describes as the "the calcified hierarchy of mind over body" (449).

Troubled by Edny's extended absence, Huntly identifies "the idea of the wilderness" (*EH* 94) as suggesting a probable locale for Edny's putative suicide. Not only does Huntly feel that it is his duty to find and bury the man he assumes is dead, but he also embraces an excuse to plunge into the expansive, entangled recesses of "rugged, picturesque and wild" Norwalk (*EH* 19), a physical and symbolic landscape wherein Brown adapts depictions of picturesque landscapes to his own innovative purposes. According to Berthold,

> Charles Brockden Brown pursued the picturesque in theory and practice and encouraged its early movement across the Atlantic to America.... [H]e recognized that the descriptive conventions and emotional associations of picturesque travel provided visual analogies to the romantic hero's psychological state; in this way, picturesque aesthetics mediated between nature and the ego, the "eye" of vision and the "I" of selfhood, and so helped balance the conflicting claims of wildness and disorder, on the one hand, with those of civilization and order, on the other. ("Charles Brockden Brown" 63)[12]

[12] Berthold argues, "[B]oth the landscapes and Edgar's reactions to them derive in part from the tradition of the picturesque and look forward not only to the mental landscapes of Poe but also to the more realistic landscapes of Cooper's *The Deerslayer* (1840) and Hawthorne's *The House of the Seven Gables*" ("Charles Brockden Brown" 72). This landscape also prefigures "the heart of the dark wilderness" circumscribing the ostensibly civilized outposts of Hawthorne's provincial tales and the early Puritan settings of his first two full length romances (Hawthorne, "Young Goodman Brown" 82). For other discussions of Brown's use of landscapes in *Edgar Huntly*, see Axelrod's exploration of this work and Poe's fictions (29–46). See Kafer for his exploration of the connection between Norwalk and the ancestral lands held sacred by Delaware Indians and which led to murderous attacks on white settlers (167–70). See Kafer on Norwalk 171–76; Battistini asks a provocative question concerning Brown's sprawling cultural conflicts and configurations: "Why write a novel in which a Quaker sleepwalks into the very territory stolen in 1737, encounters and murders Delaware warriors, and investigates an Irishman for murder?" (329).

For Huntly, the unknown world of Norwalk offers an alternative to, and an escape from, the civilized world: "I love to immerse myself in shades and dells, and hold converse with the solemnities and secrecies of nature in the rude retreats of Norwalk" (*EH* 94–95). Berthold makes the crucial distinction that the domain of Norwalk is not the same as the wild, unmediated wilderness. Instead, Norwalk is situated "on the fringe of civilization, quite near houses, farms, and villages" ("Charles Brockden Brown" 73). Berthold elaborates:

> Norwalk is a rugged but not forbidding or inaccessible place and is sharply distinguished from the wilderness beyond, a fact obscured by psychological approaches to the text.... Norwalk is the known wilderness—the wilderness named, charted, and admired. It is neither as dangerous nor as wild as the unknown regions beyond.... It is a definable borderground that provides the sensitive observer with the wild and rugged beauty of the picturesque. ("Charles Brockden Brown" 74–75)

Situated beyond the reach of the fledgling settlements that mark the incipient presence of Eurocentric civilization, this landscape constitutes a seemingly inexhaustible resource that feeds the expansion of human consciousness: "Every new excursion indeed added somewhat to my knowledge. New tracks were pursued, new prospects detected, and new summits were gained" (*EH* 97). Norwalk, then, constitutes a middle space, a contested world marginally humanized and minimally known, a place that provides access to the untamed wilderness beyond, where savage Indians dwell and from where they launch murderous incursions. It is also a culturally contested space, the version of the wilderness already undergoing modifications that could either eventuate in the complete establishment of an imperial civilization (as the Anglo-Americans would have it) or a return to an unmediated, primal domain supporting the indigenous inhabitants (as the marauding Indians wish to do by extirpating the invaders). Norwalk thus reflects a physical externalization of the partially known, partially conscious self that experiences the process of change and therefore projects, as it were, a double of the human mind: "My rambles were productive of incessant novelty, though they always terminated in the prospect of limits that could not be overleaped" (*EH* 97). This landscape feeds the incremental, though continually truncated, acquisition of knowledge. Wild, tangled, a strange world without fixed and established rule, Norwalk exemplifies the protean possibilities inherent in Americanized transformation. This arena provides partial access to inexhaustible secrets and unrestricted vistas of immensities beyond imagination. Norwalk suggests the inexhaustibility of the phenomenal world, while simultaneously manifesting the human mind's innate, inherently dangerous, tendency to expand the reach of experience and consciousness through energies of hegemonic, political domination.

In his search for Clithero Edny, Edgar Huntly travels into the dark cave beyond the mediating space of Norwalk and thus carries within him the peripatetic essence of the Eurocentric colonial imperatives, especially its self-congratulatory, though specious, ideology of First Discovery. The cave constitutes a liminal entry way "into spaces hitherto unvisited, and to summits from which wider landscapes might be seen" (*EH* 98). To enter the cave will be to follow Edny and possibly reach the site of his supposed suicide.[13] Preoccupied as he is with "incessant novelty" (EH 97), Huntly fails to comprehend that what might seem new to him was not new to his predecessors. The wilderness beyond and within Norwalk has been, and remains, an ancestral and well-traveled landscape inhabited by generations of Indians. Viewed within this novel's conflict between indigenous and colonial cultures, what Brown in the preface reductively foregrounds as "incidents of Indian hostility, and the perils of the western wilderness" (*EH* 3), Huntly's perspective becomes ironically self-deflating. The extravagant image of himself as Original Conqueror reflects an unwarranted exuberance regarding his own achievements as well as the arrogance inherent in his cultural

[13] See Lueck for her discussion of how Brown transforms the picturesque in relation to the British tradition of the picturesque tourist (25).

posture: "Since the birth of this continent, I was probably the first who had deviated thus remotely from the customary paths of men" (*EH* 103). He believes he is not only the initial explorer, but he also uses language that asserts his right to possess this landscape. Huntly steadfastly believes that the workings of his mind are at one with the actual configuration of the phenomenological world.

His sense of rapture over the thrill of First Discovery dissolves when he looks across a chasm and sees Edny hiding where no person had been supposed to tread. When the anchorite suddenly disappears, Huntly clings to his notion that Edny intends suicide and immediately assumes that he leaped into the gorge to his death. Driven by a desire to assert a "benign influence," Huntly imagines that Edny might have retreated into an adjacent "aperture or pit" (*EH* 106). To solve the problem of traversing the abyss, Huntly goes home to get an ax so he can chop down a tree "whose trunk was to serve me for a bridge" (*EH* 108). In just such a way are this landscape's labyrinthine entanglements subverted by the application of human ingenuity. He begins the march of progress—in this case, the incremental appropriation, and destruction, of the wilderness. In taking the ax and cutting down the tree, Huntly transfigures nature into an identifiable human construct. Tree becomes bridge and constitutes a synecdoche of the encompassing colonizing process.[14] Huntly enacts in microcosmic form those cultural processes that convert nature into proliferating, though innately ambiguous, structures that typify western civilization. Scott Bradfield sees such actions as part of a cultural dynamic in which the evolution of the American romance becomes a consequence of re-conceiving Anglo-European tales—in this case, the imperial conquest of the wilderness—

[14] Doolen argues, ". . .Brown's writings persistently deny the existence of a clear temporal boundary between British colony and American republic. In this version of literary nationalism, colonialism—a system of territorial acquisitions, capitalist exploitation, and the domination of non-whites—was part and parcel of the Bildungsroman of a rising republic with imperial designs in North America" (352). Levine reads *Edgar Huntly* "as a text that blurs national and racial identities and obscures (and unfixes) historical trajectories" (*Dislocating Race and Nation* 41).

via a series of transgressive acts: "By constantly transgressing the 'inaccessible' Edgar surrenders himself to irresistible progress. Every limit he confronts compels him to transgress it, and every act of transgression leads him to the brink of another, still further limit to be transgressed" (27).

Huntly's reconstructive actions are all meant to seem very rational. With the same directness with which he chops down a tree to make a bridge, he attempts to amend the fault-lines of Edny's mind. Huntly tries to apply the balm of rational (or rationalizing) explication:

> How should I convince him that since the death of Wiatte was not intended, the deed was without crime; that, if it had been deliberately concerted, it was still a virtue, since his own life could, by no other means, be preserved; that when he pointed a dagger at the bosom of his mistress he was actuated, not by avarice, or ambition, or revenge, or malice? He desired to confer on her the highest and the only benefit of which he believed her capable. He sought to rescue her from tormenting regrets and lingering agonies. (*EH* 110)

Huntly once again, unwittingly it seems, indulges the notion that attempted murder can be construed as "the highest and only benefit," just so long as Edny's motives have an exalted, self-justifying (if self-deluding) premise. He does not find anything wrong with the Irishman wanting to kill Mrs. Lorimer so that she will no longer have to suffer from "tormenting regrets." This brand of rational (or rationalizing) speculation simply appears as more sophistry: the self-justifying, interpretive process leads him to his only applicable measure of moral rectitude. His highly problematic presentation of himself as moral arbiter coalesces with his preposterous and impetuous desire to create the illusion of a providentially engineered miracle. After Huntly crosses the gorge on his new-made bridge, he finds Edny sleeping. Rather than awakening him and presenting the food he brought, Huntly decides he will assume a divine office. He simply leaves the refreshments with the idea that when the sleeper awakens, he will believe that these provisions were gifts from a deific agent reflecting "a kind of heavenly condemnation of his [alleged suicidal] purpose" (*EH* 111–12).

Once again, Brown presents the protean artificer as one who plays at being God. Like Carwin, Huntly uses a manipulative ploy to create the illusion of divine intervention. Once again, Brown depicts the danger of the artist figure—this author of experience—let loose in life. For example, after returning home, Huntly believes himself authorized to invade the privacy of Edny's strong box, even though Mr. Inglefield declared that "[t]his box contained nothing with which others had a right to meddle" (*EH* 114). In reconceiving the locked box incident from "The Man at Home," Brown indicates that Huntly conveniently views himself as a "mechanist" (*EH* 115): "I looked upon this [box] therefore with the eye of an artist, and was solicitous to know the principles on which it was formed. I determined to examine, and if possible to open it" (*EH* 116). This box is meant to represent a possible repository of secrets and may even reflect a simplified, symbolic double of Clithero. In this instance, Huntly anticipates Hawthorne's various practitioners of "the Unpardonable Sin," prying like Ethan Brand or Roger Chillingworth into another person's secrets and exploiting such knowledge for malign purposes.[15] Whereas Huntly can open the box, he cannot close it. To snoop into protected interiors is to launch an invasive, self-indicting venture that can neither be reversed nor covered up. Indeed, Huntly emerges as a misdirected artist-figure, who relies, to his own detriment, on self-authorized intentionality. Even though Huntly wishes to correct Edny's obsessive claims of diabolical causality, he has his own problems. He no more controls the disruptive power of the unconscious than Edny does.

[15] See Hawthorne's "Ethan Brand" for the "Unpardonable Sin" (87) and Hawthorne's presentation of Roger Chillingworth, especially in Chapter XI, "The Interior of a Heart," in *The Scarlet Letter* (139–46).

Primal Energies Erupt: A New American Action Hero

When Huntly finds that letters written to him by the late Waldegrave are missing, he feels as baffled and frustrated as he does when his uncle reports having "distinctly heard some one pacing to and fro with bare feet, in the long room" (*EH* 136). The packet of letters was secured in an extremely safe location: "I was not conscious of having taken it away, yet no hands but mine could have done it" (*EH* 134). Nor could anyone but Huntly have paced "so solemnly and indefatigably across the *long-room* for near an hour" (*EH* 136, emphasis in original). In the aftermath of these enigmatic events, Huntly does not rest with an acceptance of inscrutability. In the attempt to solve these mysteries, Huntly creates a skein of speculative scenarios. He imagines that the letters were purloined "by some malignant and inscrutable destiny" (*EH* 135). He believes the letters could only have vanished through supernatural agency: "Human artifice or power was unequal to this exploit. Means less than preternatural would not furnish a conveyance for this treasure" (*EH* 138).

Neither "malignant destiny" nor "preternatural" beings were responsible for perpetrating these disruptive events. Huntly himself, while sleepwalking, paced the room for hours. Huntly himself, while sleepwalking, absconded with the letters. Essentially, his conscious self no longer controls his actions. Sleepwalking is to this novel what disembodied voices are to *Wieland*—a powerful, interruptive force that creates dramatic mystery and opens the way for the transformation—indeed, the disintegration—of ostensibly stable forms of identity. Huntly's sleepwalking propels him into a whole new plot that grows out of itself with no apparent relation to the life he lived or the person he seemed to be. As sleepwalkers, Edgar Huntly and Clithero Edny are doubles and alter-egos.[16] Both characters reflect how the unconscious

[16] For discussions of character doubling in *Edgar Huntly*, see Krause, "Historical Essay" 325; Christophersen 129–30; Watts 126. Witherington details how Brown's

mind can usurp the tenuous structures of ego consciousness. Unlike Huntly, however, Edny remains trapped within the constrictive, highly destructive master-narrative of demonic possession. Huntly, on the contrary, re-invents who he is, revealing a protean capacity for remaking the acting self in response to specific histrionic exigencies. As Brown in his major novels delights in demonstrating, the performing self is malleable and can be reconstructed and deconstructed by arbitrary circumstance, by the conscious application of will, and by the irruptive power of the unconscious. Brown relentlessly dismantles the notion that the conscious self is an unwavering, reliable agent. As Beverly R. Voloshin notes, "*Edgar Huntly* turns in part on what happens in such gaps in consciousness.... The buried life is the real mystery of the novel" (265).[17] Up to this point in Brown's work, self-making has been coincident with the expression and acquisition of personal power. Carwin, for example, simultaneously revels in and fears the exercise of his biloquial power—a power that not only finds issue in protean forms of imposture, but also has the capacity to dominate other people and thereby direct what transpires on the social stage. As Carwin indicates, the conscious mind reconfigures the acting self in highly determinant and willful ways. Neither Edgar Huntly nor Clithero Edny, however, has control over their respective sleepwalking selves. When the sleepwalking Huntly hides Waldegrave's letters, he is impelled to act according to the dictates of an irruptive, seemingly purposeless, unconscious process. He acts without cognition, consciousness, and memory. In this instance, he is like Edny, who digs frantically beneath the storied elm, yet has no memory of doing so. Huntly, therefore, becomes the unwitting prisoner and dupe of his own past deeds. In seeking

---

exploration of doubles and doubling extends beyond the delineation of character to include a complex language of "classical parallelisms, the doubling of noun or adjective or verb phrases, and a carefully modulated reinforcement of ideas through contrast of similarities" (176). Also see 176–80. As Miles notes, "Doubling...is a principle source of Gothic horror" (411).

[17] Voloshin links Brown's exploration of doubling and repetition to his critique of Locke's view of the self (274–75).

outwardly for the perpetrator, he does little more than accentuate his own confusion. Brown's focus here is on the independent force of unconscious compulsion as it transforms the performative self into a being who acts without volition.[18]

The depths of the unconscious mind become the tangled, psychological equivalent of the wilds that exist beyond the picturesque borderworld of Norwalk. The unmediated wilderness exists outside the margins of what is known, out beyond the ego-realm of civilized self-knowledge, and becomes manifest as an undifferentiated, experiential domain from which emerge the energies and acts of human savagery—both native and colonizing. It is here that one meets the frightening realities of a rampaging, vengeful, indigenous America inscribed within xenophobic stereotypes that (ironically) depict Indians not only as Other but alien.[19] It is here where one recognizes that the Quaker Huntly rejects the pacifistic tenets of his creed and enacts extreme forms of violence. As Robert Battistini notes, "*Edgar Huntly* imagines a Pennsylvania Quaker imagining cultural others from whom he is deeply alienated—Irish immigrants, the Delaware, Scots-Irish settlers—and considers local conflicts against the backdrop of the wider Atlantic and the imperial world that shapes them" (330). It is here where one meets the naked horror of a full-blown, murderous, colonial processes dramatized through the wildness of a savagely re-created, self-displacing Edgar Huntly. The social and political constructs of

---

[18] Silyn Roberts locates Brown's *Edgar Huntly* within the tradition of the "American adventure tale" with its emphasis on the presentation of conflicting, chaotic, and seemingly random events: "To put it mildly, the adventure tale is emphatically *not* the kind of tidy, unified narrative we might expect from a 'realist' novel. Rather, it asks to be read as something like a generic 'assemblage,' less a taxonomic category than a set of discursive relations, stitching together narrative components that may seem unrelated and discordant but whose very heterogeneity dictates how we apprehend their meaning" (445, emphasis in original).

[19] See Gardner's exploration of issues pertaining to the relation of Americans and aliens within the political cauldron associated with the various Alien and Sedition Acts of 1798 (433). For Gardner's discussion of Huntly's incursion "into the savage landscape" (443) in relation to his Indian massacre, see 444–48.

civilization and the self-made embodiments of personal order give way and crumble before the power of the unconscious. When Huntly awakens in total darkness in a state of pain and disorientation, Brown continues to dismantle the coordinates that give continuity and direction to Huntly's identity and world. After falling asleep in his bed, Huntly wakes up in a nightmare of pain and darkness: "Then I was in perfect health; now my frame was covered with bruises and every joint was racked with pain" (*EH* 161). He finds himself caught within both an epistemological mystery and experiential crisis. Possessing sensation without knowledge, he is bereft of any notion of how he came to be in this predicament. As with the mysteries surrounding the night-pacer and Waldegrave's letters, Huntly responds to his lack of knowledge by developing an explanatory fiction that blames his situation on some unknown, magical artificer: "The author of my distress and the means he had taken to decoy me hither, were incomprehensible. Surely my senses were fettered or depraved by some spell" (*EH* 164). Having plunged into experiential and psychological chaos, Huntly enlists Gothic plots and the prospect of supernatural agency as failed, explanatory paradigms.[20]

After awakening bruised and confused in the depths of a wilderness cave following an extended episode of "Noctambulation" (*EH* 260), however, Huntly decides to rebel against his "fettered" condition and counteract whatever "spell" has so mysteriously trapped him. Unlike Edny, Huntly repeatedly abandons fixed conceptions—for example, the notion that he has been victimized by some maleficent, supernatural agent—in favor of improvised responses to emergent, usually threatening, exigencies. Repeatedly, he finds himself in strange, new phenomenological and psychological circumstances. Repeatedly, he must reconstruct his acting self. Indeed, the wilderness without reflects the wilderness within. At first, he descends into an instinctual, gruesome, masochistic form of savagery: "I felt a strong propensity to bite

[20] Axelrod discusses Poe's borrowing of words and situation from the cave scene for use in "The Pit and the Pendulum" (36–42).

the flesh from my arm. My heart overflowed with cruelty, and I pondered on the delight I should experience in rending some living animal to pieces, and drinking its blood and grinding its quivering fibres between my teeth" (*EH* 164).[21] He considers cutting his own body with a tomahawk and drinking his blood. After climbing out of the pit, he attacks a panther, feeds on it, and later consumes his own sweat. In this scene, Brown pushes language toward the limits of dramatic representation. As Berthold notes, "Often considered the most gothic section in the book, the cave scene provided a model for similar scenes of enclosure and darkness in the writings of Poe and others. And with good reason. It is a terrifying, even repulsive plunge into atavistic horrors as grotesque as any in fiction" ("Desacralizing the Gothic" 130).

Brown not only depicts the bizarre dissolution of Huntly's earlier social self but indicates that the ineluctable fact of his own brand of colonizing, Eurocentric savagery constitutes a culturally specific embodiment of, and identification with, the ferocious Other, both Indian and Irish. Most significantly, however, such an inclusive form of savagery reflects a universal ontological axiom, an elemental attribute buried within any human being, and *not* exclusively an idiosyncratic, signature-attribute of either the Eurocentric Huntly, the dark-skinned, indigenous Other, or the wild Irish immigrant. Consequently, the elevated status accorded to an ostensibly rational, civilized Eurocentric individual does not inherently reflect a fixed quality of being but remains a provisional, malleable attribute that can lead anyone into aberrant forms of improvised, unsettling behavior. Brown's message here is that human beings oscillate between civility and savagery as along a rising or sliding scale. One's civilized attributes—one's respectable social identity—can be enhanced or debased. To descend into savagery, as it were, is to give unimpeded vent to those elements normally repressed or displaced by the mores dictating acceptable social behavior. At one point, Brown's imagery reflects how ontological distinctions

[21] Axelrod explores Brown's passing reference to "self-cannibalism" (18) as it relates to Huntly's descent into savagery (18–20).

between humans and beasts are not absolute but conditional. When tracking the wayward Edny through Norwalk, Huntly sees a panther. What heightens the ferocity of the beast is its "cry which...by its resemblance to the human voice, is peculiarly terrific, [and] denoted him to be the most ferocious and untamable of that detested race" (*EH* 124). By conflating human and bestial attributes, in depicting Huntly's own declension into savagery, Brown continues his assault on the stability and efficacy of the social self and, by extension, the encompassing civilized sphere. Thus, if the social self is a constructed entity that can easily give way to the irruptive emergence of a compulsive, savage ur-self, then the grandiose, self-congratulatory structures of civilization—this realm of law, altruism, benevolence, culture, religious and societal order—rest on very shaky ground: in fact, such structures are little more than self-authorizing and self-generated fictions.

To the extent that savagery lurks beneath the ego-veneer of any human being, then there is, at least, an implicit irony—stemming from a kind of ideological blindness—in the degree to which the once rational, altruistic (if naïve) Edgar Huntly so quickly devolves into the savage, scheming, bloodthirsty, psychologically addled Edgar Huntly. As Stephen Rachman observes, "For Brown, Gothic anxiety's proper métier was not the trapdoor-riddled monk's castle or the black robe but the mental conditions aroused by fears of madness, disease, bankruptcy, politics, the ordinary violence of human passion, and, on the American frontiers, Native American treachery and captivity" (369–70). The chief irony inherent in this particular dramatization of Gothicized horror resides in the alacrity with which he turns himself into an effective killing machine. Although fearing the savage Indians, he becomes an accomplished savage himself. In reflecting on one of his murderous forays, he writes, "All my education and the habits of my life tended to unfit me for a contest and a scene like this. But I was not governed by the soul which usually regulates my conduct. I had imbibed from the unparalleled events which had lately happened a spirit vengeful, unrelenting, and ferocious" (*EH* 192). From out of the chaos of violent, primal energies steps Huntly as an American action hero: "In spite of the force and uniformity with which my senses were impressed by external objects, the transition I had undergone was so wild and inexplicable; all that I had performed; all that I had witnessed since my egress from the pit, were so contradictory to precedent events, that I still clung to the belief that my thoughts were confused by delirium" (*EH* 194). Ironically, the more violent Huntly becomes, the more he can be identified as a double of the stereotyped savage Indians.[22]

In attempting to prepare the reader for Huntly's momentous "transitions," Brown's preface not only introduces the aesthetic and psychological dimensions of his "new performance"—this emergent creation of American novelty—but he also foregrounds the dominant geographical and cultural complexes animating the novel. In promising "a series of adventures, growing out of the condition of our country" (*EH* 3), Brown prepares to shift the reader's gaze from the suburban, patrimonial lands of *Wieland* and the urban, disease-stricken domains of *Ormond* and *Arthur Mervyn* toward engaging a proliferation of strange, liminal narrative possibilities. The picturesque domain of Norwalk is where the Native Americans once lived and thrived and now it is the place where a roving band of Indian warriors has returned to terrorize the colonizing, European invaders. In his prefatory note, Brown's bid to advertise his distinctly American tale leads him to refer to "incidents of Indian hostility, and the perils of the western wilderness" (*EH* 3). Thus, Brown calls attention to the colonial conflict between savage European settlers on the hunt for marauding enemies of civilization, on the one hand, and the dwindling, demonized Indian band reduced to terroristic guerilla warfare, on the other.[23] By

[22] Rebhorn argues, "[W]e discover a hybrid form of consciousness that troubles the distinctions between Native American and white, conscious and unconscious, mind and body" (466).

[23] Brown's portrait of the combative Indians is not without an empathetic dimension. Chief among the vestigial cohort of avenging Indians is Old Deb. Krause argues, "Indeed, in Old Deb, Brown gives us a notable exception to the racist stereotypes visited on her younger kinsmen.... The lone surviving representative of

frequently identifying the Indians as savages, Huntly condones his own extreme violence against them on the grounds that he pursues a justified revenge for the wholly imagined assumption that the Indians have slaughtered his two sisters and his uncle—a notion that turns out to be mostly untrue. His sisters survived and his uncle died not as an innocent victim but in close combat with the Indians. Huntly is all too ready to accept without challenge those determinate conclusions spawned by his hyperactive imagination.

After he makes his way toward the mouth of the cave, he finds a young, white female captured by a "swarthy band" of sleeping Indian kidnappers (*EH* 175). Huntly attacks and kills the unsuspecting sentry. In the moment of action, Huntly reconfigures his "ill fate" (*EH* 178) and becomes the "author" of a violent action: "[The Indian] had not time to descry the author of his fate" (*EH* 179). Huntly's relentless, unconflicted desire to extirpate the demonized, savage horde replays the stereotypical ideology of the heathen Indian popularized more than one hundred years before in Mary Rowlandson's *Captivity Narrative*, where Rowlandson's ordeal as described in this first Indian captivity narrative became a testament to the power of providential purpose.[24] In *Edgar Huntly*, Brown's focus on irruptive psychological causality and exigent contingencies eliciting savage responses has the effect of displacing assertions of a providential order in favor of speculations regarding either the sphere of malign supernatural agencies or the

---

Delaware interests in Norwalk...Deb, like Edny, is another of Brown's shadowy figures, hovering on the fringe of what she sees as violating settlements" ("Penn's Elm" 474). Also see Krause for his discussion of Brown's use of sources and historical referents ("Historical Essay" 357–90).

[24] Hamelman examines relationships between Rowlandson's *Captivity Narrative* and Brown's treatment of Indians and wilderness encounters in *Edgar Huntly* (171–75). The full title of Rowlandson's narrative of 1682 is *The sovereignty and goodness of GOD, together with the faithfulness of his promises displayed; being a narrative of the captivity and restoration of Mrs. Mary Rowlandson, commended by her, to all that desires to know the Lord's doings to, and deals with her. Especially to her dear children and relations* (Rowlandson 269).

presence of such morally neutral forces as fate, necessity, and destiny: "Some ill fate decreed that I should not retreat unobserved" (*EH* 178). Huntly repeatedly uses words like "fate" and "destiny"—"my destiny was propitious" (*EH* 198)—to describe circumstantial encounters. When holed up at Deb's hut with the freed young woman, Huntly is by now "satiated and gorged with slaughter" (*EH* 199). He sees that a "savage…was now approaching the theatre of carnage, to ascertain [his companions'] fate" (*EH* 199–200). Here, "fate" is just another word for an event that already happened. The "fate" awaiting the alleged savage is also no more than Huntly's impending savage act: "Fate has reserved him for a bloody and violent death" (*EH* 200). Huntly also takes note of the seemingly arbitrary way that his fated troubles come tumbling one after the other: "Surely my fate has never been paralleled!…No sooner was one calamity eluded, than I was beset by another" (*EH* 223). Such a sequence reflects random events operating without pattern or order, a kind of picaresque skein of accidental encounters.

Animating the "capricious constitution" (*EH* 195) of Huntly's mind is his insistent preoccupation with postulating an array of explanatory fictions. Brown does not grant interpretive priority to any particular causal configuration, whether providential, fated, or self-actualized. Instead, he dramatizes the protean process whereby human beings *create* potentially credible, if speculative, narrative constructs that might explain, if only briefly, the twisted, discontinuous events that comprise the human story. Huntly's mind percolates with overheated energies fueled by his "own distempered imagination" (*EH* 164). The result, according to Berthold, is that "gothicism gave way to nationalism" ("Desacralizing the Gothic" 136). Early in the cultural life of the nation, Brown shows how the American action hero becomes a powerfully expressive fact and symbol—one that emerges through the irruptive, dominating force of extreme violence.[25] What *is* American is

[25] As Gardner explains, "[F]or Brown the threat of the Native American presence has less to do with questions of what it means to be civilized than with the

Huntly's hegemonic extension of his will over the land and, consequently, over its original inhabitants. His tale depicts the protean energies that characterize the expanding nation, while at the same time dramatizing a moral and political critique of how such violence confers horrific consequences on Indians and Huntly himself.

The Failure of Benevolence Redux

Sarsefield's re-appearance in Huntly's life opens the way for the resolution of specific mysteries. Sarsefield answers questions regarding how Huntly managed to find his own gun in the possession of the Indians; he explains how the sleepwalking Huntly wandered the backwoods of Norwalk; Sarsefield explains what happened to Waldegrave's letters; he provides information regarding the safety of Huntly's sisters and the death of his uncle. In his resemblance to Thomas Cambridge in *Wieland*, Sarsefield speaks as a stable man with focused, ratiocinative powers. By reading clues and developing sensible inferences, he cobbles together a story of past events and arrives at credible conclusions: "Having formed a plausible conjecture as to him who walked in the Long-room, it was obvious to conclude that he who purloined your manuscripts and the walker were the same personage.... Men have employed anxious months in search of that which, in a freak of Noctambulation, was hidden by their own hands" (*EH* 260). The cognitive force that impels Sarsefield's explanations stands in opposition to the force that drives a sleepwalker to perform bizarre actions neither willed nor remembered. Brown delineates two versions of the construct that is the self—one version characterized by the energies of rational discourse; the other version characterized by anarchic energies of unconscious compulsion. The sleepwalking Edgar Huntly seems to be driven by the urge to scatter those things that are most important to him. By hiding Waldegrave's letter, he demonstrates how the unconscious self

---

question—newly urgent in the United States in 1799—of what it means to be American" (429).

sometimes acts in opposition to the wishes and best interests of the conscious, rational mind. In this configuration, the two selves remain at war. Huntly remarks on the affinities that exist between himself and his sleepwalking double:

> Clithero had buried his treasure with his own hands as mine had been secreted by myself, but both acts had been performed during sleep. The deed was neither prompted by the will, nor noticed by the senses of him, by whom it was done. Disastrous and humiliating is the state of man! By his own hands, is constructed the mass of misery and error in which his steps are forever involved.... How total is our blindness with regard to our own performances! (*EH* 278)

Huntly recognizes the dangers that obtain when rational powers of mind and will are absent. The conscious self must develop the means necessary to neutralize those actions driven by "phantoms too indistinct to be now recalled" (*EH* 278). As a rational being with a tempered judgment, Sarsefield embodies this novel's predominant force of order. His presence carries with it the possibility of narrative closure. His explanations counteract the dangers of runaway subjectivity, even as they de-romanticize many of the novel's outrageous, seemingly inexplicable events.

It is not so surprising or coincidental that Sarsefield reappears on the scene. Some years before, he was Huntly's confidant and mentor. In fact, his primary purpose in returning to America with his wife, the former Mrs. Lorimer, was to find Huntly and reclaim him as a surrogate son. Sarsefield's presence also allows Brown to connect the Huntly plot with the antecedent Clithero plot. What *is* surprising is that Sarsefield finds Huntly alive after presumably seeing him dead. Sarsefield not only resolves plot incidentals and stabilizes a highly volatile social situation, which includes helping Huntly reclaim himself from savagery, but he also expresses a new belief in the power of miracles. His character reconciles, and indeed normalizes, the unification of rational and supernatural modes of discernment. As part of this normalization process, he specifically affirms the possibility of providential agency. After mourning Huntly's death and then finding him alive, Sarsefield remarks, "Well, I have lived to this age in unbelief. To credit or trust in miraculous agency was foreign to my nature, but now I am no longer skeptical" (*EH* 242). During his pursuit and attempted "extirpation" of the Indian guerilla warriors, "these detestable foes" (*EH* 250), Sarsefield also becomes spokesman for the Eurocentric colonizing forces convinced of their affinity with supernatural agency: "Some invisible power seemed to be enlisted in our defence and to preclude the necessity of our arms" (*EH* 255). Sarsefield asserts that Huntly's exploits as an Indian-killing action hero could only have been successful with the aid of "supernatural means" (*EH* 256). In a novel mostly bereft of providential claims, Sarsefield does not bring "miraculous agency" into the text as a fact but simply as another interpretive possibility: his assertion of beneficent causality stands in dialectical opposition to Edny's demonic master-narrative and to those numerous evocations of fate and necessity.

Whereas Sarsefield resolves incidental mysteries and asserts the efficacy of divine intervention, he also underscores the inescapable limits of human subjectivity and (inadvertently) the dangers of investing confidence in his own ideological and ontological superiority, especially when reflected in the ironic ways in which Sarsefield and Huntly each mistake the other for demonic, Indian savages. In this novel, who, or what, *is* savage does not have a fixed cultural, ideological, racialized, or geographical referent. Rather, savagery often derives from an offensive, violent response to a series of accusatory postulations founded on preconception, bias, and misapprehension. In the process of reconstructing the Edgar Huntly action hero narrative, Sarsefield recounts his confusing experiences in "the theatre of action" (*EH* 251) and describes his mistaken perceptions. Simply put, he does not know who or what he is shooting at; he merely presents a series of suppositions: "There was something likewise in the appearance of the object that bespoke it to be man; but if it were man, it was, incontrovertibly, a savage and a foe" (*EH* 257). When Sarsefield is shooting at Huntly, he believes he is shooting an Indian savage. When Huntly is shooting at Sarsefield, he is convinced he is shooting at an Indian savage. Neither is actually shooting at the indigenous American enemy, but both are locked within their own perceptions that tell them they are doing so. From their respective points of view, they are simply mistaken and trapped within a self-deceptive framework established by limited vision and ideological preconceptions. In these instances, the performative self becomes an actor within a racist, culturally ordained plot that reduces the indigenous Other to a stereotypical embodiment of archetypal evil. Sarsefield's notion that the figure he is shooting at is "incontrovertibly a savage" is actually controverted. The social forms that trumpet the righteous superiority of the colonizers are nothing more than ironic assertions farcically contradicted by facts: both white men think they are shooting at dark-skinned savages.

Neither Sarsefield nor Huntly sees the continuing mix-up over who has Huntly's gun and the alacrity with which it changes hands as anything more than a remarkable series of surprising events. One must step outside their self-justifying Eurocentric ideology to grasp the political implications regarding the various possessors of the gun.[26] The gun belongs to Huntly until his uncle takes the gun to shoot some Indians. An Indian takes the gun, shoots the uncle, and keeps the gun. Huntly finds this gun in the cave and shoots an Indian. When Huntly is mistaken for dead, Sarsefield picks up the gun and assumes it was fired not by Huntly, who he believes is dead, but by an Indian. Sarsefield wonders, "What was I hence to infer respecting the person of the

[26] See Calcaterra's exploration of guns as depicted in *Edgar Huntly* and in American culture and how this gun culture stands in opposition to archival Native American holdings. In her cross-cultural reading, Huntly's use of guns facilitates his descent into murderous violence. This convoluted business concerning who owns the gun reflects what Levine identifies as "the 'Brownian moment'… those moments in Brown's fiction when there is a destabilization or collapse of binaries that uphold the identity and coherence of self and republican nation" (*Dislocating Race and Nation* 46)

last possessor?" (*EH* 258). In a world dominated by protean reconfigurations and misapprehensions, anyone can use the gun. Power simply comes with possession. Savagery is not a matter of ontological depravity inherent in a specific individual or racialized identity but a matter of behavior, of actions, that lead one from order to dis-order, from social forms of civilized deportment, discourse, and laws toward an extravaganza of violence, confusion, and mayhem. In their desires to hold the land as their own and use violence to enact their purposes, the colonizer and the Indian are in fact inverted images of one another. Sympathy for the nativist position, however, can only be reached by rejecting the savage stereotype promulgated by Sarsefield and Huntly and by recognizing that the Indians are trying to repossess Norwalk and the wilderness beyond. Indeed, they have a natural right to regain what they once fully possessed. Like the Europeans, the Indians will use any instrument of power available to them.

With the return of Sarsefield, Huntly also finds himself in a position to explore whether "the narrative of Clithero [was] the web of imposture or the raving of insanity" (*EH* 261). Impelled by his ingenuous, enduring desire to save Edny and bring him within normative, social relations, Huntly is like Arthur Mervyn in that he proposes to construct new social forms by enacting the arts of benevolence. Huntly wonders whether he might reunite Edny and the former Mrs. Lorimer: "Was it possible to bring them together; to win the maniac from his solitude, wrest from him his fatal purposes, and restore him to communion with the beings whose imagined indignation is the torment of his life?" (*EH* 265). "Indignation" against Clithero Edny, however, is not "imagined." Unsurprisingly, Sarsefield despises him for his attempt to murder his wife. According to Sarsefield, Mrs. Lorimer made Edny into the well-adapted person he had once appeared to have been, "for he was her own work. His virtues were the creatures of her bounty." Sarsefield is appalled that Edny could "[l]ift a dagger to destroy her who had been the author of his being and his happiness" (*EH* 276). From this perspective, the former Mrs. Lorimer must be seen as a failed "author," another indication of the dangers inherent in any human being attempting to re-form the life of another person. Huntly's attempt to impose his benevolent design conflicts with Sarsefield's unwavering conviction that Edny is an irrevocable maniac, a man alien to any possibility of reestablishing a normative, social identity. Sarsefield is even convinced that he is the agent of diabolical forces: "An agent from Hell had mastered his faculties. He was become the engine of infernal malice against whom it was the duty of all mankind to rise up in arms and never desist till, by shattering it to atoms, its power to injure was taken away" (*EH* 276). Whereas Huntly can use the protean power of self-making to return from savage depths and reconstruct an operative, social self, Edny, on the contrary, cannot escape the dictates of his fate and remains entangled within an isolated, idiosyncratic, self-justifying, insane mindset.

In his misguided attempt "to benefit a man" (*EH* 287) and "outroot a fatal, but powerful illusion" (*EH* 288), Huntly makes the mistake of telling Edny that the former Mrs. Lorimer is alive and currently in New York. Rather than seeking forgiveness and reconciliation, Edny uses this information to pursue his original, murderous design: "If she be alive, then am I reserved for the performance of a new crime. My evil destiny will have it so. If she be dead, I shall make *thee* expiate" (*EH* 289, emphasis in original). In finding that he cannot control the events he set into motion, Huntly recognizes his repeated failures as an authorial agent: "How little cognizance have men over the actions and motives of each other! How total is our blindness with regard to our performances!" (*EH* 278). Having admitted the limitations of his powers, he still finds a way to embrace an explanatory fiction. In this state of extremity, he even expresses the hope for providential intervention: "May heaven avert the consequences of such a design" (*EH* 283). Having surrendered the power of manipulation, he can do little more than hope that providence will guide Sarsefield in capturing and restraining Edny. Having lost faith in his own powers, Huntly nevertheless needs a narrative structure that will explain human actions: "Heaven grant that some means may suggest themselves to you of intercepting his approach. Yet I know not what means can be conceived." He evokes the possibility of providential intervention, even as he indicates the tenuousness of this hope. He even suggests that the concept of providence rests on little more than a "visionary and fantastic base" (*EH* 290). Thus, Huntly joins Clara Wieland and others in revealing how providential agency assumes shape as a self-authorized projection of imagination and desire. When it comes down to his wife's safety, however, Sarsefield does not rely on providence. Instead, he uses his New York connections to keep Edny from killing his wife, although her agitation upon discovering the maniac's proximity causes her to suffer a miscarriage. Sarsefield realizes that there is no protection from Edny except in his incarceration, and no resolution to the problem he poses except in his death.

Huntly fails not only when attempting to apply arts of benevolence; he also fails as a detective. His originating search for Waldegrave's murderer gives way to various digressions: to his self-consuming search for Clithero Edny; to his descent into savagery; to the reconstruction of his social identity; and to his admitted failure to become a beneficent author of Edny's reclamation. The anticlimactic, gratuitous discovery of Waldegrave's murderer has nothing to do with Huntly's busy, frequently aberrant, endeavors, nothing to do with the emergent energies of Huntly's actions. It turns out that Waldegrave was a random victim of a passing Indian guerilla warrior: "Queen Mab...readily confessed and gloried in the mischief she had done; and accounted for it by enumerating the injuries which she had received from her neighbours" (*EH* 280). One of her henchmen had killed Waldegrave but refrained from scalping him "least he should afford grounds for suspicion as to the authors of the evil" (*EH* 281). In depicting Huntly's multiple failures, Brown presents the culminating instance of the dangers inherent in the artist figure, who attempts to control the lives of other people. Repeatedly, Brown dramatizes that the likes of Carwin, Welbeck, Ormond, Huntly, and Wiatte have difficulty directing the consequences of their disruptive, overbearing antics. In his final words from his second letter to Sarsefield, Huntly admits to the dangers associated with his misinformed and misdirected attempts at altruism. In concluding his letter to Mary Waldegrave, Huntly acknowledges that he "erred, not through sinister or malignant intentions, but from the impulse of misguided, indeed, but powerful benevolence" (*EH* 290).

Peter Kafer sees *Edgar Huntly* "as a psychological purgative" that stamps paid Brown's preoccupation with Gothic forms and his tumultuous explorations of aberrant behavior and symbolic landscapes (185). As expressed in the conclusion of the *Second Part* of *Arthur Mervyn*, published after *Edgar Huntly* in 1800, and reflected in his last two epistolary novels published in 1801, Brown moves away from the projected, imaginative world of sleep and dreams toward safer havens, toward the embrace of providential confinements and societal norms, away from volatile, subversive energies of the uncontained, creative daemon to an acceptance of narrative limitation and epistolary convention. His last two novels, while well crafted, under-appreciated epistolary performances, enact Brown's farewell to the protean possibilities of narrative self-making and his career as an American novelist.

Coda: 1801

"I shall not fall hereafter into that strain."

The End of Extremity

Throughout the strange, involuted reaches of *Edgar Huntly*, Charles Brockden Brown gives expression to a host of savage energies that not only challenge in livid, unapologetic fashion conventional standards of taste and behavior but also postulate that a Human Being—at least as figured in the deranged Clithero Edny and the protean Edgar Huntly—cannot be contained, or explained, within rational, or logical, categories. In seeking to solve a murder mystery, Huntly details how he stalked a maniac; lost himself in somnambulistic wandering; woke up in a cave, slew a panther, and drank its blood; how he unleashed a saturnalia of murderous violence against a marauding, dispossessed Indian band seeking to reclaim a primordial wilderness from colonizing invaders. In displacing his sociable, well-adjusted acting self, Huntly seems less recognizable as a person than a force—the living embodiment of anarchistic, imperial fervor, a man who enacts without moral self-scrutiny a swarm of violent, self-justifying dictates. As the personification of colonial mandates, especially as expressed through his professed conviction of racialized, ontological superiority, Huntly displays the dangers inherent in the transformative energies Brown associates with the protean power of narrative self-making. As a letter-writer, Huntly initially sees the compositional act as a therapeutic means to regain his "ancient sobriety" (*EH* 5). Through a lengthy epistolary process, Huntly hopes to divest himself of this destructive identity and recover a state of balanced normality that he presumably enjoyed prior to his descent into barbarism. Whether the completed process of telling his story fulfills this office is left to the reader to ponder.

The experiential and psychological extremity of *Edgar Huntly* differs in degree but not kind from Brown's earlier attempts to dramatize both the outer limits of human behavior and the ineluctable power of naturalistic forces. Brown's major novels dramatize a cavalcade of shocking acts and disruptive, chaotic circumstances—for example, the elder Wieland's bizarre, combustive death; Theodore Wieland's ostensibly God-directed slaughter of his family; Ormond's frenzy to possess Constantia Dudley's body, whether alive or dead. In *Ormond* and *Arthur Mervyn*, the encompassing, indiscriminate agency of the yellow fever epidemic shreds the social fabric. What characterizes Brown's problematic period of novelistic invention is not only his aspiration to compose American tales from the fertile grounding of Eurocentric literary forms, but his attending belief that such tales must bring into collision the conventional realm of quotidian experience and those protean, often deconstructive, forces that challenge and undermine social and political constructs reflective of Enlightenment principles.

Whereas *Edgar Huntly* constitutes Brown's most troubling, yet most fully realized American tale, it was without question the least amenable to the dictates of popular taste. James Brown, Charles' brother, assumed the chastising voice of a Representative Reader and critiqued Brown's unsettling achievement in this novel. In an April 1800 letter, Charles responds to James' contention that he went too far. After granting the essential validity of his brother's assessment, Brown makes a devastating admission regarding his failure to find and please a large, appreciative audience: "Your remarks upon the gloominess and out-of-nature incidents of Huntly, if they be not just in their full extent, are, doubtless such as most readers will make, which alone, is a sufficient reason for dropping the doleful tone and assuming a cheerful one, or, at least substituting moral causes and daily incidents in place of the prodigious or the singular" (*L* 463). In the aftermath of *Edgar Huntly*, possibly at James' instigation, Brown engaged in some aesthetic soul-searching. His letter signals the depth of his concern over the viability of his career as a novelist, especially his realization that if were to satisfy "most readers" he would not merely have to alter his "tone" but radically reconceive his subject. It was clear that he could not be commercially successful while giving vent to uninhibited investigations prompted by his wayward muse—for example, anything on the order of an American protagonist waking in a cave, imagining self-cannibalization, and drinking restorative blood from the pulsing arteries of a lurking panther. He concluded that he could not be a commercially viable novelist while dramatizing liminal and bizarre expressions of human behavior, especially as figured in the antics of rogue, fiction-making performers. No longer, in short, could he begin a novel with something as audacious as a madman digging ferociously under a politically evocative elm tree—the site of a recent murder—and then propel the story as it careens from there. In resolving to put away "the prodigious or the singular," in resolving to delineate "moral causes and daily incidents," Brown makes a momentous, and decisive, declaration regarding future, novelistic ventures: "I shall not fall hereafter into that strain" (*L* 463).

And he did not. The first sign of Brown's aesthetic transformation—his avoidance of extremities so characteristic of his experiments with the novel form—seems to appear in the conclusion of the *Second Part* of *Arthur Mervyn*, which was published in the summer of 1800, a few months after his letter to James. However weird, or comedic, one might find the "lost mamma" locutions with which Mervyn describes his feelings for fiancée Achsa Fielding, it is nevertheless clear that Brown is intent on displacing the unruly, ambiguous energies that hitherto impelled this story along its winding path (*AM* 429). In pursuit of narrative closure, he strong-arms his materials toward an ostensibly "cheerful" embrace of marital resolution. After depicting a wasting Mervyn's recovery from yellow fever, after dramatizing a city devastated and depopulated by disease and death, after delineating the depraved criminal machinations of Welbeck and other harrowing exploits and horrific events, after having Mervyn reject the free-thinking Eliza Hadwin and her assertive, proto-feminist self-advertisements, Brown directs Mervyn—formerly an errant, impetuous, and ambiguous proponent of disinterested benevolence—away from extremity and toward his impending, fortuitous marriage into wealth and ostensible security. Even if one might justly contend that the conclusion's celebratory epithalamion operates in parodic ways, one must also recognize the determinant consequences of Brown's seemingly slapdash decision to conclude this proliferating narrative of individual and communal wreckage with anticipations of concord, serenity, and *please no more trouble*!

Following the publication of *Arthur Mervyn*, the *Second Part*, Brown redirected his fiction-writing energies in a more conventional "strain." He began *Clara Howard; in A Series of Letters* in fall 1800. He was likely at work on this novel on November 2, 1800 when he encountered Elizabeth Linn for the second time and initiated a long, conflicted courtship that culminated with their marriage on November 19, 1804. Implicit in Brown's literary ventures from 1801 onward was the need to establish a professional, economically-sound foundation sufficient to provide for the well-being of a prospective family. Casting his novel-writing ventures in a conventional "strain" was a pragmatic act designed to court commercial viability—an act that could be successful, he must have believed, by avoiding the strange, disconcerting reaches dramatized in his four published novels. Following the December 1800 publication of the final issue of *Monthly Magazine*, Brown surrendered his weighty editorial responsibilities. Earlier that year, he had written and published at least ninety pieces of non-fiction, mostly essays and reviews. With the magazine behind him, he was free throughout the pivotal year of 1801 to try-out revised notions regarding the demands of popular authorship. In this cause, he composed two courtship novels. Donald A. Ringe contends that Brown

> must have begun *Jane Talbot* by early 1801, perhaps while he was still at work on *Clara Howard*. We know that *Jane Talbot* was at least planned by early March, and since Brown speaks of its publication in his letter to Elizabeth Linn, he had probably begun the writing and may even have carried it well forward. Though he gave up the book for a while, he must have

> returned to it during the spring while *Clara Howard* was going through the press, for by late June...Brown was still at work on it. (445)

In this process, Brown modified, but did not entirely reconceive, the nature of his artistic practice. In these novels, Brown retains "many of the devices of sentimental fiction" (Ringe 434). In casting both novels in the epistolary mode, he accentuates the emergence of present-time consciousness as he dramatizes each letter-writer's unfolding compositional process. While exploring in both novels the vicissitudes of courtship, especially in relation to the meddling of oppressive or incompetent parental figures, Brown steadfastly avoids outrageous incidents and concentrates on commonplace occasions of life. Some "doleful" elements infiltrate the narratives, operating not through the agency of a death-dealing plague but in relation to individuals suffering from debilitating diseases: Edward Hartley conveniently languishes for many pages on his sick bed; Henry Colden in *Jane Talbot* partakes in an extended vigil at Thomson's bedside. Most notably, Brown abandons his dramatic depictions of protean, self-making characters—the "strain" that dominates *Wieland*, *Ormond*, *Arthur Mervyn*, and *Edgar Huntly*. The largest issue here concerns not simply how Brown changed as a novelist in the pacifying attempt to reach a popular audience. Rather, the completion and publication of *Clara Howard* and *Jane Talbot* demonstrate that Brown's attempt to achieve success in America concerns not only his embrace of highly conventional applications of the epistolary form, but most importantly his celebration of highly specific Anglophile concerns—an aesthetic project most evident in *Clara Howard*. However well-written and entertaining, these last two novelistic ventures did not find an audience. Their publication brought Brown face to face with unavoidable, commercial failure—few sales and virtually no reviews—and ended his career as a novelist.

Edward Hartley, the Anti-Edgar Huntly

Brown's "Introduction" to *Clara Howard* distinguishes itself from the prefatory materials of his earlier novels in its avoidance of ominous portents and in its flaunting of an extremely cheerful, self-congratulatory tone. Edward Hartley's "Introduction" situates him in the aftermath of those events that he will subsequently depict chronologically in a stream of interactive letters. Exuding a hyperbolic sense of exuberance at having fully achieved an unambiguous state of beneficence, Hartley summarizes for an unnamed correspondent his amazing transformation from an orphaned, impoverished, watchmaker's apprentice and a life of "rustic diffidence" and "inveterate humility" (*CH* 3) to a condition of wealth and hauteur emanating from his experience of upscale, marital bliss. He has been "crowned with every terrestrial felicity" (*CH* 3). In locating Hartley within the compositional present, Brown positions the "Introduction" as a teasing *critical* narrative that imposes a determinant interpretive framework for containing those felicities already actualized but yet to be narrated. In preparing to describe "how all these surprising things came about" (*CH* 3), Hartley retains a minimum of suspense as he evades answering the not-so-mysterious question of who the wealthy heiress is. The narrative itself recounts a series of emotional fulminations concerning a most narrow premise. Even though at the outset of these epistolary exchanges, one finds a plentiful supply of self-regarding gloom, misery, and Weltschmerz—Hartley writes, "But I am tired of the pen already; of myself; of the world" (*CH* 6)—such lugubrious acts of rhetorical self-dramatization have already been offset by the joyous effusions pervading the "Introduction." Essentially, Brown's authorial purpose is to use his favored epistolary devices to explore recognizable "moral causes" as they emerge in "daily incidents" (*L* 463). Brown thereby tames—or avoids—those discordant energies permeating his earlier novels in a manner brother James would approve.

What impels the plot of *Clara Howard* is essentially a narrowly configured, concocted problem that drives Hartley's erratic, frequently stalled quest. He made the mistake of betrothing himself to the ostensibly indigent Mary Wilmot not out of love but duty. Subsequently, he fell in love with wealthy Clara Howard and she fell in love with him. Clara, however, has a vacillating conviction that Hartley's promise to Mary preempts his ability to change his mind. Therefore, he must frustrate both their lives to uphold this most dubious notion of honor. Clara carries these ethical scruples to a somehow-not-quite-human point of self-abnegation. She feels that to surrender Hartley's hand to Mary would be to enact a heightened (and divinely sanctioned) form of disinterested benevolence, thereby allowing her to achieve "a purer delight than in gratifications merely selfish and exclusive" (*CH* 24). Clara's questionable principle derives from her notion that Mary Wilmot is a poor, shy victim in need of saving. Clara wonders, "Can I riot in bliss, and deck myself in bridal ornaments, while she lives pining in dreary solitude, carrying to the grave an heart broken by the contumelies of the world; the horrors of indigence and neglect; and chiefly by the desertion of him on whom she doated?" (*CH* 77).

The stream of letters dramatizes the consequences deriving from Clara's nagging, misinformed manipulations of the pliable, befuddled, and irresolute Hartley, while at the same time depicting how Mary Wilmot is by no means contained by Clara's mistaken assertions. In fact, Clara's premises collide with a number of competing descriptions of the elusive Mary Wilmot—that she is a fallen woman; that her friend and benefactor Sedley is a wanton, villainous rake; that she has money that possibly belongs to a wayfaring man named Morton. Brown spins a mystery yarn wherein multiple plot lines intersect, tangle, and engender confusion. Clara forces Hartley to pursue a woman who, for reasons best known to Mary, seems to be trying to get as far from him as possible. Complicating the emotional jumble are Clara's transient doubts that further manipulate and perplex Hartley. At one point, she reverses course and opines, "Come to me my friend. Exert all thy persuasive eloquence. Convince me that I have erred in resigning thy heart and hand to another, in imagining the claim of Mary better than mine" (*CH* 35).

Delineating the emotional and epistemic oscillations of multiple characters constitutes a core attribute of Brown's novelistic aesthetic and links *Clara Howard* to his preoccupation in his earlier novels (and in *Jane Talbot*) with enlisting the epistolary form to dramatize multiple characters' unsettled play of mind. Nevertheless, the center of Brown's reconfigured aesthetic resides in his insistent attempts to cast his work within a Eurocentric framework, a process that leads Brown to reject recurrent claims in his first four published novels with writing American tales. It is no accident that the name Edward Hartley is a syllabic analogue to Edgar Huntly. Essentially, Edward Hartley continually defines himself as a kind of anti-Edgar Huntly. In making what amounts to an oddly irruptive ideological manifesto, Hartley summarily rejects the politics, aesthetics, and social mores associated with Brown's brand of American novelty in favor of associating Hartley's own identity, attributes, and predispositions within specifically Eurocentric categories. In fact, he sees America as little more than a hollow imitation of Anglophile forms and values that derive from a spate of literary influences:

> The ideas annexed to the term *peasant*, are wholly inapplicable to the tillers of ground in America; but our notions are the offspring, more of the books we read, than of any other of our external circumstances. Our books are almost wholly the productions of Europe, and the prejudices which infect us, are derived chiefly from this source. These prejudices may be somewhat rectified by age, and by converse with the world, but they flourish in full vigor in youthful minds, reared in seclusion and privacy, and undisciplined by intercourse with various classes of mankind. In me, they possessed an unusual degree of strength. My words were selected and defined according to foreign usages, and my notions of dignity were modelled on a scale, which the *revolution* has completely taken away. I could never forget that my condition was that

> of a *peasant*, and in spite of reflection, I was a slave of those sentiments of self-contempt and humiliation, which pertain to that condition elsewhere, though chimerical and visionary on the western side of the Atlantic. (*CH* 53, emphasis in original)

If within his native sphere he is nothing more than a "peasant," then he can only escape this indigent state and achieve his goals through the fairy-tale flourish of a fortuitous marriage to a European heiress. In the figure of Edward Hartley, Brown rejects the paradigm of the American Proteus. Hartley wants nothing to do with that political, social, and aesthetic process of transformation and subversion that elevates the likes of Carwin and Ormond toward self-made positions of power ostensibly capable of transfiguring society and challenging providential notions of divine authorship. Conversely, Hartley seeks not *novelty* but propriety as epitomized by the insular, protective, wealthy world of the Howards. No amount of narrative self-making can lead him into the social class that Clara Howard inhabits. Only Clara and her father can bring him there.

As a passive actor dependent on other people's decisions, Hartley must wait to receive Clara's hand in marriage. In displacing these subversive energies impelling the American tale, Brown enacts a process whereby Mr. Howard—a kind of fairy godfather—constructs Hartley's path to felicity. Concerning Mr. Howard, Hartley writes, "But now my old preceptor had started up before me, and, like my good genius, had brought with him gifts immeasurable, and surpassing belief. They existed till now in another hemisphere; they occupied an elevation in the social scale, to which I could scarcely raise my eyes; yet they were now within a short journey of my dwelling" (*CH* 54). Unlike Edgar Huntly, the issue at the heart of Edward Hartley's life concerns not newness or the explosive discovery of some hidden primal self ever-ready to erupt into violence. Instead, Hartley recognizes that he is not, nor can he be, a self-determining actor. He is allured by tantalizing gifts from "another hemisphere," gifts that promise an elevation in "social scale" that can be conferred but not earned. He is little more than the plaything of contingency and coincidence. His fate remains completely in the hands of high-class English benefactors.

Throughout the novel, Hartley remains subject to the will and whims of two strong-minded women. It is no accident that he spends much time prostrate with illness. After getting sick, he recounts how events happen to him and around him. He writes and reads letters, of course, but he can do little, or nothing, to help himself. He is shown to be consistently wrong in his conjectures. He is convinced, for example, that Mary's money comes by way of an elusive Mr. Morton. Her money turns out to be an anonymous gift from Sedley. Edward also believes pernicious gossip. Rather than being a rake, as wagging tongues maliciously allege, Sedley turns out to be a stalwart and faithful man, who loves Mary and is willing, without recompense, to provide for her well-being. Conversely, if Hartley will escape his "peasant" status, he will only do so by following rigid conditions prescribed by Clara Howard, "[t]his heiress of opulence and splendour, this child of fortune" (*CH* 54), a woman who makes no pretention to possessing, or desiring, values associated with an inchoate, American society.

As the narrative proceeds, Hartley finds himself suspended between seemingly irreconcilable stipulations. On the one hand, Mary Wilmot knows that Hartley does not love her. In fact, she flees from him, it seems, because she rejects the notion of marrying for anything less than love. To make Clara Howard happy, Hartley repeatedly makes clear that he will follow the dictates of duty and marry the very woman who will not have him. The rigidity of Clara's ethical dictates, despite her occasional and short-lived ambivalence, makes her loathe to pursue her own happiness. Clara will indulge "no selfish gratification" (*CH* 78). At one point, when considering the possibility that Hartley might convince Mary to free him from his much-regretted commitment, Clara contorts this reasonable resolution of the novel's informing conundrum into a warped indictment of Hartley's rhetorical powers: "If [Mary] withstand your eloquence, it will be because you have betrayed your cause, or because she acts from a romantic and groundless generosity with regard to me" (*CH* 109). Clara's persistence leads to potentially dire consequences. In fact, when seeking to actualize Clara's mandate, Hartley eventually catches up with Mary Wilmot. He proposes marriage and she turns him down. Now, he finds himself in the position of possibly marrying neither Mary nor Clara. What is crucial here is not Brown's creation of a state of faux suspense, but his depiction of the potential costs of Hartley's state of frenzied, emotional duress. Ironically, he threatens to become what amounts to an avatar of Edgar Huntly—the protean, sleep-walking marauder, who awakens in a cave and experiences ontological devolution. If Hartley cannot marry, he claims that he "shall hasten to embrute all my faculties. I shall make myself akin to savages and tygers, and forget that I once was a man" (*CH* 134). That is, he will become just like Edgar Huntly in his most ferocious state.

This novel, however, only dabbles in the protean modality of the American tale of transformation, especially as manifested through its momentary evocation of savage forms of personal disintegration. With this conclusion, Brown transforms earlier preoccupations with the irruptive power of ostensibly supernatural forces into a sentimental trope that celebrates the happy resolution of preceding vicissitudes. Mary Wilmot will marry the faithful Sedley and Clara Howard will marry the fortunate Edward Hartley. With his fate decided for him, Hartley comes back from the edge and recoups human status: "I am once more a reasonable creature" (*CH* 144). By marrying out of the American way, he is now allied in love, finally and forever, with his "heavenly monitor" (*CH* 144). With this conclusion, Brown conflates (and diminishes) his earlier preoccupations with the irruptive power of ostensibly supernatural forces into little more than sentimental tropes.

Elizabeth Linn, the Anti-Henrietta

From the start of Brown's literary career, he believed that the written word could possess the immediacy of direct speech. He wrote his address to the Belles Lettres Club for oral presentation. Frequently, he asserted how letters were analogous to, even another version of, the spoken word. For Brown, the unfolding, emergent process of epistolary exchange mirrored the improvisational intensities of conversation. This incipient attribute of Brown's aesthetic achieved early actualization in his spring 1792 series of letters to Bringhurst and Wilkins. By casting his letters as forms of direct speech, Brown created the framework within which he could experiment with developing irruptive, proto-fictional narratives featuring projected, self-reflexive authorial voices like Julius Brownlow and C.B.B. In the seminal, faux courtship "Henrietta Letters," Brown not only celebrates the cause of gender equity but details how their impassioned correspondence had the power to translate physical absence into spiritual presence. The performative nature of epistolary address, especially the figuration of writing *as* speech, became a foundational element of Brown's aesthetic innovations in his six published novels.

During the decisive year of 1801, as Brown was composing *Clara Howard* and *Jane Talbot* and thereby making a bid to revive his career as a publishing novelist, he was also involved in what turned out to be one of the most important personal and literary ventures of his life. Throughout the early months of his extended courtship of Elizabeth Linn, he wrote her a clustered series of highly revelatory letters beginning in February 1801 and ending in late May 1801 that reaffirmed his conviction that the written word could mirror speech. One can easily imagine Brown, ever the multi-tasker, putting aside his work on one or another or both novels, and launching into an effusive letter to Elizabeth, who lived not far away and who he likely was to see in a few hours. It may not be too much to say that Brown's entrenched love for the physicality of writing brought him to a state where he experienced a peak coalescence of mind and body similar to what he describes in the "Rhapsodist" essays of 1789. In these spirited letters to Elizabeth, Brown worked strenuously to put himself on the page. In one of his epistolary moods, he represents himself on February 17, 1801 as an intensely supportive friend seeking to repair her fragile self-image: "I often smile, wonderingly, when you express dissatisfaction with your personal appearance, & profess your belief that all others must despise & dislike!...There is one eye, my friend, that sees you often, in which every thing about you, is lovely & engaging" (*L* 474). In assuming his frequent, favored role of counselor, he casts himself as a teacher inculcating a series of highly conventional lessons. In a March 23, 1801 letter, he celebrates the providential order as a steadfast resource for achieving the fullest measure of self-actualization: "What is my third [lesson]. Perhaps it ought to have gone first, but let it come now—Rely, in all things, on the wisdom & goodness of that providence, to whom you ascribe universal presence & unlimited power. Trust to him, for giving, sooner or later, here or elsewhere, repose to all your earthly cares; fruition to all your just hopes" (*L* 506).

In these letters, he appears to be intensely alive, intensely at one with the literary performance he hopes will project the essence of his being into the mind and soul of the woman with whom he is falling love. In a February 28, 1801 letter, for example, Brown not only indicates that writing is a form of direct speech, but he also reveals that his words have the power to translate physical absence into dialogic presence. In this letter, he inscribes a fictive scenario, wherein his words possess experiential immediacy:

> "I must not see her," said I, just now. "Well." I'll take up the pen, at least; & write a few words; &, thus, unless she interdicts me, will I always do, when I am desirous of her company, & must not seek it.
>
> 'Tis a kind of Conversation, is it not—My *love*? (*L* 480, emphasis in original)

In the same letter, he goes on to banter with the seemingly transgressive implications of the word "love": "And now, the pen does not speak it out; only whispered it: So don't be angry" (*L* 481). Brown's whimsical, rhetorical play nevertheless reinforces the high seriousness of his investment in the power of language. In a letter of April 3–4,

1801, he sounds a cautionary note: "My imagination was sometimes in danger of becoming too strong for me" (*L* 525). Nevertheless, he draws on his powers of literary conjuration to bring her absent self into spiritual presence:

> Were not your midnight prayers more than usually eloquent. I thought they were, for you must not suppose me absent. No. I see you vividly. Shall I paint you, as I see you? I hear you distinctly, & endeavour to banish the unwelcome truth that Walls & Streets are actually between us? (*L* 525, emphasis in original)

Through his epistolary art, he seeks to overcome obstacles posed by space, time, and matter.

These courtship letters provide telling evidence for the biographer. Brown emerges as intermittently rhapsodic and depressed, confident and apprehensive, considerate and hectoring. At times, both Charles and Elizabeth (as reflected indirectly in Charles' representations of her letters and behavior) come across as moody and emotionally insecure—in need of constant reinforcement that the other is not consistently prepared to give. In the case of Elizabeth's relation to Brown, her seeming reticence and querulousness is either the cause or consequence (or both) of his insistent craving for her to love him as he wants to be loved. (See April 16, 1801, *L* 548). It is not hard to imagine Elizabeth feeling overwhelmed and intimidated by her beau's lavish, rhetorical performances.

Especially in the series of letters beginning late in March 1801 and extending through April 1801, Brown (wittingly or not) attempts to reconceive the C.B.B.-Henrietta interaction within the context of his budding romance with Elizabeth. In what seems an attempt to shape the untidy complexities of their gestating relationship into a redacted version reminiscent of his faux courtship narrative, Brown drew upon a foundational experience that informed the development of his authorial self. Maybe now, in this momentous situation wherein he believed his future happiness was at stake, his art could shape the course of his life. Brown seems to assume the role he gave to C.B.B., even as he cajoles and begs Elizabeth to become what would amount to be a real-life version of Henrietta. Elizabeth, however, would not play along. His responses to her indicate that she shunned his invitations to indulge in rhapsodic, verbal display. Apparently, Elizabeth was troubled by the notion that this well-known, prolific novelist was critiquing or parsing her words: "For my Love to talk of refusing to write because she does not write <u>well</u>, is very strange" (*L* 514, emphasis in original). On the contrary, it was not so strange that Elizabeth resisted his appeals to put herself fully on the page, to engage with him in an epistolary form of competitive repartee. It is highly unlikely that Elizabeth in March 1801 knew anything about the "Henrietta Letters," but she seemed to be unsettled, even troubled, by the manipulative energies driving their exchanges and could not have missed Brown's florid enthusiasm for romanticizing her through the medium of *her* written words. Elizabeth knew that she walked upon the earth and was decidedly not an ethereal embodiment of his effusive idealizations. She even seemed to fear that he might make some literary use of her "<u>pennings</u>" (*L* 492, emphasis in original). In fact, when she did write to him, she apparently insisted that he return the letter to her after he read it: "You scarcely ever put epistolary pen to paper.... What your cautious pen indites, you insist upon having immediately returned" (*L* 491). Emphatically aware of her compositional limitations, she seems to have resisted his penchant for hyperbolic praise: "The beauty of your phrazes, I might praise with sincerity; their correctness & their elegance; but how unfeeling & absurd should I be to have an eye for these qualities, in a paper that contains the effusions of your heart" (*L* 514).

A recurrent theme in these letters involves Brown's desire to have her *talk* to him through her letters and for her to write to him with an enthusiasm that matches his own. In a letter of April 9, 1801, Brown writes: "Do, I entreat you, write a little for me.... Write any thing, so it be not cold; austere, direfully omenous.... How talkative has been my pen! I shall, presently, have filled a little volume: & how few; how rare; how sparing your returns" (*L* 532). At one point, Brown expresses frustration over how they continually revisit old subjects: "You talk of your own incapacities, of my fastidiousness; After all that I have said upon that subject, you still dwell upon the same topics" (*L* 560). If she will not deign to exist in a kind of C.B.B.-Henrietta state of interactive mutuality, then Brown (quite fastidiously) offers to cast himself as her mentor and thereby spur her on to new epistolary heights: "Writing is of more benefit than you imagine. You wish for intellectual improvement. You beseech me to supply you with the means. The most powerful means of your own improvement & that of my pleasure are the same, namely; the use of the pen." In instructing her on "the essense of epistolary composition," he implores her to "Write something dayly. Narrative; rhapsody; no matter what; but let something be written every day. The pen is a discipliner of the thoughts. It summons reason; reflection; memory. It gives durability to fleeting moments. It furnishes me with ever new & ever fresh tokens of your existance & your love" (*L* 560).

This restive comedy plays out via Brown's repeated insistence on Elizabeth becoming the companionate correspondent she had little, or no, wish to be. In a letter of April 29, 1801, Brown writes, "I wish I could cure thee, my love, of thinking thyself a Simpleton, & me a fastidious Hypercritic" (562). Brown's fastidious, hypercritical attempts to will into existence the C.B.B.-Henrietta interaction informed their correspondence for a few months, but by May 1801 the disconcerting strains became less pronounced and eventually disappeared. Perhaps Brown realized he did not need to strong-arm his way into her heart through the display of his ardent, compositional prowess. Perhaps Brown disciplined his own thoughts and told himself to stop nagging. For whatever reason, he put away the artifice of literary self-making designed to contort Elizabeth into playing a wholly inappropriate role of his creation. Perhaps he recognized that her greatest gift to him was her recurrent insistence on presenting herself as a woman formed on her own terms—one who did not need to be coached, or badgered, into playing epistolary games. Perhaps by late May 1801, Elizabeth succeeded in deterring him from trying to make her into a version of his own desires. Maybe, by then, she stood before him as simply the person she was. It was no doubt of value to their slowly evolving relationship that he came to have his fullest life with her not within the compass of written words, but in the day-to-day incidentals that shaped their interdependent, common lives—experiences that did not need to be sanctioned, or extended, by profuse, epistolary testimonials.

During 1801, the year Brown gave up his career as a novelist, he may have found that he could court his love without the aid of his literary genius. In fact, the dissolution of his career as a publishing novelist cannot be separated from the gestation of his love for her and his sense that she healed, or relieved, a tension, or stress, that in a letter of April 1, 1801 he associates with those years that coincide with his development as a novelist: "What a dreary interval of six or eight years has been my life, & to whom but my good angel, in Eliza's form, am I indebted for the joyous & serene element that now surrounds me" (*L* 517). The so-called "dreary interval" corresponds to the time when he did not know—and was not in love with—Elizabeth, but this sweeping pronouncement not only takes him back to 1793 and the early years of his literary apprenticeship but also includes his three-to-four-year period of prolific creation—an "interval" that includes the publication of four novels and a multitude of essays, reviews, and poems. It is possible that by the end of 1801 he saw his novel-writing career as being economically, and even emotionally, incompatible with his prospective marriage to Elizabeth Linn. Perhaps, the search for an American tale came to seem a misdirected, played-out indulgence for which he no longer had time, taste, patience, or need. On March 10, 1801, he makes a cryptic admission: "I mean not to publish 'Jane Talbot.' My reasons for a change of plans, I will tell you, when I have all your ear" (*L* 492). Brown's rejection of the "prodigious or the singular" in his last two published novels culminated in a final effort at achieving commercial success as a novelist (*L* 463). In this epistolary moment, he may have been in the mood to give it all up. If he could not be successful writing as his daemon compelled him to write—in the unbridled ways that characterized his first four published novels, especially *Edgar Huntly*—then why bother with fiction at all? He had not lost his love for the physical and mental exertions of composition. Fiction was one of many authorial forms.

By the end of 1801, Brown left behind that part of his life dedicated to fiction-making in novels and fiction-making in letters. He went on to embrace practical solutions associated with having a career that he hoped would combine professional and financial stability with marriage to the woman he committed to loving on her own terms. A diminutive coda to this telling episode concerning Elizabeth Linn as C.B.B.'s anti-Henrietta does not appear until January 9, 1802 when Brown—in the role of mentor— sent a copybook to Mary Linn, Elizabeth's younger sister. He counseled her to read, reflect, and write a great deal. Regarding the question of whether Mary might soon expect a letter from Elizabeth, Brown remarks, "I have taken the liberty to urge her to write to you, by the present opportunity, which is safe & speedy, but she answers— 'No. She hates writing. It is always a painful task'" (*L* 574–75).

"The Critical Spot"

In an October 31, 1801 letter, Brown congratulates Anthony Bleecker, a fellow member of the Friendly Club, on his ability to balance an abiding devotion to an active literary life with exacting demands of the legal profession:

> I never yet saw you seated at this table, without some poetical or literary solace within your reach; some conductor to the flowery Elysium of the poets, in the midst of the austere guides and crabbed implements of the law. In this respect, it is rare to meet with one that resembles you; who retains the pure taste of a literary devotee, without disrelish and aversion for naked science and mere business. (*L* 570)

Bleecker would surely have reminded Brown of his own conflicts with the legal profession, his eventual inability—or refusal—to find a way to balance a literary life with the "crabbed" demands of the legal profession. Later in this letter, Brown wonders about Bleecker's attempts to learn the "tangled maze" of written and spoken French and uses this occasion to meditate on exigencies associated with navigating difficult points of passage, of transitional challenges, especially the process of navigating tempestuous struggles and achieving a state of calm resolution: "I suppose there is, always, in every pursuit, a point that may be termed the critical spot; a point where the difficulties multiply, as it were, on a sudden, and where the patience or the penetration, is put to the hardest test; and this being past, as ships pass a sand bar in a river, you suddenly glide into still deep water" (*L* 570). Brown wrote this letter four and a half months after the publication of *Clara Howard* and two months before the publication of *Jane Talbot*. Brown's first novel of 1801 was a commercial and critical failure and it is hard to imagine that he was optimistic concerning the success of *Jane Talbot*. As it turned out, "The first editions of *Clara Howard* and *Jane Talbot* seem to have elicited no critical response in American magazines when they appeared in 1801" (Ringe 452).

At some unknown point, in responding to the literary failures of 1801 and the new life possibilities of his great love, Brown undoubtedly encountered a "critical spot." He passed what no doubt was a difficult "test" and made the decision to give up writing American novels. There is no documentary evidence indicating that such a decision—however it exactly came about—occasioned anger, angst, regret, or complaint. In fact, the evidence suggests that he did not seem to miss writing American novels at all. He passed "the sand bar," as it were, and found "still deep water." Having concluded that his opportunities for success as a novelist were behind him, having realized that a future with Elizabeth Linn required a stable, economic foundation, he renewed his commitment to a professional life in letters with a focus on cultural and political discourse within non-fictional modes. As Steven

Watts points out, "Brown's series of early nineteenth-century realignments...set the stage for an important new public role: bourgeois cultural critic" (155). Throughout 1802, he wrote numerous pieces of prose and verse for *Port-Folio.* By 1803, he assumed the editorship of *Literary Magazine* and also published the first of his political pamphlets—*An Address to the Government of the United States of America: on the Cession of Louisiana to the French*. He resumed the prolific pace of non-fictional productions—reviews, essays, poems—that characterized his crowded, professional year of 1800, except that now he was not attempting to write novels for the threadbare American marketplace. After the failure of *Jane Talbot*, Brown returned to fiction with the serialization of *Memoirs of Carwin* in late 1803. After publishing the portion of the story composed in August and September 1798, Brown fitfully continued Carwin's first-person account of his experiences in Ireland with the strange, manipulative, and duplicitous Ludloe, who served as ostensible mentor but actual oppressor. Certainly, Brown saw Francis Carwin's truncated, autobiographical narrative as a ready source for magazine copy, but he had trouble moving the story toward any satisfying resolution. This narrative ran intermittently in the *Literary Magazine* from November 1803 before concluding mid-scene in March 1805.

Many mysteries beyond the scope of the present study attend the trove of faux historical materials that have come to be identified among scholars as Brown's Historical Sketches— "Sketches of a History of Carsol" (printed in Dunlap, *The Life*, I, 170–258) and the more prolix "Sketches of a History of the Carrils and Ormes (printed in Dunlap, *The Life*, I, 262–396). These sketches bear no resemblance to Brown's six published novels and appear to be expository summaries rather than dramatic enactments. Perhaps mirroring the aesthetic tastes of Elizabeth Linn Brown, William Dunlap in the biography favors the faux histories and finds Brown's published novels not only deficient in focus and structure but creatively self-indulgent. The early part of the following passage was composed by Paul Allen and appears near the end of his truncated biography. It is notable that Dunlap retains this passage both as a way to justify Brown's rejection of "his first mode" and then to anchor Dunlap's emphatic contention that death had kept Brown from fully realizing his authorial powers:

> His novels are therefore evidences of what he *might* have done, not of what he has accomplished. It was the excess of his genius that prevented him from excelling. He loads his heroes with incredible and mysterious adventures, trusting to the fruitfulness of his own fancy to find the means of extrication.... Before writing the 'Sketches of a History of Carsol,' and 'Sketches of a History of the Carrils and Ormes,' Mr. Brown had seen the inconveniences and mischief arising from his first mode, and I doubt not but he would have given in these works, if he had lived to finish and fill up his plans, volumes which would have delighted, instructed, and satisfied the reader. (*The Life*, I, 261, emphasis in original; Allen 389)

In these expansive faux histories, Brown rejected an aesthetic of narrative self-making within his American novels in favor of sweeping, non-dramatic, third-person generalized summaries of a fictionalized European past. Perhaps Brown saw these sketches as opportunities to create a hybrid product combining fictionalized persons and events and actual, historical contexts. Perhaps Brown attempted to realize some of the more extreme implications of Edward Hartley's embrace of Eurocentric contexts. Perhaps Brown was looking to develop a wholly new kind of novel, with a more objectified, dispassionate voice. In any case, the voluminous sketches provide indices to Brown's developing ideational interests in the aftermath of his novel-writing career, especially his views on the matter of history. It is also possible that Brown, with his abiding love for the physicality of writing, saw the sketches not in light of their eventual completion and publication, but simply as private compositional excursions, off-handed hobbies of a sort, where he could write for his own pleasure without regard to his contemporary time and place, without regard to audience, without regard to making money, and yet still give his burgeoning thoughts about these fictional personages a claim to aesthetic permanence within the margins of his proliferating pages.

"I Cannot Be Happier than I Am"

After 1801, Brown's courtship of Elizabeth Linn continued for almost three years through greater and lesser degrees of strain. Following their marriage on November 19, 1804, Brown experienced moments when he believed his life was fully realized—a stunning admission for this career melancholiac. He was in love. He was writing and editing. He was providing a living for his family. In a letter written to Dunlap three month after the wedding, he portrays himself as existing in an exhilarating (though tenuous) state of equipoise:

> As to myself, my friend, you judge rightly when you think me situated happily. My present way of life, is in every respect, exactly to my mind. There is nothing to disturb my felicity; but this sense of the uncertainty & mutability that sticks to every thing human. I cannot be happier than I am. Every change, therefore, (and change is unavoidable,) must be for the worse. My business if I may so call it, is altogether pleasurable, &, such as it is, occupies not one forth of my time. My companion possesses all that an husband can wish for, &, in short, as to my own personal situation, I have nothing to wish for but that it may last. (*L* 631)

On the day Brown wrote this letter, Elizabeth was likely pregnant. Their twin sons, William Linn Brown and Charles Brockden Brown, Jr., were born on August 10, 1805. These thoughtful lines offer an extended epitaph as Brown died from tuberculosis at age thirty-nine less than five years later on February 22, 1810. When Brown composed this summative statement, he knew that any desire for human perfection must remain an alluring, illusive fiction in a steadfastly protean world.

Works Cited

Allen, Paul. *The Life of Charles Brockden Brown*. Edited by Charles E. Bennett. Scholars' Facsimiles & Reprints, 1975.

Apap, Christopher. "Irresponsible Acts: The Transatlantic Dialogues of William Godwin and Charles Brockden Brown" in *Transatlantic Sensations*. Edited by Jennifer Phegley, John Cyril Barton, and Kristin H. Huston, 23–40. Ashgate, 2012.

Auerbach, Jonathan. *The Romance of Failure: First-Person Fictions of Poe, Hawthorne, and James*. Oxford University Press, 1989.

Axelrod, Alan. *Charles Brockden Brown: An American Tale*. University of Texas Press, 1983.

Arner, Robert D. "Historical Essay." *Alcuin; A Dialogue* with *Stephen Calvert. The Novels and Related Works of Charles Brockden Brown: Bicentennial Edition*. Edited by Sydney J. Krause, S. W. Redi, and Robert D. Arner, vol. 6, 273–312. Kent State University Press, 1987.

Barnard, Philip. "*Historical Sketches*." Barnard, Emmett, and Shapiro, 171–87, in *The Oxford Handbook of Charles Brockden Brown*. Edited by Philip Barnard, Hilary Emmett, and Stephen Shapiro, 171-87. Oxford University Press, 2019.

———. Barnard, Philip, Hilary Emmett, and Stephen Shapiro, editors. *The Oxford Handbook of Charles Brockden Brown*, Oxford University Press, 2019.

Barnard, Philip, Elizabeth Hewitt, and Mark L. Kamrath, editors. *Letters and Early Epistolary Writings. The Collected Writings of Charles Brockden Brown*, vol. 1, Bucknell University Press, 2013.

Barnard, Philip, Mark L. Kamrath, and Stephen Shapiro, editors. *Revising Charles Brockden Brown: Culture, Politics, and Sexuality in the Early Republic*. University of Tennessee Press, 2004.

Barnard, Philip and Stephen Shapiro, editors. *Wieland; or, The Transformation: An American Tale with Related Texts*, by Charles Brockden Brown. Hackett Publishing, 2009.

Barton, John Cyril and Jennifer Phegley, "Introduction: 'An Age of Sensation…Across the Atlantic.'" In *Transatlantic Sensations*, Edited by Jennifer Phegley, John Cyril Barton, and Kristin H. Huston, 1-22. Ashgate, 2012.

Barton, John Cyril, Jennifer Phegley, and Kristin N. Huston, editors. *Transatlantic Sensations*. Ashgate, 2012.

Battistini, Robert. "Brown's Philadelphia Quaker Milieu." In *The Oxford Handbook of Charles Brockden Brown*. Edited by Philip Barnard, Hilary Emmitt, and Stephen Shapiro, 318-34. Oxford University Press, 2019.

Bell, Michael Davitt. "'The Double-Tongued Deceiver': Sincerity and Duplicity in the Novels of Charles Brockden Brown. *Early American Literature* vol. 9, no 2 (1974): 143–63.

Bennett, Charles E. "Charles Brockden Brown: Man of Letters." In *Critical Essays on Charles Brockden Brown*. Edited by Bernard Rosenthal, 212-23. G. K. Hall, 1981.

———. "Introduction." *The Life of Charles Brockden Brown*. By Paul Allen. Scholars' Facsimiles & Reprints, 1975, v–xxii.

Bercovitch, Sacvan, editor. *The Cambridge History of American Literature*. 1590–1820, vol. 1. Cambridge University Press, 1994.

Berthoff, Warner. *American Trajectories: Authors and Readings 1790–1970*. Pennsylvania State University Press, 1994.

Berthold, Dennis. "Charles Brockden Brown, *Edgar Huntly*, and the Origins of the American Picturesque." *The William and Mary Quarterly*, vol. 41, no. 1 (1984): 62–81.

———. "Desacralizing the American Gothic: An Iconographic Approach to *Edgar Huntly*." *Studies in American Fiction*, vol. 14, no. 2, Autumn (1986): 127–38.

Blair, Walter and Hamlin Hill. *America's Humor: From Poor Richard to Doonesbury*. Oxford University Press, 1978.

Bloom, Harold. *The Daemon Knows: Literary Greatness and the American Sublime*. Spiegel & Grau, 2015.

Boyd, Sarah. "Brown, the Visual Arts, and Architecture." In *The Oxford Handbook of Charles Brockden Brown*. Edited by Philip Barnard, Hilary Emmett, and Stephen Shapiro, 488–504. Oxford University Press, 2019.

Bradfield, Scott. *Dreaming Revolution: Transgression in the Development of American Romance*. University of Iowa Press, 1993.

Brown, Charles Brockden. *Alcuin; A Dialogue* with *Stephen Calvert*. *The Novels and Related Works of Charles Brockden Brown: Bicentennial Edition*. Edited by Sydney J. Krause, S. W. Redi, and Robert D. Arner, vol. 6. Kent State University Press, 1987.

———. *Arthur Mervyn; or Memoirs of the Year 1793, First and Second Parts. The Novels and Related Works of Charles Brockden Brown: Bicentennial Edition.* Edited by Sydney J. Krause, S. W. Reid, Norman S. Grabo, and Marvin L. Williams, Jr., vol. 3. Kent State University Press, 1980.

———. *Clara Howard* and *Jane Talbot. The Novels and Related Works of Charles Brockden Brown.: Bicentennial Edition.* Edited by Sydney J. Krause, S. W. Reid, and Donald A. Ringe, vol. 5. Kent State University Press, 1986.

———. *Edgar Huntly; or, Memoirs of a Sleep-Walker. The Novels and Related Works of Charles Brockden Brown: Bicentennial Edition.* Edited by Sydney J. Krause and S. W. Reid, vol. 4. Kent State University Press, 1984.

———. *Letters and Early Epistolary Writings. The Collected Writings of Charles Brockden Brown.* Edited by Philip Barnard, Elizabeth Hewitt, and Mark L. Kamrath, vol. 1. Bucknell University Press, 2013.

———. "The Man at Home." In *The Rhapsodist and Other Uncollected Writings.* Edited by Harry R. Warfel, 27–98, 1943. Scholars' Facsimiles & Reprints, 1977.

———. *Ormond; or, The Secret Witness. The Novels and Related Works of Charles Brockden Brown: Bicentennial Edition.* Edited by Sydney J. Krause, S. W. Reid, and Russel B. Nye, vol. 2. Kent State University Press, 1982.

———. "The Rhapsodist." In *The Rhapsodist and Other Uncollected Writings.* Edited by Harry R. Warfel, 1–24, 1943. Scholars' Facsimiles & Reprints, 1977.

———. *Wieland; or, The Transformation: An American Tale* with *Memoirs of Carwin the Biloquist. The Novels and Related Works of Charles Brockden Brown: Bicentennial Edition.* Edited by Sydney J. Krause, S. W. Reid, and Alexander Cowie, vol. 1. Kent State University Press, 1977.

———. *Wieland; or, The Transformation. An American Tale, with Related Texts.* Edited, with an introduction and notes by Philip Barnard and Stephen Shapiro. Hackett Publishing, 2009.

Calcaterra, Angela. "*Edgar Huntly*'s Gun Violence and Indigenous Mechanisms of Peace." *PMLA*, vol. 136, no. 1, January (2021): 55–71.

Calvin, John. *Institutes of the Christian Religion.* Edited by John T. McNeill, translated by Ford Lewis Battles. Westminster Press, 1960. 2 vols.

Christopherson, Bill. *The Apparition in the Glass: Charles Brockden Brown's American Gothic.* University of Georgia Press, 1993.

Clark, David Lee. *Charles Brockden Brown: Pioneer Voice of America.* AMS Press, 1952.

Cody, Michael A. "Brown's Early Biographers and Reception, 1815–1940s. In *The Oxford Handbook of Charles Brockden Brown.* Edited by Philip Barnard, Hilary Emmett, and Stephen Shapiro, 522–36. Oxford University Press, 2019.

Colacurcio, Michael J. *The Province of Piety: Moral History in Hawthorne's Early Tales.* Duke University Press, 1995.

Cowie, Alexander. "Historical Essay." In *Wieland; or, The Transformation: An American Tale* with *Memoirs of Carwin the Biloquist. The Novels and Related Works of Charles Brockden Brown: Bicentennial Edition,* 311–48. Edited by Sydney J. Krause, S. W. Reid, and Alexander Cowie, vol. 1. Kent State University Press, 1977.

Crevecoeur, J. Hector St. John de. *Letters from an American Farmer.* Introduction and Notes, Warren Barton Blake, Dutton, n.d.

Cronin, James, editor. *The Diary of Elihu Hubbard Smith.* American Philosophical Society, 1973.

Davidson, Cathy N. "The Matter and Manner of Charles Brockden Brown's *Alcuin.*" In *Critical Essays on Charles Brockden Brown.* Edited by Bernard Rosenthal. 71-86. G. K. Hall, 1981.

_____. *Revolution and the Word: The Rise of the Novel in America.* Oxford University Press, 1986.

Doolen, Andy. "Brown, Empire, and Colonialism." In *The Oxford Handbook of Charles Brockden Brown.* Edited by Philip Barnard, Hilary Emmett, and Stephen Shapiro, 351–65. Oxford University Press, 2019.

Downes, Paul. "Constitutional Secrets: 'Memoirs of Carwin' and the Politics of Concealment." *Criticism,* vol. 39, no. 1, Winter (1997): 89–117.

Dunlap, William. *Diary of William Dunlap (1766–1839),* vol 1. Benjamin Blom, 1969.

———. *The Life of Charles Brockden Brown.* Philadelphia: James P. Parke, 1815.

Edwards, Justin D. "Engendering a New Republic: Charles Brockden Brown's *Alcuin, Carwin* and the Legal Fictions of Gender." *Nordic Journal of English Studies,* vol. 2, no. 2 (2002): 279–301.

Elliott, Emory. "Narrative Unity and Moral Resolution in *Arthur Mervyn.*" In *Critical Essays on Charles Brockden Brown.* Edited by Bernard Rosenthal, 142-63 G. K. Hall, 1981.

———. *Revolutionary Writers: Literature and Authority in the New Republic, 1725–1819*. Oxford University Press, 1982.

Ellis, Scott. "Brown and the Yellow Fever." In *The Oxford Handbook of Charles Brockden Brown.* Edited by Philip Barnard, Hilary Emmett, and Stephen Shapiro, 384–98. Oxford University Press, 2019.

Emerson, Ralph Waldo. "The American Scholar." In *Ralph Waldo Emerson: Selected Essays*. Edited by Larzer Ziff, 83-105. Penguin Books, 1984.

Faherty, Duncan. "*Wieland*; or, The Transformation of American Literary History." In *The Oxford Handbook of Charles Brockden Brown.* Edited by Philip Barnard, Hilary Emmett, and Stephen Shapiro, 47–60. Oxford University Press, 2019.

Fliegelman, Jay. *Prodigals and Pilgrims: The American Revolution against Patriarchal Authority, 1750–1800.* Cambridge University Press, 1982.

Fleischmann, Fritz. "Brown and Women's Rights." In *The Oxford Handbook of Charles Brockden Brown.* Edited by Philip Barnard, Hilary Emmett, and Stephen Shapiro, 288–301. Oxford University Press, 2019.

Franklin, Benjamin. *Autobiography*. Edited by J. A. Leo Lemay and P. M. Zall, Norton, 1986.

Gabler-Hover, Janet. *Truth in American Fiction: The Legacy of Rhetorical Idealism*. University of Georgia Press, 1990.

Galluzzo, Anthony. "Brown, the Illuminati, and the Public Sphere." In *The Oxford Handbook of Charles Brockden Brown.* Edited by Philip Barnard, Hilary Emmett, and Stephen Shapiro, 335–50. Oxford University Press, 2019.

_____. "Charles Brockden Brown's *Wieland* and the Aesthetics of Terror: Revolution, Reaction, and the Radical Enlightenment in Early American Letters." *Eighteenth-Century Studies*, vol. 42, no. 2, Winter (2009): 255–71.

Gardner, Jared. "Alien Nation: Edgar Huntly's Savage Awakening." *American Literature*, vol. 66, no. 3, Sept. (1994): 429–61.

Giles, Paul. "Antipodal America: Charles Brockden Brown, New Holland, and the Constitution of US Literature." *Reading Across the Pacific: Australia-United States Intellectual Histories.* Edited by Robert Dixon and Nicholas Birns, 23–37. Sydney University Press, 2010.

Gilmore, Michael T. "Charles Brockden Brown." In *The Cambridge History of American Literature.* 1590–1820, vol. 1. Edited by Sacvan Berkovitch, 644-60. Cambridge University Press, 1994.]

———. "Letters of the Early Republic." In *The Cambridge History of American Literature.* 1590–1820, vol. 1. Edited by Sacvan Berkovitch, 541-57. Cambridge University Press, 1994.

Godwin, William. *The Adventures of Caleb Williams or Things As They Are.* Edited by George Sherburn. 1794. Holt, Rinehart, and Winston, 1963.

———. *An Enquiry Concerning Political Justice, and Its Influence on General Virtue and Happiness.* Vol. 1. London: G. G. J. and J. Robinson, 1793. Online Facsimile. http://files.libertyfund.org/files/90/0164–01_Bk.pdf

Grabo, Norman S. *The Coincidental Art of Charles Brockden Brown.* University of North Carolina Press, 1981.

———. "Historical Essay." In *Arthur Mervyn; or Memoirs of the Year 1793, First and Second Parts. The Novels and Related Works of Charles Brockden Brown: Bicentennial Edition.* Edited by Sydney J. Krause, S. W. Reid, Norman S. Grabo, and Marvin L. Williams, Jr., 447–75, vol. 3. Kent State University Press, 1980.

Hamelman, Steve. "Rhapsodist in the Wilderness: Brown's Romantic Quest in *Edgar Huntly.*" *Studies in American Fiction*, vol. 21, no. 2, Autumn (1993): 171–90.

Hawthorne, Nathaniel. "Ethan Brand." In *The Snow-Image and Uncollected Tales.* Edited by William Charvat, et al., 83–102. *The Centenary Edition of the Works of Nathaniel Hawthorne*, vol. 11. Ohio State University Press, 1974.

———. "The Hall of Fantasy." In *Mosses from an Old Manse.* Edited by William Charvet et al., 172–85. *The Centenary Edition of the Works of Nathaniel Hawthorne*, vol. 10. Ohio State University Press, 1974.

———. "My Kinsman, Major Molineux." In *The Snow-Image and Uncollected Tales.* Edited by William Charvat, et al., 208–31. *The Centenary Edition of the Works of Nathaniel Hawthorne*, vol. 11. Ohio State University Press, 1974.

———. "Young Goodman Brown." In *Mosses from an Old Manse.* Edited by William Charvet et al., 74–90. *The Centenary Edition of the Works of Nathaniel Hawthorne*, vol. 20. Ohio State University Press, 1974.

Hewitt, Elizabeth. "History and Romance: Fictionality in Charles Brockden Brown." *Early American Literature*, vol. 57, no. 2, (2022): 537–42.

———. "Letters." In *The Oxford Handbook of Charles Brockden Brown.* Edited by Philip Barnard, Hilary Emmett, and Stephen Shapiro, 225–36. Oxford University Press, 2019.

Hinds, Elizabeth Jane Wall. *Private Property: Charles Brockden Brown's Gendered Economics of Virtue.* University of Delaware Press, 1997.

Homer. *The Odyssey of Homer.* Translated by Richard Lattimore. Harper & Row, 1967.

Horne, William C. *Making a Heaven of Hell: The Problem of the Companionate Ideal in English Marriage Poetry, 1650–1800.* University of Georgia Press, 1993.

Hsu, Hsuan L. *Geography and the Production of Space in Nineteenth-Century American Literature.* Cambridge University Press, 2010.

Hughes, Merritt Y., editor. *Complete Poems and Major Prose.* By John Milton. The Odyssey Press, 1957.

Irwin, John T. *The Mystery to a Solution: Poe, Borges, and the Analytic Detective Story.* The Johns Hopkins University Press, 1994.

"Isaiah." *Holy Bible,* The Washburn College Bible. Edited by Bradbury Thompson, 927–96. Oxford University Press, 1980.

Kafer, Peter. *Charles Brockden Brown's Revolution and the Birth of American Gothic.* University of Pennsylvania Press, 2004.

Kamrath, Mark L. *The Historicism of Charles Brockden Brown: Radical History and the Early Republic.* Kent State University Press, 2010.

Kazajian, David. *The Colonizing Trick: National Culture and Imperial Citizenship in Early America.* University of Minnesota Press, 2003.

Krause, Sydney J. "Historical Essay." In *Edgar Huntly; or, Memoirs of a Sleep-Walker. The Novels and Related Works of Charles Brockden Brown: Bicentennial Edition.* Edited by Sydney J. Krause and S.W. Reid, 295–400, vol. 3. Kent State University Press, 1984.

———. "Penn's Elm and *Edgar Huntly*: Dark 'Instruction to the Heart.'" *American Literature*, vol. 66, no. 3, Sept. (1994): 463–84.

Leask, Nigel. "Irish Republicans and Gothic Eleutherarchs: Pacific Utopias in the Writings of Theobald Wolfe Tone and Charles Brockden Brown." *British Radical Culture of the 1790s.* Edited by Robert M. Maniquis, 91–111. Huntington Library, 2002.

Letter, Joseph J. "Charles Brockden Brown's Lazaretto Chronotope Series: Secret History and 'The Man at Home.'" *Early American Literature*, vol. 50, no. 3, (2015): 711–35.

Levine, Robert S. "Arthur Mervyn's Revolutions." *Studies in American Fiction*, vol. 12, no. 2, Autumn (1984): 145–60.

_____. *Conspiracy and Romance: Studies in Brockden Brown, Cooper, Hawthorne, and Melville*. Cambridge University Press, 1989.

_____. *Dislocating Race and Nation: Episodes in Nineteenth-Century American Literary Nationalism*. University of North Carolina Press, 2008.

Lindberg, Gary. *The Confidence Man in American Literature*. New York: Oxford University Press, 1982.

Looby, Christopher. *Voicing America: Language, Literary Form, and the Origins of the United States*. University of Chicago Press, 1996.

Lueck, Beth L. "Charles Brockden Brown's *Edgar Huntly*: The Picturesque Traveler as Sleepwalker." *Studies in American Fiction*, vol. 15, no. 2, Spring (1987): 25–42.

Martin, Ronald E. *American Literature and the Universe of Force*. Duke University Press, 1981.

Martin, Terence. *Parables of Possibility: The American Need for Beginnings*. Columbia University Press, 1995.

Miles, Robert. "Brown's American Gothic." In *The Oxford Handbook of Charles Brockden Brown*. Edited by Philip Barnard, Hilary Emmett, and Stephen Shapiro, 411–25. Oxford University Press, 2019.

Miller, Nicholas E. "*Ormond; or, The Secret Witness*." In *The Oxford Handbook of Charles Brockden Brown*. Edited by Philip Barnard, Hilary Emmett, and Stephen Shapiro, 61–75. Oxford University Press, 2019.

Miller, Perry. "The Marrow of Puritan Divinity." *Errand into the Wilderness*. Edited by Perry Miller, Harper and Row, 48–98. 1964.

Milton, John. *A Mask Presented at Ludlow Castle 1634*. In *Complete Poems and Major Prose*. Edited by Merritt Y. Hughes, 86–114. The Odyssey Press, 1957.

Nye, Russel B. "Historical Essay." *Ormond; or, The Secret Witness. The Novels and Related Works of Charles Brockden Brown; Bicentennial Edition*. Sydney J. Krause, S. W. Reid, and Russel B. Nye, 295–314, vol. 2. Kent State University Press.

O'Shaughnessy, Toni. "'An Imperfect Tale': Interpretive Accountability in *Wieland*." *Studies in American Fiction*, vol. 18, no. 1, Spring (1990): 41–54.

Parker, Hershel. *Herman Melville: A Biography,1851–1891*, vol. 2. Johns Hopkins University Press, 2002.

Person, Leland S, Jr. "'My Good Mamma': Women in *Edgar Huntly* and *Arthur Mervyn*." *Studies in American Fiction*, vol. 9, no. 1, Spring (1981): 33–46.

[Professor Newman's Address]. "Address Delivered before the Benevolent Society of Bowden College, Tuesday evening, Sept. 5 1826. By Samuel P. Newman." *The Quarterly Journal of the American Education Society*, vol. 1, July (1827): 7–9.

Rachman, Stephen. "Brown and Physiology." In *The Oxford Handbook of Charles Brockden Brown.* Edited by Philip Barnard, Hilary Emmett, and Stephen Shapiro, 369–83. Oxford University Press, 2019.

Rebhorn, Matthew. "Coagulating Consciousness: Neural Historicism and the Onto-Possibilities of *Edgar Huntly*." *Early American Literature*, vol 56, no. 2, (2021): 441–69.

Ringe, Donald A. "Historical Essay." In *Clara Howard* and *Jane Talbot. The Novels and Related Works of Charles Brockden Brown; Bicentennial Edition.* Edited by Sydney J. Krause, S. W. Reid, and Donald A. Ringe, 433–74, vol. 5. Kent State University Press, 1986.

Roeger, Tyler. "Agrarian Gothic: Carwin, Class Transgressions, and Spatial Horrors in Charles Brockden Brown's *Wieland*." *Literature in the Early American Republic: Annual Studies on Cooper and His Contemporaries*, vol. 6, (2014): 85–111.

Rombes, Nicholas. "'All Was Lonely, Darksome, and Waste': *Wieland* and the Construction of the New Republic." *Studies in American Fiction*, vol 22, no. 1, Spring (1994): 37–46.

Rosenthal, Bernard, editor. *Critical Essays on Charles Brockden Brown*. G. K. Hall, 1981.

Roth, Philip. *American Pastoral.* Vintage International, 1998.

Rourke, Constance. *American Humor: A Study of the National Character.* Harcourt, Brace, Jovanovich, 1931.

Rowlandson, Mary. *A Narrative of the Captivity and Restoration of Mrs. Mary Rowlandson. The Norton Anthology of American Literature: Beginnings to 1820*, 9th ed. Edited by Robert S. Levine, 269–301, vol. A. W. W. Norton, 2017.

Samuels, Shirley. "*Wieland*: Alien and Infidel." *Early American Literature*, vol. 25, no. 1, (1990): 46–66.

Scheick, William J. "The Problem of Origination in Brown's *Ormond*." In *Critical Essays on Charles Brockden Brown*. Edited by Bernard Rosenthal, 126-41. G. K. Hall, 1981.

Schmidt, Leigh Eric. *Hearing Things: Religion, Illusion, and the American Enlightenment*, Harvard University Press, 2000.

Shakespeare, William. *The Tempest*. Edited by Peter Holland. Pelican, 1999.

Silyn Roberts, Sian, "Brown and the Novel in the Atlantic World." In *The Oxford Handbook of Charles Brockden Brown*. Edited by Philip Barnard, Hilary Emmett, and Stephen Shapiro, 439–54. Oxford University Press, 2019.

Smith, Elihu Hubbard. *The Diary of Elihu Hubbard Smith*. Edited by James E. Cronin. The American Philosophical Society, 1973.

Smith Stocker, Abigail. "Brown and the Woldwinites." In *The Oxford Handbook of Charles Brockden Brown*. Edited by Philip Barnard, Hilary Emmett, and Stephen Shapiro, 273–87. Oxford University Press, 2019.

Stamphone, Christopher. "A 'Spirit of Mistaken Benevolence': Civilizing the Savage in Charles Brockden Brown's *Edgar Huntly*." *Early American Literature*, vol. 50, no. 2, (2015): 415–48.

Stern, Julia. "The State of 'Women' in *Ormond*; or, Patricide in the New Nation." In *Revising Charles Brockden Brown: Culture, Politics, and Sexuality in the Early Republic*. Edited by Phillip Barnard, Mark L. Kamrath, and Stephen Shapiro, 182-215. University of Tennessee Press, 2004.

Teute, Fredrika J. "'A Republic of Intellect': Conversation and Criticism among the Sexes in 1790s New York." Barnard, Kamrath, and Shapiro, 149–81.

Tomkins, Jane. *Sensational Designs: The Cultural Work of American Fiction 1790–1860*. Oxford University Press, 1985.

van Leeuwen, Evert Jan. "'Though Hermes never taught thee': The Anti-Patriarchal Tendency of Charles Brockden Brown's Mercurial Outcast Carwin, the Biloquist." *European Journal of American Studies*, vol. 5, no. 1, (2010): 1–17.

Verhoeven, W. M. "'This blissful period of intellectual liberty': Transatlantic Radicalism and Enlightened Conservatism in Brown's Early Writing." In *Revising Charles Brockden Brown: Culture, Politics, and Sexuality in the Early Republic*. Edited by Phillip Barnard, Mark L. Kamrath, and Stephen Shapiro, 7-40. University of Tennessee Press, 2004.

Voloshin, Beverly R. "*Edgar Huntly* and the Coherence of the Self." *Early American Literature*, vol. 23, no. 3 (1988): 262–80.

Wallace, James D. *Early Cooper and His Audience.* Columbia University Press, 1986.

Warfel, Harry R. *Charles Brocken Brown: American Gothic Novelist.* Octagon Books, 1949.

Waterman, Bryan. "Later Years, 1795–1810." In *The Oxford Handbook of Charles Brockden Brown.* Edited by Philip Barnard, Hilary Emmett, and Stephen Shapiro, 24–43. Oxford University Press, 2019.

———. *Republic of Intellect: The Friendly Club of New York City and the Making of American Literature.* Johns Hopkins University Press, 2007.

Watt, Ian. *The Rise of the Novel: Studies in Defoe, Richardson and Fielding.* 1957. University of California Press, 1974.

Watts, Steven. *The Romance of Real Life: Charles Brockden Brown and the Origins of American Culture.* The Johns Hopkins University Press, 1994.

Weinstock, Jeffrey Andrew. *Charles Brockden Brown. Gothic Authors: Critical Revisi*ons. University of Wales Press, 2011.

Weldon, Roberta F. "Charles Brockden Brown's *Wieland*: A Family Tragedy." *Studies in American Fiction*, vol. 12, no. 1, Spring (1984): 1–11.

West, Lisa. "Early Years, 1771–1795." In *The Oxford Handbook of Charles Brockden Brown.* Edited by Philip Barnard, Hilary Emmett, and Stephen Shapiro, 7–23. Oxford University Press, 2019.

White, Ed. "Carwin the Peasant Rebel." Barnard, Kamrath, and Shapiro, 41–59.

Witherington, Paul. "'Not My Tongue Only': Form and Language in *Edgar Huntly.* In Critical Essays on Charles Brockden Brown.. Edited by Bernard Rosenthal, 164-83. G. K. Hall, 1981.

Woertendyke, Gretchen J. "History, Romance, and the Novel." *In Revising Charles Brockden Brown: Culture, Politics, and Sexuality in the Early Republic.* Edited by Phillip Barnard, Mark L. Kamrath, and Stephen Shapiro, 155-70. University of Tennessee Press, 2004.

Index